Contemporary Approaches to the Study of Religion

Religion and Reason 27

Method and Theory
in the Study and Interpretation of Religion

Mouton Publishers
Berlin • New York • Amsterdam

Contemporary Approaches to the Study of Religion in 2 Volumes

edited by
Frank Whaling
University of Edinburgh

Volume 1: The Humanities

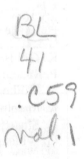

Mouton Publishers
Berlin • New York • Amsterdam

Library of Congress Cataloging in Publication Data

Main entry under title:
Contemporary approaches to the study of religion.

(Religion and reason ; 27)
Contents: v. 1. The humanities —
1. Religion—Study and teaching—History—20th century
—Addresses, essays, lectures. I. Whaling, Frank,
1934-   . II. Series.
BL41.C59 1983   291'.07   84-14807
ISBN 3-110-09834-2 (v. 1)

CIP-Kurztitelaufnahme der Deutschen Bibliothek

Contemporary approaches to the study of religion:
in 2 vol. / ed. by Frank Whaling. — Berlin ;
New York ; Amsterdam : Mouton

NE: Whaling, Frank [Hrsg.]

Vol. 1. The humanities. — 1984.
(Religion and reason ; 27)
ISBN 3-11-009834-2

NE: GT

Typesetting: Permanent Typesetting, Hong Kong.—Printing: Druckerei Hildebrand,
Berlin.—Binding: Lüderitz & Bauer Buchgewerbe GmbH, Berlin.
                                                    Printed in Germany.

Contents

Preface

The two volumes of *contemporary approaches to the study of religion* were conceived as a sequel to Jacques Waardenburg's *classical approaches to the study of religion* published in 1973. Waardenburg had told the story of the development of the study of religion as an academic enterprise from its beginnings in the nineteenth century until the time of the Second World War. The aim of the present volumes is to bring the story up to date from 1945 to the present day.

It became evident that this was a mammoth task that called for the energies and abilities of more than one person and the space of more than one book. A team evolved to write two books, and these two volumes are essentially the product of a team. The team is excitingly international including as it does two scholars from Germany, one from New Zealand, three from Great Britain, two from the United States, two from Holland, and for good measure one who divides his time between Britain and the United States. Although lacking the presence of a non-western scholar, with this qualification the team is cosmopolitan and representative.

After it had been decided that this project was to be a team effort, the question remained of how recent developments in the study of religion were to be described and analysed. One possibility was to proceed historically: to begin at 1945 and to show year by year how methods and ideas had evolved. Although not impossible, this approach would have been difficult even for one person to attempt. It would, of necessity, have involved a good deal of repetition, and the likelihood of repetition would certainly have been increased through the presence of a team.

In place of a historical narrative, an alternative procedure has been adopted. Each member of the team has summarised the developments in the study of religion since 1945 in the area of his or her own expertise. In volume one, Ursula King analyses historical and phenomenological approaches, Frank Whaling looks at comparative approaches, Kees Bolle sums up studies of myths and other religious texts, Ninian Smart

grapples with the scientific study of religion in its plurality, and Frank
Whaling places the study of religion in its global context and looks at the
relationship of the philosophy of science to the study of religion. In
volume two, David Wulff investigates psychological approaches,
Michael Hill, Günter Kehrer and Bert Hardin share the task of interpreting sociological approaches, Tony Jackson deals with social anthropological approaches, Jarich Oosten looks at cultural anthropological approaches, and Wouter van Beek reflects on cultural anthropology and
the many functions of religion. In this way, a breadth and depth of
expertise is brought to bear upon this important topic.

This does not mean that there is never any overlap of subject matter.
Names such as Lévi-Strauss, Pettazzoni, Eliade, Dumézil, Wilfred
Cantwell Smith, and so on, inevitably crop up in more places than one,
and this is to the benefit of the whole. Our practice has been to include a
bibliography after each chapter, even though some of the books appear
more than once. The only exception applies to Ninian Smart's typically
perspicacious small chapter. Insofar as the books on that bibliography
are all found elsewhere, it has simply been left out.

Whether our age contains academic giants such as Müller, Weber,
Durkheim, Jung, and the like, who loomed large in Waardenburg's
work is debatable. The five modern scholars mentioned above, supplemented by others such as Widengren, Zaehner, Parrinder, Berger,
Smart, Panikkar, Wach, Brandon and Nasr, to name but a few, are hardly
negligeable. However a feature of our age is the rapid development of
varied currents in the study of religion, some of which are small yet not
unimportant. It is to the credit of the members of our team that they
have dealt with both the smaller and the larger streams within the wider
river of their own approach, and that, while doing justice to their own
area, they have not lost sight of the total field of religious studies.

I am grateful to my colleagues for their endeavour. They have
brought to this project a plurality of nationalities, a plurality of methods,
and a plurality of insights. This means that these two volumes are not
wedded to the approach of any particular school in the study of religion,
they take an overview of them all; it means that the scholars involved are
flexible enough to enhance the work of a team.

The coordination of a team so talented and yet so scattered has inevitably led to delays, and I am grateful to my colleagues for their patience. Thanks are due also to Lamin Sanneh and John Carman of the Harvard Center for the Study of World Religions for advice and hospitality during the editing of this project. Above all I am happy to pay tribute to the unfailing help and encouragement of the General Editor of the *religion and reason* series Professor Jacques Waardenburg, whose original book inspired this series of two volumes on *contemporary approaches to the study of religion*, and whose advice has accompanied everything that has been done.

Introduction: The Contrast between the Classical and Contemporary Periods in the Study of Religion

FRANK WHALING

Edinburgh

This introduction, although it relates mainly to the issues raised in the first volume of this series *contemporary approaches to the study of religion: THE HUMANITIES*, is intended also to introduce the reader to the outstanding issues raised in the second volume *contemporary approaches to the study of religion: the social sciences.*

As was mentioned in the Preface, the two volumes of *Contemporary Approaches to the Study of Religion* are conceived partly as a sequel to Jacques Waardenburg's *Classical Approaches to the Study of Religion* (1973). However the format of the two projects is different, and this difference in format illustrates the contrast between the classical and contemporary approaches to the study of religion. It would be virtually impossible to repeat in these volumes the exercise undertaken by Waardenburg because the study of religion in the age he was dealing with—from Max Müller to World War II—grappled with materials, methods, techniques, and problems of a less complex nature than those that dominate the study of religion today. This is not to say that there is no continuity between the so-called classical and contemporary periods. Nevertheless, to give a framework to our introduction, we shall

highlight the differences between the era of the classical approaches and
that of today.

Waardenburg, in his book, gives a succinct history of the development of the study of religion from the time of Müller to about 1945,
and then he includes an anthology of extracts on method and theory
of research from the work of over forty scholars who were pioneers,
indeed giants, in the field. It was possible to employ this stratagem
in regard to the classical period because specialisation and diversification were less rampant than they are today, scholarly disciplines
and academic knowledge generally were less developed, and the world
itself was a less complex place. Today, as we shall see, there is an
extraordinary ramification within the study of religion, a vast growth
of academic knowledge of all kinds, a springing up of new seeds within
the field, and a complexification and globalisation of the context wherein
religion is studied that make easy generalisations, reliance upon a select
anthology, and a one-person treatment difficult if not impossible. These
volumes, therefore, are not an anthology, and they are not by one
person. They are the work of a team who aim to summarise, insofar
as they are able within the covers of one work, the contemporary
approaches to the study of religion. This summary is not a compilation
of select passages of key authors (the bibliographies contain not far short
of two thousand entries and such a selection would, of necessity, have
omitted much relevant material); it does not attempt to impose a
particular viewpoint (the authors were born in a number of different
countries and now work in different universities in three different
continents); it is a narrative of the main developments and discussions
since World War II in the fields of history and phenomenology of
religion, comparative religion, the study of myths and other religious
texts, anthropology of religion, sociology of religion, psychology of
religion, the scientific study of religion in its plurality, and the study of
religion in a global context. However although an account is given of a
vast corpus of material gathered from varied parts of this complex area
of study—a more ambitious account than has been attempted before—
an endeavour is also made to give an integrated overview of the whole
field. Indeed when the project was first conceived it was hoped that it
would be possible so to summarise the mass of developments since 1945

that an integral and acceptable way forward would be opened up for the *whole* study of religion. It must be admitted that this grandiose aim has not been completely fulfilled. Such a stage has not yet been reached; an overall philosophy of the study of religion has not yet been fully conceptualised; a single paradigm is not yet in sight. Nevertheless, in the course of this work, a number of suggestions are made as to how, on the basis of past research and present directions, future programmes may proceed. While the authors are under no illusions that they have achieved a complete breakthrough, they are hopeful that the comprehensive nature of their account and the breadth and depth of their narrative will not be without significance for the future. Quite apart from any contributions of method or content made by these two books, the very fact that scholars from Tübingen in Germany (Günter Kehrer and Bert Hardin), Edinburgh in Scotland (Tony Jackson and Frank Whaling), Wheaton, Massachusetts in the United States (David Wulff), Wellington in New Zealand (Michael Hill). Leeds in England (Ursula King), Los Angeles in the United States (Kees Bolle), Lancaster (UK) and Santa Barbara (USA) (Ninian Smart), Utrecht in Holland (Wouter van Beek and Jacques Waardenburg—general editor of the series), and Leiden in Holland (Jarich Oosten) have banded together to produce this work may represent in itself a portent for the study of religion of an interdisciplinary, international, and interlinked future.

Before we focus upon the differences between the modern period and the classical period dealt with by Waardenburg, there are three points that need to be made. Firstly, there is *some* continuity between this volume and that of Waardenburg. Some of the great names of the past mentioned by Waardenburg inevitably figure in the present work. Moreover, although our purpose is to tell the story of the development of the study of religion after 1945, some of the chapters go back before that date in order to put their account of the later developments into a wider focus. There are no rigid breaks within the web of history. Any particular date, even a dramatic date such as 1945 which marks the end of the Second World War, must inevitably be arbitrary. Nevertheless periodisations, however arbitrary, are useful and in the case of this work the basic cut-off point is 1945 and the limits set by Waardenburg's work.

Our second point is that, like Waardenburg, we do not aim to cover all aspects of the study of religion. This would be both impossible and (even if possible) undesirable. Our purpose is not to summarise the *content* of the various religious traditions of the world. This is done with reasonable adequacy by bibliographical reference volumes such as Charles Adams's *A Reader's Guide to the Great Religions* (1977, 2nd ed.), and other encyclopaedic volumes in different fields of study and specialised disciplines. Indeed one of the basic problems in the whole field of religious studies is the sheer volume of information that is being amassed. As early as 1905 Louis Henry Jordan was writing in *Comparative Religion: Its Genesis and Growth*, (1905: 163):

> The accumulation of information, indeed, has never slackened for a moment; and the special embarassment of today is the overwhelming mass of detail, still rapidly increasing, which confronts every earnest investigator.

This accumulation of data has not lessened since 1905, and after 1945 the whole process has been exacerbated by the fact of quicker communication, both in transport and electronics. At a basic descriptive level, the history and anthropology of religion continue to supply scholars with a plethora of data of many different varieties. The volume of data grows yearly, if not daily, and it provides the raw material for hypotheses or theories in the study of religion. Wider studies must continue to depend upon the basic researches of the historians and anthropologists of religion. However, endless description is not an end in itself; to give it control and direction there is the need for methodological sophistication and wider categories of interpretation. Such a need was recognised as early as the last century in methodological prophecies such as that of Burnouf (1872, 2nd ed., *La Science des Religions*, trans., p. 1):

> This present century will not come to an end without having seen the establishment of a unified science whose elements are still dispersed, a science which the preceding centuries did not have, which is not yet defined, and which, perhaps for the first time, will be named science of religion.

Such an optimistic forecast can now be seen to be naive, yet the need for methodological clarification remains as urgent as ever. In this book, there will be some reference to content, for method and content can (and should) never fully be separated, but our main concern is for methods and theories rather than for content per se. We will deal with contemporary approaches to the study of religion rather than the contemporary content of the study of religion which is generally 'taken as read.'

Our third point is that, insofar as these works are written in English, the references and quotations from books in all languages are mostly given in English, and reference to the original works is made elsewhere, usually in the bibliographies of the end of the chapters. This does not detract from the international coverage. As we have stated before, these books are written by an authentically international team and our only slight regret is that is has not been possible to include a non-western scholar in the team.

(1) *Increasing diversification in contemporary approaches*

An obvious difference between the classical and contemporary approaches to the study of religion is the increasing diversification of methodological discussion in our own time. Not only has the mass of accumulated religious data multiplied, so also has the variety of methodological reflection upon those data. It is not merely the case that the number of methodological approaches with a serious interest in religious data has increased, there has also been an intensification of discussion about religion *within* each approach. Growing specialisation within each approach has resulted in a growing ramification of discussions about religion and, in addition to this, new 'seeds' have sprung up ranging from the 'ecology of religion' to the 'academic dialogue of religions.' The pity is that some of this discussion is virtually unknown. The temptation is for scholars of one nationality or language group to know only each other's work, or for the scholars of one discipline to be acquainted solely with the research in their own discipline (or part of their discipline). These books are an attempt to gather together and to put into some sort of order the diverse discussions about method and theory since 1945. Thus each author summarises the main trends within

his or her own area: Ursula King writes on the history and phenomenology of religion; Frank Whaling on comparative approaches to the
study of religion; Kees Bolle on the study of myths and other religious
texts; Tony Jackson, Wouter van Beek and Jarich Oosten on anthropological approaches to the study of religion; Michael Hill, Günter Kehrer,
and Bert Hardin on sociological approaches to the study of religion;
David Wulff on the psychology of religion; Ninian Smart on the scientific study of religion in its plurality; and Frank Whaling on the global
context of the study of religion. Within each section certain basic
questions are addressed either implicitly or explicitly, and to help focus
the discussion. In each approach the basic method involved is described,
and questions are raised as to what the method is attempting to do in the
study of religion, whether or not it is complementary to other methods,
and whether it is centred outside the study of religion or is basic to it.
The basic position implied within the approach concerned is also investigated: is it one of neutrality or are truth claims implied, and if so are
those truth claims related to a particular discipline, to religion in general,
or to a particular religion? The question of definition is also raised: what
definition(s), if any, is (are) implied in the approach concerned? A
further area of interest relates to the scope and nature of the data used in
a particular approach: are they first or second hand, do they arise out of
primal religion, historical religions, or the major religions, are they
concentrated more upon the study of one particular religion and if so
which one? The main part of each section focusses upon a description
and discussion of the major trends within the approach concerned.
Attention is also given to the future prospects envisaged for each area.
Clearly the above concerns: method, standpoint, definition, nature of
the data, trends, and future prospects, are interrelated. Some of the
implications arising out of the elucidation of these concerns will be dealt
with later in the introduction. We are content, for the moment, with
pointing out the complex nature of the discussion of theory and method
within each of the above-mentioned approaches, and with outlining the
criteria whereby we have sought to bring order to each section and
potential integration to the whole.

It is important to stress at this point that although each chapter of
these books necessarily contains a large amount of bibliographical

material—and to this extent they are equivalent in the sphere of theory and method to Adams's *A Reader's Guide to the Great Religions*—they transcend mere bibliographical description and are cast in the form of narrative. It is our hope that scholars with particular interests in history and phenomenology of religion, comparative religion, myths and texts, anthropology of religion, sociology of religion, psychology of religion, scientific study of religion in itself, and the global context of religious studies, after they have read the summaries of their own area and their own volume will read the other volume so that they can obtain an overview of the wider discussion. Although our work is significant in that it brings together and orders a vast amount of material within *each* approach, its more important function is to summarise the general field of method and theory in the study of religion in a way that has never been so fully attempted before. There is an urgent need for scholars of religion to supplement their areas of specialisation with a total view of the field as a whole, and a major aim of these volumes is to contribute to this end.

(2) *Greater research involvement of social and humane sciences*

Another major difference between the classical and contemporary approaches to the study of religion is the increasingly complex relationship between the humane sciences, and especially the social sciences, and this sphere of research. Durkheim, Weber, Freud, Jung, and James may have departed from the scene, but it is possible to submit that, in the contemporary situation, any theory or method of investigation in any of the social (and humane) sciences is or may be applied to the study of specific sets of religious data. In order to do justice to the range of involvement in the study of religion by the contemporary social sciences, we have put into the second volume chapters which deal with the anthropology, sociology, and psychology of religion. However, the overall perspective is by no means confined to the social sciences. Indeed the five chapters of volume one, although concentrating upon a particular approach, are more wide-ranging. Ursula King's brief, namely history and phenomenology of religion, takes her (after a comprehen-

sive survey of the detailed trends within those areas) into a wider
investigation of hermeneutical and integrally scientific approaches arising out of or implied in history and phenomenology of religion. Frank
Whaling, although limiting his discussion of comparative religion to the
actual classification and comparison of religion, points out that systematic comparisons of religion(s) have been attempted by phenomenological typologists, depth psychologists, social and structural anthropologists, sociologists, and (more widely) historians and (less appositely)
theologians of religion, and therefore comparative religion (although
not a synonym for the total study of religion) involves within itself a
range of approaches and calls forth an overview within the circumscribed area of comparison. Kees Bolle, in a detailed review of the study
of myths and religious texts, ranges over a number of approaches relating to these themes including the historical, structural, and phenomenological. Within the total structure of the book, therefore, the first
three chapters of volume one, by King, Whaling, and Bolle, are more
wide-ranging in that their subject matter carries them beyond one
particular methodological perspective, and the six chapters of volume-
two concentrate upon particular social scientific approaches. The final
two chapters of volume one revert to a more wide-ranging treatment:
Ninian Smart reviews the plurality of methodological approaches
within the 'scientific' study of religion, and Frank Whaling examines,
under the heading of the global context of the study of religion, the
work of some key non-western scholars, the implications for the study
of religion of recent developments within the philosophy of science, and
the influence of the global environment itself upon our notions of the
place of the study of religion within the wider academic context. Within
the overall planning of the volumes, a balance has therefore been struck
between the six chapters related to the social sciences that concentrate
upon the methodological findings of particular disciplines, and the five
chapters related more implicitly to the humanities where the treatment is
geared as much to themes as to disciplines. It is our hope that this way of
dealing with the material illustrates the sheer variety of contemporary
approaches, the complexity of treatment within and between different
approaches, and a balance between the minutiae of detail and wider
connecting themes.

The structure of the books outlined above allows for a certain amount of, but not too much, overlap between the sections. The six chapters dealing with the social scientific approaches complement each other and contain comparatively little repetition. The five wider-ranging chapters deal occasionally with overlapping names or themes but when this happens the difference of perspective brought to the name or theme in question both extends the discussion and contributes to a potentially more integrated overview. Some names inevitably recur. A glance at the index and the various bibliographies will guide the reader in this respect. The bibliographies are placed at the end of each chapter (with the exception of Ninian Smart's whose entries are all available elsewhere) and, in order to save space and prevent undue repetition, and in contrast to Waardenburg, (1973), there is no composite or separate bibliography.

(3) *Importance of improved communications for the study of religion*

Another factor that played only a minor role in the period of the 'classical approaches' but is more important in contemporary studies is the fact of quicker communication. A new prophet arising in Africa, a new religious movement arising in some part of the West, a new indigenous expression appearing in the third or fourth worlds can now be investigated on the spot by anthropologists, psychologists, sociologists, or historians taking a airplane out of Heathrow or Kennedy airport or going by train or car to the area concerned. The present-day scholar has access not only to books written by travellers or scholars, as was the case in former days, but also to tape-recordings, films and so on, that record in sight and sound the formerly barely accessible data of various religious groups ranging from nomads and peasants to syncretistic sects. The relationship of scholars of religion with present-day religious phenomena is already, by the fact of improved communications media, very different from that which pre-1945 scholars had with the religious phenomena existing in their time. Quite apart from questions of 'pure' methodology, theory, philosophy, ideology and so on, the sheer development of the technical and other devices of the communications media has made religious data accessible in a way undreamt of by scholars before World War II. The influence of the media is also potentially important with regard to the exchange of information and documentation between scholars in the field, the rise of bibliographies, and the eventual need for the storage of increasingly computerised information. It raises the possibility that the 'flavour' of religious studies may change with ever-increasing card-indexes, standardised reporting systems, quantificatory analyses, and the like. We are at the very beginning of reflection on these matters, and they are not dealt with at length or in depth in this book. These 'communication issues' do, however, exercise a subtle influence upon three questions referred to in this volume. In the first place, there is a discernible shift of attention in religious studies generally away from a more obvious involvement in the history of past religions to a greater interest in present developments. This shift is aided and abetted by other factors we will have cause to consider later in the introduction, but if it continues it will represent an important change. Thus the focus of all the chapters of this book, including the one on phenomenology and history of religion, although not neglectful of the past, is geared more obviously to present religious developments than would have been the case before 1945. Second, the social scientific approaches of volume two, notably the chapters by David Wulff and Michael Hill, bring out the increasing use of quantificatory data in religious research. The balanced nature of the presentations of Wulff and Hill masks the extent to which sheer statistics and quantificatory data are becoming dominant in some of the social scientific investigations of religion. This leads us to our third point. Insofar as the silicon chip is already beginning to affect scholarship, and computers have become part of the apparatus of much research, there is the need for reflection upon the consequences of this trend for the study of religion. What kind of data can computers store? According to what criteria should the ordering of these data be organised? Is computer information exhaustive, or complementary to other kinds of information? Although this work does not deal with this question directly in a specific chapter, it deals with it indirectly by its investigation of the complementarity of different approaches, the complementarity of different methods within each approach, and the relevance for the study of religion of the different views of science and scientific information built into the modern philosophy of science.

(4) *Implications of the western nature of much religious research*

A fourth factor that is assuming more importance within the contemporary study of religion in contrast with the situation that pertained at the time of the classical approaches is an increasing concern for the implications of the fact of the western nature of much past research. This book brings out clearly, in several places, the various strands within 'western' scholarship. For example, Whaling chooses three American scholars, three British scholars, and four continental European scholars (two French, one Italian, one Scandinavian) for special mention as comparativists; Bolle reviews the work of American, British, Dutch, German, French, Italian, and Scandinavian scholars of myths and religious texts; Smart implies a similar international range in his piece; and King likewise gives a comprehensive survey of the contributions to the history and phenomenology of religion of American, British, German, Dutch, French, Italian, and Scandinavian scholars. Ursula King mentions, but does not follow, Waardenburg's primary distinction between three main geographical areas in the study of religion: the developing countries of the third world, socialist countries of marxist inspiration, and western countries and his secondary fourfold subdivision of European countries according to language groups and cultural traditions into the Latin areas of France, Italy, and Spain, the Protestant areas of Britain, Scandinavia, and Holland, the Germanic areas of Germany, Austria, and North Switzerland, and the Slavonic areas of Eastern Europe. It would appear that Waardenburg's divisions, although suggestive, are too linguistically and geographically based and that, to give but two qualificatory examples, Dutch and German scholars have inclined towards a more phenomenological approach, and Swedish and Italian scholars have inclined towards a more historical approach, in spite of their geographical differences.

However, in his larger divisions, Waardenburg is right. Although this book traces in detail the contributions of scholars of different western nationalities to different approaches—and this in itself is salutary because past surveys have tended to proceed consciously or unconsciously according to national categories—the wider question that is emerging is whether the study of religion has not been too much dominated by *western* categories. What is the significance of the fact that religions outside the West have been studied in a western way and, to a lesser extent, that religions outside Christianity have been studied in a Christianity-centred way? To what extent has this pre-1945 attitude of often unconscious superiority been superseded in the contemporary situation? To what extent have western scholars of religion subsumed the whole spiritual creation of mankind under one interpretation of religion and then absolutised it? To what degree, in spite of the concern for *epoché* and *Einfühlung* fostered by the phenomenological approach, do western scholars feel that it is *they* who must research and interpret the religion of others for these latter? Can and should scholars from other cultures study western religions in the West, can and should western and non-western scholars study western and non-western texts together, can and should western anthropologists interpolate the views of the people of primal tribes into their academic investigations? One suspects that we are only just beginning to reflect seriously upon these matters. In this volume, they are touched on by Ursula King who intimates the problem, by Kees Bolle who stresses that explanations of a myth must be capable of being presented to the narrators of the myth and not just to western colleagues, and by Frank Whaling who in the final chapter reflects upon the global context of the study of religion.

(5) *Greater involvement of marxism, interreligious dialogue and non-western scholarship*

Related to the last paragraph, a further factor differentiating the contemporary from the classical period is the greater awareness of the involvement of what may loosely be termed 'ideologies' in the contemporary study of religion. In the post-1945 era we can spot the influence of 'ideologies' upon the interpretation and the concrete study of religion and religions. This involvement can take at least three forms. First, there are forthcoming more marxist studies of religion in relation to ethnographic studies, studies of Africa and Asia, the theory of scientific atheism and dialectical materialism, discussions of institutionalised religion, and searchings for the roots of religion in terms of social conflict, escape, or projection. Second, there is the rise of inter-faith dialogue and understanding, especially between Christianity and other religions, which has had an impact upon the interpretation of present-day religious expressions, and in the light of which encounters of religious attitudes and systems are seen to be basically peaceful and constructive. Third, there is the immense interest which scholars from independent countries take in their religious and cultural tradition, which leads to a rediscovery in terms of their own culture of their own religious heritage, but also to scholarly selections and evaluations which can be explained by reference to the present-day spiritual, social, and psychological needs of the traditions concerned. The word 'ideology' with its emotive overtones does not perhaps convey the correct reso-nance to do justice to the contribution that is being made by marxist, interfaith dialogue, and renascent non-western religious scholarship. This is especially the case as the notion is arising in some quarters that western positivistic science or phenomenology can also operate as an 'ideology,' and this leads us back to some of the points made in the last paragraph. However, the question remains as to whether the study of religion is destined to become an arena for competing 'ideologies,' whether there is a bedrock and substratum of data and theories to which our 'ideologies' can contribute and which they can amend constructively without producing a cacophony, or whether the study of religion itself has an ideology-critical function. This range of issues is addressed directly in the final chapters by Ninian Smart and Frank Whaling. Smart attempts to draw the boundary lines that demarcate the study of religion from unduly 'ideological' approaches, and Whaling analyses the contri-bution made to the study of religion by a number of noted non-western scholars.

(6) *Truth-claims, philosophy, and theology*

Our next contrast relates to the status of truth claims, philosophy, and theology in regard to the study of religion and this, of course, is not a post-1945 development but a variation within a graph of relationship that has been a source of debate since the last century. This area of discussion has been, and remains, an exceedingly complex one. Within the confines of this book, it is discussed implicitly or explicitly in three different ways. In the first place, it is pointed out in various places that 'truth claims' are not necessarily confined to philosophy and theology, and that much depends upon what we mean by 'truth claims'—are they methodological or ontological, general or specific, 'first-order' or 'second-order?' For example, Kees Bolle points out that myths lay claim to veracity, and that scholars of mythology have been wont to distinguish *mythos* from *logos*, the 'true' word from the conceptual endeavour of man. According to this notion, theological 'truth' which has the status of *logos* is at a lower level than mythological 'truth' although the latter is pluralistic rather than monolithic. It is clear that greater specificity as to the different levels and motivations of views of 'truth' is required; after all any respectable discipline, method or approach would hardly disclaim all concern for 'truth' of some kind. Different chapters allude to this problem in their own way.

The second sphere of interest relates to the search for a general philosophy of religion. When this work was planned originally it was hoped to include a chapter on the philosophical approach to the study of religion. However, this did not prove to be possible because, in the present state of affairs, any such chapter would be too specific. What we are seeking for and have not yet found is a philosophy of religion that is universal in application, that can deal responsibly with religious diversity, and that can moderate over (rather than isolate itself from or dominate) the other approaches to the study of religion. This book, although it lacks a chapter on the philosophy of religion as such, conducts such a search implicitly in a number of places. Ursula King's sections on hermeneutics and the search for an integral science of religion form one such attempt, Frank Whaling's pieces on the philosophical emphases of non-western religious scholarship and on the implications for the study of religion of the philosophy of science form another attempt, and the whole of Ninian Smart's chapter implies a general philosophical approach to the study of religion. Although they are not completely in agreement, together with the more specialist chapters, they indicate the parameters within which the search for a universally applicable philosophy of religion may continue.

The third sphere of interest is that of theology of religion. The contributors are in agreement that theology as traditionally conceived is separate from the study of religion in the sense that, although it provides data for such study, its categories do not and cannot dominate it. They agree also that institutional considerations have tended to accentuate the differences between the two educational domains. They agree too that insofar as theology operates from within particular religious traditions and focusses upon the *nature* of transcendent reality, its concerns are different from those of the study of religion. The situation is further complicated by the fact that theology is often equated with Christian theology or the theology of a particular religious tradition other than Christianity, although this need not necessarily be the case. At certain places in this volume, some unease is expressed at the confrontational attitudes sometimes implied between monolithic views of theology and the study of religion. In various sections some of the following points are made: theology need not be confined to Christian theology, it need not be confined to any particular religious community, and it can be conceived in universal rather than particular categories; it can be viewed broadly as synonymous with the whole data of religious tradition (when its meaning is so confined) or narrowly as relating to knowledge of God or transcendence; even when viewed as *parti pris*, some of the issues raised (for example historical criticism in Christian theology) are directly relevant, and most of the data mentioned are also relevant; some of the matters that are supposedly the prerogative of theology, namely commitment and dialogue, may be seen to be wider in that the commitment of believers may be a necessary interest of phenomenological *Einfühlung* and dialogue may be an academic category related to the study as well as the practice of religion; the so-called 'exclusion of the transcendent' that has been a feature of much social scientific investigation whereby the social scientist leaves aside all judgements about the existence of religion's transcendent objects, neither affirming nor denying their reality, remains a useful working methodological tool but, as David Wulff comments, it is a negative rather than a positive injunction and leaves out of account the possible significance of the transcendent in the fundamental structure of religious consciousness; and finally, although religious sociology, anthropology, psychology, history, phenomenology, comparison and so on viewed as handmaids of theology or any particular religious community are ruled out, nevertheless the suggestion is made, especially by King, that any truly integral science of religion can hardly exclude any reference to theology of some sort. Intricate questions are involved in this discussion, notably whether any reference to transcendent categories should be declared out of court in the study of religion (as a number of social scientists have suggested), whether reference to the transcendent as experienced by the believer or tradition being studied is legitimate, and indeed required, as suggested by Ninian Smart, or whether ultimacy as such must be brought into the methodological discussion (as tends to happen in practice, rather than by methodological fiat, in the work of many non-western scholars and in the work of a number of western scholars of non-western religions). In this volume, Ninian Smart argues for the exclusion of traditional theology and the transcendent as a permanent and ultimate category from the study of religion in favour of concentration upon the transcendent as experienced, Frank Whaling attempts a longer and more intricate exercise of demarcation between the study of religion and theology more narrowly defined, Ursula King seeks ways to reconceptualise the role of theology within a more integral study of religion, while Kees Bolle refers to the theme more indirectly.

(7) *Definitions of religion*

Our seventh contrast, which like the discussion of truth-claims, philosophy and theology is a continuing rather than a new one, is bound up with some of the issues we have already considered, and concerns the vexed question of definitions. In the course of these two volumes countless definitions of religion are mentioned or assumed, and to summarise them here would be unnecessarily to lengthen the size of this introduction. Perhaps one of the reasons why western philosophy of religion has found it difficult to grapple with the study of religion is because that study has not been amenable to agreement on any one definition of religion. Conversely, one of the probable reasons why the study of religion has not become even more important than it is lies in the fact that it has not been content to settle upon an agreed set of given data which would constitute it as a rigid discipline wherein a particular definition would be universally appropriate. Thus the question of 'definitions' is necessarily part of our wider discussion of methods and theories.

It raises deeper questions as to whether the different approaches to the study of religion with their various implied definitions are complementary or opposed, as to what is meant by the term 'science' in the science of religion, as to whether the study of religion is a discipline or a field of studies, and as to whether the seeming impossibility of settling upon an overall definition of religion can be circumvented without opting for the approach of one school at the expense of others. Our volume does not solve the problem of definition although it does pose it, and it does open up the various definitional alternatives, in a more comprehensive way than is usually the case. However, there is another sense in which this book performs a more restricted and yet equally valuable task in the sphere of definitions. Attention is paid in various places to the need for a more exact definition of certain terms that are important in the study of religion. Thus Bolle argues for a more sophisticated definition and analysis of myth; Whaling makes a case for a tighter analysis of what we mean by comparative religion, theology, history of religion, anthropology of religion, dialogue, and faith; King investigates closely the meaning of history, phenomenology, science, hermeneutics, understanding, and interpretation; and implied in Smart's piece is the need for conceptual analysis of terms. Clarification of terms and concepts within these more limited areas is important; the advances resulting from such clarifications may contribute to the emergence of a more general view of what is meant by 'religion.'

(8) *Scope and nature of the data*

Another difference between the classical period of the study of religion and the contemporary situation lies in the contrast between the scope and nature of the data considered worthy of study. In the classical period, there was relatively greater stress put upon the data of primal religion, archaic religion, religions of antiquity, and the classical forms of the major living religions. Anthropologists such as Tylor and Frazer, sociologists such as Durkheim, and psychologists such as Freud theorised on the basis of the data of primal religion. When they ventured into comment upon the major religions, the likelihood was that their data would be taken from their own Judaeo-Christian tradition. At the present time, the situation is different. Not only has there been an explosion of knowledge in regard to *all* the religious traditions of mankind, the greatest relative accumulation of data has encompassed the major living traditions. There are a number of reasons for this relative switch of interest, and an analysis of them leads to some interesting conclusions.

(a) One reason is the relatively less prominent position of anthropology in the contemporary study of religion. During the classical period, the data of the primal religions provided the jumping-off point for some of the formative early theories of religion. Part of the motivation for this was the notion that study of primal religions could provide knowledge by means of which one could trace the origins of living religions, above all the Judaeo-Christian tradition. The origins theory is no longer viable, and with the exception of the work of Lévi-Strauss, anthropology is less significant in theory-formation.

(b) Another reason lies in the change of emphasis within sociology of religion. Durkheim's famous definition: (*The Elementary Forms of the Religious Life*, 1915: 62)

A religion is a unified system of beliefs and practices relative to sacred things, that is to say, things set apart and forbidden—beliefs and practices which unite into one single moral community called a church, all those who adhere to them

was erected, in the main, on the basis of research into primal religion with a more static flavour. Present-day sociology of religion has a greater interest in contemporary religion and change. To give but one example, the important recent debate about secularisation focusses upon the nature and definition of religion, and the decline or otherwise of religion in the contemporary situation. As we saw earlier, the increasing importance of modern communications systems also tends to rivet attention more prominently upon the modern religious situation.

(c) A third reason lies in the rediscovery of autochthonous religious traditions in a number of recently independent nations. As we saw earlier, the focus of religious attention and study inevitably falls upon the major religious traditions that are the basis of religious life in those nations. In his study of seven major non-Christian or non-western scholars, Coomaraswamy, Radhakrishnan, Suzuki, Buber, Nasr, Mbiti, and Chan, Whaling shows how their interest is centred upon both the past and present development for their own tradition.

(d) Another reason lies in the increasing western interest in major non-western religions. Factors lying outside the academic study of religion have contributed to this growth of interest: the immigration of Hindus, Buddhists, Muslims, and Sikhs into the West, the stimulus of south and east Asia upon commonwealth and north American troops who were in these regions during the Second World War, the steady trickle of western converts to eastern religions, the effects especially upon North America of political events in Korea and Vietnam, the aftermath of empire in Britain, the continuing spread of eastern sects into the West, the interest in Islam generated by the oil crisis and events in the Middle East. Before World War II, there were relatively few members of eastern religious traditions living in the West or even visiting the West, and there was not the same urgency to become acquainted with other religions in order to understand current affairs. The effect of the above-mentioned quasipolitical developments has been to focus more attention upon the major religious traditions in their contemporary as well as classical forms.

(e) A further reason lies in the fact that, especially since World War II, religions are in a sort of permanent change everywhere in the world. In addition to eastern religions entering the West, eastern religions in the East and western religions in the West find themselves in increasingly dynamic flux. The pre-1945 situation of more static and stabilised systems is no longer with us and 'religious change' is the order of the day. New religions are multiplying in Japan, numerous indigenous African Churches are springing up yearly, new sects are sprouting in different parts of the West. How to interpret religious change may have been viewed originally as a problem for the social scientists of religion, but it has since become a vital problem for historians and all students of religion, especially if attention in focussed not only on changes in institutional religion but also on religious interests themselves. The awareness is growing that such interests may appear and disappear much' more rapidly than was realised before World War II. The general effect of the obvious presence of religious change around the world is to create a greater relative interest in the contemporary religious scene and in the major living religions.

(f) A sixth reason lies in the apparent concern for the present state of western culture and religion among scholars of religion in both East and West. Whether that concern be for the seeming weakness of Christianity in the West, for the growing materialism of western civilisation, for the possible help that eastern religions can give to the West, or for the possible danger that eastern cultures face from the West, the inclination once again is to focus upon the present context and upon the major religions. Even a scholar such as Eliade, who involves himself mainly in the data of primal and Indian religions, is motivated to alter the mindset of contemporary western culture and religion through providing the West with creative contact with these other worldviews. Eliade's grappling with past religious forms is motivated therefore by a concern to help the present situation. The past for its own sake is no longer an end in itself.

(g) A final reason lies in the growing interest since World War II in religious education in schools, especially in Britain and the United States. The American constitution had banned the teaching of denominational or dogmatic religion in state schools, but this ban did not apply to the non-evaluative teaching of other world religions or the descriptive teaching about Christianity. Since 1945 such teaching has gradually become far more important in American schools. In Britain, the pre-war stress upon Christian education as a nurturing or even proselytising process has been replaced by a greater emphasis upon the teaching of world religions and a less theological emphasis upon the teaching of Christianity. Within both America and Britain therefore recent trends in religious education have highlighted the importance of the teaching of the living major world religions in schools. This is a natural development in that for curriculum and educational reasons it would have been much less feasible to teach primal or archaic religion to children. However, there is inevitably some interaction between the teaching in schools and the teaching in higher educational institutions within the same lands. Yet again we see the pendulum swinging in the direction of the contemporary living major religions away from the archaic or primal religions.

Consequences of increasing interest in major religions

There are at least two important consequences for the study of religion arising from this increasing interest in the major living religions in their contemporary as well as classical forms. In the first place, there is a correlation between the data used by scholars and the approach they adopt towards their studies. Had Wilfred Cantwell Smith not begun his career in Islamic studies, had Eliade not gone to India or used the data of primal religions, had Dumézil not immersed himself in Indo-European studies, it is likely that their theoretical approach to the study of religion would have taken a different course. Data and theory are interlinked. A change in the type of data used is therefore likely to be reflected in changing patterns of theory emerging from the switch in data. An inceasing number of present-day scholars make predominant use of the data of the major living religions in their contemporary as well as classical forms. The increasing use of the data of the major living religions, and the increase of theorising on the basis of those data, constitute a contemporary development that is little remarked but is of obvious long-term significance. It is intimated at various places within the pages of this volume.

The second consequence relates to the seeming difference within western scholarship in relation to the types of data that are used. We have seen how continental European scholars are more likely to make greater use of the data of the religions of antiquity, the classical forms of the major religions, and (to a lesser extent) primal religions, whereas Anglo-Saxon scholars are more likely to use the data of the major living religions in their contemporary as well as classical forms. This is, of course, by no means a water-tight division. European scholars have done some fine work upon the major religions in their contemporary as well as classical forms, and Anglo-Saxon scholars have done some noted work upon the religions of antiquity, the classical as well as contemporary forms of the major religions, and primal religions. However the fact that this seeming division of interest is more than a mere rule of thumb is illustrated by the heated methodological debates, described by Dr. King, that characterised the International Association for the History of Religions (IAHR) and its conferences during the 1960s and have rumbled on quietly ever since. This discussion is not merely a debate as to whether the study of religion is more scientific, historical, empirical, and academic rather than more philosophical, theological, hermeneutical, and dialogical in tone, it is also a debate over data. European scholars are not only more likely to emphasise the historical-philological, approach as the royal road along which the study of religion must march, they are also more likely to employ that method upon archaic or classical data. Lying behind this preference there are causes rooted in the academic background of the study of religion in Europe that are clearly important. Other causes too are brought our or implied in this book: the general lack of an imperial background on the continent to make the study of eastern religions more urgent, the smaller presence of immigrants belonging to eastern religions, the lesser presence and impact of eastern religious sects, a greater ignorance of continental European languages among noted non-western scholars who generally wrote and thought in English, a lesser interest in developing new forms of religious education involving world religions in southern European countries influenced by Roman Catholic norms of Christian education or in northern European countries with relatively little contact with world religions, a concern for the state of their own religion that was apt to arouse more concern in theological than religious studies circles, and relatively less contact with religious change in the wider sense either at home or abroad. In short, differences of approach are not unrelated to the use of certain types of data, and the reasons for the use of certain types of data may have both academic and non-academic roots within certain cultures and language groups. To put it another way, the selection of religious data by scholars and their study of religion 'abroad' are related to some extent to the cultural and religious consciousness 'at home.' We are not aware that this point has been made so forcibly before, and we hope it will lead to a deeper realisation of some of the non-academic reasons for differences in approach that appear to be totally academic in character. It is perhaps significant that the Netherlands, which was an imperial nation, and which makes constant as opposed to peripheral use of the English language, forms a kind of bridge between the continental and Anglo-Saxon proclivities, employing as it does an umbrella of approaches (as Kees Oosten, van Beek and Bolle illustrate) arising out of a varied set of data.

(9) *The study of religion: A discipline or field of studies?*

Our ninth point of contrast between the classical and contemporary periods in the study of religion concerns the question as to whether the study of religion is a discipline or a field of studies, whether it is a science or an art, and whether the elements that compose it are complementary or opposed. This is probably the key question of all. After all, the study of religion, as we have summarised it, straddles a number of disciplines; the 1980 IAHR congress at Winnipeg held twenty sections on topics ranging from African Religion to Women in Religion. Through these various disciplines, through these different sections at IAHR and other conferences, 'messages' are passed from one mind to another. But what is it, if anything, that these disciplines, these approaches, these conference sections, these 'messages' have in common? Compared with this extraordinarily complex state of the field, the study of religion before 1945 looks like another world.

And yet perhaps the difference between the two periods, although grounded in fact, is more one of perception. A perusal of histories of the study of religion such as those of Waardenburg and Sharpe shows that, although the accumulation of data and the volume of writing on theory and method were less, the work done on the study of religion by the 'giants' of the earlier period was varied. The question is whether the scholars and movements included by Waardenburg and Sharpe as being engaged in the study of religion in the pre-1945 period considered *themselves* to be engaged in the study of religion, or in the study of something else. To some extent the same question remains today and is raised throughout this volume: are sociologists, psychologists, anthropologists, historians, phenomenologists, comparativists, and other scholars of religion primarily scholars of religion, primarily scholars of the discipline concerned, or both? Part of the reason for the growing interest in phenomenology of religion that arose out of the work of Kristensen and van der Leeuw and that grew to a peak in the earlier post-World War II period was the feeling that the component of 'religion,' however viewed, had been underemphasised in the pre-war period when, it was felt, the so-called study of religion had often been divided into discretely separate sections that focussed upon different oriental languages and literatures per se or upon history, sociology, psychology, theology, and other disciplines as such which, from the standpoint of the study of religion, were often viewed in a covertly exclusivistic or reductionistic fashion. The corollary of this attempt by phenomenologists to give a greater integration to the study of religion and to emphasise that 'religion' was at the heart of this study was the tendency on the part of some phenomenologists to downplay contributions from those methods which saw the study of 'religion' as part of a greater whole rather than as an end in itself. The ambience of the present discussion has therefore shifted by comparison with the pre-war period.

Within the pages of these books, this area of concern is considered at different levels within different chapters, sometimes explicitly and at other times implicitly. Complete agreement is not reached as to a single paradigm, but some tentative general principles do emerge.

(a) In the first place, the study of religion has to do with the study of all religious traditions and all methods of studying religion. No religions are excluded from the study of religion whether they be ancient or modern, primal or major, living or dead. Contemporary fashions may veer towards a preference for the study of certain kinds of data, but no principle of exclusion can be applied to any data that are part of the history of religion. The same principle of non-exclusion applies to the various methods of studying religion. No methods are excluded whether they centre exclusively upon religion or not, whether they belong to the social sciences or the humanities, whether their approach is inductive or hermeneutic, whether they focus upon data or persons. The only exception applies to the type of method that centres upon one religion and explicitly applies its categories to others as tends to happen within theology and to a lesser extent within philosophy. Even then the data rather than the truth-claims involved remain relevant. To the extent that different methods, disciplines, and approaches feed into the study of religion, it does appear to be a field of studies rather than a discipline in the normal sense of the term.

(b) There is also implied within these books the need for a complementarity of approaches. Although each section focusses upon a particular approach and in this respect advances its claims, this does not imply that other approaches are inappropriate or that any one approach should dominate the field. However, in spite of the variety of materials, issues, theories and angles thereby introduced into the study of religion, the stance of complementarity does not obviate the need for overall integration within the field.

(c) Furthermore, although it is agreed that the study of religion must be founded upon a bedrock of data provided by empirical studies especially within the history and anthropology of religion, there is also a virtual consensus that it is naive to view such studies positivistically or exclusivistically. The axioms of such positivism: that there is an external world of religious data, objectively present, observable by induction, that can be dispassionately described by empirical language as a series of propositions corresponding to objective facts—are no longer seen to be inductively self-authenticating but dependent upon prior theory. Hermeneutics of a heuristic type are therefore found to be necessary even within the social scientific approaches. Moreover the accumulation of data is not enough. Interpretative categories and other approaches are necessary that transcend positivism in the attempt to bring order to the overall study of religion.

(d) In the fourth place, although doubts are raised as to the present direction and future viability of phenomenology of religion as a 'discipline,' there is tacit agreement that the phenomenological categories of *epoché* (suspending judgement in order to understand) and *Einfühlung* (empathy with the [religious] position of others) are generally helpful within the total study of religion.

(e) It is also agreed that the study of religion is different from natural science insofar as it deals with data that involve persons rather than data that centre upon objects in nature. The study of data involving persons relates the study of religion to the humanities as well as to the social sciences, to the arts as well as to the sciences. When religion is perceived as a religion of persons it can be seen in terms of the religion of groups of persons (sociology and anthropology of religion), the religion of individuals (psychology of religion), the faith and intentionality of persons (phenomenology and hermeneutics), the myths and texts of persons (the study of myths and texts), and so on. This involvement of religious data with persons, their social groupings, their individual religious experiences, their conscious commitment, their unconscious moulding by heredity or environment, their history, means that the study of religion has to do centrally with man.

(f) In the sixth place, there is a reasonable, although not total, agreement that the study of religion should have wide rather than narrow limits. Ninian Smart is willing to contemplate that communism, humanism, and nationalism, should be within the same species as religion. More importantly there is reasonable agreement that, whether the limits of the study be drawn wider or not, there should be a wider integration within the whole field. This task is attempted in different ways by Ursula King, Frank Whaling, Kees Bolle, and Ninian Smart. They are not in full agreement about the minutiae of any proposed solution, but they do agree that the task is important. Frank Whaling makes the point that, although widely differing methods and data are fed into the comparative approach to the study of religion, comparative religion remains a recognisable and important endeavour. It is supportive of, but not subordinate to, the approaches that feed into it; it is neither superior nor inferior to them; it is not reduced to any of the methods that service it, whether they be strongly hermeneutical or empirical; its function is to coordinate and direct the overall comparative enterprise as a means to the end of understanding religious traditions and religious man. Within the restricted sphere of comparison, it provides a possible model for the role of the study of religion in relation to the various approaches that feed into it. Ninian Smart's chapter deals directly with the way in which a whole set of disciplines in interplay make up the study of religion. He analyses the roles of structured empathy, phenomenological typology, sociology of religion, anthropology of religion, psychology of religion, history of religions and iconography within the study of religion, and he points out that there is an overlap between the scientific study of religion based upon the aforementioned disciplines and five other enterprises which, because they are expressive, proclamatory and philosophical rather than descriptive and value-free, are not inherently part of the study of religion, namely: constructive traditionalism, philosophical theology, theological positivism, pluralistic theology, and dialogue. Ursula King, in her discussion of the possibility of an integral science of religion, glances at various proposals that have recently been made to combine the multiple perspectives and questions of the study of religion in a more integral manner. She emphasises in particular the work of Georg Schmid, *Principles of Integral Science of Religion* (1979), as being illustrative of a new desire on the part of scholars of religion to reflect on the *whole* field of religion (including its transcendent reality), on the *role* of the study of religion, and on the premises and methods whereby that role can be fulfilled. In short, while maintaining a wide view of the complex nature of the contemporary situation, this book also offers significant clues as to how future integration may be achieved.

Lastly, it is also agreed that, in spite of the search for integration, and the possible complementarity of approaches, there remain a number of different, but flourishing approaches within the study of religion which provide helpful, alternative methods and levels of interpretation. In a later chapter, Frank Whaling analyses how the different approaches to science intimated by the philosophy of science have their counterparts in the different approaches to the study of religion, and how methodological reflection within the study of religion can be aided by recent work done in the philosophy of science.

(10) *Relevance of the contemporary global context*

Our final and brief contrast between the classical and contemporary approaches touches upon the relevance of the present-day global context for the study of religion. Global events since 1945 have drawn together the peoples of the planet into a closer unity of shared danger, opportunity, and reflection on their future. This situation is vastly different from that which pertained before World War II. Part of the final chapter glances briefly at the relationship between the study of religion and wider scholarship, and at the opportunity afforded to the study of religion to play a creative role in the contemporary situation. One of its main tasks is to study world religions which are global in setting, and it straddles a number of disciplines and interests which have as their areas of concern the study of cosmic matters, namely nature, man, and transcendence. As Ninian Smart comments, the fact that so often the wider study of religion has been suspected from the side of faith and neglected from the side of reason has contributed to the lopsidedness of the human sciences. That the study of religion should play a creative role in contemporary scholarship is important not only for the study of religion but also for the world of learning in general.

We hope that readers will find out two volumes a worthy successor to Jacques Waardenburg's *Classical Approaches to the Study of Religion*. We hope also that they will be read widely and commented upon at length. May the constructive comment that must be forthcoming when people wrestle with the issues contained in a book of this immense scope serve creatively to advance the cause of the study of religion. Our purpose has been so to summarise the contemporary approaches to the study of religion that momentum may be given to such an advance at an inter-disciplinary, intercultural, and interhuman level.

2

Historical and Phenomenological Approaches to the Study of Religion

Some major developments and issues under debate since 1950

URSULA KING

Leeds

If one examines the major developments in the history and phenomenology of religion over the last thirty years, there can be no doubt that there has been a considerable growth of activities. This is apparent from the number of publications, the frequency of conferences and the range of issues under debate. A lively discussion by an increasing number of scholars around the world is taking place as to the very nature of the subject. The year 1950 does not mark a completely new beginning but it provides a convenient watershed for a survey of recent developments. The middle of the twentieth century saw the emergence of a new era when in the wake of the Second World War a post-colonial world was born. It saw the birth of numerous new nations as well as the growth of a new kind of internationalism, not to mention the many new problems linked to quickly expanding populations and an equally quickly shrinking globe, developments which were not without significance for the study of religion.

1950 is also the year when the International Association for the History of Religions (IAHR) was formed, soon to be followed by the foundation of new national sections, the establishment of new journals as well as the renaming of old ones, the launching of new bibliographical ventures and the concern for greater international cooperation. Another reason for starting at this date is the fact that the major developments in the study of religion have been described up to 1950 by Jacques Waardenburg in his *Classical Approaches to the Study of Religion* (1973: 2 vols.; see especially 'View of a Hundred Years' Study of Religion,' I, 1–73). A general survey for the years following that period has not been undertaken so far although several excellent studies exist which analyse specific developments and arguments in greater detail than is possible here. Articles apart, the most up-to-date survey in book form is found in the concluding chapter of Eric Sharpe, *Comparative Religion. A History* (1975: 267–93, 'Twenty Years of International Debate, 1950–1970').

When Professor C. J. Bleeker, in his capacity as general secretary of the IAHR, addressed the XIIth International Congress at Stockholm in 1970, he explicitly stated that 'It would be a great source of satisfaction if we could get to know the results the history of religions has reached in the past twenty years, in which direction the study is moving, and whether there has been progress in the discipline. Unfortunately, we have no systematic surveys of the whole field of research.' It would be a challenging task indeed for a group of scholars to collaborate in such a venture for, as Bleeker went on to say, 'the type of scholar who is capable of surveying the total field of the history of religions, or at least great parts of it, seems to be slowly dying out. This is why it is impossible at present to satisfy the desire which we all feel to know what has happened in this branch of scholarship during the past twenty years' (Bleeker 1975b: 27).

However, it is perhaps less the case that such a type of scholar is dying out than the fact that the material available for surveying has become so voluminous that it is impossible for any single individual to provide a comprehensive summary on his or her own. The study of religion, as presently conceived and pursued by many scholars around the world, is much wider than 'the total field of the history of religions' of which Bleeker spoke. It represents an increasingly international and multi-disciplinary as well as an interdisciplinary field of studies and research. It would be presumptious for any one scholar to claim that such rich and varied developments could be adequately surveyed in any other way than by close international collaboration and the intensive team-work of specialists in the various disciplines which have a bearing on the study of religion. The present article is offered as a modest attempt to survey recent literature within the given constraints of space and time, and to ask how far current publications implicitly demonstrate or explicitly contribute to the major issues in the methodological debate of the contemporary history and phenomenology of religion.

There has been much discussion over recent years as to what constitutes the proper subject area and the specific method(s) of the history and phenomenology of religion and whether these two approaches to the study of religion are separate, interrelated or even identical or, on the contrary, opposed to and exclusive of each other. This debate has gained enormous momentum, especially over the last ten years or so, as is evident from a large number of publications and also from several conferences which have expressed an explicitly methodological concern. Although the size of the debate is considerable, the area of common agreement is perhaps less large than one might hope for. There is a growing trend towards greater methodological self-awareness and closer analysis of the presuppositions of one's research among many scholars today, yet much further clarification is still needed in this area.

What is available to anyone surveying the scholarly harvest in the history and phenomenology of religion during the last thirty years? In other words, what research results have been produced in the form of books, articles and conference proceedings? What are the major concerns of the scholars of religion belonging to the present generation and where is the discipline going in the future? Important too, what are the organisational developments which have affected the production of scholarly works, facilitated intellectual exchange and stimulated the debate on methods?

Given these questions, the approach adopted here will of necessity be synoptic; it may occasionally involve critical comparisons and will attempt an analysis of some of the conceptual tools currently used in the history and phenomenology of religion. It must be emphatically stated that this chapter can neither reflect all the discussions and developments which have taken place around the world nor can it provide a complete bibliography of relevant publications in all major languages. The emphasis lies primarily on the analysis of the recent practice and discussion of methods found in the history and phenomenology of religion. The aim is not to give a survey of developments country by country (for this see *Religion*, Special Issue, August 1975) nor to discuss publications in this field in a strictly chronological order. The need for this is adequately filled by such indispensable bibliographical reference works as the *International Bibliography of the History of Religions*, published by the IAHR from 1954–80, now replaced by *Science of Religion—Abstracts and Index of Recent Articles* (before 1980: *Science of Religion Bulletin*) published by the Free University of Amsterdam, the quarterly issues of the *Bulletin Signalétique: Sciences Religieuses*, published by the Centre National de Recherche Scientifique in Paris and the *Religious Studies Review*, published by the Canadian Council on the study of Religion. In fact, the most recent publications will be drawn on rather more frequently as they are less well known than earlier studies; they possess the additional advantage of incorporating discussions about preceding works.

The present survey will mainly, but not exclusively, focus on a third-level analysis of the data provided by research in the history and phenomenology of religion over recent years. At the first level, many specialised studies and monographs exist which cannot be directly taken into account here. At the second level, various reference works have been produced which bring together and, in certain cases, integrate a host of individual data into an overall framework. These works often, but not always, include analytical reflections and discussions of the methods underlying such attempts at integration. At the third level, an analysis of the materials and methods found in such reference works and in many other sources can be undertaken in order to map out the common core of the history and phenomenology of religion and to explore their fluid boundaries. It should be clear by now that this survey will mainly be concerned with works which have attempted an integration of subject-matter or have made a significant contribution to the current debate about methods in the two fields under review here. In actual practice this means that most examples will be taken from post-1960 publications for it is only after that date that the methodological debate came in a new way fully into its own.

To counter any possible criticism at the outset, it must be mentioned that only a limited range of arguments can be examined here. Thus, this chapter is far from exhaustive nor can it be as truly international as it should be. I am painfully aware of the diverse constraints working against a fully international conception of the science of religion as a scholarly discipline. Although international in scope and intention, the study of religion is not always approached from such a wide and integral perspective in the works of all scholars. There is the obvious built-in defect that individual scholars only have access to limited data, not merely because of their chosen field of specialisation but even more because some major modern languages are not easily accessible. Few can follow the latest developments in the study of religion around the world. For western scholars this is particularly true with regard to eastern languages, especially Japanese and Chinese, and also with regard to recent developments in the study of religion in Eastern European countries and the USSR. Out of necessity rather than choice the present survey refers largely to western publications. To some readers, especially eastern ones, it may thus appear unduly western-centred, a shortcoming for which I apologise although I know that it is to a large extent unavoidable at present.

Even if one examines major publications in western languages, one cannot help but notice a certain duplication of work undertaken by different scholars working in different languages, often unknown to each other. In spite of growing collaboration, there is still a lack of close communication and, as a result, a lack of urgently needed clarification about the objects and methods of the discipline. A repetition of similar arguments occurs in this debate of many schools and voices; in fact, sometimes there seems to reign more of a cacophony than harmony. If we can pick out some of the main melodies, interpret the reigning leitmotifs and possibly discover a new note here and there which may stimulate further reflections on the part of the reader, then the present survey will have been amply worthwhile.

1. What are the historical and phenomenological approaches?

Towards the end of his important address on *Religionswissenschaft*, given at the inaugural meeting of the American Society for the Study of Religion in 1959, Erwin R. Goodenough pleaded that at 'the present stage of the Science of Religion, we would do well to ask small questions until we have established a methodology we can all approve and use' (Goodenough 1959: 94). But more than twenty years later have we come any nearer to this aim of a generally approved methodology? Over the last decade or so the cry for methodological clarification has repeatedly been raised; the number of papers, monographs, and conferences devoted to methodology has grown fast, previously developed methods have been criticised and found wanting, several new methods and theories about the study of religion have been proposed. There can be no doubt that a vigorous, if not always sufficiently rigorous debate about methodology has come into existence; at the same time many works are still being published which include little or no theoretical reflection at all. There is much need for a clarification of the terminology in use and for a critical examination of the objects and methods specific to the study of religion. Scholars with enough imaginative grasp and vision to reflect on the future have clearly perceived that the most urgent requirements for a further creative development of the subject are a well formulated research programme and bolder theory formation.

However, the plea for greater methodological awareness does not in itself answer the question whether the classification, analysis, and interpretation of religious data on as comprehensive a scale as possible represents basically one single discipline, a wide field of related but different studies, or whether it is a science, a craft, or possibly even an art, only to be mastered by a few extraordinarily endowed and creative scholars. All these possibilities have been suggested and one may venture the opinion that these differences of approach in handling data from the complex and multidimensional reality that is religion allow for creative tension which reflects the healthy state and vitality of the discipline, if indeed this is the right word. For although large areas of

agreement have been reached in the way scholars understand and practise their research, a general lack of consent exists as to what the study of
religion is or ought to be called. The fluidity of terms given to this
subject in the English-speaking world alone is baffling. Intellectual
fashions of the day have repeatedly affected common usage. There are a
great many names in circulation but none has become so universally
accepted as to be definite. The debate about what the subject ought to be
called has oscillated a great deal over the years; it is closely interwined
with the *Methodenstreit* in general, i.e., the arguments about respective
methods and their problems are closely interrelated with what is perceived to be the nature of the subject (see the excellent survey article by
R. Pummer 1972). Thus, the problem of definition is a matter of central
concern, for the name given to a subject both reflects and in turn affects
the choice of suitable objects and methods of study.

The multidisciplinary thrust and new directions taken by the study of
religion in the last two decades or so has been institutionally recognized
by the founding or renaming of university departments devoted to
religious studies (sometimes called 'department of religion,' especially in
North America). However, this term can be both a help and a hindrance
as its adoption does not by itself settle the methodological debate or
clarify the boundaries of the subject area. It is certain that many different
orientations, not all consistent with each other, have found umbrage
under this new term. However, the conception of religious studies
definitely expresses a new development which does not represent a
sudden, sharp break with the past but is to some extent continuous with
what went on earlier in the study of religion. Yet it is also a new attempt
to go beyond the mere collection, description, and empirical analysis of
religious data and seek an interpretation within a wider theoretical
framework which allows a more systematic perspective. This effort to
develop an integral approach and a more comprehensive theory of
interpretation for the study of religion may be the hallmark of what
could eventually prove to be the most stimulating and promising aspect
of the contemporary methodological debate.

Before the developments of recent years can be fully reviewed, an
initial mapping of the territory will be of help. Anyone eager to discover
the route taken by the subject in recent years can easily be confused by

the abundance of contradictory signposting and the many different roads which have been taken. Which are the ones pointing in the right direction for the study of religion not to end in a future cul-de-sac?

The contemporary study of religion covers a wide range of interests and methods which often complement each other. A special difficulty of the methodological debate is the question whether all methods are equally important, whether some are more indispensable than others, and whether any particular method is so crucial that it lays the foundation for all others. The present chapter concentrates on the historical and phenomenological approaches which, if not understood in the narrowest sense, raise many difficult issues about meaning and interpretation. History and phenomenology are here discussed together because theoretical debates about their nature and method are often closely related. To enter the debate at its simplest level, an attempt will be made to state briefly what is meant by the 'historical' and 'phenomenological' approach when protagonists argue about the respective appropriateness of these methods for the study of religion.

Both the historical-descriptive presentation as well as the systematic analysis and classification of religious data belong to the history of the study of religion. Both approaches are an integral part of the nineteenth century inheritance of the subject and both have found further refinement in subsequent theory and practice. If anything, the historical approach is easier to define; it has been better established and longer practised. It has also produced more works of scholarship. What is precisely understood by the historical approach is frequently related to the wider discussions about the nature of history as an academic discipline. The protagonists of a strictly historical approach emphasize the use of historical-critical methods, a rigorous practice of philology and other subsidiary disciplines necessary for the study of history, and insist on factual-descriptive expositions, not infrequently accompanied by a minimum of interpretation as to the meaning of the data presented.

It is necessary to stress again and again that the plurality of religions in the present world and the variety of cultures moulded by different religious traditions cannot be adequately understood without a thoroughly historical study of the origin, growth, and development of particular religions, affected by the ongoing dynamic of continuity and change. At an earlier stage, the sharp emphasis on the knowledge of historical facts arose perhaps from the need to counteract the general ignorance of non-western religious and cultural traditions in the West. It was not only the concern for historical truth but also the need to free the study of religion from the dominance of *a priori* theological and philosophical speculation which required a strong insistence on the use of the historical method.

The historical-philological method has yielded a rich harvest for the study of religion. But it would perhaps not be incorrect to say that, in certain overworked areas at least, it has also led to a surfeit of data suffering from a lack of integration. In some cases it has had the unfortunate result of an isolationist position whereby individual scholars, through their overspecialisation in one specific aspect or period of a particular religion, have been unable to relate their knowledge to wider questions and concerns, whether those of the study of religion or of the intellectual life and scholarship of their time.

But history itself is open to a wide range of interpretations and cannot be practised without a concern for systematic reflection and theory, a point proved by the existence of very different philosophies of history. (The American serial publication *History and Theory* regularly examines different theoretical orientations affecting the study of history; see especially Beiheft 8, 1968 'On Method in the History of Religions,' edited by J.S. Helfer.) History may be understood in a very narrow or much wider sense. There exists what might be called the descriptive and the interpretative use of history. Each approach has its own adherents and means of expression. For example, the French journal *Revue de l'Histoire des Religions* (founded in 1880) still carries a programmatic statement today saying that 'the review is purely historical; it excludes any work of a polemical or dogmatic character' (back cover; my translation). Many French scholars have favoured this strictly historical approach, perhaps best exemplified in the work of the *École Pratique des Hautes Etudes* (Paris) but it has well-known protagonists among other European scholars too, particularly in Scandinavia. At the other end of the spectrum lies the American journal *History of Religions* (founded 1961 and subtitled 'An International Journal for Comparative Historical Studies;' edited by M. Eliade, J. Kitagawa, and J. Smith) which since its inception 'has been instrumental in providing materials and creating a methodology for the study of world religions' (publicity brochure). However, on closer inspection one discovers that apart from Eliade's own important statements and a few other articles on methodology, most contributions deal primarily with historical-factual data.

Another important aspect of the history of religions as practised today is the question of which period of history is most emphasized in the work of particular scholars. Is the research primarily concerned with the religions of the past or with the living religions of the present? However, such a distinction between extinct and living religions may be unjustifiable, as has been argued, because it implies wrong assumptions about historical discontinuities. But while it is legitimate to give due prominence to the formative period of a religious tradition or to the exemplary height of its development, one wonders why in many works this is accompanied by a neglect for the present, too often only considered in terms of loss and decline. Is there a marked preference for classical rather than modern materials among historians of religions in the strict sense so as to bypass the problem of meaning which grows more urgent and difficult the nearer one gets to the present? But is religion even in the far-away past not too often seen primarily in terms of ideas and institutions in isolation from the concrete context of a particular society? All these questions have been asked and, depending on the answers given, particular orientations result in the study of religion, as will be seen later. At present it is enough to be aware of their existence and realize that when the term 'history of religions' is used to describe a methodological stance, the emphasis may well lie on the factual-descriptive approach which, however, begs further questions of a theoretical and essentially philosophical kind about the nature of factual data and their explanation.

In contrast to the history of religions approach in the narrow sense some scholars understand 'history' to mean an enquiry of such magnitude that it embraces most phenomenological studies whilst others regard the phenomenological approach as clearly distinct from the historical one. Phenomenology is then primarily understood as a systematic and comparative classification of all religious phenomena whatever they are. Undertaken at its widest, this must also include the historical development of these phenomena and this leads, from a different angle, back to the question of the relative importance and relationship of history and phenomenology. Several sides have been taken in this debate which goes back to an earlier part of this century. It is a debate beset with many philosophical thorns, few of which have been removed so far (see Sharpe 1975: 220–50; the Dutch contribution to phenomenology is discussed in Waardenburg 1972).

In contrast to the historical approach which is always diachronic, the phenomenological approach presents data in a synchronic, classificatory manner, frequently irrespective of any historical sequence. Thus, in the view of many, it appears to be too ahistorical if not to say anachronistic at times. The term 'phenomenology of religion' was first used by Chantepie de la Saussaye (in his *Lehrbuch der Religionsgeschichte*, 1887) prior to the development of Husserl's philosophy of phenomenology. It described the attempt to investigate the essence and meaning of religious phenomena and to group phenomena in a typological manner independent from space and time. The early phenomenology of religion was thus a discipline of classification used by many different scholars. However, this early empirical phenomenology is distinct from the classical phenomenology of religion developed in the first half of the twentieth century and perhaps best known through the work of the Dutch scholar, Gerardus van der Leeuw (especially his *Religion in Essence and Manifestation: a Study in Phenomenology*, trl. 1938, 1st ed. 1933). The specific methodological principles characteristic of this classical phenomenology were initially dependent on Husserl's influence but it must be emphasized that the subsequent developments of the phenomenology of religion remained unconnected with philosophical phenomenologies or the more recent discussions about phenomenology in the social sciences.

At its simplest, phenomenology seeks to understand the phenomenon of religion or, rather, specific phenomena of religion. The phenomenological method is summed up by the use of two distinct principles, derived from Husserl, namely the *epoché* and the eidetic vision. The *epoché* is often described as 'bracketing', that is to say, a suspension of judgment on the part of the investigator as to the truth, value, and in some cases also the existence of the phenomenon. The eidetic vision aims to grasp the essence of phenomena by means of empathy and intuition. Whereas the use of the *epoché* is pursued to achieve detachment and some kind of pure objectivity, the intuitive grasp of the essentials of phenomena in their wholeness clearly introduces a large measure of subjectivity. Thus, phenomenological methodology is characterized from the outset by an inherent tension, if not to say contradiction, of its underlying principles.

Phenomenological discussions have been influenced by developments in biblical interpretation or hermeneutics and the philosophical explorations of German *Verstehensphilosophie*. Large claims have been made on behalf of the phenomenology of religion; the most significant of these was that the phenomenological approach 'provided a path to the understanding (*Verstehen*) of religion, and to a grasp of its essence (*Wesen*), by means of an as far as possible value-free examination of its manifestations (*Erscheinungen*)' (Sharpe 1975: 220).

Traditional phenomenology has been largely practised by Dutch and German scholars of an earlier generation whose work has come in for much criticism recently. In spite of the investigation of numerous religious phenomena, little theoretical advance seems to have been made and much phenomenological work lacks methodological rigour and precision. The field is characterized by an extreme fragmentation so that one can discern almost as many different phenomenologies as there are phenomenologists. More frequently than not the term 'phenomenology of religion' appears to refer to a general approach rather than a specific method. This approach emphasizes the need to distance oneself from speculative and normative *a priori* categories in the study of religious phenomena; it also pleads for an overall orientation where the scholar investigates what the believer believes himself rather than what others believe about him.

Through the use of *epoché* and the search for objectivity, phenomenology may seem to share the aims of descriptive science but on closer examination it appears, as Oxtoby has pointed out, that '*Epoché* and eidetic vision are neither critical nor objective in the commonly understood sense of critical objectivity. Just as *epoché* suspends criticism, eidetic vision suspends objectivity. There is nothing outside one's intuitive grasp of a pattern which validates that pattern ... phenomenological expositions of religion are in fact very personal appreciations of it, akin more to certain forms of literary and aesthetic criticism than to the natural or even the social sciences' (Oxtoby 1968: 597). In the opinion of many scholars phenomenology represents an extremely subjective approach in strong contrast to the objective approach of the history of religions. Furthermore, much phenomenological work depends on specific theological assumptions, derived in particular from liberal Protestant theology. The apologetic and theological presuppositions of several phenomenologists have been pointed out; Van der Leeuw in particular considered himself always primarily as a theologian (see 'Gerardus van der Leeuw as a Theologian and Phenomenologist', in Waardenburg 1978a: 187–248). Much phenomenology may thus be considered as theological propaedeutics.

The methodological presuppositions of phenomenology imply several philosophical assumptions regarding the essence of religion and the nature of religious experience, too easily assumed to be the same in all people and places. Another practical difficulty arises from the vast multiplicity of religious phenomena. No phenomenologist can ever deal with all phenomena and the particular ones chosen for investigation are often dealt with in isolation from the wider context necessary for their explanation. Moreover, the very choice of phenomena to be studied must rest on criteria other than those supplied by the phenomena themselves.

Although the phenomenology of religion seems to have reached few answers and little clarity, it has raised important questions many of which are still with us today. One wonders how far the emphasis on 'bracketing' in the search for objectivity has not led to a 'bracketing out' of some of the most central and decisive questions of religious existence, namely those of ultimate truth and value, of the focus of the transcendent, and the place of its revelation to man. This also raises the further difficulty of what difference there may be between investigating a historical 'fact' about religion(s) and understanding a religious 'phenomenon'. Does one need to distinguish between 'understanding a religion' and 'understanding a faith other than one's own' and if so, wherein lies the difference between these two approaches? Furthermore, why is the 'history of religions' usually expressed in the plural whereas the 'phenomenology of religion' is always referred to in the singular?

These and similar issues point to the difficulties of interpretation in

the study of religion. It is true that historical and systematic considerations have from the earliest days of the discipline been combined with
reflections about the understanding and interpretation of religion. But it
is only recently that a more concerted and systematic effort has been
developed to create a unified, adequate method and a comprehensive
hermeneutic for the study of religion. This has included a new look at
phenomenology and a critical reconsideration of its nature and method
(see especially the important plea for methodological awareness made
by Waardenburg (1978a), and the discussion in Honko (1979:
141–220)). It has also been argued that the term 'phenomenology of
religion' is so ambiguous as to be misleading and consequently should
be abandoned in order to avoid any association with philosophical
phenomenologies. Instead, it might be replaced either by the term
'systematic *Religionswissenschaft*' or 'the comparative study of religion.'
To many scholars this is unacceptable, however, as the latter term
appears to be too closely associated with an earlier, less methodologically aware understanding of 'comparative religion.'

The search for clearer concepts, definitions, and methods is still going
on. There seems to exist a built-in dialectical relationship between the
historical and systematic aspects of the study of religion since its beginning. Whether this inherent tension will ever be resolved and transcended by a more comprehensive and integral approach is at present
much debated. The historical and phenomenological approaches are
generally understood to be non-normative, that is to say, to describe and
examine facts, whether historically or systematically, without judging
them from a particular theological or philosophical standpoint. Whether
this is at all possible or can only be practised on a limited range of data
and questions, has come in for much discussion recently. However, only
the future can show whether currently proposed methodologies will
prove to be of more lasting value than those of previous generations.

The phenomenological approach, in spite of serious shortcomings,
has much to commend it as it is closely connected with the attempt to
develop a hermeneutic appropriate to the study of religion as an integral
part of human knowledge and experience. At any one period, the study
of religion is always closely related to and dependent upon the general
understanding of religion dominant at that time and related to the wider

intellectual and cultural developments of society. During the nineteenth century, scholars were fascinated by the question of the origin and evolution of religion, now largely abandoned, whereas twentieth century studies have been dominated by questions about the nature and essence of religion and, more recently, its meaning and function in society.

Many of the issues mentioned so far have found both protagonists and antagonists among contemporary religion scholars. The most characteristic feature of the methodological debate since World War II is not an either/or position—*either* the historical *or* the phenomenological approach—but a critical reexamination of the classical approaches to the study of religion and the attempt to develop a more differentiated and comprehensive methodology than before. Besides the critical evaluation of the legacy of an earlier *Religionswissenschaft* and 'comparative religion' this includes a strong concern for definitional issues, the attempt to refute any kind of reductionism in the understanding and explanation of religion, however closely connected to other branches of knowledge and their methods, and an increasing appreciation of the wider cultural role of the study of religion.

Waardenburg's indispensable survey of the *Classical Approaches to the Study of Religion* (1973a) already emphasized the fact that the study of religion is less one particular discipline than a field of studies with a strongly interdisciplinary character. In his view it is this rather than a specific object or method which distinguishes it most from other disciplines. Many specialists belonging to a wide range of disciplines and working with different methods and theoretical assumptions contribute to our understanding of the complex and multidimensional phenomenon of religion. Whether this multiplicity can ever be theoretically accounted for by one comprehensive theory is at present very much open to debate.

Not all scholars will see the important methodological issues in the same way as they are presented here. But whatever their methodological stance, even when it is primarily one against the consideration of methods, their arguments form part of the wider developments which have taken place since the 1950s. To understand particular aspects and arguments of the current methodological discussion it is necessary to see them within a much wider regional and international context. Before specific arguments about the history and phenomenology of religion are examined in detail, it is imperative to give first an outline of the growth of the debate at the international level. This will be done by considering the main areas of the contemporary scholarly network in the study of religion, by describing the organisational innovations which have greatly facilitated and strengthened research in this field, and by looking at important reference works and handbooks which have been published in the history and phenomenology of religion over recent years.

2. Growth of the international debate

2.1 *Geographical distribution of the participants in the debate*

It is important to stress the growing international and intercultural character of the study of religion today. From its early beginnings in Western Europe more than a century ago, the systematic study of the religious heritage of mankind has now grown into a worldwide pursuit which links together scholars from many different nations. The major emphasis and approach to the study of religion may vary widely but, in one form or another, the subject is represented among the teaching and research interests of numerous contemporary universities and colleges. In some of the newly founded nations, and sometimes in the older ones too, the study of religion is also not unrelated to a renewed search for origins and spiritual roots. Different motivations and divergent cultural and scholarly traditions help to explain the wide range of attitudes taken towards what are considered to be the objects and most appropriate methods of the study of religion.

To locate the participants in the contemporary debate, it may be helpful to give a brief overview regarding the major geographical distribution of the subject. Waardenburg (1978b) has distinguished three main geographical areas in the contemporary study of religion, namely the developing countries of the third world, the socialist countries of marxist inspiration, and western countries (North America and Europe, with four further subdivisions according to language areas and different cultural traditions in Europe). But in spite of these linguistic and cultural subdivisions, Waardenburg's main categories seem to be less related to geographical areas than to current political alliances. It is very difficult indeed to delineate neat geographical boundaries for the study of religion. It may be more accurate to speak of overlapping circles with fluid boundaries and a shifting centre of gravity.

Looked at from a different point of view, one might distinguish five major areas with different cultural, religious, and scholarly traditions, representing different clusters of interest and related to wider historical and political developments: (1) The historical roots of the subject developed in continental Europe and several west European countries possess major centres for the study of religion. There is a strong historical tradition in Holland, Britain, France, Germany, Italy, and Sweden whereas the development of the phenomenology of religion is particularly closely associated with Holland and Germany. (2) More recently, North America has become an important centre for the study of religion (with numerous university departments and college courses in the USA and Canada), bringing with it a marked methodological shift in the understanding of what the subject is and ought to be about. There exists a considerable disagreement over method between scholars from the USA and certain European countries, in Scandinavia and Italy for example. By and large, the North American developments have been characterized by a search for a more integral approach to the study of religion as can be seen from the continuing debate about an appropriate hermeneutic or theory of interpretation, especially as initiated by the so-called 'Chicago school'. Profound methodological differences notwithstanding, the European and North American centres have so far generated most activity and been the major contributors in the debate about methodology. (3) However, over the last two decades or so, participants from other areas have entered the methodological debate and made important contributions. They range from the Middle East (Israel) to South East Asia (India and Thailand) and the Far East (Japan, Korea, Australia). Eastern developments in the study of religion have been influenced by earlier work done in Europe and even more the USA, but these influences have been blended with strong indigenous traditions, especially in India and Japan. Unfortunately, far too little is generally known about these important eastern developments. (4) An even heavier curtain of ignorance divides the West from the socialist countries of East Germany, Poland and the USSR—in all of which the study of religion is pursued in one form or another. East Germany has a longstanding tradition in the study of *Religionswissenschaft*, particularly at the University of Leipzig which has perhaps remained more closely in contact with western developments than any other university in a socialist country and maintains a high standard of historical-critical scholarship. Lively methodological discussions are taking place in Poland but the emphasis is very much on a rigorously defined scientific approach, based on a narrowly understood objectivity close to verging on 'scientism'. Both in Poland and the USSR the sociology of religion is an important discipline. Soviet scholars, particularly members of the philosophical and oriental sections of the Academy of Sciences, are also carrying out considerable research in the history of religions but few of their publications find their way to the West. It is impossible to discuss the manysided aspects of the study of religion in the USSR here. Comparatively little information is directly accessible to the western student but a survey of developments is now available in the recently published study by J. Thrower, *Marxist-Leninist Scientific Atheism and the Study of Religion and Atheism in the USSR* (1983). (5) Another important area of development in the study of religion is represented by the African subcontinent. Research work and teaching in different subjects is carried out in West, East, Central and Southern Africa with a great increase of activities in recent years, to be distinguished from research on African religions which has been going on much longer. A possibly further area to be considered is South America but little information regarding research developments in the study of religion seems to be available.

In fact, the general lack of information on worldwide developments represents a serious lacuna in current scholarship if one seeks a well-informed assessment of the scholarly network and scope of the study of religion which would adequately show its intellectual and cultural importance for the modern world. Specialised studies on specific countries apart, the best and most easily accessible international survey currently available is the one undertaken by the British journal *Religion* (August 1975) although it is by no means comprehensive. Articles of various length and depth deal with the study of religion in continental Europe, Scandinavia, and Great Britain; with North America; with South Asia, Japan, Australia and New Zealand; with developments in different African countries; and briefly, with the academic study of religion in Israel. Unfortunately, the issue contains no information on any of the socialist countries. It is not only regrettable that scholarly interests and orientations are so closely dependent on political and linguistic divisions but it is also abundantly clear that the future viability of the subject will depend on much closer international collaboration and a more comprehensive and rigorous methodology. However, these necessary developments will not be brought about if overspecialised scholars maintain a cultural ghetto mentality and remain unable to relate their particular researches to wider concerns. Although much remains to be done to develop a more adequate international network of scholarship, it is true to say that the realization of a truly global framework is closely interrelated with the development of the *International Association for the History of Religions* (IAHR) during the last three decades. This is not the place to review in full the history of the IAHR and its discussions, examined in considerable detail in Eric Sharpe's *Comparative Religion* (1975: 267–93; see also the monograph by Bleeker (1975a)). However, contrary to Sharpe, it would seem that the developments connected with the IAHR provide more than merely 'a convenient focus' (Sharpe 1975: 268) for recent methodological discussions. The initiative of the IAHR in developing an organizational structure for promoting conferences and publications has been of central importance in the development of the methodological debate over recent years, especially as the IAHR has organised two conferences explicitly devoted to methodology, and brief reference must be made to some of its activities insofar as they have affected the methodological debate since World War II.

2.2. *The growth and development of the IAHR*

The development of the IAHR, founded in 1950 by primarily
European scholars at Amsterdam, represents an innovation without
being a completely new beginning, for its organisation is built on earlier
foundations laid during the first half of the twentieth century. The
IAHR continued the custom of holding international congresses in the
study of religion, first begun in Paris in 1900. Six congresses had been
organised when the seventh was convened in 1950 at Amsterdam. It was
during this congress that 'The International Association for the Study of
the History of Religions' (IASHR) was formed, with its name subsequently being shortened to the 'International Association for the
History of Religions' (IAHR, Rome 1955). The continuity with the
earlier congresses has been consciously maintained and recognized by
the fact that the first IAHR congress is number VII in the series.
However, the earlier congresses (I–VI) had always been prepared by an
ad hoc committee with no permanent organisation during the interven-
ing years. It is only since the foundation of the IAHR in 1950 that there
has been a continuing international body with its own journal (*Numen*
1954–), an international secretariat, and a continuous flow of publications (*Supplements* to *Numen*, and most important, the *International
Bibliography of the History of Religions* 1954–80, now replaced by *Science of
Religion Abstracts and Index of Recent Articles* (1980–).

Between 1950–80, eight international congresses have been held; in
addition, five regional conferences were organised between 1964–79.
Detailed information about these can be found in the published
Proceedings of each congress (up to 1980), the reports in *Numen*, and the
survey up to 1970 in Sharpe (1975). As the information about the
congresses held so far is not easily accessible in one place, all relevant
data have been gathered in a diagram (see Table 1) which readers may
find helpful for reference. Without wishing to repeat discussions found
in Sharpe, some of the most significant developments which have a
bearing on our investigation may be mentioned here.

Milestones in the development of a fuller methodological awareness,
accompanied by the realization that many different perspectives exist
side by side in the study of religion, are represented by the IAHR

Table 1. CONGRESSES

INTERNATIONAL ASSOCIATION FOR THE HISTORY OF RELIGIONS (IAHR—1950–80)

Six international congresses in the history of religions preceded the IAHR:
I Paris (1900), II Basel (1904), III Oxford (1908), IV Leiden (1912), V Lund (1929), and VI Brussels (1935).

	Date	Place	President	Secretary	Published Proceedings
VII	1950	AMSTERDAM	Van der Leeuw (Holland)	Bleeker (Holland)	Amsterdam 1951
VIII	1955	ROME	Pettazzoni (Italy)	Bleeker	Leiden 1959
IX	1958	TOKYO	Pettazzoni (Italy)	Bleeker	Tokyo 1960
X	1960	MARBURG	Widengren (Sweden)	Bleeker	Marburg 1961
XI	1965	CLAREMONT	Widengren (Sweden)	Bleeker	Leiden 1968
XII	1970	STOCKHOLM	Simon (France)	Brandon (England) d. 1971	Leiden 1975
				Sharpe (England) 1971–75	
XIII	1975	LANCASTER	Simon (France)	Werblowsky (Israel)	Leicester 1980 (contains details of all congress proceedings since 1900; see pp. 180–1.)
XIV	1980	WINNIPEG	Simon (France) Schimmel (Germany/USA) newly elected	Werblowsky (Israel)	Waterloo 1983

Table 1. (*cont.*)

Regional IAHR study conferences:

Date	Place	Theme	Publication	
1964	STRASBOURG	Initiation	C.J. Bleeker ed.,	*Initiation*, Leiden 1965
1966	MESSINA	Gnosticism	U. Bianchi ed.,	*Le Origini dello Gnosticismo*, Leiden 1970
1968	JERUSALEM	Redemption	R.J.Z. Werblowsky and C.J. Bleeker eds.,	*Types of Redemption*, Leiden 1970
1973	TURKU	Methodology	L. Honko ed.	*Science of Religion, Studies in Methodology*, The Hague 1979
1979	WARSAW	Methodology		unpublished so far

congresses in Tokyo (1958), Marburg (1960), and Claremont (1965). The international methodological discussion was taken further at the regional conferences in Turku (Finland) (1973) and Warsaw (1979).

During the first two decades of the IAHR, the centre of activities in the study of religion was found in Holland, Sweden and, to some extent, Italy. The first two congresses (Amsterdam 1950, Rome 1955) continued to reflect the historical and philological research interests of earlier generations. Thus, there was little explicit reference to methodological issues. There were also few eastern delegates present at the early congresses. The first congress outside Europe, and so far the only one held in the East, was organised in Tokyo (1958) and for several reasons it is of particular importance. It brought with it a greater awareness of the East-West components in the study of religion although the IAHR counted among its official eastern members only Japan and Israel at that time. However, from Tokyo onwards the IAHR developed into a more fully international body and the methodological debate soon came into its own. Whilst western scholars became painfully aware of their ignorance regarding the development of research in the East, a considerable gulf appeared between eastern and western interpretations of the essence and manifestation of religion (see Sharpe 1975: 271).

Werblowsky (1958), in his report on the Tokyo Congress (see *Numen* 5) writes: 'the emancipation of the study of religions from "religious studies" (whether theology or religious philosophies) is not yet fully recognised by many students of the subject. Particularly in the East this development . . . has not yet greatly progressed.' Werblowsky points out that this danger has been recognized by the IAHR through the conscious choice of 'history of religions' in its name. Even though the latter is meant to include many other disciplines, it indicates a resolve to adhere to strictly historical and scientific standards, whereas a broader designation might easily encourage less strict, unscientific criteria.

The Tokyo Congress also included an East-West Symposium, sponsored by UNESCO on 'Religion and Thought in the Orient and Occident: A Century of Cultural Exchange'. Its major subjects of discussion were: (1) the characteristics of oriental and occidental culture; (2) the influence of the West on the East; (3) the common concern: the problems of an emerging world civilization. At the conclusion of the

Tokyo Congress it was recommended that the IAHR should give greater emphasis to the study and research of eastern religions and their relations to the West. It should also stimulate scholarly and popular publications in the field of the history of religions since these will promote mutual understanding between East and West. For this purpose, a series of specific recommendations were submitted to UNESCO, pointing out the important cultural function of the scientific study of the history of religions in its different branches in fostering a better appreciation of eastern and western cultural values (for the full text see *Numen* 5, 1958: 238–40). Since the Tokyo Congress, the East-West relationship and participation are an indispensable aspect of the IAHR but the suggestions made then to hold a further East-West symposium and international congress in the East have so far not been realized (a congress planned to be held in India in 1963 unfortunately could not be organized for various reasons).

The next congress at Marburg, in 1960, was in many ways 'a watershed, for the simple reason that there methodological discussion established itself for the first time as an integral part of IAHR procedure' (Sharpe 1975: 277). It was realized that the different methodological positions do not divide neatly along East-West lines. In the West, too, the intuitive method found its supporters and there was a growing pressure on scholars to make a contribution to the reconstruction of cultural and religious life. Professor Bleeker (1960), the secretary general of the IAHR at that time, outlined what he considered to be 'The Future Task of the History of Religions.' Although international understanding may be a by-product of the scholar's work, it can never be his primary aim. Discussions revolved around the scientific and scholarly orientation of the study of religion and the term 'phenomenology of religion' appeared to be especially confusing to some. R.J. Zwi Werblowsky circulated a statement regarding 'the basic minimum presuppositions' of the scholarly studies aimed at by the IAHR which found support from many well-known scholars present at Marburg. It emphasized that there was no question of an 'East versus West' situation in terms of the criteria and standards brought to bear on the study of religion: 'The history of religions is a branch of the humanities, not of theology and still less of international politics; it is simply there, to be discussed as dispassionately as possible on the principle of truth for its own sake' (in Sharpe 1975: 278; see also the ardent plea made subsequently by Werblowsky (1960) to protect the IAHR from dilettantes, theologians and idealists).

However, the tension over different methods had by no means been resolved. It came even more to the fore at the Claremont Congress (1965), the first international congress held in North America. Sharpe thinks that at Claremont 'the ideal of disinterested, objective scholarship *for its own sake*, while not abandoned, had been relegated to a position of only relative importance' (Sharpe 1975: 284). This shift in the overall orientation was not unrelated to the different perspectives of study which had been developed by both Mircea Eliade and Wilfred Cantwell-Smith. The latter in particular shows a much greater openness to the 'religious approach' championed by several eastern scholars. In Brandon's assessment, made from the traditional perspective of historical scholarship nurtured by the academic traditions of Europe, there existed a tension between the European concern with the history of religions and the American disposition to concentrate on the existing situation. He termed the latter, quite wrongly, the 'sociological approach' in contrast to the critically historical one. Although he noted that the emphasis of the Claremont Congress was on 'the present and future significance of religion in human culture' (quoted in Sharpe 1975: 285), he thought it unlikely that the European tradition of scholarship would succumb to the new American approach which stressed a dialogical disposition.

In the years to come, European scholarship tended, on the whole, to be dominated by the purely historical approach. Thus, the understanding and practice of the history of religions in America and Europe seemed to drift apart. However, this tendency was to some extent overcome through developments at the Stockholm Congress (1970) which 'marked both an end and a beginning. What had ended was perhaps the period in which scholars had locked themselves into a rigid methodological "either-or" and had failed to recognise the essentially complementary character of alternative approaches. What had begun we cannot yet know: we can only hope, and work' (in Sharpe 1975: 290f.; see also the address given by C.J. Bleeker (1975b) at Stockholm on 'Looking Backward and Forward').

The methodological discussion has fully come into its own during the seventies, as is evident from the many specialised publications in this field as well as the numerous journal articles devoted to discussing alternative approaches to the study of religion. The IAHR Congress at Lancaster (1975) included a separate section on methodology (chaired by Professor N. Smart). The Winnipeg Congress, in 1980, the second international congress to be held in North America, also comprised among its twenty different sections one on 'methodology and hermeneutics' (chaired by Professor W.G. Oxtoby).

The need to clarify methodological questions was recognised by holding a regional study conference entirely devoted to the 'Methodology of the Science of Religion' at Turku in Finland (1973). While the initiative came from the IAHR, the main responsibility for organising the conference was undertaken by the Finnish Society for the Study of Comparative Religion (founded in 1963, with its annual publication of *Temenos*) which enlisted the support of UNESCO and other organisations. In the words of the organisers, the aim was 'to review central problems within the methodology of the science of religion, and to attempt by means of active discussion to evelute the strength of old and new methodological trends, and their directions of development' (*Temenos* 8, 1972: 5). The need for such a conference was more explicitly discussed in *Numen* 19 (1972: 241):

The methodology of the science of religion was unanimously regarded as a timely and relevant theme. Recent developments in the field have been characterized by acute criticisms of traditional approaches and the impact of increasing inter-disciplinary exchange. Certain new modes of thought have revealed new vistas for comparative religion. The classic topics of debate have become somewhat uninspiring for the younger generation of scholars. Looking around they have noticed the increase of empirical field-work, the trend towards operationalization of scientific terms and the possibilities of confronting problems at various levels of abstraction. Regardless of one's theoretical allegiance there certainly exists a need for a more general evaluation of the present methodological situation....

The conference explored different methodological approaches under three main themes: (1) oral and written documentation of religious tradition; (2) the future of the phenomenology of religion; (3) religion as expressive culture (for a report see *Temenos* 9, 1973: 15–24; the papers and discussions of this important conference are now available in print (Honko 1979)).

The second methodological conference of the IAHR was held in Warsaw in 1979, at the joint invitation of the Polish Society for the Science of Religions (founded in 1958 and affiliated to the IAHR in 1970 with its own journal *Euhemer*—The Science of Religions Review, published since 1957) and the Institute for Philosophy and Sociology of the Polish Academy of Sciences. Papers and discussions were again grouped around three themes: (1) methodological problems in the history of religions; (2) religions in the process of social development; (3) religion in relation to secular culture. So far, no published proceedings are available yet but, to judge by the opinions of participants, no new perspectives seem to have emerged. Although participation was lower than at Turku (39 as compared to 49 participants), the special importance of this conference lies in the fact that it represents the first official gathering of history of religions scholars in a socialist country.

At the Rome Congress (1955) twelve different member groups were listed (including already the 'Japanese Association for the Science of Religion'). At present, the IAHR consists of about 20 member associations based on individual countries. These include one association in Africa (Nigeria), one in Latin America (Mexico) and three in Asia (Japan, India, and Israel). In addition to the national member groups, international scholarly organisations have become affiliated to the IAHR as, for example, the International Old Testament Society, the International Association for Buddhist Studies, and the Society for Mithraic Studies. Nationally based associations for the study of religion become officially affiliated at international congresses. Several national associations have been formed in recent years, such as the New Zealand Association for the Study of Religions (1979), the Swiss Association for the Study of Religion (1978), and The Australian Association for the Study of Religions (founded in 1976 with its first national congress held in Adelaide; see V.C. Hayes (1977)). There are a number of other countries where the study of religion at university level is growing but where no national associations have been formed so far. Departments of religious studies can be found, among others, at universities and colleges in South Africa, Sri Lanka, and Thailand (especially at Mahidol University, Bangkok). Among the delegates of the Winnipeg Congress (1980) there were, for the first time, several participants from the People's Republic of China. The Australian, Belgian, Nigerian, and Swiss associations were newly affiliated to the IAHR and it was decided to hold the next IAHR Congress in 1985 in Sydney (see R.J.Z. Werblowsky's report on the Winnipeg Congress in *Numen* 27, 1980: 292–4).

Besides the information on the study of religion in different countries contained in the 1975 survey of *Religion*, the founding of national associations and their development can be followed through regular reports in *Numen*. The most obvious source for further information about particular developments are the journals published by national associations; see, for example, L. Honko's 'The Finnish Society for the Study of Comparative Religion in 1963–1973' in *Temenos* 9, 1973: 5–14. The development of the Canadian Society for the Study of Religion, (founded in 1965 and affiliated to the IAHR in 1970), is described by E. Combs in 'Learned and learning: CSSR/SCER, 1965–1975' and published in *Sciences Religieuses/Studies in Religion* 6, 1976–77: 357–63, the new journal launched by Canadian scholars in 1971. The recent developments of the British Association for the History of Religions (founded in 1954 and affiliated in 1955), can best be followed in its quarterly Bulletin, unfortunately only available in cyclostyled form. The activities of the Polish Society for the Science of Religions (founded in Warsaw in 1957 and affiliated to the IAHR in 1970), are briefly described by W. Tyloch in *Euhemer* 3 (113), 1979: 3–8. For a detailed study of the historical development of Polish studies on religion, see P.O. Szolc (Scholz) 'Religionswissenschaft in Polen' (1971: 45–80); A. Kee, 'The Study of Religion in Poland' (1980: 61–7); and M. Pomian-Srzednicki, *The Politics and Sociology of Secularization in Poland*, (1982). A great deal more could have been written about the development of national associations but I shall now proceed to a discussion of some major publications which illustrate the complex threads of the contemporary debate regarding the study of religion.

2.3 Recent reference works and handbooks

Over recent years, a number of important handbooks and reference works have been produced in both the history and phenomenology of religion. In looking at some representative titles one may ask whether the authors are at all method-conscious in the presentation of their data and if so, what methods they advocate for the study of religion. If, on the contrary, they remain methodologically inarticulate and unaware, what methods do they implicitly practise?

It has been maintained that, due to the different orientations of the subject, a comprehensive work on the history of religions, by its very nature, requires several authors whereas a book on the phenomenology of religion must be written by one author in order to bring across a unitary conception of the phenomena under review. If one surveys the publications since 1950, it is apparent that a greater number of books has been devoted to the historical study of the major religions, both ancient and modern, than to specialised works in the phenomenology of religion. Excellent reference works in the history of religions exist in several European languages, especially German, French and English, not to forget Dutch, Scandinavian, Italian, and Russian publications. The West European works in this field have been critically analysed by Kurt Rudolph (1973; 1979) and I shall only selectively refer to the most important books.

Since the sixties, several new handbooks have been produced which have gained high praise from critics, notably the German series *Die Religionen der Menschheit* (1961–, edited by C.M. Schröder), the French publication *Histoire des Religions* (1970–6, edited by H. Puech), and the two volumes edited by C.J. Bleeker and G. Widengren, *Historia Religionum. Handbook for the History of Religions* (1969–71). Each is different in conception and structure and each serves a different purpose. Ideally, the handbooks in the three languages should be consulted together as they complement each other and, if read critically, they provide a good opportunity for a fruitful cross-fertilization of ideas. Published closely together in time, they will remain standard reference works for years to come.

Die Religionen der Menschheit (RM) is an ambitious and monumental project. Originally planned to have thirty-seven volumes, it will probably now have forty-two of which twenty-two had been published in Germany by 1979, with additional translations into French and English. Each title is the work of one or several specialists in the history of religions and the series represents without doubt the best collection of handbooks dealing with the history of particular religions giving an overall view of their development. It comes rather as a surprise, however, to discover that the books do not include any discussion of the purpose and plan of the series nor do they consider methodological issues. The historical approach used in the series is nowhere discussed nor is there a general preface introducing the entire series. Without introduction or explanation the series begins with a first volume on phenomenology by Friedrich Heiler (1961); one of the last volumes planned is a *Geschichte der Religionswissenschaft*. As this work is still outstanding, it is uncertain whether this history will be confined to strictly historical-descriptive data or include an analysis of different methodological approaches underlying the practice of *Religionswissenschaft*. If one views the series as a whole, there is no attempt at integration and an impression of particularity, if not to say fragmentation, cannot be avoided. No general framework has been provided, no systematic or comparative questions have been asked, no methodological issues have been raised, even though the project is not without its own classificatory schema.

The French series *Histoire des religions* is also a collective, but nevertheless much briefer work comprising three volumes which have been judged the best single reference work in the history of religions available at present. Here, the treatment of particular religions is also classified according to historical and geographical criteria but, in contrast to the German series, this work begins with a thorough methodological discussion by Angelo Brelich (1970: 3–59) dealing with the presuppositions and problems of the history of religions. Considered to be one of the best introductions to the entire field, its arguments will be examined later. The series concludes with an article on the history of the history of religions as a discipline (III, 1279–1328). As this covers only an outline of the major developments and remains rather brief, the forthcoming volume of *RM* on this subject will certainly fill a need (for a recent review of *Histoire des Religions* and other publications, see R.J.Z. Werblowsky (1979: 250–5)).

The individual contributions to *Histoire des Religions* remain unconnected, however, in spite of the excellent introduction. Each article stands on its own so that the reader is still confronted with 'unconnected monographs', a difficulty which the editors of the English series, *Historia Religionum*, sought to overcome by inviting all contributors to follow the same basic outline in presenting their subject. Each author was asked to submit a 'short description of the essence of religion', 'historical development', 'conception of the deity', 'worship (cult, ethics, myth or doctrine)', 'conception of man (creation, nature, destiny: path of salvation, personal and general eschatology)', 'religions of the past: subsequent influence; religions of the present: present religious situation', 'short history of the study of the religion', 'selected bibliography' (Preface, I: VII). This scheme, with suitable adaptations where necessary, is first applied to the religions of the past (vol. I), and then to the religions of the present (vol. II). As is evident from the outline, historical and phenomenological approaches are here interwoven with the aim to present 'an organic unity' in marked contrast to other handbooks of the history of religions where one 'never gets a survey of the history of religions presented as a unity and thus revealing not only the individual peculiarities of the religions of the world, but also, and more particularly, the similarities in their structure, the formal parallels in their development and their most hidden interrelation and interdependence.' The two editors, Bleeker and Widengren, present their handbook as 'a description of the religions of the world in such a manner that their ideological parallelism is made manifest' and they hope that their new venture 'will stimulate further the systematic study of the history of religions' (I: VII, and VIII). The conception of the editors, only briefly stated in the succinct preface, is fully expressed in Bleeker's 'Epilegomena' (II: 642–51) from which a particular phenomenological stance becomes fully apparent.

Not all contributors were able to conform to the original outline with the same satisfactory results. The shortcomings of the handbook have been pointed out by several critics (see Rudolph 1973a; Waardenburg 1975a; Penner 1976). Although it may be too strong a criticism to say that *Historia Religionum* 'is not a history in the proper sense of the word' (Waardenburg 1975a: 28), its presentation certainly raises the question of how far the framework, developed for comparative purposes, is such a straightjacket as to distort historical data. If the editors wanted a survey of the history of religions which would at the same time present the unity of religion and reveal its structure, this goal has not been achieved. In the opinion of one reviewer, it is not only the contributors who do not agree on this issue, but not even the editors express clearly what constitutes the essence and structure of religion.

Other recently published handbooks in the history of religions are either revised editions or reprints of earlier works. This is true of the well reviewed and detailed Italian series *Storia delle religioni* by P. Tacchi Venturi (originally published in 2 vols., 1934), now available in revised form in five volumes (edited by G. Castellani, Turin 1970 f.), but perhaps hard to find outside its country of origin. Its substantial introduction on 'La storia delle religioni' by Ugo Bianchi (I: 1–171) discusses at length the object, method and problems of the history of religions up to the present day. A fuller account of the contents of the five volumes is found in Rudolph 1973a: 411–2. Bianchi's introduction is now available in English translation as *The History of Religions* (1975)—see especially Part I 'Object and Methodology of the History of Religions' which also contains a brief section on 'The organization of studies concerning the history of religions,' and Part IV 'Modern Problems of Methodology and Interpretation' which, among others, includes a discussion of Otto, Pettazzoni, and Eliade, and of 'The "history of religions" and "comparative religion" in the USA'.

The German translation of the Scandinavian work by J.P. Asmussen and J. Laessoe, *Handbuch der Religionsgeschichte* (translated and edited by C. Colpe, 1971–2), although published recently, contains primarily older material. It is based on a revised work by J. Pedersen (1948) which in turn relied on a much earlier study by E. Lehmann (1924). The German editor has followed the arrangement of the original Danish edition (Copenhagen 1968). Much of the material seems old-fashioned which, given its age, is perhaps not surprising. There is little systematic reflection on the ordering of the material; in fact, much emphasis is laid on earlier ethnographic and archaeological evidence. The distribution of the articles leaves the reader with the impression that the history of religions, far from being an international discipline working within a global perspective, is a western branch of scholarship heavily over-shadowed by its own history, steeped in a fascination with the origins of western civilization, the ancient Near East, and a traditional classicist and orientalist interest of a particular kind (compare 66 pp. on Sumerian religion, 56 pp. on gnosticism and mystery religions, 28 pages on Mandeism with 49 pp. on the whole of Hinduism and a mere 21 pp. on Tibetan 'lamaism'!). The most valuable addition is the new section, supplied by the German editor, on 'Synkretismus, Renaissance, Säkula-risation and Neubildung von Religionen in der Gegenwart' (vol. 3).

In marked contrast to *Historia Religionum*, the three volumes of *Handbuch der Religionsgeschichte* lack a unitary conception. Instead of an overall framework they present a 'mixture of geographical, cultural-historical and chronological points of view' (Rudolph 1973a: 411). Other reviewers have been more outspoken. Reacting to both the content and mode of presentation, N.Q. King has written that much of the handbook

is the work of European brahmins pontificating about the religion of other people. There is too little use of books by Indians and other Asians who can speak of their religion from inside. The texts and artefacts are not allowed to speak for themselves. There is little hint that the writers are aware of the modern academic ferment in this subject outside Europe and America .... In most of the articles there is a tendency to treat History of Religion as a strictly scientific, objective, cut-and-dried self-contained discipline and to neglect the interweaving of attention to music, art, devotion, ritual, hagiography and first-hand impression with the sequence of major historical happenings (*Scottish Journal of Theology* 26, 1973: 378).

King's criticism might be applied to other publications. Only highly motivated students will find the necessary determination and patience to plough through the dull and arid pages of certain books in the history of religions. By and large it is true to say that the field is not noted for an original and imaginative presentation of its materials. Here, too, the issue of methodology is paramount. To advance the subject beyond the narrow circles of erudite *literati* it will be necessary to develop a greater self-critical awareness, promote theoretical reflections and work on a refinement of methods adequate to the study of religions.

It may not be out of place here to refer to a recent British publication addressed to mature students. In 1977, the Open University produced a variety of study materials for programmed learning. Integrated with a network of radio and television programmes, especially made for the course, the fourteen textbooks produced by a team of scholars introduce the student to the historical development of the major religions of the past and present as well as to some central theoretical perspectives. As with *Historia Religionum*, the contributors were given a particular outline beforehand which was to be used in the presentation of their material. But here the chosen framework was expressed in the form of three questions relating to the human religious search asking 'from what? by what? and to what?'. It is interesting to see that again not every one of the twenty or so contributors was willing to conform to the imposition of such a structure. The books have called for scholarly criticism pointing out the 'quasi-religious' character of these questions which in certain cases can lead to a distortion of historical data (see 'Man's Religious Quest. A review of Open University materials,' *Religion* 9, 1979: 116–39). Yet in spite of certain obvious shortcomings, this course on the history of religions in the wider sense represents a highly original venture. Through the efforts of teamwork, the results of the study of religions over the last hundred years are made available to a large public far beyond the traditional limits of the university world. The potential consequences of such a step of introducing historical and systematic thinking about the religious traditions of mankind within a comparative and scholarly context to society at large cannot be fully assessed at present but should not be underestimated. It is important to know that the methodological reflections include, among others, materials drawn from the phenomenology and sociology of religion. The textbooks also comprise a short history of the study of religion and introduce some of the major issues of the current scholarly debate, although admittedly rather brief and incomplete (see especially the book units 1–3 *Seekers*

and Scholars, and units 31–32 *Quest and Questioning*, Milton Keynes 1977).
Besides the handbooks comprising several volumes, shorter one-volume works are also available as introductions to the history of religions. *Religions of Mankind. Today and Yesterday* (edited by H. Ringgren and A.V. Ström, 1967) claims to summarize modern research and emphasises that religions are expressions of faith and life rather than mere objects for curiosity and study. However, careful examination reveals again that this is a rearranged text of an earlier Swedish work (3rd ed., 1964). Besides the systematic discussion of religious pheno-mena in the introduction, the main sections follow a primarily ethnolo-gical, historical, or geographical orientation with no overall conclusion.

By contrast, T.O. Ling's *History of Religion East and West* (1968), widely used as a textbook for students, implies a thematic approach and unitary conception throughout. Each chapter treats individual religious traditions in a parallel manner. This helps to outline major develop-ments and allows for comparisons but it leads to a certain amount of discontinuity within the religious traditions themselves. Also curious is the use of the singular 'History of Religion' in the title which may create the idea of a false unity imposed from without on the diversity of the data. Although someone might produce a more definitive work in the future, there are at present few books available in the history of religions which make as stimulating reading as this one. Such an introduction can motivate many a student to take the challenge of the subject seriously by proceeding to more demanding and specialised works.

The German work by E. Dammann *Grundriss der Religionsgeschichte* (1972, 2nd ed. 1978) has mainly been written for theology students. It is characterized by a distinct emphasis on living religions and new reli-gious movements of today. By contrast, S.A. Tokarev's *Die Religion in der Geschichte der Völker* (1968) is based on Marxist philosophy, underlin-ing the evolutionary development of religion in history. The book is a translation of an earlier work by one of the leading Soviet historians of religion, now available in a new two-volume edition in Russian *Religiya v istorii narodov mira* (Moscow 1976). Another Russian work on the history of religions is by I.A. Kryvelev, *Istoriya religii* (1975).

These examples of currently available surveys must suffice to give an idea of the growth of publications in different languages over recent years (for more detailed bibliographical information consult the *International Bibliography of the History of Religions*; see also the excellent survey of works published since 1968 by Waardenburg (1975a) and the review article by Rudolph (1979); a survey of Italian publications is found in Culianu (1981) who mentions no less than 101 books in the history of religions published in Italy since 1975).

There can be no doubt that more and more historical materials relating to the study of religion have become accessible to a greater number of readers. The results of specialised research have been incorporated into widely available handbooks and surveys, especially if one thinks of large reference works such as *Religion in Geschichte und Gegenwart* (7 vols., Tübingen 1957–65), not to mention many still very valuable older publications and the newly established journals in the history of religions. It has been noted, however, that there is a marked current trend away from purely historical-descriptive works towards a more systematic treatment of religious data, involving a greater acknowledgment of the need for methodological and theoretical reflections. Waardenburg's survey (1975a) expresses this by distinguishing recent works in the 'history of religions in the proper sense' from those publications which deal with 'the study of religion in a wider sense' or with 'method and theory in the study of religion,' and it is only to the two latter categories that he assigns the term *Religionswissenschaft*. Ninian Smart in his book, *The Phenomenon of Religion* (1973a), proposes a different distinction of studies, namely: (1) histories of religions; (2) historical-dialectical studies (with (1) and (2) further subdivided into holistic, divisional, aspectual, and itemized histories); (3) phenomenological and structural studies (with further subdivisions); (4) dialectical-phenomenological studies (where sociology, anthropology, psychology and philosophy of religion are included; see Smart 1973a: 45–8).

Works in the phenomenology of religion are an integral part of the systematic reflection of *Religionswissenschaft*. However, there is a greater tendency on the whole to incorporate certain phenomenological perspectives rather than to produce specific works wholly devoted to the phenomenology of religion. Yet several such works have appeared in recent years. The most substantial and widely acclaimed is G. Widengren's revised *Religionsphänomenologie* (1969), based on earlier

Swedish editions (1945, 1953). This is all the more surprising if one considers that Widengren has been called 'one of the most powerful advocates of the "purely historical" approach to the study of religion' (Sharpe 1975: 243). It appears that for Widengren the phenomenology of religion is the systematic counterpart of the history of religions; the synthesis of the former is based on the historical analysis of the latter so that no phenomenologist can ever work without the historical method. Some scholars are of the opinion that this publication combines in an ideal manner the philological-historical method with a systematic presentation of the data. In fact, Bleeker ranks the work so highly that he thinks no one in his generation possesses either the imagination or the energy to create something new after Widengren's *Religionsphänomenologie*—the book represents a milestone in the history of the discipline (C.J. Bleeker 1971c). This appreciation is shared by Rudolph (1971a) who considers the work a pioneering attempt to reclaim the name of phenomenology for the integration of historical researches and systematic reflections within a truly comparative framework of *Religionswissenschaft*.

One of the most recent, but much more modest, publications in the phenomenology of religion is Günter Lanczkowski's *Einführung in die Religionsphänomenologie* (1978a). Primarily written for students, it includes a discussion of many earlier reference works and provides a succinct and helpful survey of the field. Unfortunately, the author seems to be little aware of the complexities of recent methodological discussions at the international level. No attempt is made at a comprehensive presentation of phenomenology; one is left with the impression that the work depends far too much on earlier German publications without taking into account recent works in the English language.

Friedrich Heiler's *Erscheinungsformen und Wesen der Religion* (1961) is a copiously documented work, based on an earlier German publication (1949). Its introduction discusses the concept of religion, presents a brief history of the systematic study of religion and develops a model of the phenomenological method which has been strongly criticized for its theological presuppositions (Sharpe 1975: 244 f.). In Heiler's analysis of religious phenomena historical and phenomenological approaches are closely intertwined. He is also one of the few who considers the personal attitude of the researcher as an important factor in the selection and presentation of data. However, his stance is too narrowly normative here, influenced by a particular understanding of faith which uses the phenomenological method as a substitute proof for the existence of God and is too dependent on Otto's idea of the Holy. Kurt Rudolph describes Heiler's work as 'eine theologische Religionswissenschaft und eine religionsgeschichtliche Theologie' whilst admitting that the volume provides a mine of information about historical data (see his 'Die Problematik der Religionswissenschaft als akademisches Lehrfach' 1967). Meanwhile, C.J. Bleeker judged Heiler's book as 'ein sehr verdienstliches Werk ... in dem aber die neueren Ansichten über die Methode und Struktur der Phänomenologie nicht verarbeitet sind' (*Numen* 14, 1967: 162).

The phenomenological work of another German scholar has now become widely available, particularly in India, through its recent translation into English. Gustav Mensching's *Structures and Patterns of Religion* (translated by H.F. Klimkeit and V. Srinivasa Sarma, 1976) presents a general typology of religions and of particular religious phenomena. Its systematic framework is provided by a specific approach to 'comparing and understanding' and 'the unity of religions.' Far fewer historical data are cited in support of the main arguments than is the case in Heiler's work. The overall perspective of the book reflects many of the earlier concerns of Otto and van der Leeuw and much of the secondary literature is out of date.

Much more theoretically aware in the discussion of method and the analysis of comparative historical data is the handbook *Phenomenology of Religion* (1973) by Mariasusai Dhavamony. It stresses the empirical character of 'historical phenomenology,' understood as the combined use of the historical and phenomenological method. The author considers the elucidation of the essence of religious phenomena as the legitimate aim of phenomenology, to be achieved on strictly empirical and not on philosophical or theological grounds (1973: 3–27). This approach is then illustrated by a comparative discussion of wide-ranging religious phenomena, concluding with a part on the 'scope of religion and salvation.' To some, the orientation of the book may still appear to be too dependent on theological perspectives but on the whole the main themes of the study of religion are introduced in a systematic and critical manner. Written for students and the general reader, this work deserves to be more widely known, for its clarity of structure and style provide a helpful introduction to the contemporary study of religion. It also includes a more up-to-date bibliography than some better known works in this field.

Earlier works in the period under discussion include W. Brede Kristensen's *The Meaning of Religion* (translated by J.B. Carman, 1960), representing post-humously published lectures given before 1953 (for a discussion of Kristensen's work see Sharpe 1975: 227–9; other Scandinavian and German publications on phenomenology are also considered in pp. 242–6). Two well established and still widely used earlier works which present a systematic classification of religious phenomena, each set in a very different framework, are Joachim Wach's *The Comparative Study of Religions* (1958)—see the critical review by R.J.Z. Werblowsky (1959)—and Mircea Eliade's *Patterns in Comparative Religion* (1958). The latter is a translation of Eliade's earlier French work *Traité d'Histoire des Religions* (1949) with a different introduction. The thematic presentation of certain religious phenomena, largely drawn from archaic and exotic thought-forms and compared at the level of symbolism with little reference to their wider historical and social context, is here considered as 'history of religions,' as the original title of the work clearly states. The work is even described as a 'science of religions' (see preface to the French edition) although Eliade's methodological stance is very different from what this term has come to mean in more recent debates.

If one compares the titles of recent publications, it is evident that fewer handbooks have been produced in phenomenology than in the history of religions. Perhaps more books and articles exist discussing the phenomenological method from a theoretical point of view than fully developed phenomenologies where this method has been consistently applied. In general it is true to say that the historical handbooks contain too little methodological self-reflection whereas phenomenological works, due to their systematic orientation, usually include a discussion regarding the specific objects and methods of studying religious phenomena. This often implies the consideration of how far it is legitimate to separate the phenomenological from the historical perspective or vice versa. But most phenomenologies are not rigorous enough in the examination of their underlying assumptions and remain bound by a preconceived framework.

Over recent years, the absence of a common body of theory in the contemporary study of religion has been repeatedly pointed out and new avenues to remedy this situation have been explored. Given the use of very different and even disparate methods in the study of religion, the subject of methodology has come into its own, implying the examination of existing methods and the development of new ones, producing a whole body of metatheory for *Religionswissenschaft*. I shall list some of the most important books published over the last decade or so, giving an idea of the wide range of questions raised in the study and interpretation of religion today. However, the substantive issues discussed in these works will only be examined in the next section on the methodological debate.

The best orientation about current theoretical developments can be gained by studying the works which continue to appear in the series *Religion and Reason* (RR), begun in 1971 and explicitly devoted to 'method and theory in the study and interpretation of religion' (edited by J. Waardenburg). The series comprises almost thirty titles so far, including the recently published papers of the IAHR methodology conference held in 1973 at Turku in Finland (*Science of Religion. Studies in Methodology*, 1979). Another recent title is J. Waardenburg's *Reflections on the Study of Religion* (1978a), bringing together many of his earlier papers which reconsider the nature of the phenomenology of religion and its relationship to the history of religions. The work provides a valuable description, assessment, and critique of the so-called 'classical phenomenology of religion' and pleads for phenomenological research in a new style. Other titles of particular interest to the methodological debate are G. Schmid's *Principles of Integral Science of Religion* (1979) and D. Allen's *Structure and Creativity in Religion. Hermeneutics in Mircea Eliade's Phenomenology and New Directions* (1978); J.E. Barnhardt, *The Study of Religion and Its Meaning. New Explorations in Light of Karl Popper and Emile Durkheim* (1977); T.P. van Baaren and H.J.W Drijvers, editors, *Religion, Culture and Methodology*. Papers of the Groningen Working-group for the Study of Fundamental Problems and Methods of Science of Religion (1973); M. Pye and R. Morgan, editors, *The Cardinal Meaning, Essays in Comparative Hermeneutics* (1973) and R.D. Baird, *Category Formation and the History of Religions* (1971). For a critical review of the early volumes of RR see Rudolph (1979).

Questions of methodology were also at the centre of an earlier study conference organised by the Italian section of the IAHR on 'Problems and Methods of the History of Religions, 1959–69,' held in Rome. The conference proceedings were published as a Supplement to *Numen*, edited by U. Bianchi, C.J. Bleeker, A. Bausani as *Problems and Methods of the History of Religions* (1972) (see the review by N.G. Holm (1972)). Several important papers deal with the place of phenomenology and the problem of definition in religion.

In reviewing a work by Mensching, H. Biezais has said that it may be difficult to speak of a German *Religionswissenschaft* truly independent from theology (*Temenos* 8, 1972: 160 f.). This may be true of the older generation (Biezais refers to the last forty years), but there can be little doubt that there are many signs indicating a search for greater methodological clarification and a striving for the independence of the discipline. Wide-ranging methodological concerns are reflected in several collective works. The conference proceedings of the *Deutsche Vereinigung for Religionsgeschichte* (the German section of the IAHR) are entitled *Der Religionswandel unserer Zeit im Spiegel der Religionswissenschaft* and are edited by G. Stephenson (1976). The last section of this volume is explicitly devoted to *methodologische Versuche*. The volume of articles on *Selbstverständnis und Wesen der Religionswissenschaft* edited by G. Lanczkowski (1974) is a useful compilation of material found in different journals and includes German translations of methodological discussions previously published in *Numen* and IAHR (conference proceedings). Another collective work on *Theologie und Religionswissenschaft*, edited by U. Mann (1973), is more oriented towards theology as the title indicates. A more specialised survey of methodology is found in the article by C.H. Ratschow, 'Methodik der Religionswissenschaft' in *Enzyklopädie der geisteswissenschaftlichen Arbeitsmethoden* (1973: 347–400). However, it only lists publications up to 1966 and has met with detailed criticisms regarding its presuppositions (see Stephenson 1975: 201–8).

Important questions as to the way in which the study of religion may be considered scientific are raised in N. Smart's book, *The Science of Religion and the Sociology of Knowledge. Some Methodological Questions* (1973b). Another work which analyses in great detail the objects and methods of the science of religion is the study by M. Meslin, *Pour une science des religions* (1973). It is characterized by a humanistic emphasis and includes a history of the study of religion as well as an analysis of contemporary approaches to the phenomenon of religion. By contrast, the collective work, *Introduction aus sciences humaines des religions* (edited by H. Desroche and J. Séguy, 1970) possesses a stronger orientation towards the social sciences. It provides informative surveys on different methods in the study of religion and the section on phenomenology is considered to be a basic contribution to this field (see Isambert 1975: 217–40).

Few books on methodology will have gone through as many editions as the essays edited by Mircea Eliade and Joseph Kitagawa, *The History of Religions, Essays in Methodology* (1959–1973). This collective work must not be confused with the subsequent publication, also edited by Joseph Kitagawa together with M. Eliade and C. Long, *The History of Religions, Essays on the Problem of Understanding* (1967). Besides older material (i.e., J. Wach's 'The Meaning and Task of the History of Religions,' originally written in 1935), the latter includes several articles attempting a particular hermeneutics of comparative religious data. This hermeneutical concern is at the centre of Eliade's own work, best represented in his collection of articles, *The Quest. History and Meaning in Religion* (1969). These three volumes have exercised considerable influence by stimulating much argument and critical debate and they continue to be often cited. However, they primarily belong to the middle of the period under review here, namely the 1960s, representing a fluid, transitional stage towards the growth of greater methodological awareness and critical theory which have come into their own since the 1970s. The best summary statement in article form about current methodological concerns is J. Waardenburg's 'Religionswissenschaft New Style. Some Thoughts and Afterthoughts' (see especially part IV, 'Methodological and Theoretical Issues' (1978b: 189–220)). It outlines the major developments since the 1960s and emphasizes the growing need for fundamental research with regard to problems of method and theory.

Another very helpful survey which takes the reader up to the early 1970s is R. Pummer's 'Recent Publications on the Methodology of the Science of Religion' (1975). Here the publications are grouped under specific themes such as the problem of defining religion, the category of understanding, the meaning of explanation in the science of religion, the role of comparison, and the multimethodic nature of the study of religion, all of which are discussed in considerable detail. A recent, more descriptive literature survey is G. Lanczkowski's 'Literaturbericht zur Religionswissenschaft' (1978b: 285–320) which is unfortunately not up-to-date, however.

The most recent publications indicate very clearly that the study of religion, as currently conceived, is undergoing a great deal of change involving much critical self-examination and a search for clearer self-definition. As with all change, this implies both continuity and discontinuity with what went on beforehand and may well lead to a 'new style' *Religionswissenschaft*. In Waardenburg's opinion such a 'new style' study of religion rests 'not only on the discovery of new facts previously unknown, but also on a further refinement of the way in which facts can be ascertained and interpreted. Investigations of method and theory are highly relevant for the assumptions and the existence of the study of religion itself as a distinct field of scholarly research' (1978b: 189).

New surveys and handbooks in the history and phenomenology of
religion continue to appear. One can note a marked increase in publications primarily devoted to discussing theoretical questions and I shall
now analyse in some detail the major issues prominent in the methodological debates of the last thirty years.

3. The methodological debate since world war II

The contemporary methodological debate possesses an important
historical dimension often unduly neglected. The ongoing discussions
about the most appropriate methods for the study of religion often relate
to earlier work in this field or continue to rely on unexamined assumptions of previous generations. The majority of present-day scholars
would probably concede the multi- or poly-methodic nature of the study
of religion and the potential vastness of its objects in both time and
space. Such a general statement can easily be agreed upon but it does not
solve specific difficulties when it comes to detailed methods and procedures. At present, the methodological debate consists of numerous
interwoven themes and overlapping areas, often difficult to disentangle.
However, some dominant themes can definitely be noted although there
is no orderly progression of argument nor a general consensus about
methods which has emerged since the end of World War II.

For analytical purposes, four major issues may be distinguished in the
current methodological debate, namely: (1) the debate about the history
of religions; (2) the debate about the phenomenology of religion; (3) the
debate about hermeneutics; (4) the debate about the science of religion.
These four themes have been singled out for their dominance in recent
discussions, the volume of which has greatly increased since the early

1970s. These topics constitute neither four distinct and completely separate enquiries nor must they be viewed as following each other in chronological succession. On the contrary, they are best considered as four interrelated areas of the ongoing methodological debate about the study of religion today. Although specific arguments pertaining to these four themes are often interwoven in practice, they are here distinguished and treated under separate headings so as to gain clarification about the characteristic thrust of each. I shall now look at each area in turn by examining some representative arguments and contributions produced over recent years.

3.1 The debate about the history of religions

The term 'history of religions' is still widely used today to describe a wide range of non-theological approaches to the study of religion. But there has been much debate as to the precise meaning of 'history' in this context. Is it simply intended to be a mere fact-finding exercise, solely concerned with the analysis of descriptive data, the study of original sources, particularly ancient religious texts requiring philological expertise or does it, on the contrary, require a wider theoretical framework which makes use of comparative data and systematic classifications, leading to typologies and generalisations?

Both positions are held and in terms of the actual works of scholarship produced, as distinct from methodological reflections about them, Waardenburg (1975a) has conveniently divided the field into 'history of religions in the proper sense' (dealing with 'general studies', 'religions of the past', 'religions existing at present' and 'comparative studies') and 'the study of religion in a wider sense' which he equates with *Religionswissenschaft*, a term also applied to works on 'method and theory in the study of religion.' Several other scholars have little room for the history of religions in the narrow sense; they simply equate the term with its wider meaning and understand it as the direct equivalent of *allgemeine Religionswissenschaft* (Goodenough 1959, Kitagawa 1968, Streng 1968, Baird 1971). This immediately raises questions about other systematic approaches to the study of religion, particularly about phenomenology.

Mircea Eliade has characterized this tension among the students of *Religionswissenschaft* as follows:

The different historical and historicist schools have reacted strongly against the phenomenologists' claim that they can grasp the *essence* and the *structure* of religious phenomena. For the historicists, religion is exclusively a historical fact without any trans-
historical meaning or value, and to seek for 'essences' is tantamount to falling back into
the old Platonic error. (The historicists have, of course, neglected Husserl). This tension
between phenomenologists and historicists corresponds in some measure to the irreduc-
ibility of two different philosophical temperaments. For this reason, it is difficult to
suppose that one day the tension will completely disappear. Besides, the tension is
creative; by virtue of this tension *Religionswissenschaft* escapes dogmatism and stagnation.
('The History of Religions in Retrospect: 1912–1962', *The Journal of Bible and Religion* 31,
1963: 98–109; a revised version is found in *The Quest*, chp. 2).

One of the most lucid and conceptually clear statements about the
object and methods of the history of religions in a strict sense is found in
Angelo Brelich's 'Prolégomènes à une Histoire des Religions' (in Puech
vol. I, 1970: 1–59); in Puech's opinion this comes close to a '*storicismo
assoluto*' (*ibid.:* XIX). Brelich does what few authors do, namely, he
presents a conceptual elucidation of both terms of the conjunction
'history of religions.'

By first asking 'What is religion'?, he highlights some inherent difficulties in the cross-cultural use of this historically and culturally conditioned concept. For him, a historian can neither accept the objective
existence of the sacred as pre-given nor postulate a religious dimension
as innate to man, as is usually done in the phenomenology of religion.
The permanent dilemma of historical enquiries consists in the fact that
history does not know 'religion' in the singular but knows only a
plurality of religions, and yet it requires a unitary concept of 'religion' to
look at religions in the plural. One may also point out that the modern
study of religion is in addition based on unitary concepts of 'history' and
'humankind' without which a universal 'history of religions' within a
global framework could hardly be conceived.

Brelich rightly emphasizes, however, that our unitary concept 'religion' is a societal and cultural one, having been defined at a special
epoch and in a specific milieu. Thus, 'religion' has no eternal meaning
but is a historic product of our own culture, subject to changes through-

out history. Although it is true to say that all historically known civilizations include certain manifestations which may be termed 'religious,' only post-classical western languages possess a separate word for 'religion.' Our concept 'religion' applies to a whole set of phenomena which separate 'religious' from other cultural manifestations. Other civilizations do not have this separating concept. If insufficient attention is paid to these contextual differences, similarities may be seen in phenomena which strictly speaking are not comparable. Many false generalizations in works on the history of religions are due to this lack of conceptual differentation (this point has been more fully developed by W. Cohn (1969)).

In terms of procedure Brelich pleads for an initially empirical investigation of what is included under the term 'religion,' followed by a critical sifting of the data in order to obtain a functional definition of religion which can serve further scientific investigation. In fact, he admits that religion can never be exactly defined but, rather, its field can only be circumscribed. He also emphasizes that religion must always be discussed with reference to a particular 'human group' and 'society,' for empirically there exists no individual religion but only the religion of groups to which individuals belong. Even religious founders are no exception here as they always somehow relate to a surrounding religious milieu, even when refuting it.

After clarifying the concept 'religion,' Brelich goes on to ask 'What is the history of religions?.' He sees the autonomy of this discipline as given by its object and methods. Its autonomous object consists in religious as distinct from other cultural manifestations of human groups. Its most distinctive method is the use of comparisons, founded on the unity of human history rather than on a so-called common 'human nature' or a uniform 'evolution.' However, this raises the difficulty of how far one can conceive a unity of human history independently from a certain unity of human nature and development. For Brelich, only the consistent use of the comparative method can elucidate the data of the history of religions and account for the originality of each religion. Others might consider this systematic task to be part of the phenomenology of religion but in Brelich's understanding the latter suffers from the defect that it considers concrete religious phenomena on a merely horizontal level, treating them as 'variables' of the presumably same fundamental phenomenon. However, this leads back to historical questions about the origin and development of these phenomena in a wider historical and social context and the need to distinguish clearly between the qualitative differences found in diverse expressions of one and the same phenomenon.

Brelich also states the need for close collaboration among different scholars specialising in particular aspects or periods of the history of religions. No scholar can produce a work like Frazer's *Golden Bough* singlehandedly anymore. Any history of different religions must of necessity be based on teamwork. But in spite of the diversity of the data, the unity of the history of religions as a discipline is warranted by the existence of a common language, a common problematic and a common methodology—except of course that Brelich's narrowly circumscribed methodology will not find general approval. His exposition presents the history of religions in the narrow sense of *Religionsgeschichte*, to some extent opposed to the science of religion or *Religionswissenschaft*, equated with the search for the essence of religion. The emphasis lies entirely on the *faits religieux*, on the priority of history from which phenomenology can alone receive its facts. Henri Puech has summed up Brelich's methodological stance by saying (1970: Vol. I: IX): '*Etudier les faits religieux en eux-mêmes et pour eux-mêmes indépendemment de tout préjugé, de tout jugement de valeur, au même titre et sur le même plan que n'importe quelle autre catégorie de faits accessibles à l'expérience et à l'observation humaine.*'

Jean Bottero (1970: esp. 108–24), too, pays close attention to the use of a strictly historical method in the study of religions. Significantly, he refers to 'histories of religions' rather than to 'history of religions' for there can only be a multiplicity of histories dealing with specific religious systems through which alone the 'phenomenon of religion' finds expression. Epistemologically, one can refer to the 'history of religions' in the singular in terms of one coherent discipline of knowledge whose methodology is that of '*histoire tout court*'. If Brelich primarily emphasizes the social dimension of religion, Bottero's starting-point is quite the opposite by giving priority to the individual religious experience or feeling ('*le sentiment religieux*,' '*un phénomène essentiellement individuel*') which leads to social expression. In many ways Bottero seems to share Otto's approach to the numinous yet in the study of religious systems, often co-extensive with social and cultural systems, he wishes to remain strictly scientific and leave all generalizations to philosophers. Thus, the question about the appropriate method of the history of religions is identical with the question about the nature of the historical method. Here, Bottero clearly distinguishes between 'history-as-knowledge' (*'histoire-connaissance'*) and 'history-as-becoming' (*'histoire-devenir'*). The former is at great distance from the latter and even at its best can only achieve a fragmentary knowledge of the past. Thus, there is always a place for conjectures and hypotheses in the development of historical knowledge. Bottero places equal emphasis on the need for archaeology and philology in the study of religious systems, together with the appropriate attention to the wider historical, geographical, and social context. However, after a detailed discussion of the methods of analysis, criticism, and synthesis, he states in an almost complete *volte-face* that a true historian of religions

'*doit se laisser mener par une compréhension totale de son objet d'études, et, par conséquent, vu la constitution de ce dernier, par une profonde communion à la religiosité qui en est l'élément premier et essentiel, communion que peut seule lui assurer une expérience personnelle du sentiment religieux*' (1970: 122).

One wonders whether this is an afterthought, or is it the return of phenomenological presuppositions otherwise not admissible? For Bottero remains emphatic in denying that there ever could be one single 'history of religion' as a quintessence of the diverse histories of religious systems. Such a goal, although conceivable, would be unrealistic in face of the insurmountable difficulties of the objective limits of historical knowledge. Religion as such does not exist except in and through diverse religions with their countless concrete expressions. Thus, history in general and the history of religions in particular is as limited or limitless as the ongoing development of human knowledge. That Bottero has a very clear idea of what the term 'history' implies is also evident from his outspoken criticism of Eliade: '*Par exemple, le titre d'Histoire des religions que M. Eliade a donné à son traité connu* [1949] *me parait pour le moins un abus de langage*' (1970: 126, n.15). But one might well ask whether the idea of human knowledge itself does not structurally require the conception of unity which both encompasses and transcends the fragmentary multiplicity of its constituent parts.

Many arguments in the methodological debate focus around two questions: what is meant by 'history' in the history of religions? and, what is the historical method in the study of religion? If the ideal of objective scholarship is to achieve a historical and analytical understanding of religion as a human phenomenon, is it enough to apply the methods of philology, archaeology, ethnology, and anthropology? The stringent demands for objectivity and scholarly precision are of prime importance but will they not ultimately leave us with fragmentary results or even a destructive analysis, if not in some way complemented by synthesis? The attempt to seek the latter is perhaps often misunderstood as a flight into pure subjectivity, too easily seen as abandoning the necessary detachment and objective criteria required for research.

The Swedish scholar, Geo Widengren, one of the best known champions of a strictly historical approach, regards the phenomenology of religion as the systematic counterpart of the history of religions (see his work *Religionsphänomenologie* (1969) and also the preface to *Historia Religionum*)). In his presidential address to the IAHR Congress at Stockholm (1970) he reaffirmed the predominantly historical character of the study of religion ever since the beginning of the discipline. Although recognizing the importance of the growth of phenomenology, he expressed his misgivings about its 'overwhelming domination,' seeing it as

a characteristic trait of our time, which as we all know is extremely anti-historical—in marked contrast to the preceding century and the period up to the First World War. Since then there has been an ever growing hostility against all historical research and against every historical interpretation of facts, except for those having to do with "modern" times (the term "modern" being in general very vaguely defined) (1975: 20).

In his plea for a renaissance of historical studies, Widengren bypasses the *real* difficulty, acutely felt by other scholars using the historical method, namely the problem of what is the nature of historical interpretation. There never exists a 'pure' religious datum; to make historical 'facts' available always involves the formulation of historical meaning, implying evaluative criteria of some kind, not deducible from the facts themselves. Not every historical moment or 'fact' is necessarily of equivalent value. To arrive at historical understanding and discern a pattern of development, the historian must interpret his 'facts' within a much wider context and it is well known that no two historians interpret the same facts in the same way.

In reflecting on the problems of historical methodology in the study of religions, Frederick Streng has written:

In order to deal significantly with religious data, then, as *religious* it is a false procedure to interpret the phenomenon of religion simply in terms of that which is not religious. On the basis of this assumption, I would say that one cannot even begin to write a history of religions that is based on a positivistic presupposition. The fact that the historian deals with human phenomena rather than simply physical phenomena requires him to use interpretive techniques that permit the humanness—and in terms of religious history, the religious character—to be expressed.

Because the "facts" of the historian are different from the empirically provable evidence of the physical scientist, the assertions made by the historian are capable only of degrees of probability. The historian's facts are the products of human existence; his aim is to understand people through these products rather than to dissect "objective events". (1968: 160 f.)

Streng is one of those who strongly advocates the use of both historical and phenomenological methods in the history of religions, equated again with *allgemeine Religionswissenschaft*. For him, this also includes the self-consciously raised question about the meaning of religious phenomena and the nature of understanding, bringing him close to modern hermeneutical concerns to be considered later.

It is generally true to say that the understanding of the history of religions in the narrow sense is largely, though not exclusively, found among European scholars. A much wider interpretation is given to the history of religions in North America with, at its extreme, Eliade's use of this term which often implies an ahistorical, if not to say antihistorical, perspective. To some extent, however, this opposition between a narrow and a wide sense of the term is misleading. The IAHR, for example, has always represented a wide variety of different scholarly methods and disciplines even though the term 'history' has been retained in its name. Thus, the very existence of the IAHR embodies the wider understanding of 'history' as a discipline. This was explicitly stated by its former general secretary, C. J. Bleeker (1960, reprinted in 1961), chiefly known as an ardent phenomenologist, when he addressed the Congress at Marburg, in 1960, on 'The future task of the history of religions.'

He reviewed the methodological debate up to that time and attempted to clarify the underlying principles of the history of religions and the phenomenology of religion. In his formulation of "regulative ideas" for the conduct of the history of religions Bleeker combined theoretical with practical concerns. He asked scholars a) to investigate more closely the question what is religion? in order b) to gain a clear picture of the different types of religion and c) to assess the value of religion for the present and the future. More historically oriented and methodologically aware scholars would perhaps not agree with Bleeker's statement 'that the study of the history of religions should give its contribution to the clarification of present religious questions' nor would they accept his 'regulative ideas' formulated to 'stimulate the practical application of the results of purely scientific research' (Bleeker 1961: 238). Sharpe (1975: 277) describes Bleeker's address as 'the first methodological pronouncement of its kind at a congress'; this is historically incorrect and seems surprising, coming from such a strongly historically oriented scholar. The 1908 Congress at Oxford already included a section on the 'method and scope of the history of religions' with, among others, papers on 'Les sciences auxiliaires de l'histoire comparée des religions' (Goblet d'Alviella), 'Das Verhältnis von Religionsgeschischte und Religions-psychologie' (Titius), 'The Relation of Comparative Religion to the History of Religions' (Jordan), and 'Comparative Religion and Sociology' (Hobhouse) (see *Transactions*, Oxford 1908, vol. II). Questions about the appropriate method in the study of religion and about the nature of the historical method have been raised ever since the first congress in Paris, 1900; for this reason the French scholar Clavier (1968) prefers to speak of the 'resurgence' rather than the newness of the methodological problem.

Ten years after Marburg, at the IAHR Congress in Stockholm, in 1970, Bleeker once again surveyed the major developments in his address on 'Looking Backward and Forward' (1975b: 23–32). Bleeker expressed the ambiguity of the situation in the following words:

the study is steadily moving in the direction of an increasingly refined specialization. This means a loss in breadth of vision. It can also involve a gain in precision of study procedure. . . . In the meantime a new problem is arising, concerning the ultimate aim of the history of religions. Numerous studies are appearing which stick fast in philological or historical researches, clever and illuminating though these may be. Philology and history are of course indispensable auxiliaries of the history of religions. But they have no higher value than maidservants' (1975b: 27).

One may query whether there must be an overall aim of the history of religions which goes beyond the discovery of historical knowledge and truth and, moreover, whether a clear conception of such an aim is possible before the question of method has been adequately clarified. For Bleeker there exists an overall aim, namely, the perception of the essence of religion:

It is imperative that historians of religions should clearly realize what the ultimate aim of their studies is, viz., insight into the essence and the structure of religion in the manifold forms in which it appears. This is the criterion for the value of their researches. The history of religions is an autonomous discipline. Its very nature prescribes a critical, independent and yet congenial study of the religious phenomena so that their inner religious logic becomes transparent (1975b: 30).

For Bleeker, this is achieved through a particular phenomenology and therefore history as such plays a subservient role. However, Bleeker's practical aim, for which one may have considerable sympathy, goes far beyond the possibilities of scholarly investigation. It is ultimately a religious and spiritual aim, not as unequivocal as he makes out, and open to many further questions when he concludes:

Let us not forget that we are living in a period in which religion and cultural values are compelled to fight for their very existence. The question arises: What will be the future of religion and of our civilization? Science cannot corroborate, nor can it renew a faltering faith and a decaying culture. Nor can the history of religions. But it could make its contribution to the solution of the crisis by presenting a clear picture of the intrinsic value of religion. The history of religions, studied impartially and critically, shows that religion has always been one of the noblest possessions of humanity, and that it has for the most part served to spiritualize culture. This is a truth which might bring new hope to the present generation, a generation which is struggling for more spiritual certainty and for a culture permeated by the ideas of justice and peace (1975b: 32).

Bleeker does not so much investigate the precise nature of the historical method as pronounce ideas of a general kind for conducting research on religion. However worthy his aims, they include causes which for others can only be by-products of their scholarly work. This at least is the view of Kitagawa who sees the primary object of the history of religions as 'the scholarly task of "integral understanding" of the structure and meaning of man's religious history, in elucidation of the fact that in order to be really human in every culture and every phase of history, man has always seen the total aspect of existence in relation to sacral reality' (1968: 201). Kitagawa makes a basic distinction between the study of specific religions and the history of religions as a discipline in a technical sense. By equating the latter so strictly with a 'scholarly enquiry into the nature and structure of the religious experience of the human race and its diverse manifestations in history,' he is open to the objection that his particular view of *Religionswissenschaft* is much closer to hermeneutic phenomenology than it stands for a historical discipline with a consciously formulated method.

Contrary to the view of Bleeker and others, the search for a precision of method does not necessarily include a loss of vision. It all depends what is subsumed under the idea of 'vision,' for a refinement of method can lead to a more differentiated and enriched result. The analysis undertaken by Robert Baird in his book *Category Formation and the History of Religions* (1971) has demonstrated that a close examination of basic categories can produce greater clarity and distinction in the orientation of research. For Baird, the history of religions is neither normative nor merely descriptive. It cannot be isolated from other disciplines on whose work it depends but it is not to be equated with or subsumed under them for it possesses its own distinct methodology. His functional definition of history is that 'history is the *descriptive study of the human past* ... historical study cannot be the study of "the Sacred"'. Baird admits that history has numerous uses but 'to *use* historical knowledge is to go *beyond history*' (1971: 32, 33). However, in Baird's understanding religion is ultimate concern, a position in turn dependent on a prior theological standpoint derived from Tillich. Thus, for Baird the history of religions is concerned with both historical *and* religious questions:

The history of religions, then, is systematic in that it asks the religious question at various points in history. The religious question, involving ultimacy, involves a systematic answer. But it is also historical in that the answer is fully rooted in the cultural setting and is related to the shifting of the subordinate and the ultimate at various times and places. The history of religions is further historical in that it makes no attempt to give any more than an accurate description of the religious dimensions of the human past (1971: 36 f.).

Perhaps fewer would query this statement than the definition of the history of religions, also given by Baird, as 'a description of the ultimate concerns of men and communities in the past (including the immediate past which we sometimes mistakenly call the present)' (1971: 35). However, he emphasizes the historical givenness and particularity of these concerns and dissociates himself from Kitagawa by saying that the historical study of religions cannot mean to study historical religions in their wholeness.

Baird affirms the possibility of religio-historical knowledge by which he means 'accurate descriptions about man's religious past' (1971: 37). He also discusses the limits of applicability of the statements an historian of religion makes although 'the descriptive study of the human past can never answer ultimate questions on the normative level, the religious question is probably the most significant *historical* question that one can ask' (1971: 52).

Although Baird closely examines fundamental categories of the history of religions, he is more concerned with defining the object of the discipline, as he understands it, than with a detailed analysis of its method. In fact, his insistence on the descriptive study of the human past begs the further methodological question about the nature of description. There cannot be *pure* description which does not also involve some kind of explanation.

The most vigorous defence and illuminating analysis of a strictly historical-comparative method, already advocated and practised at an earlier stage by Pettazzoni, comes from the Italian scholar Ugo Bianchi (1972, 1975, 1979). Bianchi objects to Baird's definition of religion as 'ultimate concern' by arguing that is is of no use if one is not at the same time prepared to define the categorical quality of what is 'ultimate.' In

Bianchi's view the problem of a definition of religion can only be solved through inductive research which

is not a matter of a selection of facts or aspects operated *a priori*, but rather a matter of penetration. This penetration is realized through the progressive and articulated extension of the historical knowledge of the enquirer, in relation to the different milieus that he is methodically considering.... Only this dialectic between contact with the object and progress in the conceptual determination of it makes it possible to surmount the impasse ... of a definition that is at the same time the presupposition and the aim of research... (1979: 317).

According to Bianchi, the historical-comparative method establishes and compares historical-cultural milieus and complexes and investigates historical processes linked to the categories of genesis and development. For this, the historian of religions has to be in constant contact with the concrete data of religion and religions. Only then will he be able to perceive 'those real "continuities" (which does not exclude oppositions or radical innovations) which provide the basis for a general concept, but of inductive origin, of religion' (1979: 317).

The three essential qualifications of the historical-comparative approach are for him: (1) the concept of a 'historical typology' which allows for the development of types of beliefs, etc., in terms of a series of concrete affinities derived from the study of the historical process rather than being abstract 'ideal types;' (2) the concept of 'analogy' to bring out the comparative similarities and differences between phenomena; and (3) the concept of the 'concrete or historical universal' applied to the vast continuity of religion 'as a family of phenomena that, though various and often irreducibly different, nonetheless do show, if not always a continuity or real connection in a historical succession proved by facts, at least some affinities of character and of function (but not of function only); affinities that should not be less profound than the differences themselves. Of course these affinities too will have to result from the pertinent application of the historical-philological method' (1979: 321).

It is not always easy to see what is concretely meant by statements such as these. One of the main issues seems to be whether the history of religions has a distinct method of its own and therefore represents a distinct discipline or whether the history of religions works with the same methods as other historical disciplines. The Dutch scholars T.P. Van Baaren and H.J.W. Drijvers (1973) object to the view of the history of religions as an autonomous subject but see it instead as one of the branches of the science of religion which does not differ from other subdivisions of the science of history in its method of working (especially see 1973: 35–56 and 57–77). Drijvers has also pointed out that there is no single historical method but only a number of different methods used in accordance with the problem under investigation. Theoretically, he distinguishes four stages of progression in the application of historical methods:

1. Examination of the facts on the basis of the available data;
2. Formulating an explanatory hypothesis;
3. Analysis of the implications of this hypothesis;
4. Checking these implications by means of additional data.

For every interpretation of data a theory is needed; this holds good for the setting up of the problem, for the ordering of the data found, for the formulating of an hypothesis as well as for the whole process of argumentation, so that the function of theory in the science of history and consequently in history of religions is the same as in other sciences, that is to supply questions to the researcher whereby information is turned into data that can be used scientifically (1973: 62).

Many historians show little interest in theory but simply practise some kind of historical positivism in their accumulation and description of historical 'facts.' There is no lack of data and factual information in the history of religions (although much more needs to be collected still), but there is a lack of explanatory theories which can be tested, adjusted and retested. So far, the history of religions, like other human sciences, belongs to what has been described as the 'underveloped' areas of research (Pummer 1972: 121). Whether in history or in the history of religions, isolated facts have little value on their own. To collect the necessary data is often not the most challenging problem but to explain or relate them within a wider context is a more difficult task. This is where the role of theory formation is most important for a theory 'has the heuristic function of making events comprehensible and explicable, and therefore we often need more theories to approximate to reality, and these theories must not be too comprehensive to be workable.... All-embracing theories are only too apt to pass for reality itself, as depicting all that happens in the world in a single consistent theory that explains every fact. Such theories, however inspiring, no longer have any heuristic value; they cannot be made to work' (Drijvers 1973: 63).

There seems to be a large area of agreement about the need for more theory in the study of religion but very little consensus about what this theory should be. The demand for further critical theory formation has been equally stimulated by the absence of theoretical perspectives in much historical work as by the presence of all-inclusive theories found in much phenomenological work. In the quest for a solid, workable methodology there is a discernable development away from subjective value categories and arbitrary deductions towards inductive generalisations which can be backed by evidence. This is a healthy development and much more research in fundamental methodological and theoretical issues is needed. But it is one of the symptomatic dilemmas of the discipline that at present very few scholars are actively engaged in such research into fundamentals. This is a fact deplored by Smart (1978) who wished that 'more historians of religion were bolder in theory' (see also the detailed discussion in Waardenburg, 1978a).

To sum up the many issues raised in the current methodological debate about the history of religions, the following questions seem to recur most frequently: Should the discipline be understood in a narrow sense and be restricted to historical/factual/descriptive matters, or should it be interpreted in the wider sense of *Religionswissenschaft*? Should it include a systematic hermeneutic which might elucidate the meaning of religion and relate past religious history to the contemporary self-understanding of human beings?. Put differently, the history of religions may be considered as part of the wider cultural and intellecutal or, if one prefers, scientific history; alternatively, it may be understood as an autonomous discipline in its own right, with its own method. But this still leaves unanswered a host of further questions such as what is the historical method(s), what is the nature of historical generalisation, what is the place of philology and other subsidiary disciplines in historical studies, and how legitimate is the use of the comparative method? A further problem is posed by the relative emphasis given to the study of the distant and more recent past and the comparative importance assigned to extinct and living religions. Is the main emphasis placed on the origin and full development or possibly the decay of religions, on continuity or change, or on the dynamic of the geographical and cultural transplantation and acculturation of religions? This points to the continuing problem of diversity and unity in the history of religions, the existence of different histories of religions as against the attempt to present one unitary history of religion. There is always the tension between the ideal of objectivity versus the problem of subjectivity involved in the choice of a particular perspective which shapes the interpretation of the basic facts.

Even when the immense historical diversity of religious traditions is acknowledged, there remains the difficult question whether religions are fully theoretically accounted for if they are solely taken as historical phenomena. Their inherent, though diverse, claims to embody trans-historical meanings and values point to a focus or rather a multiplicity of foci which may have to be somehow accounted for by criteria other than those of history. All these questions involve the clarification of fundamental conceptual issues such as how one defines 'history' and 'religion' and, moreover, what such terms as 'meaning,' 'understanding' and 'interpretation' are thought to imply. At a certain level this is closely related to the nature of language and how far it can adequately express or even reflect the fullness of human experience. It is precisely such questions which find fuller elucidation in the discussions about the phenomenology of religion.

3.2 The debate about the phenomenology of religion

The survey undertaken so far shows that it is not easy to draw a sharp distinction between the subject-matter of the history of religions and the phenomenology of religion and fully separate their respective methods, at least not when these terms are understood in their widest sense. Generally speaking, the phenomenological approach has stressed the need for objectivity by insisting on a value-free, detached investigation, as far as possible free from all presuppositions, and it has upheld an ideal of accurate scholarship which is sympathetic towards its data. The aims of phenomenology have been variously expressed as the search for patterns and structures, or for the essence of religion behind its multiple manifestations or as understanding the unique quality of religious phenomena, particularly religious experience, or even of comprehending the role of religion in history and culture. Yet it is hard to see how some of these and similar aims can be combined with a non-normative approach to the study of religion.

The interdependent relationship between historical and phenomenological approaches has formed the substance of many methodological arguments over recent years and created much confusion in turn. At the simplest level, one can distinguish between a descriptive phenomenology, more empirically grounded in the examination of data, and an interpretative phenomenology which seeks to grasp a deeper meaning of religious phenomena; in some works both approaches are fruitfully combined. The search for an adequate theory of interpretation for the cross-cultural and comparative study of religious phenomena has also led to the development of an explicitly hermeneutical phenomenology, particularly in North America. Further distinctions have been drawn more recently between the 'classical' or 'traditional' phenomenology of religion (comprising both the descriptive and interpretative variety) and 'new style' phenomenological research (see especially Waardenburg 1972a, 1972b, and 1978a); the latter might simply be called 'neo-phenomenology.' I shall examine the argument for and against phenomenology in its descriptive, interpretative, and 'new-style' orientation in turn but will consider the debate about hermeneutics in a separate section.

The term 'historical phenomenology', used by several authors (Bianchi 1979: 317; Dhavamony 1973: 8–11, 15–21; Smart 1973a: 40), is perhaps the most appropriate to describe a strongly historically grounded, but systematically and comparatively oriented study of religious phenomena. In emphasizing the empirical basis and non-normative orientation of phenomenology, it comes close to the meaning of earlier designations such as 'comparative religion,' 'the comparative study of religion' or even *allgemeine Religionswissenschaft*. Religious phenomena are here systematically studied in their historical context as well as in their structural connections. In discussing the method of the historical phenomenology of religion, Dhavamony underlines the close and systematic relation between theorising and experience in the development and use of the scientific method:

'Observation and experiment furnish us with evidence for generalisations and hypotheses which are tested (verified or falsified) by making deductions from them and comparing these with the results of further observations and experiments'. However, phenomenology faces the particular problem that its 'field of study consists of religious facts that are subjective: the thoughts, feelings and intentions of people expressed in outward acts.... In other words, religious phenomena are objectively ascertainable but subjectively rooted facts' (Dhavamony 1973: 16).

Thus Dhavamony maintains the principle of *epoché* to realize the necessary objectivity in letting the facts speak for themselves. Whilst it belongs to the task of the phenomenologist to explain the meaning of religious phenomena, he cannot consider the grounds on which religious beliefs are held or ask whether religious judgements possess objective validity, for this belongs to the domain of philosophy of religion or theology. The methodological principle of the eidetic vision aims to grasp the meaning and intentionality of religious data which are expressions of an inner religious experience and faith. Dhavamony discusses the complexity of different types of understanding operating at different levels and emphasizes that the understanding of the meaning of religious phenomena is always and solely achieved through the understanding of expressions or what others might call manifestations. Summing up the phenomenological method he writes:

The phenomenological method does not just yield a mere description of the phenomena studied, as is sometimes alleged, nor does it pretend to explain the philosophical essence of the phenomena; for phenomenology is neither merely descriptive nor normative... But it does give us the inner meaning of a religious phenomenon as it is lived and experienced by religious men. This inner meaning can be said to constitute the essence of the phenomenon; but then the word essence should be understood correctly; what we mean is the *empirical essence* (emphasis added) that is in question here. Phenomenology of religion is an empirical science, a human science which makes use of the results of other human sciences such as religious psychology, religious sociology and anthropology. Still more, we can even say that phenomenology of religion is closer to the philosophy of religion than any other human sciences which study the religious phenomena, for it studies the religious phenomena in their specific aspect of religiousness (1973: 27).

Geo Widengren, author of the well received handbook *Religions-phänomenologie* (1969), has relatively little room for methodological reflections even when he explicitly writes 'Some Remarks on the Methods of the Phenomenology of Religion' (1968) where he largely reviews the methods of earlier phenomenologists. Widengren considers the phenomenology of religion practised by most modern scholars as a systematic, but non-historical sub-discipline of the history of religions (see his '*La méthode comparative: entre philologie et phénoménologie*', 1971, which with slight stylistic modifications is also in Bianchi, Bleeker, Bausani, 1972). Widengren subscribes to a general principle formulated by Bleeker:

la phénoménologie prend sur soi d'arranger les faits dans un ordre systématique, pour essayer ensuite d'en saisir la portée et le sens; somme toute, elle cherche à les comprendre en tant que faits religieux, sans les violer en aucune manière en tant que faits historiques (Widengren 1971: 171 f.).

However, Widengren's discussion of the phenomological method still remains at the descriptive level for he in no way analyses the methodological difficulties involved in the 'description' and 'interpretation' of 'facts' or in the elaboration of 'types' and 'structures.'

La méthode phénoménologique, en se basant sur la philologie et la méthode comparative, comprend donc les stades suivants: 1. la description des faits; 2. l'arrangement des faits dans un ordre systématique; 3. l'interprétation des faits pour comprendre la signification; 4. l'essai d'établir un type, une structure, un méchanisme, sans violer en aucune manière les faits historiques mais aussi sans confondre phénoménologie et histoire (Widengren 1971: 172).

He does, however, point out serious shortcomings in the overall approach of some phenomenologists and his valid criticisms in this respect should be given due consideration:

It surely must be something wrong with a methodological approach where the greatest living religions are not asked to give their contributions to the phenomenological researches, but obscure African or Indian tribal beliefs or even modern folk-lore are heavily drawn upon. In this regard Heiler deserves to be praised for having extensively quoted both Christian and Indian illustrative examples. That Islam so little has been utilized for phenomenological research is regrettable. To some extent, however, this is due to the fact that some highly important phenomena such as e.g. myth, sacrifice, and confession of sins, are extremely difficult or even impossible to illustrate from Islam (Widengren 1968: 260).

In spite of the praise for Heiler expressed in this passage, Widengren and Heiler cannot be further apart in their understanding of the phenomenological method. Heiler's handbook on phenomenology (1961) begins with a long section on methodological questions where three different possibilities of finding the essence of religion are discussed (see *'Die phänomenologische Methode'* (1961), also translated in Waardenburg, 1973a: 474–8). First, one can approach the study longitudinally by surveying individual religions from a geographical-historical point of view; second, one can undertake a cross-section by treating several types of religion comparatively; third, one can envisage the study of religion in terms of concentric circles. The latter represents Heiler's own method but includes the earlier perspectives of his mentors Nathan Söderblom and Rudolph Otto. In his own words

this method treats the religion of mankind as a whole, and views the lower and higher forms of religion together. Every single manifestation is traced from its most primitive to its most spiritual form. In concentric circles we penetrate from the outer manifestations to the inner ones, to the experiences, and finally to the intended object (quoted in Waardenburg 1973a: 475).

Heiler has expressed his methodological model through a diagram of three concentric circles which progressively move from the outer to the inner world of religion. At the periphery lies the world of outer manifestations (*sinnliche Erscheinungswelt*), followed by the world of ideas and the rational element (*geistige Vorstellungswelt*), which in turn is followed by the world of psychic experience, the dimension of values and the mystical element in religion (*psychische Erlebniswelt*). At the centre of these three circles is found the object of religion itself, i.e., 'divine reality,' whether revealed or hidden.

Criticisms of Heiler's method are directed to the fact that this model, however inspiring for discussion, is not a universally applicable one but has been constructed on the premises of Christian theology. Furthermore, he emphasizes personal pre-suppositions in the attitude of the researcher which go far beyond what is either necessary or legitimate from a scholarly point of view.

Besides the necessary scientific requirements for the study of religion he speaks of three religious postulates: '*Ehrfurcht vor aller wirklichen Religion*'; '*persönliche religiöse Erfahrung*'; '*Ernstnehmen des religiösen Wahrheitsanspruches*' (Heiler 1961: 17). Heiler's presuppositions are untenable: '*Die phänomenologische Methode dient . . . ihm als Gottesbeweis . . . Diese wenigen Belege zeign sehr klar, dass Heiler im Grunde genommen eine theologische Religionswissenschaft oder "religionsgeschichtliche Theologie" vertritt, was nicht auschliesst, dass sein Werk eine Fundgrube religions-geschichtlichen Materials ist*' (Rudolph 1967: 36). For a recent discussion of Heiler's work, see C. J. Bleeker (1978).

Heiler's strong insistence on the need for religious experience as part of the scholar's equipment would be shared by few western scholars. It brings Heiler perhaps much closer to certain eastern, particularly Indian scholars, such as Radhakrishnan for example. However, in spite of this insistence Sharpe thinks that Heiler's work 'kept to the phenomenological rules' although indirectly it might imply a great deal about inter-religious *rapprochement* (Sharpe 1975: 279). Heiler's religio-practical motivation is much more explicit in the paper he delivered at the IAHR Congress in Tokyo, in 1958 (see, 'The History of Religion as a Way to Unity of Religions', in Heiler (1960: 7–22), and discussed in Sharpe (1975: 272 f.); see also Heiler's 'The History of Religions as a Preparation for the Cooperation of Religions' (1959: 132–60)).

Most scholars do not ask for special personal qualifications from the researcher practising the phenomenological method beyond those inherently belonging to the subject matter. But it is here that the greatest difficulty arises. Is religion a special area or dimension of human experience demanding a specific method for its understanding and explanation? Moreover, is it necessary for such a method to include some 'extras' over and above what is required in the study of other areas of human experience so as to be fully appropriate to the study of religion?

Different answers can and have been given to these questions by scholars of religion in both East and West. Many difficulties in the debate about the phenomenological method arise from the fact that not enough careful attention has been paid to the nature of method and the way it works in concrete detail. 'Method' is all too often simply understood in terms of wide philosophical generalisations rather than precisely defined in terms of a rule or rules for procedure in specific cases. It is this lack of precision and conceptual distinctions which has bedevilled the debate up to now and taken much force out of the argument for a distinct phenomenological method. To define the historical method is comparatively easy if one restricts it to the factual-descriptive or even the historical-comparative approach. By contrast, to handle the issues raised in phenomenology is much more difficult and calls for a great refinement of method. The fact that many phenomenological works cope only poorly with methodological questions and unjustifiably blur many distinctions is not sufficient evidence that the questions posed are not of vital importance for a systematic understanding of religion.

One of the best known contemporary representatives of traditional phenomenology using wide philosophical generalisations is the Dutch scholar C. Jouco Bleeker, closely influenced by the earlier work of Van der Leeuw. However, Bleeker himself disclaims any philosophical presuppositions as he is emphatic in wanting to keep phenomenology at a distance from all philosophical implications. The nature of his phenomenological work can be seen from the collection of essays *The Sacred Bridge. Researches into the Nature and Structure of Religion* (Bleeker 1963) and from his frequent methodological statements on the history and phenomenology of religion (see Bleeker 1959, 1960, 1969, 1971a, 1971b, 1971c, 1972, 1975b). I shall draw here on one of his latest and clearest statements on 'The Contribution of the Phenomenology of Religion to the Study of the History of Religions,' a paper originally delivered to the regional IAHR Study Conference in Rome in 1969 (in 1972: 35–45).

Bleeker finds it easy to describe the history of religions for in his view there 'can hardly be any difference of opinion about the character of the history of religions. It aims at what its name expresses, i.e., the study of the historical development of the religions of the past and the present, primarily of separate religions or of certain segments thereof. In order to reach a scholarly level, this study should be founded on knowledge of the sources of information, primarily of the texts' (1972: 38). Although phenomenology uses facts from different religions to construct types and structures, it must not be equated with comparative religion which 'may compare religions at the best of its ability.' Bleeker is fully aware that there is still no agreement about the nature and the task of phenomenology but he distinguishes three different types of phenomenology in the post-1940 era: (1) the descriptive school which is content with a systematisation of the religious phenomena; (2) the typological school, which aims at the research of the different types of religion; and (3) the phenomenological school in the specific sense of the word, which makes inquiries into the essence, the sense and the structure of religious phenomena' (1972: 39). Bleeker counts his own work among the latter category wherein scholars have not only reflected on the aim, but also on the method of phenomenology.

This methodology-conscious reflection has in Bleeker's view resulted in a twofold meaning of the word 'phenomenology.' On one hand it is used to designate a specific discipline or independent science of religion; on the other it refers to a particular method of scholarly investigation linked to the use of the *epoché* or suspension of judgement 'in regard to the question of the truth of religious phenomena' and the eidetic vision which is the search for 'the essence and the structure of the religious facts.' Although borrowed from Husserl, these terms are only 'used in the figurative sense' and have no philosophical connections (1972: 40).

In describing the task of the phenomenology of religion, Bleeker has developed further theoretical constructs. He distinguishes three dimensions in religious phenomena which the researcher has to inquire into: (1) the '*theoria*' discloses the religious meaning of the phenomena; (2) the '*logos*' of the phenomena penetrates into the structure of different forms of religious life where four permanent categories may be distinguished (constant forms, irreducible elements, points of crystallization, typical factors); and, (3) the '*entelecheia*' of phenomena is the way in which an essence reveals itself in the dynamics or development visible in the religious life of mankind (see 1972: 42; a more detailed discussion of these concepts is found in Waardenburg 1972a: 183–90).

Bleeker maintains a difference of procedure between the history of religions and phenomenology of religion but thinks that the distinct phenomenological method can also be applied to the history of religions. Together with other Dutch scholars (see Van Baaren 1973: 44; Drijvers 1973: 48) he considers the four traditional branches of the science of religion to be history of religions, phenomenology of religion, psychology of religion, and sociology of religion. These four go hand in hand but there seems to exist a special relationship between the first two whilst the last two may be considered to be subsidiary as they supply

further data to the history and phenomenology of religion. The phenomenological method can be of help to the history of religions in five
respects:

(1) It can impel the history of religions to assess the principles of its study because it has
    evolved a distinct theory about the method how to deal with religious phenomena.
    Historians of religion who mostly work empirically by paying attention to philolo-
    gical, historical or archaeological evidence, are thus led to examine the presup-
    positions of their own work.
(2) It sharpens the eye 'for the specific nature of religion and for its function in cultural
    and social life.' By studying religion within the wider context of non-religious facts,
    the historian is 'in danger of losing sight of the true nature of religion.'
(3) It can help the historian to reach 'the true end of his study: the clarification of the
    meaning of religious phenomena.'
(4) It can give him 'insight into the essence and structure of religious phenomena' and
    help him to develop the scholarly courage and power of imagination characteristic of
    the phenomenologist. However, it is also true 'that the sometimes bold statements of
    the phenomenologist must time and again be tested and corrected by the factual
    knowledge of the historian of religions. So there can raise a fruitful cooperation
    between the two disciplines, in the line of what Pettazzoni had in mind.'
(5) The phenomenology of religion 'can induce the historian of religions to ponder on
    the definition of religion which he uses' (in Van Baaren, 1973: 43–5).

During the discussion following this paper at the Rome Conference,
several of Bleeker's underlying assumptions were called into question,
particularly by Bolgiani who argued that the relationship between
'history and phenomenology', although decisive for both the history and
science of religions, is viewed very differently by historians on one hand
and phenomenologists on the other. Without going into the difficulties
of historical methodology here, one of the most problematic aspects of
phenomenology is the complex concept of 'phenomenon' itself.
Bolgiani quite rightly pointed out that it will not do to practise phenomenology of religion as some empirical system of the classification of
data and typological approximation whilst considering the epistemological problems of phenomenology merely from a layman's point of
view: 'A phenomenology which does not aim to consider a problem of
"essences" is not phenomenology, at least in the specific sense of
modern phenomenology from Husserl onwards.' Whilst, in the view of
historians, the phenomenology of religion appears still too abstract and

conditioned by *a priori* arguments, it runs the additional risk that authentic phenomenologists regard its methodology as primitive (in Van Baaren 1973: 47).

Arguments about the aims and methods of phenomenology also took up much of the debate at the IAHR conference on methodology in Turku, Finland, in 1973. In fact, a third of the programme was devoted to 'the future of the phenomenology of religion' (see Honko 1979: 141–366) and a substantial part of this section was concerned with the evaluation of previous methods pursued in phenomenological research. As Honko has written in his introduction to the published conference *Proceedings*:

'The future of the phenomenology of religion' implies a question both about the past and the future: what is the value of the phenomenological research traditions which have dominated comparative religion for so many decades? Are they still usable, and if so, in what form? Have there arisen new approaches to research which might be attracting increasing attention? (Honko 1979: XIX).

Two new approaches which were especially mentioned were ecology of religion and anthropology of religion; both were discussed under the section on phenomenology. Very different positions were held by the participants of the debate: phenomenology of religion was considered from such diverse points of view as being the basis of the study of religion, or a comparative branch within the science of religion, or being the science of the essence of religion or mainly concerned with religious systems of meaning. For some, phenomenological studies are primarily undertaken from the standpoint of subjectivity whilst others want them to be made more empirical. Phenomenology may be understood to include historical studies or, on the contrary, it may be considered to be based on a metahistorical basis. Bleeker argued that both the name of 'phenomenology' and the traditional shape of the discipline should be maintained. Whilst others consider the history of religions and phenomenology of religion to be two essentially different disciplines, Bleeker sees them as distinct but interrelated sharing the common aim of 'the description and the understanding of religion as a human phenomenon with a deeper dimension' (in Honko 1979: 175).

However, Bleeker's views on the requirements of methodology are naive to the extreme when he affirms that the average historian of religions should abstain from speculations about matters of method but leave these to scholars in philosophy and philosophy of religion. He expressed his firm conviction:

As to methodology, there actually exists only one general rule, i.e. that one should study the religious phenomena both critically, unbiasedly, in a scholarly manner, and at the same time with empathy. Furthermore it depends on the approach to a certain side of the religions in question whether one will use sociological, psychological or anthropological standards (in Honko 1979: 176).

Yet the current methodological difficulties cannot be adequately met by merely maintaining 'that the true evaluation of methods would be to retain only those methods which let religious people themselves testify their faith' (in Honko 1979: 177). One might object that if this were correct, no scholar could ever progress to an understanding of religious phenomena which goes beyond that of the believer. Bleeker's statement, if taken to its logical conclusion, leads to a reductionism of a different sort, namely an essentialist-intuitive one which leaves many aspects and dimensions of the phenomenon of religion out of its purview. His phenomenology is based on the use of the intuitive method and it therefore seems all the more surprising that he concluded his commentary at Turku with the appeal *'retournons à la philologie et à l'histoire'* (in Honko 1979).

Bleeker's phenomenological method was critically evaluated by other scholars present in Turku, particularly by H. Biezais in his paper on 'Typology of Religion and the Phenomenological Method' (in Honko 1979: 143−61) which analyses a wide range of approaches to the phenomenology of religion and different uses of typology. Biezais's critical examination leads to the recognition 'that the phenomenological method is one-sided and, as a result of its philosophical orientation, leads to abstract generalization; it is not capable of grasping and explaining the historically given religious reality' (in Honko 1979: 148). Moreover, the demand for the use of 'historical typology' and a 'historical typology of religion,' particularly as made by Bianchi, does not remedy this situation. The case for the use of typology has not been put convincingly; the relationship between phenomenological and typological method remains confused. To arrive at some clarification in this matter, Biezais offers three alternative interpretations of the concept of types. The first two allow the typological method to be employed within the limits of empirical history of religions and make it radically different from the intuitive phenomenological method:

(1) empirically-based types of the facts studied in the history of religions;
(2) types as abstract, normative principles of a systematization carried out on the basis of the similarity or divergence of the characteristics of the phenomena in question; types operate here as a category of scientific theory (in Honko 1979: 160).

The third interpretation of types is very different from the previous two because the typological and phenomenological methods become identical here:

(3) 'By means of phenomenology, types can establish direct relationships between the object to be understood and the person understanding it, between the spheres of the empirical and the transcendental, and thus they can reveal contextual meaning. In this case, the typological method becomes a special epistemological method of speculative comparative religion' (in Honko 1979: 160).

Whilst Biezais concedes that the use of this latter type must be considered as a specific path in the history of religions, he also concludes that it passes beyond the boundaries of empirical research.

It is impossible to report here in full on all the relevant papers delivered at Turku as well as their substantial discussion (chaired and summarized by Werblowsky; see Honko 1979: 212–20). During the latter, Lauri Honko expressed the view that the past methodology of phenomenology had not been as much attacked during the conference as expected and, in any case, Van der Leeuw's methodology was hardly worth 'evaluating' anymore. With regard to the question of typology he mentioned a further possible distinction between 'core typologies' which try to express the essence of each religion, open to testing against the view of the believers, as Bleeker had suggested, and 'contrastive typologies' involving the comparison of different religions with each other (see Honko 1979: 218).

Although the question about the essence or nature of religion cannot be answered empirically, Juha Pentikäinen suggested several ways in which the phenomenology of religion could be made more empirical, namely, by studying religion from a structural point of view, by pursuing cross-cultural research, which would mean a more statistical approach to comparative religion, by introducing the ecological approach which examines the relationship between religion, environment and habitat, and lastly, by developing a 'regional phenomenology' which means 'that the drawing up of the vocabulary for a religio-phenomenological model must presuppose a general historical, ecological, and sociological analysis within a given, relatively homogeneous cultural area' (in Honko 1979: 217).

No general consensus as to the nature, method, and usefulness of phenomenology emerged at Turku. It is clear that several voices pleaded for more narrowly circumscribed aims and a more empirically grounded approach whereby a theory could be tested in practice. Theories relating to the language, symbols and meaning of religion also formed an important part of the discussion but their examination will be postponed until the next section devoted to the wider issues of hermeneutics.

In his summary of the conference, Lauri Honko stated that 'there were three disciplinary "clusters"—history of religions, phenomenology of religion, and anthropology of religion—which formed a triangle within which the major methodological discussions were carried on.' As to the debate between the phenomenology and history of religions, if any conclusion emerged it was the long familiar one that both are essential to the study of religion and complement each other. But in Honko's judgement, history had the more effective protagonists of the two at Turku:

The phenomenological front was scattered: there were a few unconditional supporters of the old phenomenology à la Van der Leeuw, but in general this approach was labelled as intuitive, metaphysical, or non-empirical, and it found little support. It is significant that none of the newer hermeneutic modes of investigation has, as yet, found acceptance in phenomenology of religion either. It became clear, however, that some people wanted to save phenomenology by creating a balance between positivism and hermeneutics, or rather between an empirical approach to research and an interpretative understanding. It was especially interesting that the reformers and supporters of phenomenology viewed the possibility of an alliance with anthropology of religion favourably, while the strongest defenders of a historical approach went into the attack against anthropology (Honko 1979: XXIII f.).

One of the clearest statements about phenomenology as a predominantly empirically oriented, scientific research method is found in an earlier article by Ake Hultkrantz (1970) of Stockholm. He defines phenomenology as 'the systematic study of the forms of religion, that part of religious research which classifies and systematically investigates religious conceptions, rites and myth-traditions from comparative morphological-typological points of view.' Thus it is in principle identical with the older 'comparative religion' or with *vergleichende Religionsgeschichte* (a view also maintained by Kurt Rudolph of Leipzig). Only if phenomenology is pursued in terms of strict, positive research, can it form durable scientific results. The main characteristics of this kind of phenomenology consist in its search for objectiveness and neutrality in questions of value, and its connection with the problems studied in anthropology (including ethnology) and folklore (see Hultkrantz 1970: 74 f.).

Together with Bleeker and others, Hultkrantz considers the phenomenology of religion as one of the four branches of the empirical science of religion. It constitutes a special field of research which works in close contact with the history of religions. But whereas phenomenology has played a relatively subsidiary role for a long time, it has now taken over the leading position in religious research, a position formerly held by the history of religions in the narrow sense. Hultkrantz lists three major points in describing the general aims of the phenomenology of religion:

(1) It seeks the forms and structures of religions, and finally of religion. But this does not imply a search for ideal types and Platonic essences. The real *essence* of religions cannot be known through studying their *forms* which are bound up with culture-historical, social and ecological presuppositions. The phenomenologist seeks to identify firm components in religious material as well as structures (which may appear as independent phenomena or as relations between phenomena) and functions of phenomena. Thus, the emphasis lies on the study of the *morphology* of religious material rather than on the development of typologies which are only of limited value.

(2) Besides compiling classifications of the contents of religion, the phenomenology of religion also seeks to *understand* religious phenomena. No specific intuitive quality is needed for this but 'just a general perception of the world of religion and of the logic of the religious conception and feeling'. Such understanding operates at two levels: firstly it seeks to understand the place of a religious trait in a certain culture, that is, what it means to those who belong to it; secondly it involves the understanding of the general import of a religious element in a wider connection, its theoretical meaning.

(3) The phenomenology of religion also provides the history of religions with a meaning by holding it together and integrating it. The strictly regionally limited, specialized historical research has led to an atomization of the history of religions so that it runs the risk of disappearing as an independent discipline or of being swallowed up by parallel anthropological or philological researches. The phenomenology of religion offers a way out of this dilemma by providing a common perspective for all historians of religion and in addition it might provide a framework 'for the new research which increasingly takes over the place of the old, philologically orientated history of religion: the study of the present-day religious situation, the religious acculturation, the emergent new forms of religion'. Thus it is only with the help of phenomenology that the history of religions can become a discipline spanning all religions (see Hultkrantz 1970: 77–81).

Hultkrantz also emphasizes that, ideally speaking, the phenomenological perspective is so extensive as to be universal; it potentially encompasses all forms, structures and elements of religion. But there exists no specifically phenomenological method, only a phenomenological perspective which makes use of certain methods also used elsewhere, particularly the comparative method, introduced early into the study of religion but refined recently, especially through the research on culture produced by American anthropologists. Comparing an earlier kind of phenomenology with that practised today in certain Scandinavian countries and also in Italy, Hultkrantz concludes

that the vices of the older research on the phenomenology of religion, hasty conclusions on the basis of material which had been quickly put together and alienated from the context, had to give way to an all-round, careful analysis of the religious material within a limited area where the researcher is a specialist. There is every reason to believe that the methods will become more refined, not least through the cooperation between phenomenologists of religion on the one side and folklorists and social anthropologists on the other (Hultkrantz 1970: 88).

Hultkrantz's view that phenomenology represents a general perspective rather than a specific method or epistemology is also shared by the French scholar Isambert (1970). He doubts the originality of phenomenology as the latter seems to consist mainly of a comparative method which is little specific in its detail, even after the introduction of *epoché* and eidetic vision (a term he considers redundant and would like to see replaced by Husserl's own '*Wesensschau*'). He considers these two principles as mere prolegomena which may open the way towards a science but they do not represent a methodology as such. He writes: '*Le bilan méthodologique de l'époché est en lui-même nul, si ce n'est pour débloquer l'entrée vers une* science' (Isambert 1970: 231).

In Isambert's view, recent phenomenologies are only derivations of the work done by earlier phenomenologists; various alternatives are now emphasized as being most important, whether they are introspection or observation, monistic or pluralistic solutions, or the search for archetypes on one hand or cultural empiricism on the other. One might accept phenomenology as a philosophy consistent in itself but in the eyes of a science concerned with religious 'facts,' phenomenological analysis can only be a transitory phase. If one wants to remain at the level of such a strictly positive science, phenomenology has to be treated as an interpretative hypothesis to be submitted to the necessary psychosociological verifications. The most important results of phenomenological developments at present are a certain mental attitude which seeks to uncover the '*signification*' and meaning of phenomena and some guiding concepts such as that of '*manifestation*,' by which Isambert understands the specific form of relationship between subject and object apparent in religious phenomena. Isambert describes as the mental attitude common to all phenomenology: '*celle d'un* respect de la signification, c'est-à-dire à la fois une intuition qui vise à se dégager de toute croyance, de toute valorisation, de toute théorie et même de tout doute, et le sentiment d'une difficulté à saisir le sens, d'une nécessité de la familiarité, de l'attention prolongée, de l'insuffisance des impressions immédiates*'. The concept of '*manifestation*' designates '*la forme spécifique prise par la relation du sujet et de l'objet dans les phénomènes religieux. L'object religieux, par définition, se voile, c'est-à-dire se montre caché. Et le propre du sujet religieux est de dévoiler tout en voilant ce que le regard cherche, mais dont il ne peut soutenir la vue*' (Isambert 1970: 240).

The criticisms of phenomenology have taken too many forms to be all individually listed here. The contention that there are as many phenomenologies as there are phenomenologists can be further extended to the conclusion that there are also as many criticisms of phenomenology as there are phenomenologies. These criticisms have ranged from phenomenology being too descriptive, without having made any theoretical contribution to the study of religion, to it being merely subjective, apologetic, pseudo-religious or even solipsistic. It has been strongly questioned whether phenomenology has a method of its own and, if so, what this might consist of and in what relationship it stands to any kind of philosophical phenomenology derived from Husserl (see especially the lucid discussion of H.H. Penner (1970)). Many critical voices have come from North America where the development of hermeneutical phenomenology has also gone farthest. The best critical overview of the classical developments of phenomenology in Western Europe, especially in Holland, is found in Waardenburg's work which combines a succinct description of the historical aspects of the discipline with a detailed analysis of its assumptions and aims in the light of contemporary new style phenomenological research on the meaning and underlying intentions of religious phenomena (see Waardenburg 1972a, and especially 1978a: *Reflections on the Study of Religion*, including among others separate sections on 'A Plea for Methodological Awareness' and 'Phenomenology of Religion Reconsidered'; the latter consists of the two important papers 'Phenomenology of Religion: A Scholarly Discipline, a Philosophy, or an Art?' and 'Toward a New Style Phenomenological Research on Religion,' pp. 91–112 and 113–37, respectively).

In Holland alone Waardenburg can distinguish five different ways in which phenomenology of religion has been traditionally understood, namely as:

(1) a classification of religious phenomena from different religious traditions;
(2) the search for basic motifs or ideas in different religious traditions;
(3) a division of religious phenomena within a fundamental structure as such;
(4) the understanding and discernment of religious phenomena according to a fundamental structure of man; and,

(5) the interpretation of man's religious history in terms of a development (direct or broken) in time-sequence.

Notwithstanding the diversity of approaches, the representatives of the classical phenomenology of religion also share a number of common characteristics in the practice of their discipline. Besides regarding religion as a non-reducible, autonomous value-category, they bring together what are considered to be 'objectively' religious facts from different times and cultures which are compared within a general encompassing framework. These comparisons and classifications are thought to be comprehensive and have universal validity. There is also a search for certain basic structures and forms, and an endeavour is made to determine the meaning of religious phenomena as such, arrived at by means of what is held to be an ideal structure or idea of religion or, alternatively, an experience of or insight into what is thought to be the essence of religious reality. Thus, classical phenomenology of religion is not founded on a strictly rational basis or derived from stringent philosophical reflexion:

It strongly accentuates the religious experience or sensitivity of the student of religion, and accepts as a part of its methodology an immediate intuition on the part of the scholar. This intuition should be able to penetrate into what is held to be the irrational side of religious experience, as the deepest foundation of religion itself (Waardenburg 1978a: 121).

Waardenburg stresses the fundamentally ambivalent position of the traditional phenomenology of religion; in the last analysis it represents a particular interpretation *of* rather than research *into* religion. It has in fact played an ideological role in the study of religion 'through being a kind of anti-theology or mirror-theology in the service of a given theology' or as 'a kind of apologetic if not of a particular historical religion, then at least of an idealized religion or of the fact of religion as such' (1978a: 128). In its resistance to positivistic reductions of religion, classical phenomenology has reduced religion to a purely religious experience or to a purely religious idea. This emphasis on ideal contents had made it incapable of paying sufficient attention to the behavioural and institutional aspects of religion. Among the many important criticisms which Waardenburg lists, the following deserve special mention: pheno-

menology has been unable to investigate a-religiosity, unbelief or atheism as authentic human possibilities; it is scientifically insufficiently
founded, for its generalizations do not apply to concrete facts of specific
religions and epistemological foundations; it has not been sufficiently
reflective and self-critical as to its methods; it has hardly entered into
discussions with other disciplines. Generally speaking, classical phenomenology has led to much intellectual confusion and, through its lack of
communication, finished up in a kind of solipsism. The hypotheses
which it has developed 'do not really make religious data intelligible and
certainly do not explain them' (Waardenburg 1978a: 129).

However, unlike certain other scholars, Waardenburg does not restrict research into religion to empirical fact-finding and rational theory-
building but has proposed a 'new style' phenomenological research
'concerned with the study of religious meanings, of human religiosity
and of the religious mental universes which man has made throughout
history.' A distinctive feature of such research is

that the meaning of the religious facts or phenomena is here not only studied as a
meaning which they have as objects in themselves or in their context, but also as a
meaning which they have for people, that is to say they are studied on a level of *intentions*.
The 'facts' of empirical research are here interpreted as human 'expressions', that is to say
as the specific traces of human problems, ideals dreams and aspirations. If there is
enough documentary material, we may reconstitute as a hypothetical probability some of
the religious intentions which prevailed, or prevail, in a given society at a given time, and
of which the religious phenomena that then occurred or occur may be considered to
provide evidence. Let us stress the wording 'as a hypothetical probability' since phenomenological statements have to be constantly verified and checked by factual research
..... As phenomenological *reflection* has moved over the last fifty years from metaphysics
to human existence, so phenomenological *research* is developing from the search for
timeless essences to a search for meanings inside time, including those meanings which
have a religious quality for the people involved (Waardenburg 1978a: 87).

This is not an entirely new approach but represents a further advance
and methodologically self-critical development vis-à-vis earlier, less
differentiated phenomenologies. It also shares a number of related
concerns with some representatives of hermeneutical phenomenology as
well as with recent attempts to develop a more integral science of
religion. As Waardenburg says elsewhere, it is a phenomenology 'new

style' centred around the investigation of 'subject's meanings' ('the
meanings which given expressions and phenomena have for given
persons and groups who are concerned or involved with them', 1978a:
40) and their underlying intentions. Although a number of examples are
listed to which these new research orientations may be applied ('analysis
of images according to their intentions and intentional perspectives,' 'of
communication in discussion and role-taking,' 'of religious expressions,' 'of significations,' or the investigation of 'religious representations;' 'religious ideals' and 'ritual action;' see 1978a: 40 f. and 117 f.),
one may object that the level of discussion still remains far too abstract;
for the methodological argument to be convincing it requires more
concrete application to specific case studies. Waardenburg maintains
that his theoretical starting points can be made operational in actual
research and that by accepting intention as a basic concept or, more
hesitantly expressed, by at least assuming the presence of explicit and
implicit intentions 'as a scholarly hypothesis of considerable probability'
(1978a: 134), further areas can be opened for research which have largely
remained outside the vision of classical phenomenology of religion such
as, for example, the confrontation between different religions, the dynamic relationship between religion and institutions as well as the
process of its institutionalization, the clash of intentions visible in the
tensions between 'religion' and the 'world.'

The particular attraction and strength of this research orientation
appears to lie in its holistic approach. The emphasis on intentions allows
for a particularly fruitful investigation of living religions and new
religious movements; it is also able to overcome the strict separation
between religion, non-religion or what some have called quasi-religion.
But besides the positive task of investigating intentions and meanings,
Waardenburg also assigns to phenomenology 'the eminently critical
function of analyzing and investigating further the concept of religion
wherever it occurs in a discipline.' It can be shown that the classical
phenomenologists who understand religion in terms of essence and
manifestations, depend just as much on a prior concept of religion in the
interpretation of religious data as the empirical scientists who largely
observe religion in terms of facts (1978a: 136). By including such
analytical-critical research into the meaning of basic concepts under the

tasks of the phenomenology of religion, Waardenburg's understanding of the discipline seems to be more akin to that of *systematische Religionswissenschaft* than to the empirical-descriptive or essentialist-reductionist orientations of phenomenologists elsewhere (German readers may like to know that Waardenburg's article on which I have extensively drawn here, first appeared in German as *'Grundsätzliches zur Religionsphänomenologie'* in *Neue Zeitschrift für Systematische Theologie und Religionsphilosophie* 14, (1972b)).

Phenomenology is not merely *vergleichende Religionsgeschichte* here (as for Hultkrantz and Rudolph, for example) but is understood as a systematic and integral approach which creatively combines current critical requirements for methodological precision with some of the most challenging questions in the study of religion by insisting on the need for research into the meaning and intentions of religious phenomena. This approach represents a synthesis of some of the best aspects of traditional phenomenologies with some of the newest methodological concerns and may rightly be considered as a neo-phenomenology which holds much promise for future studies.

It is apparent from the above discussion that there is a general dissatisfaction and wide criticism of the intuitive-essentialist approach of earlier phenomenologists. At the same time it is also clear that phenomenology still attracts much attention and, if rightly understood and practised, holds out a number of fruitful possibilities for the study of religion. We have now arrived at a period of critical re-assessment where many of the earlier questions must be asked in a more stringent form and cautious manner but the future of the discipline depends very much on the development of a more widespread methodological awareness and further clarification of the central issues in the study of religion.

Many scholars recognize that the phenomenological approach makes an important and indispensable contribution to the modern study of religion but it is by no means clear whether phenomenology should be considered an independent or subsidiary discipline to the history of religions in the wider sense, and whether there is a specific phenomenological method or merely a general phenomenological perspective in the study of religious phenomena. Many of the important questions about the form and content of religious experience, the nature of theoretical as distinct from existential understanding, the role of interpretation and explanation, the meaning of religious phenomena, and the function of language in the description of religious data are ultimately difficult philosophical issues which have been legitimately raised but not always very satisfactorily answered by earlier phenomenologists. These questions are still very much with us today, and this is perhaps nowhere more apparent than in the ongoing debate about the role of hermeneutics in the study of religion.

3.3. The debate about hermeneutics

The study of religion may be conceived in a primarily historical and phenomenological framework but even then many further questions arise about the meaning and interpretation of religious data which demand special attention. As the foregoing discussion has shown, many crucial issues relating to the understanding of religion have been debated by phenomenologists; important questions have been raised though few satisfactory answers have been found. The same may be said about the general debate on hermeneutics which overlaps to a considerable extent with phenomenological arguments but presents a more conscious attempt to develop an overall comprehensive theory of interpretation for the study of religion. It would not be inaccurate to describe several of these attempts as examples of a 'critical phenomenology' (a term used by C.H. Long 1967: 80). One might also expect that a closer examination of authors and arguments will reveal a similar diversity of positions as has been found elsewhere in the methodological discussion. Thus, there are probably as many different hermeneutics as there are conscious hermeneuticists.

It is difficult to know when the term 'hermeneutics,' originally coined in the area of biblical exegesis, was first applied to the wider study of religion. In biblical exegesis, hermeneutics has been defined as 'the science (or art) by which exegetical procedures are devised' and hermeneutical theory has arisen 'out of the awareness of the ambiguity of a sacred text and the consequent analysis of the act of understanding' (*The Oxford Dictionary of the Christian Church*, 1978: 641). This definition points to several important issues in the study of religion in general, namely, whether its interpretative procedures are a science or an art, what is involved in the act of understanding, and how far hermeneutics can offer the necessary theoretical framework or, on the contrary, might itself be problematic. The further distinction made by some theologians between 'hermeneutics' (as preliminary to exegesis) and 'hermeneutic' (as the wider study of how the message of the Bible may be expressed in the language of different cultures) does not apply to the debate within the history and phenomenology of religion; authors seem to use both terms interchangeably without implying a distinction between 'hermeneutics' and 'hermeneutic.' Similarly, the wider cultural debate about hermeneutics in contemporary literature, philosophy and the social sciences seems to be little reflected in theoretical discussions about the interpretation of religion, occasional references apart.

However, the development of and wrestling with theories of interpretation is of paramount importance in the contemporary study of religion. But there exists a wide divergence of views as to what such an interpretation can and must imply. One may distinguish between two different meanings of hermeneutics which are not always clearly kept apart: (1) in a strict sense, hermeneutics may refer to a theoretical elucidation of the interpretative process which allows for the development of a theory of interpretation closely controlled by the available data and by step-by-step analytical procedures; (2) in a much wider sense, hermeneutics stands for a theory of its own by which, it is claimed, the hidden meaning of religious phenomena can be uncovered or recovered. In the latter form, hermeneutics may become a form of cultural criticism, strongly dependent on particular philosophical and normative stances, however implicit in some cases.

Both usages are applied to the history of religions, particularly in North America, as can be seen from the following two quotations written during the same year:

The history of religions, like other disciplines, is grounded in an hermeneutic situation: that is, in an interpretative framework which establishes the possibilities and limits of critical analysis and creative synthesis ... the hermeneutic situation, taken in its totality, is the source of assumptions which operate as methodological conventions for the scholar; ... the hermeneutic situation establishes the problems and provides the heuristic devices which determine the purpose of using a particular method and the manner in which it is used (J.S. Helfer 1968: 1, 2).

When describing 'The Making of a Historian of Religions,' Kitagawa referred to the 'hermeneutical task' as

a dimension that constitutes the unique contribution of the history of religions to other disciplines concerned with religious studies. I refer to the articulation of the nature, structure, and meaning of man's religious experience, an articulation based on historical and systematic inquiry into concrete religious configurations—past and present, primitive and historic, and Eastern and Western. Granted that the hermeneutical task of the history of religions has been greatly influenced and enriched by the contributions of normative and empirical studies of religions, in the final analysis it is only the historian of religions who must carry the awesome burden of articulating what Joachim Wach termed the "integral understanding" of religious phenomena, as required by the discipline of the history of religions. This is probably the most controversial aspect of our discipline in the sense that "integral understanding" involves selectivity of data and a telescoping of the long and complex historical development of man's religions. The lack of data is not at all our problem. Our real problem, to use a phrase of G. van der Leeuw, is that the manner in which the data are "significantly organized" inevitably varies according to the personal sensitivity, religious outlook, and scholarly training of the individual historian of religions (Kitagawa 1968: 200).

This quotation illustrates how a particular understanding of the history of religions may be combined with a hermeneutic perspective and also, how the latter depends in turn on certain questions asked by earlier phenomenologists. It is particularly the so-called Chicago hermeneutical programme, based on the foundations laid by Wach and further enlarged by Eliade, Kitagawa and others, which has considerably widened the meaning of the term 'history of religions.' This overriding hermeneutic concern was outlined in Eliade's programmatic statement 'A New Humanism' with which *History of Religions* began as a new journal, published from Chicago since 1961 (see vol. 1: 1–8; reprinted in Eliade 1969: 1–11), having as one of its aims the explicit attempt 'to improve the hermeneutics of religious data.' In fact, many readers may equate Eliade's well-known plea for a 'creative hermeneutics' with the hermeneutical debate as such but several other participants and themes can be recognized in this important discussion. The following questions seem to recur most frequently:

(1) What is interpretation?
(2) What is understanding?
(3) What is meaning and, in particular, what is the meaning of religious symbols?
(4) What role does faith play in the study of religion?

For the sake of greater clarity these questions can be distinguished at the theoretical level but in actual practice they are often closely interwoven. If their implications are unpacked, they all eventually lead back to the basic problem of how one can validly describe, explain and understand the structural unity and historical diversity of religion and religious experience. Thus the problem of interpretation, together with the conceptual difficulties involved in this process, is fundamental. One may well ask what it means to improve the hermeneutics of religious data, whether it is primarily a 'reading into' rather than a 'drawing out' of meaning so that exegesis is transformed into an illegitimate *eisegesis*.

Eliade's understanding of hermeneutics has given rise to a wide-ranging discussion (see in particular the comprehensive study by D. Allen (1978)) and has frequently been criticized for its antihistorical bias and eclectic use of data drawn from the religions of non-literate peoples (for recent criticisms see the detailed studies by John A. Saliba (1976) and Guilford Dudley III (1977); also see the discussion by N. Smart (1978)). In Mircea Eliade's most recent publication, a three-volume work entitled *A History of Religious Ideas* of which two have so far appeared in English (1979, 1981), the methodological reflections are kept brief but succinctly restate what has been said at greater length elsewhere before:

For the historian of religions, *every* manifestation of the sacred is important: every rite, every myth, every belief or divine figure reflects the experience of the sacred and hence implies the notions of *being*, of *meaning*, and of *truth*.... In short, the "sacred" is an element in the structure of consciousness and not a stage in the history of consciousness. On the most archaic levels of culture, *living, considered as being human*, is in itself a *religious act*, for food-getting, sexual life, and work have a sacramental value. In other words, to be—or, rather, to become—*a man* signifies being "religious" (Preface, 1979: XIII).

Eliade is one of the few modern scholars of religion who has developed a comprehensive theory of man's religiousness set within a framework provided by the notion of universal history on one hand and the consciousness of the unity of the spiritual history of humankind on the other. Thus the hermeneutical enquiry must lead from the data of history to the search for their trans-historical meaning and value (see especially the methodological reflections brought together in Eliade's *The Quest*, 1969). In actual fact this means, however, that Eliade, in his search for meaning, assigns priority to a particular interpretation of the data which overlooks much of their historical context and closely verges on being anti-historical altogether. Thus there can be no question of identifying the history of religions in a wider sense with the hermeneutical interpretation given to it by Eliade and his disciples (see U. King's review article (1981); also F. Whaling's (1979) review).

Eliade's starting-point is the fundamental polarity between the sacred and profane. The sacred regularly manifests itself through 'hierophanies' but Eliade's examination of these manifestations draws rather too exclusively on the archaic and exotic, the spiritual universes of primitive and eastern peoples which, in his view, will open new horizons and avenues of meaning for western civilization, bound by the terror of history and its fall from primordial cosmic unity. In Eliade's view, the modern western world has reached the ultimate stage of desacralization where the sacred has become completely camouflaged through its identification with the profane. The historian of religions has an important cultural function in the contemporary world for through his hermeneutical enquiry he can transmute historical materials into spiritual messages for modern man. So far, hermeneutics is the least developed aspect of the study of religion as scholars have often neglected to study the meaning of religious data. The historical and comparative study of religions embraces all the cultural forms so far known but it must involve more than a quantitative increase in our knowledge of man; it must itself become culturally creative. If this hermeneutical task is not taken seriously, the history of religions would be reduced to a purely historiographical task and disappear as an autonomous discipline.

However, Eliade has frequently affirmed the independence and autonomy of the history of religions which he understands not merely as a historical discipline but equally as 'a *total hermeneutics*, being called to decipher and explicate every kind of encounter of man with the sacred, from prehistory to our day.' He has described the 'spiritual timidity' of many history of religions scholars as both paradoxical and tragic but thinks it not impossible to reestablish the discipline in the central position it merits. The immensity of the task should not be an excuse for delay; the search for more data does not necessarily further understanding. Eliade writes that

no man of science has waited until *all* the facts were assembled before trying to understand the facts already known. Besides, it is necessary to free oneself from the superstition that analysis represents the *true* scientific work and that one ought to propose a synthesis or a generalization only rather late in life. One does not know any example of a science or a humanist discipline whose representatives are devoted exclusively to analysis without attempting to advance a working hypothesis or to draft a generalization. The human mind works in this compartmented manner only at the price of its own creativity (1969: 58, 59).

When Eliade refers to the 'science of religion', he envisages it as such a task of integration, synthesis and creativity; he does not doubt that creative hermeneutics will finally be recognized as 'the royal road of the history of religions:' 'In the end, the creative hermeneutics *changes* man; it is more than instruction, it is also a spiritual technique susceptible of modifying the quality of existence itself. This is true above all for the historico-religious hermeneutics' (1969: 62). Today for the first time history is becoming truly universal and culture is in the process of becoming planetary. In Eliade's understanding, the history of religions 'can contribute to the elaboration of a universal type of culture' (1969: 69); in the end, it envisages 'cultural *creation* and the *modification* of man.' And he continues to say that 'all the methods of liberation of man—economic, political, psychological—are justified by their final goal: to deliver man from his chains or his complexes in order to open him to the world of the spirit and to render him *culturally creative*' (1969: 67).

In the last analysis the history of religions is given here a soteriological function which goes far beyond the limits of its possibilities. Not only must Eliade be criticized for his basically normative thrust but also for his preference of archaic to modern forms of religious life, the place he gives to religious symbolism above all other expressions of religion, and the attendant neglect of complementary theoretical frameworks for the study of religion, particularly those elaborated by the social sciences. However stimulating and insightful many aspects of Eliade's theory are, one cannot but concur with Smart's conclusion that regretfully 'his creative hermeneutic is in the end restricted—the vehicle of a certain worldview, and a means of giving life to much of man's archaic religious symbolism, and yet somehow cut off from the wider explanatory task which religion can and should perform' (Smart 1978: 183).

Eliade's approach illustrates the problematic status of hermeneutics. It raises the question of the nature and objective of interpreting religious data: can something new be created through such interpretation or is the scholar's interpretative task restricted to the examination of historically given materials?

This question of interpretation also figures centrally in the attempt to develop a 'comparative hermeneutics' relating to two or more religious traditions. A more cautious approach to a comparative framework (applied to the interpretation of Buddhism and Christianity) was explored at a symposium held at the University of Lancaster in 1972 (see M. Pye and R. Morgan (1973)). It is claimed that this 'is the first serious expression of comparative hermeneutics as an intellectual enterprise in the study of religion' which may provide the seed for future developments (1973: 196). Discussing 'Comparative Hermeneutics in Religion' (1973: 9–58), Michael Pye defines comparative hermeneutics as an essentially theoretical pursuit by which he understands 'the comparative study of *procedures* and *problems* of interpretation, as these are understood whether faintly or clearly by the representatives of recognisable religious traditions' (1973: 58). So far, however, the seed sown at this symposium does not seem to have borne much fruit, methodologically speaking. The most important problem arising from this collection of essays is perhaps the question of different levels at which interpretations and theories of interpretation may exist. Discussing these matters in his epilogue, Ninian Smart points to the underlying ambiguity of the term 'comparative hermeneutics' which could imply: (a) the comparison of the development of interpretation given by a person of a particular religious tradition; or (b) at a more reflective level, the comparison of ideas about the criteria, evolved in different traditions, as to the method of interpreting the respective materials by the traditions; or (c) it could mean both of these approaches together. At yet another, higher level of abstraction one might arrive at a 'general theory of religious interpretation' possessing 'trans-cultural validity.' But such a general hermeneutical theory is not a theory of the criteria of truth in religion nor is it a prescription for the genuine interpretation of any given tradition or of all. It is helpful to distinguish between these three different levels of interpretation—the basis (given by the believer himself), the tradition-bound theory, and the general theory of interpretation, but Smart also emphasizes that these three cannot always be kept effectively apart. There exists a dialectic tension between the descriptive and normative which ultimately cannot be escaped in the attempt of doing comparative hermeneutics. But the development of such a hermeneutics 'is part of the ongoing debate as to the right ways to study religion' (see Pye and Morgan 1973: 196–99).

The interpretation of religious data is closely interwoven with the problem of understanding which, in Kitagawa's view, is 'the central task of *Religionswissenschaft*' requiring 'a hermeneutical principle which would enable us to harmonize the insights and contributions of both historical and structural inquiries, without at the same time doing injustice to the methodological integrity of either approach' (Kitagawa 1967: 42). But the notion of understanding, so central to much of the phenomenological debate, is often not sufficiently unpacked. How far must theoretical understanding be distinguished from existential understanding, and is it necessary for the former to be grounded in the latter? It cannot be taken for granted that understanding will necessarily lead to the most satisfactory explanation of religious phenomena but this important theoretical distinction between understanding and explanation is frequently overlooked. The emphasis on understanding is often closely linked to the central place assigned to religious experience in the study of religion, for example when it is said that 'The discipline of History of Religions seeks to *understand*, from a description and analysis of all of mankind's religious expression, the *nature of religious experience* and *expression*' (Long 1967: 77; emphasis added). The methodological difficulties involved in the task of understanding religious experience are perhaps nowhere more apparent than in the comparative study of mysticism. Contrary to normative demands, no unitary answer as to the nature of either understanding or religious experience can be found. On the contrary, a critical analysis of the rich mystical materials can lead to a highly differentiated, complex picture pointing to a strong pluralism with regard to the methodological tools and levels of interpretation required for the understanding of religious experience (this is forcefully argued in the symposium edited by S.T. Katz, 1978; see especially the contributions by Steven Katz, Peter Moore and Ninian Smart.)

Many scholars might concur with the statement that the goal of the history of religions is 'to understand' but besides the difficulties inherent in the act of understanding itself, there is the problem of what 'understanding' may mean within the different western and eastern religious traditions, given their distinct semantic, philosophical and religious contexts. In Streng's view the goal of understanding in the study of religion is not

a scientific understanding in the sense of an objectifiable, empirical proof; nor is it the 'understanding' that is an appreciation or assent of the believer. To 'understand' means neither empirical absolute proof nor agreement to an unprovable interpretation of life. Rather (1) it means to enter into the mental and emotional framework of the believer to the extent that the investigator can see *how* this religious meaning is possible for the person. (2) Secondly, it means that the religious concepts, actions, and institutional forms are examined according to their relations to the psychological, social, and physical elements of human existence in a cultural context and historical situation. (3) Thirdly, it means to be aware of how the interpreter's own presupposition about such universal concepts as 'man', 'history', 'religion' contribute to his understanding of a particular phenomenon, and how the study of a particular religious phenomenon contributes to the universal images that he uses. (4) It also means that the investigator seeks to locate and expose the particular meaning of what it means to be religious in the data under scrutiny (Streng 1968: 158 f.).

One of the most detailed discussions of the category of 'understanding' is found in R.D. Baird's book *Category Formation and the History of Religions* (1971; see especially 54–125). Baird draws a distinction between the psychology and logic of understanding and offers a strictly functional definition of 'understanding' religion. It is

any valid knowledge about religion communicable in propositional form. This is not to deny that knowledge *about* religion is not the same as knowledge *of* religion in an existential and experiential sense. Nor does it deny the possibility of the latter. What is denied is that religious experience is a valid goal for the historian of religions as an academician. Academic study and research is admittedly penultimate. But such an admission should assist us in avoiding religious experience as an operative part of the methodology of the historian of religious. . . .

Furthermore, if an 'understanding' of religion is achieved when valid knowledge about religion has been acquired, then it follows that the history of religions is not to be distinguished from other disciplines in its goal of 'understanding'. . . .

There are no strictly religious data. There are human data, of which a variety of questions may be asked. To the extent that the answers to these questions are probable and valid, to that extent understanding has taken place. While certain types of religion may be mystical, *the study* of religion has no reason to be so (Baird 1971: 59).

This is a different approach to understanding than Streng's but the two perspectives are not necessarily incompatible. Baird also distinguishes several levels of understanding which he illustrates through the work of particular thinkers, indicating their method and content of understanding and the limits within which they operate. These levels are: (a) functional understanding (B. Malinowski); (b) phenomenological understanding (M. Eliade); (c) personal understanding (W. Cantwell Smith); normative understanding (H. Kraemer, H. Küng, S. Radhakrishnan). Baird is convinced that the historical and phenomenological questions cannot be asked simultaneously, nor can the historical and normative ones. The phenomenological method always implies an ontology. It is only 'a legitimate level of understanding to the extent to which one is convinced of the reality of the transhistorical structures and archetypes. These cannot be supported by merely citing historically derived data' (1971: 90). Summing up the different levels of understanding he writes:

One has acquired religio-historical understanding when he has offered an accurate description of the pattern of ultimacy for a person or community, or has accurately described the changing historical dimensions of ultimacy. Functional understanding (psychological or social) occurs when one has described the function or functions of a religious rite, belief, or myth. Personal understanding has taken place when one has described the faith of another person or group in such a way that they can affirm the description. Normative understanding has occurred when one has understood the degree of truth contained in the religious expressions under consideration. This requires that one not only has the necessary empirical data at his disposal, but also that his

normative system is true. And, it is difficult to deny ... that phenomenological understanding occurs when the data it uses is accurately reported *and* to the extent that the
ontological system on which it is based is true (1971: 125).

The wrestling with the meaning of understanding has gone a step
further in Georg Schmid's *Principles of Integral Science of Religion* (1979),
where the tasks of description, comprehension and understanding are
seen as complementary aspects of an integrally conceived science of
religion. Its methodological programme will be considered in the next
section but let it be mentioned here that in reviewing the main arguments in relation to the nature of understanding, Schmid provides a
perceptive analysis of the overall thrust and difficulties in the discussion
about understanding religious phenomena (see his sections 'On the
Theory of Understanding in the Science of Religion' and 'Understanding' in 1979: 80–9, 89–96). To Schmid, understanding 'is something like both the crown and the abyss of all efforts to perceive in
the science of religion.' That this cannot be achieved in isolation but is
interdependent on other approaches is clear from the following

Without comprehension, description leads to a hodge-podge of more or less accidentally
similar data. Without understanding, comprehension leads to a setting-in-relation of
religious data without interest in the meaning of the data. Both description without
comprehension and comprehension without understanding, measured by the task of an
integral science of religion, miss the whole and are therefore of little promise. Only
understanding asks about the meaning of religious data—not only about the relations *in*
which religious data stand but also about *the relations* which these data are *according to their
own intention* (1979: 89).

This leads to further questions about intentions, intentionality, and
the role of meaning, all of which are examined by Schmid. These issues
also found attention at the Turku conference which devoted a considerable amount of time particularly to the discussion of the meaning of
religious language and religious symbols (see Honko 1979: 429–83 and
485–545). The debate about the meaning and structure of symbols is a
very lively and fruitful one but short of writing a monograph, if not a
whole book, it would be impossible to analyse the complex and conceptually demanding aspects of the contemporary discussion on sym-

bols. Anthropologists, psychologists, sociologists and philosophers have explored numerous paths in the deciphering of symbols. In the history of religions field in a wider sense the comparative study of religious symbolism has found its best known champion in Eliade but his comprehensive approach has often been criticized as it lacks empirical grounding and the possibility of verification. Eliade completely decontextualizes symbols and interprets their meaning within a pre-given framework independent of time, place and history (for Eliade's methodological approach to symbols see his 'Observations on religious symbolism' in 1965: 189–211; see also the perceptive discussion of the different functions of religious symbolism according to Eliade and the dilemma of the 'functional fallacy' by H.H. Penner, 1968).

At Turku, Kurt Goldammer considered different aspects of symbols as revealing the depth-structure of religious experience and tried to explore a hermeneutic which might give access to this depth-dimension whereas Jacques Waardenburg examined the study of religions as sign-systems (for both these papers see Honko 1979: 498–518 and 441–57 respectively). A full discussion of these issues would have to consider recent developments in semiotics and semiology and look beyond the sign-systems of words to that of images. The important role images play in all religious traditions has been little explored so far and the field of iconography, although given more recognition recently, still provides a largely unexamined area for further theoretical analysis (attention was drawn to this point in some papers delivered at the IAHR congresses at Stockholm and Lancaster; see also the effort of documentation undertaken by the Institute of Religious Iconography at the Dutch university of Groningen and its published series on the 'Iconography of Religions' which aims 'to present major iconographic expressions systematically in a survey concerned with all religions of any importance in the world both of literate and illiterate peoples.' Of great interest is also the documentation and collection of objects in the '*Religionskundliche Sammlung*' in Marburg, originally founded by R. Otto, but considerably extended since then. At the IAHR Marburg congress a project for a further museum in Brussels was announced but I have been unable to obtain more recent information on this; see M. Mehauden '*Un "Musée comparatif des Phénomènes Religieux"*', Marburg *Proceedings*, 1961: 191–3)).

The themes of interpretation, understanding and meaning closely
intertwine in Waardenburg's new-style phenomenology where he
clearly distinguishes between several approaches to 'subjective meanings' as compared to those seeking 'objective facts' (see Waardenburg,
1978a, especially the two papers on 'Objective facts and subjective
meanings in the study of religion' and 'Toward a new style phenomenological research on religion'). Particularly valuable for stating his approach to the problem of meaning is his paper 'Research on Meaning in
Religion' (in Van Baaren and Drijvers 1973: 109–36). The emphasis on
meaning is by no means new but continues a well-known theme of
classical phenomenology although Waardenburg explores new and original ways of treating it. In his view the historian of religion encounters
the problem of meaning professionally and is compelled to admit,
especially if he works on one of the living world religions, 'that a
religious faith comprises a view on life and reality either as something
meaningful or as referring to something meaningful' (1973: 109). It is a
primary datum of the history of religions 'that within a given culture
certain things have a meaning for certain people, and that within a given
context such a meaning may have a religious quality for a particular
group or person' (1973: 110). Whilst in the classical phenomenology of
religion research on meaning largely coincided with a search for objective patterns, Waardenburg wants to analyse the contents of 'subjective
meanings' which must be distinguished from the meanings facts may
have in themselves or the meanings attributed to phenomena by certain
scholarly categories of interpretation. The earlier phenomenological
stance to go back to the facts has to be reformulated as the need to go
back to the basic intentions. The primary focus of interest should be 'the
meaning of given data for given people' (1973: 112) requiring the
analysis of the underlying intentions of religious expressions and
phenomena.

As Waardenburg himself admits, this approach is most fruitful for the
study of living religions where direct religious expressions are available.
To develop a hermeneutics of subjective religious meaning leads to an
interpretation of religious data in terms of human existence. The phenomenon of religion is approached differently today than it was fifty years
ago or earlier. This is not only due to the development of the study of

religion as a discipline but it is also related to the fact that the problems of religion and meaning are being reformulated in contemporary culture. In the past, theologians may have used phenomenology to make certain theological and philosophical pronouncements on the level of conviction rather than on that of enquiry and reflection, whereas scholars in the humanities applied the phenomenological suspense of judgement in such a way 'that religious phenomena became in practice objects of literary and historical research without too much attention being paid to their significance for the people who lived with them, or to the evident claims with regard to truth and reality as they are contained in material varying from myths to sacred scriptures' (1973: 115). In exploring the personal dimension of subjective meanings, the role of the other person has to be taken seriously:

> what the other means with his expressions, what something means to the other, what place to give him, how to relate to him, etc. Such questions are, indirectly, of fundamental importance for the interpretation of religious expressions and phenomena emanating from 'the other' with regard to whom the student somehow takes a stand. Two extreme attitudes may usefully be recalled here: on one hand the consideration of religious data as objects in themselves, not to be interpreted in terms of any human dimension or reference; and on the other hand the consideration of religious data as testimonies of a religious faith of people with whom one wants to identify oneself. Unfortunately, these attitudes were often connected with the absurd alternative of being either 'against' or 'for' religion in the study of religion itself. (in Van Baaren and Drijvers 1973: 135)

Waardenburg wants to avoid both extremes by studying religion as a self-expression of human existence in different cultures and circumstances of time and place. But objections have been raised to his preference for living religions and his approach in general for he may not have left traditional phenomenology as far behind as he thinks. For example, it may be asked how far his concept of subjective meanings differs from 'the faith of the believers' and whether it is legitimate to assume that the meaning of human existence is only uncovered in religion. Waardenburg's critics object to the strong emphasis he puts on subjective meanings and the ultimate sense of life which, in their view, is not a profitable method for historical comparisons (for these criticisms see Van Baaren and Drijvers, 1973: 166–8).

The meaning of faith and the role of the believer in the study of religion have given rise to much debate, often without the necessary conceptual clarification, however. The most perceptive plea for attention to faith is found in the work of W. Cantwell Smith (1964, 1965, 1977, 1979). Smith argues strongly against the reification and objectivization of religion; instead, he prefers to speak of cumulative religious traditions and of faith. He criticizes the phenomenology of religion for being 'object-oriented in that it has addressed itself to religious phenomena but hardly to the persons who relate themselves to some or other among these and thereby make them religious' (1979: 7). For Smith, as for Waardenburg, it is the meaning of religious data for those who are committed to them which matters most. The study of religion thus becomes the study of religious persons and their faith. Faith is first and foremost to be understood in terms of a personal relationship between subjects (God and man). To be religious is ultimately a personal act but faith also finds objective expression in community, social institutions, art, ritual, words, ideas, etc. To develop personal understanding of another person's faith, one has to enter into dialogue with the person concerned and ensure that one's statements about a particular faith are acceptable to the believer himself (for this dialogical approach see W. Cantwell Smith, 1959; a critical reply to this article is given by Per Kvaerne (1973), followed by an additional discussion from W. Cantwell Smith in *Temenos* 9, 1973: 161–72). The question of religious truth is also a crucial one for Smith but it is primarily a question about persons and not about religions. Truth is expressed and embodied through personal existence rather than found in propositions.

It has been objected that 'faith' is open to similar ambiguities as 'religion' and has been equally reified in the past. It has also been said that personal understanding of the faith of other men, although in principle applicable to all historical periods, is in practice mainly restricted to living persons with whom one can engage in actual dialogue whereas such access is impossible to persons of the past. Although drawing on a wide range of historical and comparative data, Smith's works are often considered to belong to a primarily theological perspective rather than to that of the history and phenomenology of religion. The questions he asks are valid and important for the study of religion, and always challenging, but perhaps they are best understood as providing a foundation for the radical reconstruction of theology on the basis of comparative material. Faith is a comprehensively human and even more than human quality for Smith which he distinguishes from the varieties of historically developed beliefs. Although he approaches faith and belief very differently from Eliade, he is not unlike the latter in seeking a hermeneutic position which creatively combines the religious insights of the past with the new needs of the present. This is clearly stated in the preface to *Faith and Belief* (1979) where Smith describes his work as a partial answer to the following highly important and relatively new question:

what can our present awareness of the world history of religion and comparative culture contribute to our understanding of man; and particularly, of faith.... To think clearly and to live faithfully, in the new world in which we begin to find ourselves, means a radical revising of our inherited religious—and also secular—categories.... Man is entering a new phase in his and her self-consciousness, planetary pluralist, and historical; and human society, a new phase of global conflict or community. The ideas of our new life together must themselves be new.... The new thinking is radically new, yet is based upon, and continuous with, the past: the variegated classical heritage (Smith 1979: viii f.).

(For a more detailed discussion of Smith's approach see Baird 1971: 91–106 and Sharpe 1975: 282–5; for major themes and a bibliography of Smith's work, see W.G. Oxtoby (1976)).

From a different point of view Waardenburg has argued that the concept of 'faith' can be fruitfully used in phenomenological research if it is understood as a scholarly and not a religious concept (see Waardenburg (1978a), 'The Category of Faith in Phenomenological Research', also in IAHR Stockholm *Proceedings* 1975: 305–15). He tries to see the phenomenological approach to faith as quite separate from a normative-religious-theological one. In Waardenburg's view, the scholarly speech about faith is fundamentally different from the believers' speech about it. Research on faith cannot deal with faith as a metaphysical entity in itself but is always concerned with faith in a given culture, among certain people at a particular time and place. One might almost think of Cantwell Smith when Waardenburg writes:

Scholarship which is critical towards others and itself will ... observe that a number of statements and affirmations made by scholars about the faith of other people are, when it comes to the essentials, in fact more revealing for the spiritual qualities of the scholar and the climate of his milieu than for bringing into the open a quality of faith existing "behind" the religious facts (1978a: 82).

Whilst Waardenburg points to the difficulties in perceiving a faith behind given religious expressions and the ambiguous role of any (religious or human) faith held by the researcher or of relating the study of religion to interfaith developments, he is equally emphatic in not wanting to restrict research on religion to empirical fact-finding and rational theory-building. The question of faith has been one of the most intricate problems of the phenomenology of religion since its inception and in a 'new style' phenomenology, concerned with the study of meanings, human religiosity and religious mental universes, faith still has a place as a 'limit-concept' indicating the origin of the religious meanings which are being investigated (see Waardenburg 1978a: 88). This provides a much more comprehensive base for the study of religion for if the meaningfulness of faith and its expressions were primarily restricted to a circle of believers, little advance could be made in the theoretical and practical understanding of religion at the scholarly level. This is forcefully argued by J.E. Barnhart (1977) who has undertaken a detailed analysis of the different levels of 'meaning' in relation to religion. Whilst the self-understanding of the believer is an important factor in the study of religion, it cannot provide the sole or even major basis for the understanding and interpretation of religious phenomena. If one accepted without questioning the meaning attached to religious expressions by believers themselves, this could hardly provide sufficient data for the scientific study of religion.

Many more points could be raised in connection with the hermeneutical debate about the nature of interpretation, understanding, meaning, and faith, and their respective importance for the study of religion. The debate is an ongoing one and its participants and themes well demonstrate the need for a great deal of further reflection and conceptual refinement. Generally speaking, hermeneutical issues pertain perhaps more specifically to the problems raised by the phenomenology of religion than by the history of religions, especially if understood in a narrow sense (further aspects of hermeneutics are considered in the insightful discussion on 'The Hermeneutical Situation Today' in Allen 1978: 69–101). The entire debate about methodology, and about hermeneutics in particular, has enlarged the horizon of the history of religions field to such an extent that in the mid-seventies the history of religions could be described as 'a non-normative and non-theological approach to the study of religion' whilst it was also asserted that this approach 'using comparative and phenomenological methods became especially significant and influential in religious studies among scholars all over the world in' the 1960s' (*Encyclopaedia Britannica* 1975; Micropaedia V: 66). Strictly speaking, this is mistaken as the study of religion as an academic discipline enjoys a history of more than a hundred years. But if one understands the statement as applying to a new hermeneutic orientation within the discipline, as one must, it points to important new developments which are still in the making. Both the history and the phenomenology of religion continue to pose essentially philosophical questions about the understanding, interpretation, and explanation of religious data where the issues are not clear-cut but often debatable. The inherent tension of this situation comes clearly to the fore in the contemporary debate about the possibility of a 'science of religion'.

3.4. The debate about the science of religion

The term 'science of religion' has been in use since the late nineteenth century but only in a general and imprecise sense. Sometimes it has simply been equivalent to 'comparative religion' whilst at other times it has been a direct translation of *Religionswissenschaft*. More recently, the term has also been used to describe a more integral approach to the study of religion which intends to overcome the inherent tension between the history and phenomenology of religion. Pettazzoni and Eliade, for example, speak of 'science of religion' in this sense. For others, the term refers primarily to a specific understanding of the human and social sciences which might appear to be too restrictive for studying the multiple phenomena of religion. It is interesting to note, for example, that at the IAHR Marburg Congress, in 1960, the suggestion was made to change the name of the 'International Association for the History of .Religions' to 'International Association for the Science of Religion.' However, this was not accepted and the reasons given clearly underline the limited understanding of 'science of religion' at that time. The report on the discussion states: 'The Secretary General is not in favour of this term as Phenomenology, Sociology and Psychology of Religion only have a rather small number of scholars in the sections. Moreover, "Science of Religion" would include Philosophy of Religion which is not in the field of our Association' (*Proceedings* 1961: 21 f.).

Discussing the different terms applied to the study of religion, Reinhard Pummer could still write in 1972 that 'science(s) of religion(s),' although used for a long time, was not generally accepted as a translation of *Religionswissenschaft* 'since the German term *Wissenschaft* has since Leibniz a much wider meaning than the English or French "science".... It designates every kind of disciplined research ... and not only natural science' (Pummer 1972: 103). After examining the existing theories in the study of religion, he endorsed the conclusion that, like all human sciences, the field of the history of religions belongs to the under-developed areas of research. Intense theoretical reflection on the basic premises of the study of religion is urgently required. 'What is needed are explanatory theories that are tested, adjusted and re-tested and so on, the test material being the data.' Although some scholars may find methodological discussions unattractive and secondary, they are necess-ary for 'hardly anybody will contend that it is better to follow an implicit methodology that has not been reflected on, rather than have a fully elaborate position' (Pummer 1972: 121).

In a subsequent article, however, written after the methodology conference in Turku, in 1973, and following a symposium on 'Methodology and World Religions' at Iowa University in 1974, the same author used the term 'science of religion' in a fully accepted sense without further discussion (see Pummer 1975; for the Iowa proceed-ings see Baird 1975). Pummer's article represents a comprehensive discussion of methodological publications up to 1975, and only a few aspects will be mentioned here. He points out that many methodological discussions turn around issues which have been under consideration for a long time now so that one can perceive an 'ongoing process of rethinking fundamental concepts in the attempt to clarify and refine them in accordance with the changed views in other areas.' There is also evidence of a 'continuous trend towards a more balanced study of religion that will not be as predominantly a study of texts as it traditionally has been. The inclusion of sociological, psychological, psychoanalytic, structural, etc., analyses in reflections on a theory of the science of religion should eventually lead to a more rounded approach, even though the possibilities and problems of interdisciplinary research still await exploration.' A review of the current literature shows 'the spreading of the awareness of the necessity for a comprehensive philosophy of the science of religion.' In reply to those who question the value of a continuous examination of methods, he rightly points out that methodology is not an end in itself. Yet in order to develop the scientific study of religion further now, it is necessary to discover the underlying methodological presuppositions, to delineate the limitations of a given method for a particular type of data, to adapt traditional methods or methods from other disciplines so that improved results may be obtained and last, not least, to attempt totally new approaches to the study of religion (see Pummer 1975: 179 f.).

In recent years, the term 'science of religion' has come to be much more widely used. It has acquired a more specific content relating to the ongoing discussion of what are the precise objects and methods of the study of religion, and it is with these attempts that we are concerned here. It is again indicative that the discussions on methodology at the Turku conference have been published under the title *Science of Religion* (ed. Honko 1979). Other books and articles, too, carry (science of religion' in their title, yet on closer examination it becomes clear that this term is far from unequivocal. Whilst it is true to say that the term 'science of religion' generally indicates a sharper focus on methodological questions in recent works, the expression itself covers a whole spectrum of different meanings, depending in particular on what is understood by 'science.' This wide divergence becomes apparent if we look at some of the recent publications, largely dating from the 1970s.

Two works published in the early 1970s explicitly use 'science of religion' in their title although both lean heavily on phenomenology, albeit in a different way. Michael Meslin's book *Pour une science des religions* (1973) refers to 'science' only in a general sense for he is primarily concerned with a study of the methods of analysis and understanding of *homo religiosus* in close dependence on earlier phenomenological views, especially those of Otto. According to Pummer's criticism, this cannot be considered as science however:

> To define religion as man's response to, or relationship with, the sacred either implies a theological or ontological understanding of the sacred, or, in the absence of such an understanding, requires a definition of it.... Mostly, 'the Sacred' is not defined at all; sometimes it is said that the sacred cannot be defined but only experienced. It is obvious that one thereby leaves the realm of scientific research (Pummer 1975: 164).

By contrast, Ninian Smart's work *The Science of Religion and the Sociology of Knowledge* (1973b) is much more directly concerned with the nature of explanation and the sense in which the study of religion may be considered to be scientific. He draws a clear distinction between doing theology in the sense of articulating a faith, and studying religion where theology itself is part of the *phenomenon* to be understood. Smart admits that although 'an overall strategy of a science of religion is desirable,' it has not yet been fully worked out. He then proceeds to describe the scientific study of religion as 'an enterprise which is aspectual, poly-methodic, pluralistic, and without clear boundaries' (1973b: 4, 8). This open-ended statement is made more explicit in his conclusions regarding the way in which we can speak of the scientific study of religion:

> First of all, it is scientific in the sense that it is not determined by a position within a field—that is, it begins neither from a theological nor from an atheistic standpoint. Second, though it looks for theories, it does not begin by building theories into phenomenological descriptions and it adopts methodological neutralism in its descriptive and evocative tasks. Third, this description and evocation begin in a sense from the participants and attempt to delineate the way the Focus looks from their point of view. Phenomenology thus differs from the physical sciences, because it has to deal with conscious beings who think and feel. Fourth, it is scientific in having an analogy to the experimental method, which is the use of cross-cultural comparisons. Fifth, it makes use of such methods as may be evolved in the disciplines which share in the study of religion, as being aspectual and polymethodic. Sixth, the scientific study of religion incorporates

dynamic and static typologies, which attempt to illuminate and explain religious phenomena, but relates always to the particularities of historical traditions.

It is worth stressing that the scientific study of religion is scientific in a manner
appropriate to its subject-matter; it is not simply bound to statistics and still less to causal
laws of a hard kind. Very rarely can one say in the field of religion that 'whenever X
occurs, then Y occurs', even if we can point to recurrent patterns. But this should not
discourage us from trying to put the study of religion on a scientific and at the same time
human basis (1973b: 158 f.).

In 1976, Penner concluded his retrospective review of the methodological debate with the statement that current publications and
activities 'all indicate that the science of religion is once again building
up new theoretical capital' (Penner 1976: 16). He also argued against the
widely held view that the science of religion is distinctive and non-
reductive. In his opinion, this is based on a misunderstanding of the true
function of 'reduction;' the latter is needed in developing an adequate
explanation for religious phenomena. He agrees with the anthropologist
Spiro in saying that the determinants of religion have to be analysed and
established empirically; by so 'reducing' religion to its various con-
stituents, one does not in any way destroy its essential quality but one
can explain aspects of it. In the scientific study of religion such search for
explanations is vital: 'If we do not "like" the explanation we must find
the theory *inadequate*, false, or trivial. It simply will no longer serve the
science of religion verbally to abuse other approaches to religion as
"reductionistic". All approaches to religion are reductionistic in that all
approaches assume either implicitly or explicitly some theory of interpretation or explanation' (Penner 1976: 15).

In the discussion on the evaluation of previous methods in the study
of religion at Turku a similar point was made in emphasizing the
important distinction between the widely held wish to understand and
the pursuit of science. Human understanding as the fulfilment of a basic
need might be attained in a number of ways but the difficulty arises over
the way in which understanding is transposed into scientific statement,
i.e., over epistemology:

The second step was then to arrange the perceptions—science was, indeed, merely the
ordering of perceptions—since if the understanding remained unordered, there would

be no science of religion. The difficulties, then, were twofold: the epistemological aspect, i.e. the gathering of information, and the problem of what scientific system could be built up on the basis of the information thus gathered. If, as had repeatedly been stated, the science of religion was an empirical science, then it must be pursued according to the rules imposed on empirical science by epistemology and the theory of science. Scientists of religion, after all, could not be an exclusive group with a unique epistemology, or they would never be accepted as partners in scientific discussion (in Honko 1979: 219 f.).

But as another participant in the discussion, W.H. Capps, pointed out, there are at present a great number of 'varieties of operational definitions' and 'multiple methodological interests and intentions' to be found in the study of religion. One may rightly ask 'is the science of religion a subject or a field? Is it a discipline or is it multi-disciplinary? Does it have a proper subject, or does the multiplicity of its interests prohibit a common focal point?' (in Honko 1979: 180). A great deal of further reflection is required to clarify these questions. One of the most important issues which remained perhaps unexamined at Turku, is the question of what model of 'empirical science' and which 'theory of science' are used as a basis for discussions about the science of religion. Sometimes one must question whether the underlying model itself may be out of date as far as recent developments in the social and natural sciences are concerned.

Closely modelled on the social sciences and particularly influenced by developments in cultural anthropology are some Dutch discussions on the science of religion. This is apparent from the papers of the 'Groningen working-group for the study of fundamental problems and methods of science of religion' (founded in 1968), published under the title *Religion, Culture and Methodology* (Van Baaren and Drijvers 1973). In his contribution 'Science of Religion as a Systematic Discipline. Some Introductory Remarks' (1973: 36–56) T.P. van Baaren argues that religion is a function of culture (meaning a way or form of expression), connected with and interacting with other forms of culture. Religion ought to be studied as a function of culture and this does not imply an attempt at reduction but a strong emphasis on an empirical study of religions which excludes questions of the philosophy of religion. Van Baaren holds the view that the fourfold distinction between the history of religions, phenomenology of religion, psychology of religion, and sociology of religion refers to four different approaches rather than disciplines in the study of religion but has little systematic value. For him, the systematic study of religion is not a historical discipline but a systematic one of a non-normative character: 'science of religion is not concerned with discovering the essence of *the* or *a* religion; this is a task of philosophy or theology.... It only studies religions as they are empirically and disclaims any statements concerning the value and truth of the phenomena studied' (1973: 47). 'Science of religion in all its forms consists of describing, classifying and explaining the material studied, and if need be of understanding it' (1973: 48). That means science of religion is no more subjective than other *Geisteswissenschaften* but 'it aims at reaching a maximum of objectivity and a minimum of subjectivity' (1973: 50). Similar arguments are found in Van Baaren's earlier article 'Systematische Religionswissenschaft' (1969).

Van Baaren's views are critically discussed in H. J.W. Drijvers' contribution 'Theory Formation in Science of Religion and the Study of the History of Religions' (Van Baaren and Drijvers, 1973: 57–77) which further illustrates the strong dependence on cultural anthropology, particularly on Spiro's view that religion has a cognitive, a substantive, and an expressive function and is to be explained in terms of society and personality. According to Drijver, the social sciences 'supplied the principal material for theoretical renovation in the systematical science of religion' and they 'also prove useful for history of religions in their historical aspect' (1973: 73).

The 'faith of the believer' can no longer be a legitimate subject of the science of religion. The current development is away from an earlier phenomenology of religion and a mainly historical and literary approach to the study of religion towards more strictly defined systematic and comparative research which seeks explanations rather than mere *Verstehen* in terms of an intuitive grasp: therefore the strong emphasis on correct terminology and on the formal character and descriptive precision of all terms employed. The science of religion investigates religious conceptions, values and behaviour. Whilst traditional research has been primarily concerned with religious conceptions, it is open to discussion whether renewed attention to religious behaviour is the starting-point of an entirely new science of religion based on the methodic primacy of behaviour (for a detailed discussion of these complex issues see the 'Epilogue' in Van Baaren and Drijvers 1973: 159–68).

The influence of the social sciences, particularly of cultural anthropology, was also very marked at the Turku conference where a subsection was specifically devoted to the 'religio-anthropological approach' (including a paper by M.E. Spiro on 'Symbolism and Functionalism in the Anthropological Study of Religion'). Moreover, a substantial part of the conference dealt with 'religion as expressive culture' (examining theories concerning the ritual process, the language of religion, and depth structures of religious expression). One of the main organisers, Professor Lauri Honko, summarized the discussion about anthropology as follows:

Cultural anthropology still enjoys a strong position within the scientific study of religion, not least due to its fieldwork techniques and methodology of cultural comparison. A kind of bifurcation appears for instance in the significance which anthropologists investigating religion accord to the relation 'man-the "otherworldly" (god, etc.)' in comparison with the relation 'man-society'. It is this latter relation which has always been central both for cultural and social anthropology.... Discussion arose at the conference as to whether religious symbols are manipulative in nature or not: and the dominant trend appeared to support the opinion that the existence of a symbol cannot be explained anything like exhaustively in terms of economic, social, or similar causes. If symbols are tools, they are so only in a very general sense—i.e. tools of language, thought, and living. The man-'otherworldly' relation continues to hold an important position in the metatheory of religious studies, despite the fact that some anthropologists do not consider it capable of operationalization (cf. the discussion of the term *numen*), while for some historians of religions this appeared to be a question to which different religions would in an inductive approach provide different answers. On the whole it seems that it was precisely the anthropologists and folklorists who most often came in for criticism, sometimes on the grounds that their methods of investigation were those of the natural sciences, sometimes because of their objective typologies, which were even seen as a threat to humanist scholarship (Honko 1979: XXIV).

However, such a strong dependence on the methodology of the social sciences raises the question whether the science of religion ceases to be a field of studies in its own right and is simply identical with the social sciences. The very expression 'the scientific study of religion' has, for some at least, become synonymous with research in the sociology of religion (see, for example, J. Milton Yinger's well-known textbook *The*

Scientific Study of Religion (1970), and also the American *Journal for the Scientific Study of Religion*). But many important issues arising in the study of religions, both with regard to society and individual, cannot be exhaustively dealt with by the sociological approach.

A further narrowing in the understanding of 'science of religion' is found in the quantitative and statistical researches on 'the theory and methodology of the science of religions' undertaken by the Polish Institute of Philosophy and Sociology (Polish Academy of Sciences, Warsaw). The results of these researches are published in the journals *Euhemer* and *Studia Religiozawcze* (with short summaries in Russian, English, German, and sometimes French). One of the editors, Poniatowski, speaks of a *'Metareligionswissenschaft'* and refers to the development of *'scientometrics'* in the study of religion, an approach which implies further analysis of a mainly theoretical and statistical kind of earlier research on religion. However, the heavy emphasis on quantitative data allows for little creative originality and yields perhaps few new results.

In the discussions about the science of religion much depends on whether the term 'science' is understood in a narrow, empirical-positivistic sense or in a wider, more integral manner. One must ask whether the underlying model of 'science' is primarily that of the natural-physical sciences, the life sciences, the social sciences or of the human sciences in the widest sense. If it is the latter, the interrelationship of dialectical and hermeneutical perspectives is of primary importance for the interpretation of the data; moreover, it is also less obvious what constitutes a fact or data in the human sciences. The limitations imposed on the study of religion by particular methodological models, especially those drawn from scientific empiricism, have been examined and strongly critized by several writers in recent years, (for a detailed discussion see A.M. Frazier 1970; J.F. Miller 1975; D. Wiebe 1975 and 1978).

Miller, for example, argues that science, as currently understood, possesses inherent limitations to deal with the phenomena of religion, and this for the following reasons. The scientific *criteria of causality* are unable to be met and are prejudicial to the data of religion as is the very naturalistic reductive methodological *directionality* of science. Also, the meaning criteria employed by the *experimental* scientist, especially the identification of the meaning of a term or symbol with the criterion for identifying the referent of the term or symbol, are impossible to meet in religion if that referent is God; moreover, correspondence is an adequate criterion of truth in religion. In *theoretical* science, where meaning is defined implicitly within the system and truth determined by coherence (as it must be in religion), the scientific theoretical framework is either conceptually incompatible with or inadequate for the fundamental data of religion (see Miller 1975: 147).

R.H. Penner and E.A. Yonan (1972) pointed out earlier that methodological discussions revolving around *Religionswissenschaft* have begun to recognize the essential importance of the problems of definition, reduction, explanation and understanding, but that there has been little explicit analysis of these problems. Drawing on wide-ranging discussions of what contemporary philosophers of science understand by definition, reduction, and explanation, Penner and Yonan apply their results to the science of religion in order to achieve greater clarification about its theoretical premises. Their important article (1972) has been widely discussed in subsequent literature, including G. Dudley's study *Religion on Trial* (1977), which is primarily devoted to a much wider context, namely, that of a critical examination of Eliade's methodology.

Like others, Dudley criticizes current methodological discussions in the study of religion for their undue dependence on outdated theoretical models of the natural sciences (see especially 1977: 112–38). He asks, with some justification, why phenomenologists and historians of religions should especially want to identify their discipline as an empirical science. Instead, he urges contemporary religion scholars to mount a counter-offensive against empirical positivism in the history of religions. Discussing the role of rational criticism in the natural sciences, Dudley writes:

The entire procedure of observation, inductive reasoning, and empirical verification is taken over by empiricist historians of religion from the natural sciences. They regard that procedure as a passport to objectivity that makes *Religionswissenschaft* a true science of religions. The anomaly in this dogma, and indeed in the whole dilemma of *Religionswissenschaft*, is that for nearly three decades, even before the empiricists gained their prominence in the international meetings of the history of religions, empiricism in the natural sciences has been under sweeping criticism. In fact, positivist empiricism in the sciences has been so devastatingly criticized by both philosophers and scientists that it is rather redundant to attack it again (1977: 121 f.).

Based on more recent developments in the philosophy of science, found in the works of Lakatos, Barbour, and Toulmin, Dudley proposes that the field of *Religionswissenschaft* desperately needs a methodology of research programmes built around a core theory (which, he thinks, Eliade's work can provide, a statement which will no doubt be heavily contested by other scholars). Auxiliary hypotheses can be adjusted or rejected, as the case may be, but the core theory can be pursued until all its potentialities have been explored. Such a research programme will be flexible and progressive if it leads to the discovery of new and unexpected phenomena and accounts for phenomena already known but unexplained. At present, empirical positivism is so much in trouble in the natural sciences that historians of religion are inviting problems by importing it into their own field:

To burden *Religionswissenschaft* with all the methodological dogmas of inductive reasoning and empirical verification is to bring weakness, not strength, into its methodology. What is true for history of religions is true for all the humane sciences. The answer to the sway of empirical positivism in so many university disciplines is not to draw a sharper line between the natural and the humane sciences or between the sciences and the humanities but to seek the same methodological flexibility that has become characteristic in the sciences themselves (1977: 126).

In the various discussions about the most appropriate methodology for the science of religion, however understood, the shared aim of all protagonists is to defend the autonomy of the study of religion and its independence from normative stances derived from philosophical or theological presuppositions. In this sense one can speak of the necessary critical function of the study of religion vis-à-vis established philosophical and religious traditions (for a detailed discussion of this point see K. Rudolph 1978). But from a position of counter-critique one might argue that the claim to methodological neutrality is a myth, that all description involves at least a partial explanation and evaluation. (Dudley (1977) discusses 'the normative/descriptive fallacy' and points out that it is false to suppose that scientific and normative theories are necessarily mutually exclusive. In fact, in many of our most significant scientific theories, normative and descriptive aspects are inextricably related.) Science, as traditionally understood, can only look at religion from a naturalistic point of view; yet claims relating to a supernatural referent or transcendent focus form an integral part of religion. Thus, a narrow scientific understanding of religion might well be a major category mistake if it refuses to consider important philosophical and theological questions which at some point arise in all religious traditions.

One of the most fundamental requirements of any science is that its method must be fully appropriate to its subject-matter. Many approaches to the study of religion are so narrow and reductionist that they may rightly be called 'pseudo-scientific' rather than scientific in the true sense of the word, for they are hardly commensurate with the multidimensional realities found in the institutions, expressions, and experience of religion. Whilst the classical phenomenology of religion with its intuitive approach, its emphasis on the essence of religion and the centrality of religious experience, represents perhaps an 'idealistic-essentialist' reduction of religion against which one must argue that the experiential dimension is only one aspect of religion and that other aspects require other methodologies, the pseudo-scientific limitation of the study of religion to empirical-descriptive 'hard' data represents a reductionism of another kind which has to be equally strongly criticized.

The development of both positions in their extreme form can to some extent be explained as the necessary opposition to and critique of earlier attitudes and enquiries, subsequently considered to be a serious limitation of the study of religion in the wider sense. Whilst it was historically necessary to develop the study of religion in an oppositional mode of thought against the entrenched positions of a narrowly conceived theology or philosophy, we might now be nearer the development of a more relational and inclusive mode of thought which might even recognize the convergence of the questions posed in religious studies and theology. It is perhaps this attempt which is best described as the development of an integral science of religion.

In his description of the '*Panorama des sciences des religions*' Séguy (1970) distinguishes the 'theological sciences' from the 'non-theological sciences of religion' which originally developed in opposition to the theological sciences. He considers the development of the non-theological sciences of religion as an integral part of the process of the modern secularisation of knowledge to which even theologians contribute now. But he also discerns a continuous movement from opposition through composition towards integration in the ever greater interdependence of all aspects of knowledge.

We are far from having reached such a stage of integration in the study of religion but various proposals have recently been made to combine the multiple perspectives and questions of the study of religion in a more integral manner. The vehement exclusion of philosophical questions on the part of many historians of religion is perhaps due to the fact that in practice philosophy of religion has meant a narrowly circumscribed Christian philosophy of religion without taking into account the wide-ranging philosophical questions arising from other religious and cultural traditions.

There exists now widespread dissatisfaction with scientific theories of religion because of their reductionist models. Paul Heelas, in his discussion of 'Some Problems with Religious Studies' (1978), has argued that the study of religion is characterized by competing or incommensurable paradigms. In order to develop a more coherent study of religion, it is necessary to assess these competing paradigms for 'the very nature of the religious alters depending on whether one applies, for example, a positivistic or a theological paradigm.' The fact that religious studies is at present marked by too much paradigm-dependence and faced with an invasive relativism and a phenomenal insecurity makes Heelas say 'that there is an inherent tendency for religious studies (studying the religious as phenomenon) to become something rather different (namely re-interpreting, even reconstituting, the religious in terms of paradigms which cannot be justified with respect to intra-religious criteria)' (1978: 7, 1). The relationship between the different paradigms of religious studies, theology, and a more comprehensive or integral science of religion is frequently being debated but it is impossible to summarize all relevant arguments in detail here. Charles Davis, the editor of the Canadian journal *Sciences Religieuses/Studies in Religion* (SR), which in

1970 replaced the former *Canadian Journal of Theology*, speaks of a re-convergence of theology and religious studies in terms of the further development of a methodologically coherent, unified field of studies which unites the historical, scientific, and philosophical levels of study-ing the data of religion (see Davis 1974–5). He thinks that the empirical, scientific study of religions cannot be accommodated under the title 'history of religions' or under 'phenomenology of religion.' The latter should be dropped because of its misleading associations. But he also argues against the science of religion being merely descriptive: 'Its descriptive classificatory function is only preliminary. Like sociology and the other human sciences, the science of religion has to devise explanatory concepts, models, laws, and theories' (1974–5: 215). In his distinction between structural and dialectical explanations and between the reality and existence of the objects of religion Davis depends on Smart. Reserving the term 'theology' for critical reflection upon religion (and not applying it to the communicative function of religion so often confused with theology), Davis suggests that the science of religion is a more advanced stage of systematic theology, not an essentially different enterprise. He states:

The science of religion is an empirical inquiry distinguished from sociology and psychology by its primary concern with religious data as religious. Unlike history, it deals with what is general or at least recurrent in religious experience and expression. Its aim is not just descriptive and classificatory, but explanatory. It should be productive of precise, theoretical concepts to make possible a unified grasp of the manifolds of concrete religious data and also of explanatory hypotheses and theories. Its task would seem to be a more methodical carrying out on a wider range of data of the work of ordering done by systematic theology on the data of a single tradition (1974–5: 219).

Davis's suggestion gave rise to further debates and questions which cannot be reported here but which are evidence of the search for a more integral approach to the study of religion. For a reaction to Davis's ideas see *SR* 4, 1974/75 and *SR* 5, 1975/76, as well as B.J.F. Lonergan (1976–77) and K. Klostermaier (1976–77). Davis (1981) has again restated his position in the article 'Theology and Religious Studies.'

Davis's ideas are not unlike Pannenberg's discussion (1976) of the science of religion as a critical theology of religion. Pannenberg argues that a 'mere phenomenology, psychology or sociology of religion cannot get to grips with religion's specific object, and the claims of such investigations to be sciences of religion and religions must consequently be described as problematic.' Following to some extent both Heiler and Troeltsch, Pannenberg considers the real thematic of religions to be 'the communication of divine reality experienced in them' which can only be made the object of scientific investigation in a *theology* of religions which would subject the assertions of religious traditions to critical examination and would not depend in its interpretation on a previous religious position. Pannenberg seems to think that this kind of critical theology can bridge the current gap between philosophy of religion and the history of religions (see 1976: 365; 364; 368 n., 689). However, many scholars would rightly fear that the science of religion is not given the necessary autonomy here but is being reabsorbed into theology.

A different and more truly integral approach, less dependent on systematic-critical theology, is found in Georg Schmid's important work (1979). He argues for the necessary role of a critical-reflexive but constructive methodology in the science of religion whose close examination of its own procedure is of central importance. However, methodology does not produce immovable basic laws or complete, self-contained methods but only *principles* in the sense of 'beginnings' or 'first steps leading to other steps and indicating the basic direction of these other steps ... Principles are elements of scientific perception about which science can attain clarity but which science can never hold as unshakable dogmas' (1979: 2 f.). However, Schmid also argues that such critical reflection must be applied to the whole of religion, notwithstanding the enormity of individual data. This reflection on the whole of religion must be combined with the science's reflection upon itself, that is, with a critical consideration of its own task, premises, and methods. It is precisely these three areas which Schmid's work analyses with great subtlety.

Schmid makes a clear and important distinction between *religious reality* and the *reality of religion*. However, this distinction can also appear confusing to the reader as these terms are linguistically too similar to remain sufficiently distinct. He calls *religious reality* the historically demonstrable side of religion which alone can be the object of religious-scientific research:

It means, firstly, *the enormously wide field of religious data*, which include holy writings, and other documents, prayer books, theological treatises, the formation of temples, cultic objects, pictures, symbols, songs, church offices and forms of community. We name religious reality, secondly, the whole manifold of religious life and experience which expresses itself or conceals itself in religious data: sacrifice, prayer, meditation, thanksgiving, worship, search, petition, celebration, experience, remembrance, realization, belief, hope, imitation, astonishment, rebellion, enthusiasm, confession teaching and obedient action.

In what follows, the *reality of religion* means *what is intended in all of this life and experience*, the whence and whereto of all this searching, hoping, believing and worshipping. The reality of religion means the reality for the sake of which all religious reality comes into being. . . .

As science, science of religion knows of no direct access to the reality of religion. The reality of religion is present to the science only in the witness of the religious reality. Only the religious reality is the immediate object of the science of religion, and the science researches this object systematically, this is, in awareness of method and consistent procedure within the chosen method (1979: 11f.).

Not even theology has direct access to the reality of religion. In principle, no aspect of religious reality as datum and event in the life of the individual and society is removed from critical questioning and systematic research. In Schmid's view, the specific characteristic of the modern science of religion is the bringing together of integral reflection and specific research without subsuming the one under the other. Such a systematic science of religion is different from the history of religions and also from phenomenology of religion. However, Schmid's own principles of an integral science of religion might themselves be considered to belong to a new-style phenomenological approach.

Schmid understands the science of religion as the attempt of modern man to overcome his fundamental dilemma with regard to traditional religion by means of systematic research of all religious reality. The strength of his approach lies in the fact that it embraces not only traditional religion but also modern forms of 'secular' and 'anonymous' religion outside all organised religious institutions through its attempt to critically reflect on 'the whole of religion.' As a working hypothesis he states that '*the whole of religion discloses itself in its meaning*' where meaning refers to 'what religion says to one who lives it' (1979: 64).

The major objection to Schmid's work concerns his far too inclusive definition of religion, grounded in a particular philosophical approach which focusses primarily on the individual person and neglects the wider social and historical context of religious data. 'Religion' is here mainly a personal quality rather than an objective phenomenon as when he writes:

Religion is the reality of a person . . . . Religion is the attempt to find the way beyond the individual thing to the whole. It is the infinitely manifold, continual referal and referring of man to the ground, goal, meaning and middle of all that is real . . . . Consequently, religion occurs in every human being. A person completely without religion would be a person without reality (1979: 150 ff.).

In principle, the science of religion must investigate and critically examine every form of religion but the only object to which scientific observation has direct access is the broad field of religious data. Schmid distinguishes three dimensions of religion of which religious data is the first, religious experience the second, and the reality of religion the third. Religious experience never comes directly before the eye of the re-searcher; what the science of religion can say about it, is only based on its research of religious data and their interpretation. The third dimension, the reality of religion (what others have called the transcendent focus or referent) is radically removed from direct scientific observation; it does not lie within the area of religious reality but it is *intended* in all religious reality. 'For the science of religion, this dimension is only present in the religious reality, but it is not part of that reality. Rather, the religious reality refers beyond itself to this dimension. More precisely: the third dimension is present only in the second dimension, which is indicated in the first dimension, the religious reality' (1979: 38). This schema is to some extent reminiscent of Heiler's diagram of three concentric circles (discussed above in the section on phenomenology; see p 91 f.), criticized by Schmid as 'timeless-unhistorical' (1979: 174). In all fairness it must be said that Schmid keeps his dimensions analytically more distinct and makes it clear that the science of religion is strictly limited to the first dimension of religious data. Here, three major methodological steps are clearly distinguished yet interrelated: that of the perception and descrip-tion of the data (which involves a well delineated phenomenological task); of comprehension (which concerns the relations in which a datum stands, taking into account the historical, cultural, economic, political, and social conditions of a particular time); and that of understanding (which asks about the meaning of the description and setting-in-relation of the data; it asks not only about the relation in which religious data stand but also about the relation which these data are according to their own intentions).

The integral science of religion thus consists of the description, comprehension, and understanding of the broad field of religious data. As a true 'science', however, defined as 'the systematic research of a definite area of the real' (1979: 159), it has no monopoly over research on religion but is closely interrelated with the systematic-scientific tasks of parallel disciplines. Schmid critically examines many recent publications, particularly in German, concerned with methodology and the science of religion (which stands here for *systematische Religionswissenschaft*). Of particular value is his insightful discussion of the demarcation, tension, and interrelationship which exist between the science of religion and systematic theology. His treatment of this issue is conceptually more formalized than that of either Pannenberg (1976) or Davis (1974, 1981), and perhaps more clarifying and helpful in its distinctions. Unfortunately, Schmid mentions neither Pannenberg's nor Davis's discussion of theology and the science of religion; instead, he examines at length Ulrich Mann's 'synoptic method' (1973) as a conscious correlation of theology, science of religion, philosophy of religion, and psychology of religion.

Schmid's *Principles of Integral Science of Religion* (1979) combines systematic and critical reflection with a penetrating analysis of methodological principles, offering at the same time an overall perspective of synthesis. He clearly delineates the areas of study in religion (as the only possible field of the science of religion) from those of experience and reality, yet he also systematically accounts for their interrelationship. This work of analysis and synthesis is an important contribution to greater theory formation as well as to more adequate insight and understanding. It will not doubt find its critics. (A critical review of Schmid's earlier work (1971) is found in U. Tworuschka, (1972)). One must question Schmid's far too inclusive understanding of religion, which does not sufficiently distinguish between 'religion' and 'non-religion';

similarly, his methodological boundaries between philosophy and the science of religion appear to be blurred in places. Much further work is required in working out more adequate criteria for an integral science of religion, taking into account the work of other contemporary scholars. However, criticisms notwithstanding, Schmid's work requires the closest attention as it certainly represents an inspiring challenge for the contemporary scientific study of religion, understood as an ongoing systematic and holistic task.

The foregoing survey has shown that even under the heading of 'science of religion' there exists no common consensus as to the precise nature of the study of religion. Different scholars understand 'science' as well as 'religion' in a different way. The tensions between different methodological stances, objective and subjective factors, as well as between a primarily quantitative or qualitative evaluation of the data, continue to affect much of the methodological discussions about the science of religion. Although several scholars feel that a more rigorous pursuit of methodology may raise more difficulties than it answers questions, it seems evident today that we possess a number of different, but very fruitful approaches to the study of religion which provide helpful alternative methods and levels of interpretation. They each possess particular strengths and weaknesses which need close examining so that their relative usefulness as heuristic tools becomes sufficiently clear. I take the view that this plurality of methods and positions, far from being deplorable, reflects in fact the healthy state of the study of religion and is comparable to the situation in other sciences. It is wholly mistaken to treat science in general or any science in particular as monolithic entities, for there always exists a diversity of theories and schools of thought in the practice of scientific disciplines. What is central, however, is the systematic and orderly accumulation and analysis of data and their interpretation within an overall framework which allows for the development of commonly shared conceptualizations and theories. It is this need for a common body of knowledge, for the development of conceptual skills and the necessary place of methodology in any field of studies which has yet to become more widely accepted in the study of religion. In spite of many wholly justified criticisms regarding inadequate methods, further theory formation and critical methodological reflections are of paramount importance. To proceed further with the study of religion we need to examine as closely as possible what we are doing for 'there is some merit in exhibiting what we study and how we study it with the greatest possible precision; ... if what we study and how we study it cannot be exhibited with an appropriate precision, then serious questions can be raised not only about our speaking emotive nonsense, but even more devastating than that, about our not saying much of anything worth saying at all' (G.J. Larson 1978: 459).

4. Concluding remarks: present and future perspectives

Our survey has ranged over a great number of publications and authors. It has been concerned with the clarification of current methodological issues and has focussed in particular on the debates regarding the historical and phenomenological approaches to the study of religion. There are many scholars whose contributions have not been discussed here and no injustice is intended by this, for it would seem that most works fall within one or the other category of trends surveyed above. The present article cannot be more than a summary survey of the major developments since 1950; some further publications, not explicitly referred to in our discussion, will be mentioned in the Bibliography below.

Today the study of religion has access to an immense range of data which require for their systematic study a critical methodological awareness and refined conceptual tools so that the demanding tasks of analysis, explanation, and possibly synthesis, may be undertaken in a more differentiated manner. It is clear that particular data require different methods and approaches. But in the formulation of analytically more precise questions and the ongoing search for more adequate explanations, it also becomes clear that the methodological perspectives represented by the history, phenomenology, hermeneutics, and science

of religion can to some extent be considered as an interrelated continuum. Whether acknowledged or unacknowledged, we repeatedly
encounter in the methodological debate the intersection of such fundamental questions as 'What is religion?' 'What is history?' 'What is
science?.' The kind of answer given to one of these questions will shape
the answer to the others. The criteria for answering are not provided by
the questions themselves nor by the data grouped under them; ultimately, an answer to each of these questions requires the choice of a
particular hermeneutical and philosophical stance. In fact, one may
argue that there cannot be a final answer to these issues but that the
debate is an ongoing one. Different generations of scholars have given
and will no doubt continue to give different answers to these questions.
Whilst some may consider such a situation as unacceptable, because of
its inherent uncertainty and lack of reassurance, others regard it as an
inviting challenge to continue wrestling with important difficulties in
order to achieve greater clarity and deeper understanding.

In undertaking a survey of the methodological debate one realizes the
importance of the historical dimension for understanding contemporary
arguments about methodology. Particular aspects of current controversies are often deeply rooted in a scholarly tradition extending far before
1950 or even 1930 and, in some cases, even to work done before 1900.
This point is well brought out in Eric Sharpe's wide-ranging historical
survey *Comparative Religion* (1975). A sharper awareness and more accurate knowledge of the historical problematic can also result in the
feeling that certain contemporary works are rather ahistorical and parochial or possess a quality of *déjà vu* about them, largely due to their
ignorance of earlier methodological discussions. On the other hand, an
exaggerated insistence on more rigorous methodological requirements
can result in an unproductive intellectual aridity and a lack of creative
originality, if not to say insight, in interpreting religious phenomena.

If one may characterize the present situation among younger scholars
of religion in terms of a mood, it is primarily a mood of uncertainty
which permeates much of the contemporary debate: mounting criticisms and uncertainty about the achievements of the past; doubts and
uncertainty about the direction of present developments, particularly
·when the field of study is conceived in terms of a 'science of religion';

uncertainty and disagreement about the right kind of method(s); uncertainty about the very aims of methodology and theory in the study of religion. Some of the best voiced fears regarding the value of methodology have perhaps been expressed by Wilfred Cantwell Smith. However, many of these may be due to a misunderstanding regarding the nature and role of method in the study of religion. If methodology becomes narrowly circumscribed and arid, an end in itself rather than a helpful means for the most adequate and comprehensive study of the many dimensions of religion, it must be criticized. However, if the fear of methodology is simply based on a lack of intellectual effort or on unexamined assumptions grounded in subjectivity, it must equally be critized.

The history and phenomenology of religion cannot serve as a substitute ontology or soteriology as Eliade and others sometimes seem to think. In order to grow in a dynamic and fruitful way, the study of religion must be conceived as a truly scientific enterprise, understood not in a narrow scientistic-reductionist sense but in a wider and more integral manner as the attempt to develop more refined methods of study truly commensurate to what is being studied. It is open to much debate, however, whether a further development of Eliade's work, for example, would provide the most suitable framework for a future research programme as Dudley (1977) has argued. In fact, one must seriously question whether Eliade's fundamental construct of *homo religiosus*, uncritically taken up as an interpretative category by many epigones, is not more of a hindrance than a help for the further development of the study of religion.

If one considers future prospects in the study of religion, the mood of uncertainty prevailing among the present generation does not only relate to questions intrinsic to the subject area but also to situational factors such as the uncertain status of the study of religion in universities and colleges of several western countries today. Whilst the subject as a whole has considerably expanded and continues to grow, and especially is coming more into its own in Asian and African countries, it is somewhat on the retreat in some western countries. This is linked to the general economic recession, particularly in Britain, the uncertain status of an integral science of religion within the older universities, and the institutional ramifications of traditional theology departments so that it is often difficult, if not to say impossible, to be free from theological tutelage. It may also be due to the extraordinary worldwide growth of the sociology of religion which has resulted in the taking over of research interests and projects belonging to the study of religion in a wider sense. Perhaps it may be due most of all to the general lack of consensus among contemporary religion scholars, the absence of a common core theory, of clearly stated aims and objectives, and the relatively underdeveloped links of international collaboration in spite of the existence of the IAHR. It is a fact worth reflecting on that the attendance of mostly European delegates at the History of Religions Congress in Oxford (1908) was as high or even higher than the international participation at most of the later IAHR Congresses. Although the study of religion has grown globally in many different respects, this is not necessarily reflected in a higher attendance at the IAHR Congresses. There may be many explanations for this, one of which I take to be the lack of a more fully developed international organisational structure. A more efficient network at the regional and global level would facilitate closer scholarly contact, more efficient communication and information, and ultimately perhaps the development of international data-processing in the study of religion.

We are living in an increasingly internationally oriented world where some of the scholarly legacy from the past sometimes appears to be more of a ballast than an enriching heritage. One must seriously ask how far the data presented in some works on the history and phenomenology of religion are too selective and culture-specific instead of being globally representative. What further developments will be necessary for the study of religion to become a truly integral discipline which investigates the religious history of humankind in a systematic and comprehensive manner? Widengren's plea that the study of religion has been primarily historical since its origin is no sufficient reason for pursuing historical studies in the same way as in the past. There is much need for change and especially for a greater integration and synthesis of diverse data within a truly global framework. To achieve such integration it is not enough to bring different disciplines simply together within one university department without attempting a greater theoretical elucidation of the overall

framework and its underlying assumptions. Specialisations will continue to exist side by side if no conscious effort at the interpenetration of
different perspectives is made in the work of individual scholars. Some
past approaches to the study of religion may well be outdated and block
further developments whereas other perspectives are much more open
and promising. If one is primarily interested in fuller integration and
synthesis, one must also ask how far current studies are still affected by a
'conceptual imperialism' developed in the political context of past colonialism. For example, how far are the conceptual and linguistic aspects
of the study of religion in European universities still dependent on
earlier colonial contacts or based on data and theories originally developed by colonial ethnography and anthropology? Also, how far are
many conceptual tools in the study of religion too closely dependent on
specific developments of western Christian theology? Moreover, the not
infrequent use of Latin and Greek terms in the titles of books, journals,
and articles, reflects the continuing influence of the European classical
heritage among a small western intellectual elite. But the time has come
to question whether the underlying assumptions in choosing such a
terminology are not too exclusive and may thus prove a potential
obstacle to a more comprehensive and global development of the study
of religion. The concern for the classical, for religions in the ancient
world rather than religions in their importance for society today, can
become a stumbling-block for communication and make the study of
religion appear as an obsolete pursuit. The more one reflects on present
requirements and future developments, the more one begins to see the
need for a fundamental paradigm-shift in the overall orientation of the
study of religion.

   This applies also to the handling of data relating to the study of
Christianity. Although Christianity has enjoyed a privileged position in
theological scholarship, it has not been satisfactorily represented in
comparative historical studies. It is apparent to many that the study of
Christianity could gain a great deal if it is approached from the perspectives of the history of religions and of phenomenology. Although
Christians have written on religions other than their own for many
years, it is only now that the results of a closer examination and critique
of Christianity by scholars from non-Christian traditions are beginning

to gain attention. It is encouraging to see a greater cross-cultural activity in the examination of different religious traditions. Whereas most histories dealing with non-western religions were until recently written by western scholars, we now find non-western scholars writing on their own religious tradition and that of others. We not only come across scholars of Jewish, Muslim, Hindu, Buddhist or African background writing on Christianity, but Hindus writing on Buddhism and Islam, Japanese on Indian and western religions, and so on. This development is to be welcomed and encouraged, provided sound scholarly standards are maintained.

Considering the growth of the methodological debate and the many publications in this field, particularly since the late 1960s and 1970s, one wonders how the study of religion will develop in the near future. At the moment it remains an open question whether the current state of criticism and uncertainty, the search for new developments and common areas of agreement, will provide a turning-point leading to a new breakthrough or simply prove to be an impasse fixed on a past heritage, yielding few new discoveries. Whilst Eliade and other scholars have primarily been interested in archaic ancient and exotic data of the distant past, a growing number of contemporary scholars are fostering a strong interest in the study of living religions within the wider context of society and culture. It is perhaps here that the possibility of a new breakthrough is most likely to occur in future studies.

To some extent there will always exist a dialectical tension between ·historical and systematic approaches to the study of religion as well as between the necessary research into specific data at a micro-level and the equally necessary examination of wider perspectives at a macro-level. The study of religion will of necessity be comparative, for it is not only concerned with research into one religious tradition but examines phenomena across traditions and cultures, using cross-cultural data. There has been much acrimonious debate about religion being a phenomenon *sui generis*, particularly in the older phenomenology of religion. This debate still needs further clarification. The study of religion must certainly be maintained as an autonomous subject in its own right. But whatever its own particular characteristics, this does not mean that the study of religion can claim a special or unique status within the wider universe of sciences or the circle of human knowledge. The very existence of religion as lived and practised may well point towards a reality other than itself and thereby raise important philosophical and theological questions, but the study of religion as systematically ordered *knowledge* must be closely interrelated with other areas of knowledge and open to comparable criteria of analysis and synthesis.

In Waardenburg's view (1978b), the study of religion is not a particular discipline with one specific method but rather a field of studies still best described as *Religionswissenschaft*, a term 'encompassing all studies concerned with religious data, their observation, ascertainment, description, explanation, analysis, understanding, interpretation' (1978b: 190). Some of the themes which he lists as commanding attention from contemporary scholars of religion are the following: the various kinds of meaning which religious institutions and religious data possess for communities and individuals; the connection between religious and ideological traditions and movements, and the structural similarity of their internal development; myth and symbolism and the specific meaning they convey to people as well as their relationship to the institutionalization of religion; the relationship between different religious communities and the views specific faiths have of themselves and each other; the connection between religious change and social change, i.e., what role particular values and norms of a religious tradition can play in a specific process of development; what is the role of religion in particular local or regional conflict situations; in what way does religion constitute a particular dimension of creative life, socially or individually, by giving access to deeper levels of intentionality and mobilizing constructive forms of thought and action; the extent to which research in religion is guided by theological, philosophical and ideological aims or is subservient to political or other interests; where and how do ethical questions arise in the study of religion, particularly with regard to the future of mankind? (1978b: 211–3).

All these themes require further exploration. Waardenburg is right in saying that the 'future of the study of religion lies to a great extent in the kind of problems to which it addresses itself' (1978b: 211). At the most fundamental and general level the problem of the definition of religion itself is central to methodological discussion and the self-understanding of religious studies. If one undertook a survey of all the definitions of religion in use, an article as long as this one would have to be written. Other important themes of study relate to the situation of traditional religions and modern 'a-religion' in contemporary society. This raises the question of the transplantation of religion in institutionalised form from one society and culture to another (see M. Pye 1969) and further questions about cross-cultural and interreligious encounter (see J. Pentikäinen 1976). Yet another important area of research concerns the cultural function of religion(s) and, at a second-order level, of the science of religion as an interpreter of religious and social reality. Ninian Smart, in his Gifford Lectures on 'The Varieties of Religious Identity' (1979–80) explicitly devoted one of his lectures to 'The Science of Religion as an Interpreter of Modern History' in which he pointed out that the scientific study of religion with its comparative method and its sensitivity to the symbolic life of mankind is important in the analysis not only of the religious traditions but also of secular ideologies. This view is summarized in his conclusion that 'the science of religion itself may become an important source in the interpretation of modern history and also provide the materials for a new world-view which takes account of the varieties of symbolic identity' (1979–80: 7; see also Smart 1981). This is not all that far removed from Eliade's ideal of a creative cultural hermeneutic even though Smart and Eliade differ widely as to the details and premises of such a cultural task.

The older, more empirically oriented *Religionswissenschaft* collected and accumulated a vast store of data, particularly historical data, for the study of religion. This factual-descriptive, empiricist stance was subsequently counteracted by the development of the phenomenological approach with its emphasis on *epoché* and the search for essences. Many a postulate of phenomenology still has to be taken seriously but phenomenology itself has not provided a theoretical advance nor made a great contribution to methodology. The reaction against the essentialist and subjective accounts of the phenomenologists took the form of a development away from a concern for ideas and essences to a strong emphasis on scientific facts, particularly as understood by certain proponents of the science of religion. By now, however, the validity and relative value of facts has again been called into question both by the philosophy of science and by some new developments in the integral science of religion. It is increasingly being realized that philosophical positions of one kind or another underpin the different methodological stances and to some extent this cannot be avoided. The methodological task must, therefore, always include the examination and clarification of these underlying choices of perspective, whether made explicit or tacitly assumed. In addition, it is being recognized that questions of truth claims, inherent in at least some areas of religious discourse and experience, must also in one way or another be examined and accounted for. If individual scholars choose to ignore or avoid such theoretical requirements, this does not mean they are non-existent.

Without some kind of hermeneutic, some theory of understanding and interpretation, it is impossible to systematically order and account for the variety of religious data. One can consider the history of religions, phenomenology, and hermeneutics as three interrelated approaches and tasks of an integral science of religion. So conceived, and practised in an international, intercultural, and interdisciplinary framework and spirit, an integral science of religion opens new and exciting avenues not only for the area of religious studies, but also for contemporary society and culture.

NOTE: This survey was completed in early 1980 and does not include a discussion of publications which have appeared since then, in particular G. Lanczkowski, *Einführung in die Religionswissenschaft* (1980, Darmstadt: Wissenschaftliche Buchgesellschaft) which presents an introduction to the objects and different disciplines of the study of religion. It also discusses the relationship between *Religionswissenschaft* and theology, philosophy, and other approaches. It is a brief, summary work which mainly relies on well known authors and long established material.

Readers may also be interested in the special survey of *Concilium*, 136 (1980) on 'What is Religion? An Enquiry for Christian Theology' whose guest editors are Mircea Eliade and David Tracy (see particularly N. Terrin, 'On the Definition of Religion in the History of Religions,' pp. 72–7 and L. Sullivan 'History of Religions: The Shape of an Art,' pp. 78–85.

A recent discussion of the work of the IAHR is found in the section 'Is Academic Study Disinterested?' in M. Braybrooke, *Inter-faith Organizations, 1893–1979: An Historical Directory* (1980, New York and Toronto: pp. 9–18).

Important theoretical works continue to appear in the *Religion and Reason* series published by Mouton. The following three titles appeared too late to be considered here: D.A. Crosby, *Interpretive Theories of Religion* (1981); D. Wiebe, *Religion and Truth. Towards an Alternative Paradigm for the Study of Religion* (1981); R.J. Siebert, *The Critical Theory of Religion. The Frankfurt School* (1984).

W.L. Brenneman, Jr., S.O. Yarian and A.M. Olson, *The Seeing Eye. Hermeneutical Phenomenology in the Study of Religion* (1982) raises important points for hermeneutics and must be considered in a discussion of Eliade's methodology.

The above discussion, and the language in which it is expressed, accurately reflects the major issues debated up till the late 1970s. It does not incorporate the more recent feminist critique of the study of religion. This would require a reassessment of the issues in another article.

Bibliography

Allen, D. (1978), *Structure and Creativity in Religion*. Hermeneutics in Mircea Eliade's Phenomenology and New Direction Religion and Reason 14. The Hague: Mouton.
Antes, P. (1979), 'Systematische Religionswissenschaft.' Zwei unversöhnliche Forschungsrichtungen?' *Humanitas Religiosa*, Festschrift für Harold Biezais, 213–21.
Asmussen, J.P., Laessoe, J. and Colpe, C. (1971–2), *Handbuch der Religionsgeschichte*, 3 vols., Göttingen: Vandenhoeck & Ruprecht.

Baird, R. (1968), 'Interpretative Categories and the History of Religions,' *History and Theory* 8: 17–30.
— (1971), *Category Formation and the History of Religions*. Religion and Reason 1. The Hague: Mouton.
— (1975), ed. *Methodological Issues in Religious Studies*. See 'Postscript: Methodology, Theory and Explanation in the Study of Religion.' Chico: New Horizons Press.
Barnhart, J.E. (1977), *The Study of Religion and its Meaning*. New Explorations in Light of K. Popper and E. Durkheim. Religion and Reason 12. The Hague: Mouton.
Benz, E. (1968), 'Die Bedeutung der Religionswissenschaft für die Koexistenz der Weltreligionen heute,' in IAHR Claremont Congress Proceedings, vol. III: 8–22. Leiden: E.J. Brill.
Bettis, J.D., (1969), ed. *Phenomenology of Religion*. Eight Modern Descriptions of the Essence of Religion. London: SCM.
Bianchi, U. (1972), 'The Definition of Religion (On the Methodology of Historical-Comparative Research).' In Bianchi, Bleeker and Bausani: 15–34.

— (1975), *The History of Religions*. Leiden: E.J. Brill. See 'Object and Methodology of the History of Religion,' 1–29; and 'Modern Problems of Methodology and Interpretation,' 163–200.

— (1979), 'The History of Religions and the "Religio-anthropological Approach",' in Honko: 299–321.

Bianchi, U., Bleeker, C.J. and Bausani, A., eds. (1972), *Problems and Methods of the History of Religions*. Leiden: E.J. Brill.

Biezais, H. (1979), 'Typology of Religion and the Phenomenological Method,' in Honko 1979: 143–61.

Bleeker, C.J. (1959), 'The Phenomenological Method,' *Numen* 6: 96–111; also in Bleeker 1963: 1–15.

— (1960), 'The future task of the history of religions,' *Numen* 7: 221–34; also in IAHR Marburg Congress Proceedings, 1961: 229–40. Leiden: E.J. Brill.

— (1963), *The Sacred Bridge*. Researches into the Nature and Structure of Religion. Leiden: E.J. Brill.

— (1969), 'Methodology and the Science of Religion,' in Jurji 1969: 237–47.

— (1971a), 'Comparing the Religio-Historical and the Theological Method,' *Numen* 18: 9–29.

— (1971b), 'Epilegomena,' in Bleeker and Widengren, 1969–71, vol. II: 642–51.

— (1971c), 'Wie steht es um die Religionsphänomenologie?', *Bibliotheca Orientalis* 28: 303–8.

— (1972), 'The Contribution of the Phenomenology of Religion to the Study of the History of Religions,' in Bianchi, Bleeker and Bausani: 35–45.

— (1975a), *The History of Religions 1950–1975*. Monograph produced for the IAHR Congress, Lancaster. Leiden: E.J. Brill.

— (1975b), 'Looking Backward and Forward,' in IAHR Stockholm Congress Proceedings, 23–32. Leiden: E.J. Brill.

— (1978), 'Die Bedeutung der religionsgeschichtlichen und religionsphänomenologischen Forschung Friedrich Heilers,' *Numen* 25: 2–13.

Bleeker, C.J. and Widengren, G., eds. (1969–71), *Historia Religionum*. Handbook for the History of Religions, 2 vols. Leiden: E.J. Brill.

Bolle, K.W. (1967a), 'History of Religions with a Hermeneutic Oriented toward Christian Theology?' in Kitagawa 1967: 89–118.

— (1967b), 'Religionsgeschichtliche Forschung und theologische Impulse?', *Kairos* 9: 43–53.

— (1980), 'Reflections on the History of Religions and History,' *History of Religions* 20: 62–80.

Bottero, J. (1970), 'Les histoires des religions,' in Desroche and Seguy: 99–127.

Brelich, A. (1970), 'Prolégomènes à une histoire des religions,' in Puech: vol. I: 1–59.

Brenneman, W.L., Yarian, S.O. and Olson, A.M. (1982), *The Seeing Eye*. Hermeneutical Phenomenology in the Study of Religion. University Park and London: The Pennsylvania State University Press.

Braybrooke, M. (1980), *Inter-Faith Organizations, 1893–1979: An Historical Directory*. Texts and Studies in Religion. New York and Toronto: Edwin Mellen Press.
Bulletin Signalétique: sciences regligieuses. Paris: Centre National de la Recherche scientifiqure.

Castellani, G., ed. (1970–1), *Storia Delle Religioni*. 5 vols. Turin: Unione Tipografice-Editrice.
Clavier, H. (1968), 'Resurgences d'un problème de méthode en histoire des religions,' *Numen* 15: 94–118.
Cohn, W. (1964), 'What is Religion? An Analysis for Cross-Cultural Comparisons,' *Journal of Christian Education* 7: 116–38.
— (1969), 'On the Problem of Religion in Non-Western Cultures,' *International Yearbook for the Sociology of Religion* 5: 7–19.
Colpe, C., ed. (1974), *Die Diskussion um das Heilige*. Darmstadt: Wissenschaftliche Buchgesellschaft.
— (1979), 'Symbol Theory and Copy Theory as Basic Epistemological and Conceptual Alternatives in Religious Studies,' in Honko: 161–73.
Combs, E. (1976–7), 'Learned and learning: CSSR/SCER, 1965–1975,' *Sciences Religieuses/Studies in Religion* 6: 357–63.
Crosby, D.A., (1981), *Interpretive Theories of Religion*. Religion and Reason 20. The Hague: Mouton.
Culianu, I.P., (1981), 'History of Religions in Italy: The State of the Art,' *History of Religions* 20: 250–60.

Dammann, E. (1972), *Grundriss der Religionsgeschichte*. Stuttgart: 2nd. ed. 1978: Kohlhammer.
Davis, C. (1974–5), 'The Reconvergence of Theology and Religious Studies,' *Sciences Religieuses/Studies in Religion* 4: 205–21.
— (1981), 'Theology and Religious Studies,' *The Scottish Journal of Religious Studies* 2: 11–20.
Desroche, H. and Seguy, J., eds. (1970), *Introduction aux Sciences Humaines des Religions*. Paris: Cujas.
Dhavamony, M. (1973), *Phenomenology of Religion*. Rome: Gregorian University Press.
Drijvers, H.J.W. (1973), 'Theory Formation in Science of Religion and the Study of the History of Religions,' in Van Baaren and Drijvers: 57–77.
Dudley III, G. (1977), *Religion on Trial*. Mircea Eliade and his Critics. Philadelphia: Temple University Press.

Earhardt, H. Byron (1967), 'Toward a Unified Interpretation of Japanese Religion,' in Kitagawa, Eliade and Long: 195–226.
— (1975), 'The Japanese Dictionary of Religious Studies: Analysis and Assessment,' *Japanese Journal of Religious Studies* 2: 5–12.

Eliade, M. (1958), *Patterns in Comparative Religion*. London: Sheed and Ward. *Traité d'Histoire des Religions:* Paris: Payot 1949.

— (1959), 'Methodological Remarks on the Study of Religious Symbolism,' in Eliade and Kitagawa: 86–107.

— (1961), 'A New Humanism,' *History of Religions* 1: 1–18; also in Eliade 1969: 1–11.

— (1963), 'The History of Religions in Retrospect: 1912–1962,' *The Journal of Bible and Religion* 31: 98–109; also in Eliade 1969: 12–36.

— (1965), 'Observations on Religious Symbolism,' in Eliade, *The Two and the One*, 189–211. New York: Harper.

— (1967), 'Cultural Fashions and the History of Religions,' in Kitagawa, Eliade and Long: 21–38.

— (1969), *The Quest*. History and Meaning in Religion. Third ed. 1975. Chicago and London: Collins.

— (1979), *A History of Religious Ideas*. French ed.: Paris 1976. Vol. I: London; Collins; Chicago 1981: Chicago University Press. Vol. II; Chicago 1982: Chicago University Press.

Eliade, M. and Kitagawa, J.M., eds. (1959), *The History of Religions*. Essays in Methodology. Fifth ed. 1970. Chicago and London: Chicago University Press.

Eliade, M. and Tracy, D., eds. (1980), 'What is Religion? An Inquiry for Christian Theology,' *Concilium* 136.

Elsas, C., ed. (1975), *Religion*. Ein Jahrhundert theologischer, philosophischer, soziologischer und psychologischer Interpretationsansätze. München: Piper.

Flasche, R. (1978), *Die Religionswissenschaft Joachim Wachs*. Berlin and New York: Springer.

Frazier, A.M. (1970), 'Models for a Methodology of Religious Meaning,' *Bucknell Review* 18: 19–28.

Goodenough, R. (1959), 'Religionswissenschaft,' *Numen* 6: 77–95.

Goldammer, K. (1979), 'Is There a Method of Symbol Research Which Offers Hermeneutic Access to Depth-Dimensions of Religious Experience?' in Honko: 498–518.

Gualtieri, A.R. (1967), 'What is Comparative Religion Comparing? The Subject Matter of "Religious Studies",' *Journal for the Scientific Study of Religion* 6: 31–9.

— (1972), 'Confessional theology in the context of the history of religions,' *Sciences Religieuses/Studies in Religion* 1: 347–60.

Hayes, V.C., ed. (1977), *Australian Essays in World Religions*. Adelaide: The Australian Association for the Study of Religions.

Heelas, P. (1977), 'Intra-religious Explanation,' *Journal of the Anthropological Society of Oxford* 8: 1–17.

— (1978), 'Some Problems with Religious Studies,' *Religion* 8: 1–14.

Heiler, F. (1959), 'The History of Religions as a Preparation for the Co-operation of Religions,' in Eliade and Kitagawa: 132–60.

— (1960), 'The History of Religions as a Way to Unity of Religions,' in IAHR Tokyo Congress Proceedings, 7–22. Leiden: E.J. Brill.

— (1961), *Erscheinungsformen und Wesen der Religion.* Religionen der Menschheit 1. Stuttgart: Kohlhammer.

Helfer, J.S., ed. (1968), 'Introduction' in *On Method in the History of Religions. History and Theory* 8: 1–7.

Holm, N.G. (1970), 'Der Mythos in der Religionswissenschaft,' *Temenos* 6: 36–67.

— (1971), Review of Eliade and Kitagawa, '*The History of Religions* (1970), *Temenos* 7: 131–7.

— (1972), Review of Bianchi, Bleeker and Bausani, *Problems and Methods of the History of Religions* (1972), *Temenos* 8: 139–42.

Honko, L., ed. (1979), *Science of Religion.* Studies in Methodology. Proceedings of the Study Conference of the IAHR, held in Turku, Finland, Aug. 27–31, 1973. Religion and Reason 13. The Hague: Mouton.

Hultkrantz, A. (1970), 'The Phenomenology of Religion: Aims and Methods,' *Temenos* 6: 68–88.

— (1979), 'Ecology of Religion: Its Scope and Method,' in Honko: 221–36.

International Association for the Study of the History of Religions. (1954a–1980), *International Bibliography of the History of Religions. Bibliographie Internationale de L'Histoire des Religions.* Leiden: E.J. Brill.

— (1954b–), *Numen.* Journal of the International Association for the Study of the History of Religions. Leiden: E.J. Brill.

Isambert, F.A. (1970), 'La phénoménologie religieuse,' in Desroche and Seguy: 217–40.

Jurji, E.J. (1963), *The Phenomenology of Religion.* Philadelphia: Westminster.

— (1969), ed. *Religious Pluralism and World Community.* Interfaith and Intercultural Communication. Leiden: E.J. Brill.

Katz, S.T., ed. (1978), *Mysticism and Philosophical Analysis.* London: Sheldon Press.

Kee, A. (1980), 'The Study of Religion in Poland,' *Religious Studies* 16: 61–7.

King, N.Q. (1973), Review of *Handbuch der Religionsgeschichte* vol. 2, *Scottish Journal of Theology* 26: 377–9.

King, U. (1981), 'A hermeneutic circle of religious ideas,' *Religious Studies* 17: 565–9.

Kitagawa, J.M. (1959), 'The History of Religions in America,' in Eliade and Kitagawa: 1–30.

— (1967), 'Primitive, Classical, and Modern Religions: A Perspective on Understanding the History of Religions,' in Kitagawa, Eliade and Long: 39–65.

— (1968), 'The Making of a Historian of Religions,' *Journal of the American Academy of Religions* 36: 191–201; also translated as 'Die Schulung eines Religions-wissenschaftlers,' *Kairos* 11, 1969: 264–74.

Kitagawa, J.M., Eliade, M. and Long, C., eds. (1967), *The History of Religions*. Essays on the Problem of Understanding. Chicago: Chicago University Press.

Klostermaier, K. (1976–7), 'From phenomenology to metascience: Reflections on the study of religion,' *Sciences Religieuses/Studies in Religion* 6: 551–64.

Kristensen, W.B. (1960), *The Meaning of Religion*. Lectures in the Phenomenology of Religion. The Hague: Mouton.

Kryvelev, I.A. (1975), *Istoriya Religii*, 2 vols. Moscow: Mysl'.

Kvaerne, P. (1973), '"Comparative Religion: Whither—and Why?" A Reply to W. Cantwell Smith,' *Temenos* 9: 161–72.

Lanczkowski, G. (1971), *Begegnung und Wandel der Religionen*. Düsseldorf: Diederichs.

— (1974), ed. *Selbstverständnis und Wesen der Religionswissenschaft*. Darmstadt: Wissenschaftliche Buchgesellschaft.

— (1978a), *Einführung in die Religionsphänomenologie*. Darmstadt: Wissenschaftliche Buchgesellschaft.

— (1978b), 'Literaturbericht zur Religionswissenschaft,' *Theologische Rundschau* 43: 285–320.

— (1980), *Einführung in die Religionswissenschaft*. Darmstadt: Wissenschaftliche Buchgesellschaft.

Larson, G.J. (1978), 'Prolegomenon to a Theory of Religion,' *Journal of the American Academy of Religion* 46: 443–63.

Leibovici, M. (1972), 'Méthodologie et développement de l'histoire des religions,' *Sciences Religieuses/Studies in Religion* 1: 339–46.

Ling, T.O. (1968), *History of Religions East and West*. 2nd ed. 1977. London: Macmillan.

— (1980), 'Philosophers, Gentlemen and Anthropologists: Prolegomena to the Study of Religion,' *The Scottish Journal of Religious Studies* 1: 26–30.

Lonergan, B.J.F. (1976–7), 'The ongoing genesis of methods,' *Sciences Religieuses/Studies in Religion* 6: 341–55.

Long, C.H. (1967), 'Archaism and Hermeneutics,' in Kitagawa, Eliade and Long: 67–87.

Mann, U., ed. (1973), *Theologie und Religionswissenschaft*. Der gegenwärtige Stand ihrer Forschungsergebnisse und Aufgaben im Hinblick auf ihr gegenseitiges Verhältnis. Darmstadt: Wissenschaftliche Buchgesellschaft.

Mehauden, M. (1961), 'Un "Musée comparatif des Phénomènes Religieux",' in IAHR Marburg Congress Proceedings, 191–3. Leiden: E.J. Brill.

Mensching, G. (1976), *Structures and Patterns of Religion*. Delhi: Motilal Banarsidass.

Meslin, M. (1973), *Pour une Science des Religions*. Paris: Editions du Sevil.

Miller, J.F. (1975), 'Inherent Conceptual Limitations of the Scientific Method and Scientific Models for the Study of Religion,' *Internationales Jahrbuch für Wissens- und Religionssoziologie* 9: 137–47.

Mitros, J.F. (1973), *Religions: A Select, Classified Bibliography*. Louvain and Paris: Editions Nauwelaerts.

Morioka, K. (1975), *Religion in Changing Japanese Society*. See 'List of Major Periodicals in Japan,' 222–3. Tokyo: University of Tokyo Press.

Nenola-Kallio, A. (1973), 'Report on the Study Conference of the IAHR on "Methodology of the Science of Religion" held in Turku, Finland, August 27–31, 1973,' *Temenos* 9: 15–24.

Ogden, S.M. (1978), 'Theology and Religious Studies: Their Difference and the Difference it makes,' *Journal of the American Academy of Religion* 46: 3–17.
Open University (1977), *Man's Religious Quest*. Arts/Social Sciences: An Interfaculty Second Level Course. Course material AD 208, Units 1–32; see also '*Man's Religious Quest*. A review of Open University materials,' *Religion* 9, 1979: 116–39.
Oxtoby, W.G. (1968), '*Religionswissenschaft* Revisited,' in J. Neusner ed., *Religions in Antiquity*, 590–608. Leiden: E.J. Brill.
— (1976), ed. *Religious Diversity*. Essays by Wilfred Cantwell Smith. New York: Harper and Row.

Pannenberg, W. (1973), *Wissenschaftstheorie und Theologie*. See 'Religionswissenschaft als Theologie der Religion,'361–74. English translation *Theology and the Philosophy of Science*, 1976: 358–71. London: Darton Longman and Todd.
Penner, H.H. (1968), 'Myth and Ritual: A Wasteland or a Forest of Symbols?' in Helfer: 46–57.
— (1970), 'Is Phenomenology a Method for the Study of Religion?,' *Bucknell Review* 18: 29–54.
— (1971), 'The Poverty of Functionalism,' *History of Religions* 11: 91–7.
— (1975), The Problem of Semantics in the Study of Religion' in Baird: 79–94.
— (1976), 'The Fall and Rise of Methodology: a Retrospective Review,' *Religious Studies Review* 2: 11–6.
Penner, H.H. and Yonan, E.A. (1972), 'Is a Science of Religion Possible?,' *The Journal of Religion* 52: 107–33.
Pentikäinen, J. (1976), 'The Encounter of Religions as a Religio-Scientific Problem,' *Temenos* 12: 7–20.
Pomian-Srzednicki, M. (1982), *The Politics and Sociology of Secularization in Poland*. London: Routledge and Kegan Paul.
Poniatowski, Z. (1972), 'The scientometrics of the science of religions,' *Euhemer* 3: 3–21.
— (1975), 'Twenty Years of *Numen* in the Light of Statistical Analysis,' *Studia Religioznawcze* 10: 75–99 (in Polish, with summary in English and German).
Problèmes et methodes d'histoire des religions. (1968), Mélanges publiés par la Section des Sciences Religieuses à l'occasion du centenaire de l'Ecole Pratique des Hautes Etudes. Paris: Presses Universitaires de France.
Puech, H., ed. (1970–6), *Histoire des Religions*. Encyclopédie de la Pléiade, 3 vols. Paris: Gallimard.
Pummer, R. (1972), '*Religionswissenschaft* or Religiology?,' *Numen* 19: 91–127.

— (1974), 'The Study Conference on "Methodology of the Science of Religion" in Turku, Finland 1973,' *Numen* 21: 156–9.
— (1975), 'Recent Publications on the Methodology of the Science of Religion,' *Numen* 22: 161–82.
Pye, M. (1969), 'The Transplantation of Religions,' *Numen* 16: 234–9.
— (1971), 'Syncretism and Ambiguity,' *Numen* 18: 83–93.
— (1972), *Comparative Religion*. An Introduction through Source Materials. Newton Abbot: David and Charles. See 'Introduction,' pp. 7–35, for methodological discussion.
— (1973), 'Comparative Hermeneutics in Religion,' in Pye and Morgan: 9–58.
— (1974), 'Problems of Method in the Interpretation of Religion,' *Japanese Journal of Religious Studies* 1: 107–23.
Pye, M. and Morgan, R., eds. (1973), *The Cardinal Meaning*. Essays in Comparative Hermeneutics: Buddhism and Christianity. *Religion and Reason* 6. The Hague: Mouton.

Ratschow, C.H. (1973), 'Methodik der Religionswissenschaft,' in *Enzyklopädie der Geisteswissenschaftlichen Arbeitsmethoden*: 347–400. München: Piper.
Religion in Geschichte und Gegenwart, Die. Handwörterbuch für Theologie und Religionswissenschaft, 7 vols. Tübingen: Mohr 1957–1965.
Religion (1975), Special issue on the occasion of the XIIIth Congress of the International Association for the History of Religions. Lancaster, August 1975.
Religious Studies Review. Council on the Study of Religion. Waterloo, Ont.: Wilfried Laurier University.
Ricketts, M. Linscott (1973), 'In Defence of Eliade. Toward Bridging the Communication Gap between Anthropology and the History of Religions,' *Religion* 3: 13–34.
Ries, J., ed. (1978), *L'expression du sacré dans les grandes religions*. Series *Homo Religiosus*. Louvain: Centre d'histoire des religions.
Ringgren, H. (1970), 'Die Objektivität der Religionswissenschaft,' *Temenos* 6: 119–29.
Ringgren, H. and Ström, A.V. (1967), *Religions of Mankind*. Today and Yesterday. Philadelphia: Fortress Press.
Rudolph, K. (1962), *Die Religionsgeschichte an der Leipziger Universität und die Entwicklung der Religionswissenschaft. Ein Beitrag zur Wissenschaftsgeschichte und zum Problem der Religionswissenschaft*. Berlin: Akademie—Verlag.
— (1967), 'Die Problematik der Religionswissenschaft als akademisches Lehrfach,' *Kairos* 9: 22–42.
— (1970), 'Der Beitrag der Religionswissenschaft zum Problem der sogenannten Entmythologisierung,' *Kairos* 12: 183–207.
— (1971a), 'Religionsgeschichte und "Religionsphänomenologie",' *Theologische Literaturzeitung* 96: 241–50.
— (1971b), 'Das Problem einer Entwicklung in der Religionsgeschichte,' *Kairos* 13: 95–118.

— (1973a), '"Historia Religionum". Bemerkungen zu einigen neueren Handbüchern der Religionsgeschichte,' *Theologische Literaturzeitung* 98: 401–18.

— (1973b), 'Das Problem der Autonomie und Integrität der Religionswissenschaft,' *Nederlands Theologisch Tijdschrift* 27: 105–31.

— (1978), 'Die "ideologiekritische" Funktion der Religionswissenschaft,' *Numen* 25: 17–39.

— (1979), 'Religionswissenschaft auf alten und neuen Wegen. Bemerkungen zu einigen Neuerscheinungen,' *Theologische Literaturzeitung* 104: 11–34.

Rupp, A. (1978), *Religion, Phänomen und Geschichte*. Prolegomena zur Methodologie der Religionsgeschichte. Forschungen zur Anthropologie und Religionsgeschichte. Saarbrücken: Homo et Religio.

Saliba, J.A. (1974), 'The New Ethnography and the Study of Religion,' *Journal for the Scientific Study of Religion* 13: 145–59.

— (1976), *'Homo Religiosus' in Mircea Eliade*. An Anthropological Evaluation. Leiden: E.J. Brill.

Schmid, G. (1979), *Principles of Integral Science of Religion*. Religion and Reason 17. The Hague: Mouton.

Schlette, H.R. (1970), 'Ist die Religionswissenschaft am Ende?,' *Zeitschrift für Missionswissenschaft und Religionswissenschaft* 54: 195–200.

Schröder, C.M., ed. (1961–), *Die Religionen der Menschheit*. Stuttgart: Kohlhammer. Planned series of forty-two volumes, most of which have been published.

Science of Religion. Abstracts and Index of Recent Articles. Amsterdam; The Institute for the Study of Religion, Free University.

Seguy, J. (1970), 'Panorama des sciences des religions,' in Desroche and Seguy: 37–52.

Seiwert, H. (1977), 'Systematische Religionswissenschaft: Theoriebildung und Empiriebezug,' *Zeitschrift für Missionswissenschaft und Religionswissenschaft* 61: 1–18.

Sharma, A. (1975), 'An Inquiry into the Nature of the Distinction between the History of Religion and the Phenomenology of Religion,' *Numen* 22: 81–96.

Sharpe, E. (1971), 'Some Problems of Method in the Study of Religion,' *Religion* 1: 1–14.

— (1975), *Comparative Religion*. A History. London: Duckworth.

Siebert, R.J. (1984), *The Critical Theory of Religion*. The Frankfurt School. Religion and Reason 29. Berlin: Mouton.

Smart, N. (1973a), *The Phenomenon of Religion*. London: MacMillan.

— (1973b), *The Science of Religion and the Sociology of Knowledge*. Princeton: Princeton University Press.

— (1978), 'Beyond Eliade: The Future of Theory in Religion,' *Numen* 25: 171–83.

— (1979), 'Understanding Religious Experience,' in S.T. Katz ed. *Mysticism and Philosophical Analysis*, 10–21. London: Sheldon Press.

— (1979–80), 'The Varieties of Religious Identity.' Gifford Lectures. Outline of a Series of Ten Lectures. University of Edinburgh.

— (1981) *Beyond Ideology*, Religion and the Future of Western Civilization (Gifford Lectures 1979–80). London: Collins.

Smith, M. (1968), 'Historical Method in the Study of Religion,' in Helfer 1968: 8–16.

Smith, W. Cantwell (1959), 'Comparative Religion: Whither—and Why?,' in Eliade and Kitagawa: 31–58.

— (1964), *The Meaning and End of Religion*. New York: New American Library, Mentor.

— (1965), *The Faith of Other Men*. New York: New American Library, Mentor.

— (1975a), 'Methodology and the Study of Religion: Some Misgivings,' in Baird: 1–30.

— (1975b), 'Religion as Symbolism,' in *Encyclopaedia Britannica. Propaedia*: 498–500. 15th ed. Chicago 1975.

— (1976), 'Objectivity and the Humane Sciences: A New Proposal,' in Oxtoby: 158–80.

— (1977), *Belief and History*. Charlottesville: University of Virginia Press.

— (1979), *Faith and Belief*. Princeton: Princeton University Press.

— (1981), 'History in Relation to both Science and Religion,' *The Scottish Journal of Religious Studies* 2: 3–10.

— (1981), *Towards a World Theology: Faith and the Comparative History of Religion*. London and Philadelphia: Westminster.

Spiro, M. (1979), 'Symbolism and Functionalism in the Anthropological Study of Religion; in Honko: 322–39.

Stephenson, G. (1975), 'Kritische Bemerkungen zu C.H. Ratschows Methodenlehre,' *Zeitschrift für Missionswissenschaft und Religionswissenschaft* 59: 201–8.

— (1976), ed. *Der Religionswandel unserer Zeit im Spiegel der Religionswissenschaft*. Darmstadt: Wissenschaftliche Buchgesellschaft.

Streng, F. (1968), 'What does "History" mean in the History of Religions?,' *Anglican Theological Review* 50: 156–78.

Szolc, P.O. (Scholz) (1971), 'Religionswissenschaft in Polen,' *Numen* 18: 45–80.

Sullivan, L. (1980), 'History of Religions: The Shape of an Art,' *Concilium* 136: 78–85.

Terrin, N. (1980), 'On the Definition of Religion in the History of Religions,' *Concilium* 136: 72–7.

Thrower, J. (1983), *Marxist-Leninist Scientific Atheism and the Study of Religion and Atheism in the USSR*. Religion and Reason 25. Berlin: Mouton.

Tillich, P. (1967), 'The Significance of the History of Religions for the Systematic Theologian,' in Kitagawa, Eliade and Long: 241–56.

Tokarev, S.A. (1966a), 'Principles of the Morphological Classification of Religions (Part I),' *Soviet Anthropology and Archaeology* 4: 3–10.

— (1966b), 'Principles of the Morphological Classification of Religions.(Part II),' *Soviet Anthropology and Archaeology* 5: 11–25.

— (1968), *Die Religion in der Geschichte der Völker*. Berlin: Dietz.

— (1976), *Religiya v Istorii Narodov Mira*, 2 vols. third ed., *Moscow: Politizdat*.

Tyloch, W. (1979), 'Polish Society for the Science of Religions,' *Euhemer* 23: 3–8.

Tworuschka, U. (1974), 'Integrale Religionswissenschaft—Methode der Zukunft?,' *Zeitschrift für Religions—und Geistesgeschichte* 26: 239–43.

Van Baaren, T.P. (1969), 'Systematische Religionswissenschaft,' *Nederlands Theologisch Tijdschrift* 24: 81–8.

— (1973), 'Science of Religion as a Systematic Discipline: Some Introductory Remarks, in Van Baaren and Drijvers: 35–56.

Van Baaren, T.P. and Drijvers, H.J.W., eds. (1973), *Religion, Culture and Methodology.* Papers of the Groningen Working-group for the Study of Fundamental Problems and Methods of Science of Religion. Religion and Reason 8. The Hague: Mouton.

Van Baaren, T.P., Leertouwer, L. and Buning, H., eds. (1973–), *Iconography of Religions.* Institute of Iconography, Groningen. Survey of major iconographic expressions of all religions of any importance in the world, both of literate and illiterate peoples.

Waardenburg, J. (1971–), ed. *Religion and Reason.* New Series on 'Method and Theory in the Study and Interpretation of Religion.' The Hague and Berlin: Mouton.

— (1972a), 'Religion between Reality and Idea. A Century of Phenomenology of Religion in the Netherlands,' *Numen* 19: 128–203.

— (1972b), 'Grundsätzliches zur Religionsphänomenologie,' *Neue Zeitschrift für Systematische Theologie und Religionsphilosophie* 14: 315–35.

— (1973a), *Classical Approaches to the Study of Religion.* Aims, Methods and Theories of Research. Vol. 1: Introduction and Anthology; Vol. 2: Bibliography. Religion and Reason 3 and 4. The Hague: Mouton.

— (1973b), 'Research on Meaning in Religion,' in Van Baaren and Drijvers: 109–36.

— (1975a), '*Religionswissenschaft* in Continental Europe,' *Religion.* Special issue, August: 27–54.

— (1975b), 'The Category of Faith in Phenomenological Research' in IAHR Stockholm Congress Proceedings, 305–15. Leiden: E.J. Brill; also in Waardenburg, 1978a: 79–88.

— (1976), '*Religionswissenschaft* in Continental Europe excluding Scandinavia. Some Factual Data,' *Numen* 23: 219–38.

— (1977), 'Religion vom Blickpunkt der religiösen Erscheinungen,' *Neue Zeitschrift für Systematische Theologie und Religionsphilosophie* 19: 62–77.

— (1978a), *Reflections on the Study of Religion.* Religion and Reason 15. The Hague: Mouton.

— (1978b), '*Religionswissenschaft* New Style. Some Thoughts and Afterthoughts,' *Annual Review of the Social Science of Religion* 2: 189–220.

— (1979), 'The Language of Religion, and the Study of Religion as Sign Systems,' in Honko: 441–57.

Wach, J. (1958), *The Comparative Study of Religions.* New York: Columbia University Press.

Werblowsky, R.J.Z. (1959), 'The Comparative Study of Religions—A Review Essay,' *Judaism: A Quarterly Journal of Jewish Life and Thought* 8: 1–9.

— (1960), 'Marburg—and After?,' *Numen* 7: 215–20.

— (1976), *Beyond Tradition and Modernity*. Changing Religions in a Changing World. London: Athlone Press.

— (1979), 'Histories of Religion,' *Numen* 26: 250–5.

Whaling, F. (1979), Review of *From Primitives to Zen, Religious Studies* 15: 421–3.

Wiebe, D. (1975), 'Explanation and the Scientific Study of Religion,' *Religion* 5: 33–52.

— (1978), 'Is a science of religion possible?,' *Sciences Religieuses/Studies in Religion* 7: 5–17.

— (1979), 'The Role of "Belief" in the Study of Religion. A response to W.C. Smith,' *Numen* 26: 234–49.

— (1981), *Religion and Truth*. Towards an Alternative Paradigm for the Study of Religion. Religion and Reason 23. The Hague: Mouton.

Widengren, G. (1968), 'Some Remarks on the Methods of the Phenomenology of Religion,' *Acta Universitatis Upsaliensis* 17: 250–60.

— (1969), *Religionsphänomenologie*. Berlin: De Gruyter.

— (1971), 'La méthode comparative: entre philologie et phénoménologie,' *Numen* 18: 161–72; also in Bianchi, Bleeker and Bausani 1972: 5–14.

— (1975), 'The Opening Address' in the IAHR Stockholm Congess Proceedings, 14–22. Leiden: E.J. Brill.

Yinger, J.M. (1970), *The Scientific Study of Religion*. New York: Macmillan.

3

Comparative Approaches

FRANK WHALING

Edinburgh

1. Introduction

The chief aim of this chapter is to analyse the work of a number of outstanding scholars of religion, whose main work has been produced since 1945, within the framework of an investigation of comparative approaches to the study of religion. However, as part of our main concern, we must deal with two related yet wider questions. As we shall see, the term 'comparative religion' has had different connotations within different contexts. At its widest, it can be used as an umbrella term whereby it becomes virtually synonymous with 'the study of religion'. If this were to be its accepted meaning, the title of these volumes could appropriately be *Contemporary Approaches to the Study of Comparative Religion*. Many scholars, for reasons we cannot dwell upon at this point, would feel unease at equating 'comparative religion' with 'the study of religion'. It is clear that the areas covered in these volumes, history and phenomenology of religion, comparative religion, anthropology of religion, myths and texts, sociology of religion, psychology of religion, the scientific study of religion in its plurality, and the study of religon in a global context, find their legitimate place within 'the study of religion'; it is less clear that they could all be subsumed under the aegis of 'comparative religion'. Indeed, in a narrower sense, the term has been taken to mean what the two words actually imply, namely the comparison of religions. As long ago as 1873 Max Müller wrote, 'A Science of Religion, based on an impartial and truly scientific comparison of all, or at all events, of the most important, religions of mankind, is now only a question of time' (1873, p. 34). Müller wanted the focus to be upon comparison as such, and upon comparative religion as part of a wider whole that he termed a 'Science of Religion'. The discussion has moved on since Müller's time, and the terms of debate have changed. However, the basic question as to whether comparative religion is equivalent to the whole discipline of the study of religion or whether it is one among many branches within the wider study of religion has never been fully solved. In this chapter, we shall suggest that the term 'comparative religion' should be used in the narrower sense, and we hope that some methodological confusion will thereby be resolved. But before we can pass on to this study of contemporary attempts to actually compare religions we must deal briefly with the larger problem.

The second of our wider concerns relates to the relationship between comparative religion (however defined) and theology. One of the reasons why the term 'comparative religion' came under suspicion was its implied connection with theology. According to this view the motive for much work in the comparison of religions was not the 'impartial and scientific' desire to establish patterns, similarities and differences, but the theological desire to demonstrate that one's own position was superior, fuller, or more-than-mundane compared with that of others. In other words the aim was apologetic rather than scientific—or theological rather than humanistic, to use Kitagawa's terms (1957, pp. 13–25)—and therefore the enterprise of comparative religion in this sense belonged more properly to theology than to the study of religion. In broad terms this division between apologetic comparative religion and impartial comparative religion, between theology and the study of religion, is valid. However, this separation between the two, as though they were both monolithic, has become too simplistic. Insofar as the relationship between theology and the study of religion is not treated in detail elsewhere in this book, we will address its complexities in this section, and under the heading of comparative religion, before passing on to our main investigations.

The main part of our task will be to analyse the methods and trends within comparative religion in the narrower sense, namely the ways in which religious traditions and phenomena have been impartially compared. Although circumscribed in nature, this remains a complex undertaking. It raises basic questions that we can only enumerate at this point: What is the focus of the comparison of religions? Is it religious traditions as such, and if so can they all be compared equally? Are the criteria for comparing primal and major religious traditions the same? Are religious phenomena the foci for comparison, and if so which phenomena according to what basis of selection? Are religious phenomena comparable in themselves, or as expressions of the religiousness of those for whom they are meaningful? Insofar as religious traditions themselves may form the focus of comparison, is it possible to devise models that work in regard to all of them or is this only feasible in regard to any two? Is it possible to cut structural or typological comparative cross-sections through religious phenomena, or is this unwisely to disregard contexts? Insofar as there are no essences in history because historical development is in constant flux, can we nevertheless discern patterns within history that allow of comparison across history? Are these patterns visible continually throughout many centuries, or only at specific periods? Is it possible for the same types of religious phenomena to occur with different weights in different religions and thereby to render typological comparison invalid? Is the motive of comparison to discover similarities, differences, both, or neither? Is any rapprochement possible between historical, phenomenological, typological, anthropological, sociological, psychological, and philosophical modes of comparison, or are they 'impartial' yet 'opposed'? What research models have been devised, if any, to enable long-term, fruitful comparisons to be made? It is evident that the narrowing of the meaning of comparative religion to the realm of actual comparisons opens up some of the most important questions of content and method in the whole realm of religious studies. In the course of our analysis of the comparative approach to the study of religion we shall explore in some detail the work of leading post-war scholars such as: Brandon, Dumézil, Eliade, Lévi-Strauss, Panikkar, Parrinder, Pettazzoni, Smart, Wilfred Cantwell Smith, Streng, Wach, Widengren, and Zaehner, as well as others who have made distinctive contributions. We are under no illusions that it is possible to cover the whole field in such a short compass. Our aim is to indicate the main trends, to illuminate the chief methodological discussions, and to bring out the importance in its own right of comparative religion in the narrower sense.

2. The term 'Comparative Religion'

As we have intimated in the Introduction, the term 'comparative religion' can be used in different ways. In preparing to write this Chapter, I originally contemplated analysing over a hundred titles of books written since the Second World War in which the words "comparative religion" or their linguistic counterparts are used. Space does not allow of this, and such an analysis would deflect us from our main purpose. Suffice it to say, as the reader may imagine, the meaning given to the words 'comparative religion' in these volumes varies widely. For our purposes it is sufficient to glance briefly at three well-known works: A.C. Bouquet's *Comparative Religion* (1942), *Reader in Comparative Religion* (Edited by William A. Lessa and Evon Z. Vogt, 1958), and Eric Sharpe's *Comparative Religion; A History* (1975).

2*a*.

Dr. Bouquet, who was a clergyman of the Church of England, wrote his book during the Second World War. It was published as a Pelican paperback by Penguin Books and attained such a popularity in the English-speaking world that it went through a large number of editions. Bouquet wrote in the preface:

'I believe that truth shines by its own light. I have faith that if my own creed is in any sense absolute, it cannot suffer from an unprejudiced and dispassionate exposition of the history of religion.' And so I have striven to write as a scientist, not as an advocate. Whether I have succeeded, the public must judge.

As we have seen, the public did judge by buying the book in their tens of thousands. Bouquet belonged to the same tradition as van der Leeuw in that he was able to combine a theological interest with a deep ability in the study of religion; indeed he did this institutionally by combining a Cambridge Lecturership in the History and Comparative Study of Religions from 1932–55 with the incumbency of All Saints Church Cambridge from 1922–45. His tendency was to stress belief more than practice, but he wrote impartially about other religions, and insisted upon the principle of comparing the best in religions rather than the mediocre or the worst. Importantly for our purposes, his book on comparative religion was essentially a history of religion, or rather a series of mini-histories of the main religions. After three introductory chapters, and three semi-historical chapters, he covered the traditions of India, China and Japan, Judaeo-Christianity, Islam, and Mysticism. In an 'epilogue' he finally glanced at some general theories of religion.

Bouquet followed the continental tradition of Otto, Heiler, Söderblom, and van der Leeuw in combining religious and theological interests under the heading of comparative religion. In his final chapter, after glancing briefly at theories of radical abandonment (reductionism), radical exclusiveness (truth against falsehood), and radical relativity (religions as 'hospitable caravanseries': *op cit* p. 295), he examined a fourth type of theoretical classification that he claimed was detached and descriptive. Under this heading he summarised the views of Hegel, Siebeck, Orelli, Gore, Oman, Söderblom, Berthelot, Lehmann, and Jeremias. Under a further heading of 'religions in series' he dealt with the theories of F.H. Smith, van der Leeuw, Saunders, Reinhold Niebuhr, Dewick, Kraemer, Brunner, and D.G. Baillie. The trend since Bouquet's time has been to distinguish between theological and non-theological classifications in a way that he did not find necessary.

By contrast, there is another way in which Bouquet's approach to comparative religion has remained typical of a certain approach to the subject right down to our own day. His basic method was to offer a one-by-one survey of the religions, especially the major living religions, of the world. His analysis of each tradition was basically historical. For example, he traced the development of Indian religion through nine stages: the pre-historic age, the period of the Dravidian invasions, the

Vedic period, the Brahmanical epoch, the philosophical period, the incarnation period, the age of the Muslim invasions, the period of the *bhakti* saints, and the age of European influence. Comparative Religion came to mean, in studies such as Bouquet's, the side-by-side description, mainly historical, of the religions of the world accompanied, in the introduction or conclusion, by some comments on method which were rarely applied to the religions themselves. The unexamined assumption came to be that religions, especially the great living religions, are the foci for comparison; also that the necessary data for comparison are provided primarily by the historical method. Actual comparisons were rarely made or, if they were, this was usually incidental rather than integral to the study. This general approach has been typical of a number of works written since 1945. Some have been single-author studies; some have been single works written by a team of authors; others have been multiple works. There is a continuing need for such 'overview' works, and it is significant that not only Bouquet's book but also another even more dated two volume work by George Foot Moore (1914–20) continue to sell. Examples of more recent single-author summaries of world religions are: John B. Noss's *Man's Religions* (1956); Huston Smith's *The Religions of Man* (1958); Geoffrey Parrinder's *The World's Living Religions* (1964); Ninian Smart's *The Religious Experience of Mankind* (1969); and John Hutchison's *Paths of Faith* (1969). Examples of works written by a team of authors are: Edward J. Jurji's *The Great Religions of the Modern World* (1947); R.C. Zaehner's *Concise Encyclopaedia of Living Faiths* (1959); *Religions of Mankind. Today and Yesterday* (edited by H. Ringgren and A.V. Ström, 1967); the three volume *Histoire des Religions* (edited by Henri-Charles Puech, 1970, 1972, 1976); and the two-volume *Historia Religionum* (edited by C.J. Bleeker and G. Widengren, 1969, 1971) Examples of series of works are the multi-volume *Die Religionen der Menschheit* (edited by C.M. Schröder, 1961-present) and *The Religious Life of Man* (edited by F.J. Streng, 1969ff) including volumes on *The Way of Torah: An Introduction to Judaism* (J. Neusner, 1970, 1974), *The House of Islam* (K. Cragg, 1969, 1975), *Japanese Religion: Unity and Diversity* (H.B. Earhart, 1969, 1974), *Chinese Religion: An Introduction* (L.G. Thompson, 1969, 1975), *The Buddhist Religion* (R.H. Robinson, 1970, R.H. Robinson and W.L. Johnson, 1977), *The Hindu Religious Tradition* (T.J. Hopkins, 1971), and *The Christian Religious Tradition* (S. Reynolds, 1977).

We have given a minute sample of the many handbooks that have been published since the war on 'comparative religion' in Bouquet's sense. It is not our purpose to analyse them in detail and a good survey of some of this type of literature is given by Kurt Rudolph in *Theologische Literaturzeitung* (vol 98, 1973, pp. 402–418; vol 104, 1979, pp. 13–34). In any case, the various analyses, though having merit, are derived from original research conducted elsewhere. Before passing on, however, we must note a number of points that are relevant to our main comparative task. All these works assume that there are 'religions' that can be described and analysed as discrete entities. Although seemingly self-obvious this is an *a priori* assumption that needs to be methodologically examined. Within these volumes less stress is given to primal religions, and this is due partly to the general use of the historical method which depends upon manuscripts and literate cultures. Nevertheless, primal religions are not completely neglected, nor, when examined, are they always relegated to being treated as 'survivals' of past forms; for example Black African, Oceanic, American, Arctic and Altaic religions appear in volume three of *Histoire des Religions* under the heading of 'les religions chez les peuples sans tradition écrite', and primal religions appear as one chapter out of twenty-nine in *Historia Religionum* under the heading of 'religions of the present'. However, the main emphasis is afforded to the historical religions and, especially in the Anglo-Saxon writings, to the major living religions. But there are two curious points about this predilection for the great religions. In the first place the emphasis tends to be upon these religions in their classical form rather than upon their contemporary situation, upon the past rather than the present of their 'livingness'. And, secondly, there is ambivalence in regard to the treatment of Christianity on the one hand, and communism and humanism on the other. In some cases, Christianity is extensively treated (five chapters out of seventeen in Zaehner), yet in other cases, in some examples of this genre, it is left out. As far as communism and humanism are concerned, Smart pays due attention to them by contrast with the other authors who ignore them. This is due partly to his greater willingness to grapple with the present religious climate, and partly to his approach to the study and definition of religion.

All these concerns—the stress upon 'religions', upon the historical method, upon historical rather than primal religions, upon the major religions in their classical forms, upon the problematic nature of Christianity, and communism and humanism—will be picked up later. Suffice it to say, at this point, that much of the work we have considered, although supposed by Bouquet to come under the banner of comparative religion, fits more appropriately within the framework of history of religion. Historical descriptions of religions placed side by side do not of themselves constitute comparative religion. They provide the raw material for comparative religion. The work of classifying and comparing remains to be done. This work is the true raison d'être of comparative religion as such.

2b.

Lessa and Vogt, in their *Reader in Comparative Religion*, also use comparative religion as an umbrella term, but they do so in a way different from that of Bouquet. Indeed the rubric to their title is *Reader in Comparative Religion: An Anthropological Approach*. The book contains sixty-two chapters within its ten sections which are entitled: 'the origin and development of religion; the function of religion in human society; symbolism; symbolic classification; myth; ritual; shamanism; magic, witchcraft, and divination; death, ghosts, and ancestor worship; dynamics in religion' (pp. v–vii). It is clear that although the words 'comparative religion' remain the same, their meaning is vastly different. We are now in the realm of anthropology, and indeed some of this material is used by Anthony Jackson in his chapter in the second volume on 'anthropological approaches to the study of religion'.

The majority of the chapters in the *Reader* deal with primal religious groups or less frequently with folk elements in major religions. Whereas the assumption of Bouquet had been that the historical method and the historical religions (especially the major ones) are the key to 'comparative religion', Lessa and Vogt assume that the primal religions and the anthropological method are the key. As they put it (p. 4):

The religions of the simpler societies have the advantage of being divested of the complex trappings characteristic of the faiths of civilised groups. They are more internally consistent, possessed of fewer alternatives of dogma, less complicated by sophisticated metaphysics, and freer of hierarchical structure. In short, they permit one to get down to the core—the fundamentals—of religion and its place in human life.

The implication is that myth, ritual, and symbol, as found within primal religions, are the fundamental core of religion, and that through comparing examples of them found in as many societies as possible one can generalise from the variants and build up common denominators. A further assumption is that religion is part of wider culture and it cannot be studied and compared in isolation but only as part of and in relation to a wider whole.

Lessa and Vogt, in their introduction, say much about comparison and the comparative method. They analyse the advantages and disadvantages of comparing religious phenomena, *within* a single culture, community, or nation, or *between* cultures, communities and nations. They point out that, because of the increasing emphasis upon fieldwork, the searching for universals and global typologies indulged in by Tylor, Durkheim, Freud, Radcliffe-Brown and their like is much less in vogue today (see Evans-Pritchard, 1965). However, in spite of the comparative claims that are made, most of their work, like that of Bouquet, is description of specific traditions. As they revealingly state (p. 5):

Anthropology can at least take pride in the fact that of all the social sciences it has most expanded the possibilities of comparison by adding to the general pool the thousands of case histories made available by its study of tribal societies.

It is suggestive that, at the back of their book (pp. 552–8), they recommend fifty selected monographs on particular non-western religious systems but no comparative monographs. In short, with the exception of a small number of significant articles that we will mention later, this book does not constitute 'comparative religion' but a preparation for comparative religion in the primal, anthropological sense indicated here.

Lessa and Vogt's *Reader in Comparative Religion* raises methodological questions that we will tackle later. More importantly it raises the basic question of 'What is Comparative Religion?' For Bouquet, it had been the mainly historical analysis of the world's religions, especially the major ones; for the *Reader* it is the anthropological analysis of the world's primal and folk religions. For both, the comparative intent is of importance. Bouquet may describe the great religions of the world separately, the *Reader* may offer numerous case studies of different primal religious traditions, yet the intent of both is that their studies of diverse religions should not remain as self-sufficient, discrete entities but feed into a wider comparative enterprise. However, the question remains: Is comparative religion an overarching discipline, combining the description and comparison of *all* religions, within which the history of religion and anthropology of religion are branches; is history of religion the historical description *and* comparison of the historical religions, and anthropology of religion the description *and* comparison of the primal and folk religions, so that comparative religion is redundant; or are history of religion and anthropology of religion the descriptive prologomena to comparative religion, the true role of which is comparison and classification? My contention is that the last alternative is the most correct and helpful one.

2*c*.

The dilemma is brought out even more forcibly in our third book, Eric Sharpe's *Comparative Religion. A History*. In this work, Sharpe traces the history of what he calls comparative religion from its antecedents in Greece through the rise of its modern study with Max Müller, the evolutionary theories of religion deriving from Darwinism, the early anthropological studies of totemism and magic, the varieties of religious experience stemming from William James, the developing quest for academic recognition, the theological divergences from and contributions to the study of religion centred on Otto, the later cultural and historical studies, the psychological insights hinging on Freud, the phenomenology of religion, the modern dialogue of religions, and the international debate of 1950–70. From the perspective I am adopting in this chapter Sharpe's work is quite simply a history of the study of religion rather than a history of comparative religion. He is dealing not just with comparative religion in the restricted sense of classification and comparison but also with all other methods of studying religion whether they be social scientific, psychological, historical, phenomenological, philosophical, dialogical, or even theological; whether they deal with major religions or primal religions; whether they deal with religion as a generic phenomenon or personal faith, or with religions in the plural.

Sharpe recognises his semantic problem in using the term comparative religion for the total study. As he puts it (p. xii):

> The sheer weight of material which has accumulated under the general heading of "comparative religion" is now subdivided into the history of religion, the psychology of religion, the sociology of religion, the phenomenology of religion and the philosophy of religion ... In practice it has, however, often been found necessary to continue to use some form of words which on the one hand describes the multi-disciplinary and non-confessional approach to the study of religion, and on the other separates such a study from those theological or other assessments which are entirely proper when applied within a single tradition.

After reviewing possible alternatives to the phrase 'comparative religion' such as *Religionswissenschaft*, religious studies, and history of religions, Sharpe concludes (p. xiii):

> It perhaps remains, its shortcomings notwithstanding, the only term which suggests the study, in the round, of the religious traditions of the world—including, of course, the Judaeo-Christian traditions—as phenomena to be observed, rather than as creeds to be followed.

Clearly Sharpe's view of comparative religon is even wider than that of Bouquet, or Lessa and Vogt. It implies, for him, 'the serious and, as far as possible, dispassionate study of material drawn from all the accessible religious traditions of the world' (p. xiv). His aim is unexceptional. The question remains as to whether his terminology is appropriate to his aim. It seems to me that for two reasons it is not.

In the first place, Sharpe's qualms about using the term 'comparative religion' are based upon two anxieties, namely his fear that the word 'comparative' implies a value judgement based upon either theological assessment or evolutionary scale. Having satisfied himself that the term need not carry the implication that one religion is 'better' or 'higher' than another, because the study of religion is no longer subservient to theology nor concerned with origins and evolution in the Darwinian sense, he tends to lose sight of the fact that the word 'comparison', in its impartial rather than prescriptive sense, does involve the searching for and setting up of patterns of similarity and difference. Much of the critical, historical, anthropological and other work outlined by Sharpe involves more-or-less rigorous attempts to describe particular major or primal religions in which no classificatory or comparative assumptions are present. In the attempt to save the word 'comparative' from judgmental overtones, it is possible to overlook its particular meaning as a descriptive adjective.

In the second place, some of the work in religious studies, including some of the developments indicated by Sharpe, has to do not with the religions of the world, whether major or primal, but with the religiousness of man himself. This is particularly the case with the psychology of religion. In other approaches, the focus of attention is usually one particular religion or type of religion rather than the whole spectrum of the planet's religions. For example, much work in the sociology of religion has centred upon western religion, and much anthropology of religion has focussed upon primal religion. It is therefore more difficult for the social scientific approaches to be as broadly comparative in scope as history, phenomenology, or even theology (albeit perhaps in a more prescriptive fashion). This does not make them any less a part of the study of religion, but it does make it less apt to include them within the heading of comparative religion.

2d.

To sum up our discussion, we have glanced very briefly at three books which symbolise three attempts to give a wide meaning to the term 'comparative religion'. For Bouquet it is coterminous with the study of the historical religions; for Lessa and Vogt it is coterminous with the study of the primal religions; for Sharpe it is coterminous with the general study of religion. There are three possible meanings of the term, only one of which is conveyed directly in the above-mentioned works. The first meaning, that comparison of religions is prescriptive and that it hinges upon some theological or other value judgment whereby religions are graded comparatively must be questioned. It may have had currency at an earlier period, it may do so now within the overall discipline of theology, but it is no longer a direct part of the present-day study of religion. The second meaning of 'comparative religion', that it is equivalent to the study of all the historical religions, or that it is equivalent to the study of all the primal religions, or that it is equivalent to the study of all the religions and all the methods of studying religion taken together, is too wide. Comparative religion is not to be confused with the history of religion, the anthropology of religion, or the general study of religion. It has its own distinctive role which is suggested in the meaning of the words themselves. The third meaning, and in our view the most helpful one, relates to the non-judgmental comparison and classification of religions. This is an enterprise which stands in its own right alongside the history of religion and the anthropology of religion (and other approaches to the study of religion) within the total integral task of the study of religion.

We shall eventually summarise the developments in the comparison and classification of religions since 1945, and scrutinise the place of comparative religion as such in the study of religion. Before we pass on to do this, we must first of all review the relationship between comparative religion (wide or narrow) and theology.

3. Comparative Religion and Theology

3*a*.

As we have seen, the general tendency since World War II has been for the study of religion to attempt to distance itself from theology. A typical comment is that by S.G.F. Brandon in the preface to *A Dictionary of Comparative Religion* (1970, p. 1):

For too long it was regarded as a handmaid to Theology, concerned primarily with the task of showing how other religions were destined to find their completion in Christianity. This theological involvement inevitably resulted in the evaluation of Comparative Religion as a discipline based on theological presuppositions and with confessionist interests. But now, due to a variety of causes, the claim of Comparative Religion to be considered as an academic discipline in its own right, concerned with the scientific investigation and assessment of the relevant data, is generally acknowledged.

Most scholars in the fields of comparative religion and theology would probably agree with the basic sentiments lying behind this statement. However, there are some simplistic presuppositions underlying it that require consideration. It assumes that comparative religion and theology are monolithic enterprises—we have already shown how this is incorrect in relation to comparative religion, it is equally inaccurate in regard to theology. It assumes that theology must be prescriptive (or even confessional)—this is not necessarily the case. It assumes that theology must be christian theology—this is to ignore the fact that other religions have their own 'theologies', and that a theology of religion employing universal categories is also possible. It assumes that comparative religion is a scientific discipline whereas theology is not—this raises the question of what is meant by 'science', and whether natural scientific methods (if this is what is implied) are appropriate to the study of either comparative religion or theology. It assumes that theology has found it necessary to reduce religious studies to theology whereas other disciplines have not been reductionistic—this need not necessarily happen in theology, whereas it may happen in the 'scientific' work of a Freud or a Durkheim.

The whole theological area is too important to ignore completely and in this section we shall attempt to assess its contribution to and its distinction from comparative religion, viewed within the wider context of religious studies.

3*b*.

Some of the discussion of this topic has been influenced by institutional matters. The study of religion may find itself institutionally within a Divinity Faculty, an Arts Faculty, or even a Social Science Faculty. It is a sociological truism to assert that the approach to any subject is influenced by the institutional setting. Thus, Welch (*Graduate Education in Religion*, 1971) documents the proliferation of the graduate study of religion in North America within university non-theological faculties, university theological faculties, independent schools of religion or theology, independent theological schools, and theological schools integrally related to a university. The general American trend was in the direction of the emergence of religious studies as a discipline separate from theology although more recently (*University Divinity Schools: A Report on Ecclesiastically Independent Theological Education*, 1976) there has been a greater readiness for the theological institutions to emphasise the traditional theological disciplines. Britain followed the same general pattern, although the presence of established Churches in England and Scotland has made the process slower. France has its chair in the History of Religions at the Collège de France dating back to 1880, and one at the Sorbonne dating back to 1886, together with later chairs at the Protestant and Roman Catholic faculties at Strasburg and ensuing chairs at the Catholic institutions of Lille, Lyon, Paris, and Toulouse. In Germany the vast majorities of studies in religion are conducted in the theological faculties although there are chairs at Berlin, Bonn, Erlangen, Göttingen, Leipzig, and Marburg. Likewise, Italy has chairs or institutes in the history of religions at Rome, Messina, Padua, Naples and Venice, but most religious studies are taught within the framework of the theological faculties. By contrast, in Holland, religion is studied in the faculties of Theology, Arts, and Social Sciences at the state universities of Amsterdam, Groningen, Leiden, and Utrecht, and the Catholic University of Nijmegen, and at the Protestant Free University of Amsterdam. In Spain the study of religion is located in some of the Catholic universities; in Poland the main centre is probably the Polish Academy of Sciences; and in Peking its main location is in the Academy of Social Sciences. (See Welch, *op cit*; *Religion*, Vol, V. August 1975, pp. 27–54; Waardenburg, *Numen*, 1976, pp. 219–39). It is clear from the incomplete list of institutional settings given above that the relationships between comparative religion and theology are influenced directly or indirectly by these settings. The discussion is not merely an abstract academic one, it takes place against an evolving institutional back-ground. Allied to this 'administrative' point is the recent need felt by comparative religion to understand itself as an authentic academic discipline. As Gustafson put it, ten years ago, 'very few, if any other, fields are as preoccupied with their legitimacy and as introspective about their self-understanding as religious studies' (Ramsey and Wilson, 1970, p. 330). The preoccupation, on the part of religious studies, was to distance itself from its institutional past in theological departments, and to distance itself from disciplinary entanglements with theological value-judgements, apologetics, and propagation. It is not surprising that comparative religion has been more conscious of the discontinuity than the links between itself and theology.

3*c.*

In this section, we shall try to conceptualise in a new light the problematic relationship between comparative religion and theology.

The debate hinges upon five separable but interlinked issues. In the first place there is an overlap between comparative religion and theology in regard to subject matter. The same overlap does not necessarily occur in the case of other disciplines such as psychology, sociology, anthro-pology, history, philosophy, philology, aesthetics, and so forth, which cover a far wider subject matter and can, if they wish, ignore the field of religion. This is not as possible in the case of theology. The subject matter of theology seen as a discipline usually includes description and/or interpretation of the scripture, history, ethics, doctrines, rituals, communities, religious architecture and social involvement of religious traditions which provide the raw material for comparative religion. Although the latter discipline may conceivably approach the material from a different perspective, it is unthinkable that the scholar of reli-gion would not wish to use the critically researched data provided by the theological disciplines. The deeper problem arises where theology stresses the object of its endeavours namely God (or the Transcendent, or the Ultimate). To what extent is this concern part of the province of comparative religion?

In the second place, theology is usually seen to be the conceptual vehicle used by a particular religious tradition, often Christianity. However, this need not be the case. Among the Greeks, for example, it was one intellectual strand within a wider culture. In the work of Wilfred Cantwell Smith the theology of particular religious traditions is seen as part of a wider whole, the theology of religion, wherein universal theological categories can be erected that are relevant to all the world's religions not just to one. The original complaint, that theology involves value judgments operated by one religion in regard to others, no longer operates when theology is given these two wider meanings. What is the relationship of this new thinking to comparative religion?

In the third place, theology is often restricted in provenance to Christian theology, and in some Christian theology value judgments towards other religions are still present. We shall glance briefly at seven such theological approaches to other religions. However, although such approaches may perhaps arouse the old suspicion, they cannot be ignored altogether. On the one hand, such approaches in themselves provide raw material for comparative religion; on the other hand, when employed by scholars, such as Zaehner and Panikkar, who are also historians of religion, they can provide fruitful insights enhancing the work of comparative religion. The attitude on the part of some comparative religionists that any theological input must necessarily be unhelpful is unworthy. The research must be judged by its fruits not by ideological presuppositions on the part of comparative religionists.

In the fourth place, some recent theology has become involved in the question of dialogue. This interest has fed into an overlapping discussion within comparative religion. The gist of this discussion has been that there is the need for tolerant understanding between religions, there is the need to plan a new global world of harmony between men, there is the need for the major religions to become part of this planetary ecumenism, and there is the need for comparative religion to fulfil its responsibility to mankind by helping to build up intercultural and interreligious awareness within our global village. This ideal was symbolised in Friedrich Heiler's address to the 1958 Tokyo ninth International Congress for the History of Religions:

A new era will dawn upon mankind when the religions will rise to true tolerance and co-operation on behalf of mankind. To assist in preparing the way for this era is one of the finest hopes of the scientific study of religion (Heiler 1960: 21).

This statement approximated to the position of North American scholars, such as Joachim Wach and Wilfred Cantwell Smith, but was generally distrusted by European scholars who saw their work as scientific, academic, part of the humanities, and its own justification rather than a vehicle of international understanding and somehow allied with theology. Zwi Werblowsky of Jerusalem was representative of those who insisted that there must be a rigid separation between comparative religion and theology and that the dialogical approach was really a theological attempt to bridge the gap between theology and comparative religion (Werblowsky 1960). As we shall see elsewhere in this volume, thinkers from outside the Christian theological tradition have contributed to the dialogical viewpoint including Radhakrishnan, Suzuki, Buber, Nasr, and others. Moreover, non-theologians have become engaged in dialogical concern as a function of comparative religion in its own right rather than as a function of theology. Nevertheless, the issue of dialogue is clearly important for both.

In the fifth place, theology is liable to introduce the element of faith and commitment as an integral element of theological study. To what extent are these germane to the study of comparative religion? It is important to be precise about what is meant by faith and commitment. Commitment may refer to the scholar's own commitment to pursue the truth within his own academic orbit. But this is contingent upon what view he has about his own discipline whether it be comparative religion or theology. The theologian's commitment may be to the study of theology as a scientific, philological discipline abstracted from the faith of those who produced the documents he is engrossed in, whereas the comparative religionist's commitment may be to the study of comparative religion as involving empathy with the faith of those he is studying. Commitment may refer, secondly, to the commitment of those one happens to be studying. A recognition of commitment in others does not necessarily require personal religious commitment in the researcher himself, it is rather an acquiescence on the part of the scholar that religious texts and phenomena are meaningful to people and this meaningfulness, and the intentionality and faith whereby people and communities interpret texts and phenomena, belong to the study of religion. This approach may be adopted (or not adopted) towards both theology and comparative religion. Commitment may refer, thirdly, to the personal religious commitment of the researcher. This may be interpreted as being helpful or unhelpful to the scholar in studying his own or another's religion. If the subject matter of research is a dead or a primal religion the problem may not be so acute; the normal historical and anthropological canons of study can be applied. In the case of the scholar studying his own religion, personal faith may be seen to be helpful if it is wide rather than confessional, and if it is employed to advance scholarship rather than to proselytise. The problematic case is that of a scholar with personal commitment to one religion studying another. If that scholar uses theological value judgments derived from his own commitment to evaluate the other religion he may have problems in understanding it. But if a scholar of religion uses his personal commitment as an aid in understanding the commitment of those he is studying, then he must be judged by his fruits. Again, it depends upon the scholar's vision of his discipline. If his aim is to study philology and historical contexts, his personal faith is unlikely to affect his results. If his aim is not only to understand the data and phenomena of religious traditions but also to empathise with the faith of those for whom they are meaningful the outcome must decide whether the fact of having 'faith' makes it easier to conceptualise the 'faith' of others. This, in turn, is contingent upon whether the 'faith' of others is held to be a proper concern of the study of religion. However, the question of whether the 'faith' of others is a proper concern for comparative religion has no necessary connection with theology. Theology and commitment are not necessarily linked.

It will be seen from the rapid survey we have given of the five above-mentioned issues that the relationship between theology and comparative religion is extremely complex and not susceptible to simplistic solutions. The topic deserves a book in its own right. As it is not the purpose of this chapter to dwell upon the matter at length, we shall content ourselves with reviewing the work of three scholars, Wilfred Cantwell Smith, Raimundo Panikkar, and R.C. Zaehner, whose work is major and relevant, and we shall also attempt to map out the research implications of the methodological debate encompassing theology and comparative religion.

3d. Wilfred Cantwell Smith

Smith is a good example of a scholar who is clearly and mainly a comparative religionist, and who yet takes seriously the question of God, is interested in conceptualising a universal 'theology of religion,' has been concerned with dialogue, and stresses the concept of faith. His work has been categorised as theological and dialogical. It is basically neither, His work contains very little actual theology, his so-called universal theological categories could equally be termed philosophical or comparative categories, and he downgrades the concept of belief that has traditionally been central to theology (Wiebe 1979). Although he mentions dialogue, his main concern is with 'colloquium' which has a more intellectual and academic motive. The rigour of his research is evidenced by the extent of his footnotes which constitute 161 pages compared with 172 pages of actual text in his *Faith and Belief* (1979).

Smith, a Canadian, was born at Toronto in 1916. He spent a year as a schoolboy at Grenoble in France at the age of 11, a year in Spain and Egypt at the age of 17, and eight years at Lahore on the Indian sub-continent from 1941–49. His contacts with people of other religions and other cultures have remained important to him. His parents were Presbyterian, and he was accepted onto the role of ministers of the Presbyterian Church of Canada in 1943 and of the United Church of Canada in 1961, although he has never served as a parish minister in the normal sense. In 1949 he was appointed the W.M. Birks Professor of Comparative Religion at McGill, and two years later he founded the McGill Institute of Islamic Studies which brought together equal numbers of Western and Muslim students and faculty. In 1964 he became the

Director of the Harvard Center for the Study of World Religions which combined a rigorous academic programme in comparative religion with a residential setting wherein twenty-five students from different cultures and religions could share colloquia and discourse. At Harvard, Smith's interest and expertise widened to include all the major living religions. After an interlude from 1973–78 as McCulloch Professor at Dalhousie University in Halifax, Nova Scotia, Smith returned to Harvard to direct the religion programme in the faculty of arts and science that he himself had originally masterminded. (See Willard Oxtoby's introduction to *Religious Diversity*, 1976.)

Smith's approach to the study of religion moulded and was moulded by his own experience. This is true of any creative approach or methodology. They are rarely produced in abstraction, but are a dialectical intermingling of career events and conceptual reflection.

Another assessment of Smith's importance will appear elsewhere in this book. We are content, at this point, to trace the cross-fertilisation within his work of the theological and comparative religious elements found in our five issues outlined above.

There are two basic presuppositions behind Smith's thought, namely 'God' and 'man,' and they are joined together by his personalism. Smith says a great deal about man, but he says very little about God, and what he does say about God is vague. God, in Smith's thought, is equivalent to transcendence, and has its equivalence in the Buddhist *Dharma* (1979: 20–1). Nevertheless, God is, in this vague sense, the constant, the given, the presupposition of religious studies.

As Smith puts it (1967: 36):

God is a reality about which none of us knows enough to be dogmatic or scurrilous; yet about which each of us may, through his own symbols and his own faith, know enough to live—and indeed to live in a way that is transcendently final.

Like the theologian, Smith accepts that God is given. But he does not theologise about the unobservable God, the transcendent, 'the something, or Someone, behind or beyond Christianity, or Buddhism' (1964: 17). There is a lack of definition in Smith's references to God that allows God to be available to all men equally without any clear view of what is the particularity of God within particular traditions. This is the very opposite of theological prescription, but it also precludes comparison of views of God because transcendence is an unobservable and incomparable given. Smith's views are beginning to have some influence upon Christian theology (see Hick, *God and the Universe of Faiths*, 1973)—but he is not a theologian making statements about theology, he is a historian of religion making statements about comparative religion.

Smith's second constant is man himself who is one the world over. As far as Smith is concerned, apart from God and man all else is in flux. Religious traditions evolve; faith varies from man to man and from day to day; there are no essences that endure; there are no archetypal phenomena that have meaning in themselves apart from persons; there are only 'God' and 'man' that are given and constant. Smith's view of man is universalistic and strongly personalistic, and this is, of course, a philosophical and humanistic assumption. In fact, for Smith, 'the two matters of supreme importance are the relations among persons within the total community, and the relations between men and God' (1959: 58). Persons are the locus of religious truth, not things; the link between religious tradition and faith is persons; persons are the focus of Smith's study. Even truth, faith, and religious traditions are not things in themselves—they are mediated through persons. In fact, 'intellectual formulations in the religious realm refer not directly to a transcendent reality but only indirectly, through the inner life of persons,' (1964: 166) and so we cannot talk about transcendence in itself but only as it comes to us through persons. Likewise doctrines 'can only be understood, as statements by and for persons—and also, in a primary and immediate sense, about persons. Ultimately and indirectly they are statements about transcendence' (1964: 167). Thus, Smith's stress is not upon theological beliefs, nor upon God directly, but upon persons in their religiousness. Again he is not a theologian but a comparative religionist making hermeneutical statements about his task as a scholar.

If God and man are constants, it follows that religions are not. In his *Meaning and End of Religion* (1964), Smith made this point forcibly. More than this, he startled the academic world by claiming that the very terms 'religion' and 'religions' had become reified and obsolete. He contends:

Neither religion in general nor any one of the religions is in itself an intelligible entity, a valid object of inquiry or of concern either for the scholar or for the man of faith (1964: 16).

After a long analysis of the use of the word 'religion' from Roman times to present day, Smith concludes that it has been used in four different ways. It has been used to point to personal piety whereby a person has a warm or cold or narrow religion, etc.; it has been used to point to an overt system of beliefs, practices, and values seen as an ideal, as in 'true Christianity' (1964: 48); it has been used to point to an overt system of beliefs, practices, and values seen as a sociological and historical phenomenon, as in 'the Christianity of history' (1964: 48); and it has been used to point to religion in general as 'a generic summation' (1964: 48). Smith makes the audacious claim that, 'the word, and the concepts, should be dropped—at least in all but the first, personalist, sense ... the term "religion" is confusing, unnecessary, and distorting' (1964: 48). He further shows how, after the term 'religion' had become reified from its original personalistic meaning, the term "religions,' and the terms for particular 'religions' such as Buddhism, Confucianism, Zoroastrianism, Sikhism, etc., suffered the same fate so that they came to be seen as or were conceptualised as objectified, reified entities divorced from persons and from transcendence, in other words from man and from God.

Smith's dissatisfaction with the terms 'religion' and 'religions' is basically not theological as Barth's was. He himself is primarily a historian of religion, and his first objection is a historical one. As far as he is concerned, in history there is process, flux, infinite variety, a richness too great to be defined, an unknown future, whereas 'religion' is a monolithic and static term that does not do justice to the wide variety in time and space of religious history. However, neither can man's religiousness be reduced to observable history. His second objection is that the reified term 'religion' leaves out the transcendent element in religious life, 'yet the whole pith and substance of religious life lies in relation to what cannot be observed' (1964: 123). It is desirable then to switch the focus of attention from observable religions to persons and their faith, for to understand the faith of other men it is necessary to look not so much at their 'religion' but rather at the universe through their eyes. In order to achieve this end, Smith suggests the replacement of the terms 'religion' and 'religions' by his own terms 'faith' and 'tradition.' He writes (1964: 141):

> By faith I mean personal faith ... an inner religious experience or involvement of a particular person; the impingement upon him of the transcendent, putative or real ... By cumulative tradition I mean the entire mass of overt objective data that constitute the historical deposit, as it were, of the past religious life of the community in question: temples, scriptures, theological systems, dance patterns, legal and other social institutions, conventions, moral codes, myths, and so on; anything that can be and is transmitted from one person, one generation, to another, and that an historian can observe.

For Smith, these are all-embracing terms. 'It is my suggestion,' he writes, 'that by the use of these two notions it is possible to conceptualise and to describe anything that has ever happened in the religious life of mankind' (1964: 141). Insofar as the words mean anything, therefore, 'religion' is expressive of personal faith, and 'religions' are expressive of the evolving historical milieux of religious traditions within the total religious history of mankind. This is not a theological construct, it is a new model for conceptualising comparative religion which happens to use terms such as 'God' and 'faith' that have been more familiarly found in theological writings.

In relation to comparative religion in the narrower sense, Smith's work has three consequences. In the first place, he has nothing to say about primal religions, little or nothing to say about archaic religions, and although he stresses the major religious traditions his model makes general comparisons difficult. It is necessary, he claims, to become immersed in the language and history of two traditions, usually one's own and another, and then, after long years of grappling with the deep issues involved it may be possible to draw comparisons between the two. However, comparisons in depth between traditions may find parallels between themes that on the surface seem to be very different. For example, in making his own comparison between the Christian and Muslim traditions, Smith points out that the founder of one, Christ, is equivalent to the scripture of the other, the Qur'ān, in that they represent the Word of God for Christians and Muslims. As we shall see later, there are corresponding homologies between other topics in Islam and Christianity that are superficially diverse until uncovered by research in depth. Secondly, as a result of this, phenomenological typologies that set up structural comparisons between similar types of phenomena abstracted from their traditions and symbol systems are likely to miss the point because in classifying data that are outwardly similar they may overlook the real homologies between themes that appear to be utterly different. The inference is that typological classifications of phenomena, as well as blanket comparisons of the major religious traditions, are not likely to be fruitful because the knowledge required for sensitive comparison is only possible of acquirement in regard to any two traditions. Nevertheless, thirdly, Smith's conviction that God and man are constants, even though the history of cumulative traditions may have been very diverse, leads him to seek for philosophical and hermeneutical similarities overarching cumulative traditions in the form of what he calls universal theological categories. By these, he means categories that are equally applicable to all the major religious traditions. In other words, his aim is not to set up an exclusivistic Christian theology of religion but a global theology of religion that can comprehend all the traditions of the world (see Smith, 1981). 'The theology of religions,' he writes, 'must be the product of a thinker who sees, and feels, and indeed knows, men of all religious faith as members of one community, one in which he also participates' (1969: 9). In fact, however, Smith does not define 'theology,' and what he is really striving for is not 'theology' in any traditional sense but a 'theology' of the religious history of mankind, or a 'theology' of *homo religiosus*. To put it another way, having rejected phenomenological structural typologies as quasi-Platonic abstractions and having rejected more traditional typologies between traditions (such as founders, scriptures, etc.) as being too superficial, Smith is seeking for deeper classificatory categories that are true of man *qua* man under God in all religious traditions. He conceives that these categories will be new, and he offers a few suggestions as to what they might be. So far, he has suggested four, namely the concept of faith, the concept of cumulative tradition, the concept of religious truth, and the concept of participation.

There is no time further to explicate these four terms at this point. The task of uncovering these and other categories that are apt to all religious traditions 'without distortion or reduction or transportation' (1969: 14) is a daunting and exciting one. The question is whether this task is accurately designated as theology. The concepts Smith is seeking for are not beliefs or doctrines, they relate directly to man, and they refer only indirectly to transcendence. They could just as well be designated as philosophical concepts, or even comparative concepts, with the proviso that they presuppose similarity rather than difference.

Smith's work can be questioned at a number of points—there will be a critique of his work elsewhere in this volume—but he can hardly be described as a theologian masquerading as a comparative religionist. He is not a theologian in the sense that his concern is only with his own religion, that he stresses beliefs, that he uses value judgements in regard to the religion of others, that he is unable to empathise with the faith of others, or that his concern is to define and conceptualise God—just the opposite. He is a comparative religionist who is raising the question as to what is the appropriate subject matter with which comparative religion should wrestle. In asserting that transcendence is indescribable yet not irrelevant, in suggesting that the rituals, myths, ethics, iconography, concepts, prayers, and other data of religion are significant not just in themselves but also in regard to the faith to which they point, Smith is intimating that comparative religion must be clear about the nature of its material and adapt its methods accordingly. Implicitly, he is pleading for a reorientation of both comparative religion and theology, and because of his work it is impossible to use any longer the old clichés concerning their relationship.

3e. Comparative Theological Attitudes to Other Religions

However, no other scholar has proceeded as far as Smith in thinking on these matters. Most theologians who have anything to say about other religions do so from within the ambience of their own theological system. During the period we are discussing there have been seven possible theological attitudes that one religious tradition could adopt towards others ranging from exclusivism at one extreme to relativism on the other. We shall review these briefly. They afford excellent comparative material, and one of the tasks of the next few years is to compare the attitudes that different religions have exercised towards each other. In addition to this, one or two such theological thinkers, notably Zaehner and Panikkar, have done creative work in comparative religion. As our intention is to proceed quickly we will concentrate upon Christian theologians and extrapolate from them.

(i) The first three attitudes need not detain us long. Indeed their exclusivistic nature graphically illustrates the reason why comparative religion has been so anxious to distance itself from theological comparison as such.

The first possible theological attitude is that of absolute exclusivism; the notion that other religions are misguided and wrong, they have no true access to God or to genuine spirituality, there is no possibility of compromise with them or recognition of them, any comparison with them must be in terms of truth over against falsehood. This attitude has rarely, if ever, been adapted in its absolute form although approximations to it may be found in the early Christian attitude to the mystery religions, in Tertullian, in some of the Crusades propaganda, and in some nineteenth century missionary pronouncements. More common has been the readiness to condemn one particular element, such as the sacraments or the doctrines of others. It is only in the period since 1945, in the thinking of men such as Panikkar, that Christian theologians have been ready to countenance the proposition that the sacraments of others may be their normal way to God (Panikkar 1964); otherwise, even in recent times, non-judgmental thinking about the sacraments of others has been rare. As far as doctrine is concerned, the notion that religious truth is found in exclusive doctrinal propositions is typified in the thinking of conservative evangelicals who stress the 'fundamentals' of the inerrancy of the Bible, the supernatural acts of God, the Virgin Birth, the miracles, resurrection, deity and infallible power of Christ, His sacrificial atonement and penal substitution, and the final judgement at the Second Coming of Christ (Warfield 1951).

The second possible theological attitude, not quite as stark as the first, is that of discontinuity between 'revelation' and 'religion.' Such thinking, found classically in Barth and in a modified form in Kraemer, suggests that 'revelation' represents God's downward coming to man, whereas 'religion' signifies man's upward groping for God. The qualification that Christianity as such is a 'religion' only slightly limits the exclusivism of this view in that, insofar as 'revelation' is located in the Word of God revealed in Christ, it is unlikely to be found outside the Judaeo–Christian tradition. We may note in passing that Barth comments critically upon the word 'religion.' His complaint is not like that of Wilfred Cantwell Smith who objects to the reification and confusion attendant upon the use of the word; Barth's objection is theological— 'religion' is discontinuous with 'revelation' and therefore operates within the sphere of 'unbelief' rather than that of 'faith' (1959: 34). Hendrick Kraemer, by contrast, had been a missionary in the Dutch East Indies from 1922–28 and 1930–35, and unlike Barth had a good knowledge of other religions, especially Islam. In 1927 he had been appointed to the Leiden chair in the history of religion and he wrote three books, *The Christian Message in a Non-Christian World* (1938), *Religion and the Christian Faith* (1956), and *World Cultures and World Religions* (1960), plus numerous articles directly related to this issue. Hallencreutz (1966) and Sharpe (1977) argue that Kraemer tempered the exclusivism of his discontinuity views from 1938 to his death in 1965. However, the very fact that this was the case, and the very intensity with which Kraemer attempted to 'avoid the frequently occurring identification of Christianity, one of the religions, with the Revelation of God in Christ' (see 1956: 78–83) only serves to highlight the fact of discontinuity as an important element in his thought and the theological prescription built into this notion.

The third theological attitude, which is also partly sociological, traces the supposed relationship between Judaeo–Christian theology and the rise of science and secularisation in Europe. According to this viewpoint, especially well-defined in A. Th. van Leeuwen (1964), Judaeo–Christian theology, through its concentration upon and exposition of a cluster of ideas including creation, consummation, incarnation, prophecy, history, matter, the body, this world, and so on, provided the ideological framework within which modern science and technology could arise and come to fruition. From modern science and technology there arose the process of secularisation which, insofar as it provides for man a new freedom from 'ontocratic' fetters, is an ally of the Christian Gospel which provided the seedbed for its emergence. The corollary of this view is that the other religions which were not able to prepare the way for the rise of science and technology are liable to wither away beneath the challenge of the technological process. Other variants of such secularisation theology are found in Bonhoeffer (1954), Gregor Smith (1956) and Harvey Cox (1965).

It is not our purpose to establish a critique of the three approaches outlined above. It is enough to make the point that they are theologically judgmental and therefore inimical to the true understanding and impartial comparison that lie at the heart of comparative religion.

(ii) The fourth possible theological attitude is somewhat more eirenical. We may term it fulfilment theology, the supposition that all religions have access to transcendent reality, to authentic spirituality, and to religious truth; yet these are to be found in their fulness in Christianity. Christian theology contains many subtle variations upon the fulfilment theme. Basically it can take three forms, and we shall glance at these briefly before examining the work of R.C. Zaehner who was himself both a fulfilment theologian and a skilled practitioner of comparative religion.

From time to time, in the history of both theology and comparative religion, the notion has arisen that there is a basic element in religion that is essential to it. The first type of fulfilment theology has asserted that all religions partake of this essential element, but that one religion contains it more fully than the others. Lord Herbert of Cherbury's five notions of religion, Kant's moral imperative, Schleiermacher's feeling of absolute dependence, Otto's numinous sense of the holy, Farmer's personal encounter with God are all examples of different views as to what is this basic element that is contained in all religions but fulfilled in Christianity (see Owen C. Thomas, 1969).

A second type of fulfilment theology postulates that Christianity fulfils other traditions, for example the law of Israel, and the philosophy of Greece. This approach has been present from the time of the early fathers, such as Clement of Alexandria, to the present day. Lying behind it there is often a *logos* theology: the notion that all men partake in the *logos* through creation, that the cosmic Christ informs all men, that the spirituality of all men is real, but that the religious traditions of other men are fulfilled in the perfect *logos* who is Christ Himself.

This variety of fulfilment theology is often static. The third type is more dynamic. It thinks in terms of the fulfilment of process. It supposes that the whole cosmic drama is converging upon Christ. Thus Hegel's Christianity fulfils a dialectical process of development and, for Teilhard de Chardin, cosmic evolution is moving in the direction of Omega Point and the Cosmic Christ (Chardin 1959: 279–99, 319–27).

R.C. Zaehner is a good example of a thinker who combined within himself these last two types of fulfilment theology at the same time as he practised comparative religion, and we shall pause to examine his thought at this point.

Robert Charles Zaehner

Robert Charles Zaehner was born in 1913 and educated at Tonbridge school and Christ Church, Oxford where he became a lecturer in Persian. At the age of twenty he had a religious experience of 'nature mysticism' and he retained a deep interest in the topic of mysticism. He became a Roman Catholic in 1946 and this became a key factor in his personal life. During the Second World War, Zaehner served as a press attaché and later acting counsellor at the British Embassy in Teheran. It was here that he began his influential studies in Zoroastrianism that were responsible for him gaining the Spalding chair of Eastern religions and ethics at Oxford. H.N. Spalding's aim for this chair was that the study of the major religions would lead to their comparison in such a way that they would be brought together in understanding, harmony, and friend-ship. Zaehner's predecessor, Sarvepalli Radhakrishnan, had understood this aim in one way, Zaehner himself was to interpret it very differently during his tenure of the chair from 1953 to 1974, and in the twenty books that he wrote. Although the Oxford chair was basically in comparative religion, Zaehner was not afraid to act the part of a fulfilment theologian in the work that he did. Indeed Zaehner's weaknesses were often paradoxically his strengths. For he was operating on three levels at once:

he was a professional comparative religionist; he was a convinced Roman Catholic; and he was a lay theologian. At times these three concerns operated in a helpful state of dialectical tension, at other times they became unacknowledgedly confused.

Zaehner's work may be divided into two parts. 'Of the books I have written,' he wrote, 'some are intended to be objective; others, quite frankly, are not (1970: 9). In the first group he included his three books on Zoroastrianism (1955, 1956, 1961), and to a lesser extent his books on Hinduism (1962, 1966, 1969). He was honest enough to admit the possibility, even in connection with his work on Hinduism, that his 'theistic and subjective Christian mind' may have seized on the evidence so presented and imposed its own image upon it (1970: 10). Zaehner's frankness represents a healthy caveat for the scholar. Pure objectivity may be possible in regard to objects in the natural sciences, it is less possible of achievement in the humanities. Indeed there is a sense in which Zaehner, despite his 'Christian mind,' tended to treat Hinduism as an object to be studied independently of those who practiced it. And therefore, although he may have achieved a certain impartiality, it may have been at the cost of the empathy stressed by Cantwell Smith. In his second group of works Zaehner was more admittedly theological in that he tried, as he put it (1970: 11):

to study the main texts of the non-Christian religions in their historical development, to study them, so far as is possible, from inside, and having so studied them to try to correlate them with aspects of Catholic Christianity which are of importance.

At this point he became a fulfilment theologian.

In fact, some of Zaehner's work was comparative rather than theological. By contrast with Radhakrishnan he doubted whether harmony among world religions was possible 'if, as seems inevitable, the resultant harmony is only to be apparent, verbal, and therefore fictitious' (1970: 429). Zaehner was concerned to use comparative religion to point out what he saw to be the differences as well as the similarities between types of religious life. In his inaugural lecture of 1953, and in the *Concise Encyclopaedia of Living Faiths* (1959) that he edited, he compared and contrasted the 'mystical' and 'prophetic' poles of religious life centred in

India and Israel respectively. The prophetic pole was based upon Judaism and Zoroaster, continued down into Christianity, and arose later in Islam. The mystical pole was centred upon India with Hinduism and early Buddhism, was present in China with Taoism, and it passed into the Far East through Mahāyāna Buddhism. In a somewhat simplistic way, Zaehner set up the differences betwen the two poles. On the one hand there was the stress upon revelation; on the other hand there was indifference to dogma. On the one side prophets spoke in God's name; on the other side, the immortal ground of the soul was stressed. Whereas the prophets denounced error; India breathed tolerance. The one pole stressed God as transcendent; the other pole stressed the Absolute within. The prophets witnessed to a God who created, who was good, and who desired to be known; the mystics stressed eternal life within oneself. To the prophet truth was one; to the mystic truth was many-sided. The prophetic temptation was to fanaticism and persecution; India saw religions as equal paths to the same goal. One side emphasised love; the other side emphasised spirit. For Israel man was a unified body/soul; for India matter was seen over against soul. For the one pole God and salvation were personal; for the other pole personality figured less. The prophet could countenance religious experience only of God; the mystic could experience Reality in other ways.

Objections can be raised against the too neat dichotomies outlined by Zaehner. These were exacerbated by his emphasis upon scriptures and sacred texts, and his complete neglect of primal religion. In his later work Zaehner realised that his scheme must be refined. His growing awareness of Chinese religion, especially Confucianism which was neither prophetic nor mystical, led him to attempt to do this. Nevertheless, in spite of the problems that inevitably remained, Zaehner was making a basically valid point, namely that comparative religion, impartially conceived, involves the admission of difference as well as similarity. He was also stating that the focus of comparison could rest not only upon religious traditions as such but also upon religious areas and poles.

In addition to differentiating between the religious poles based upon Israel and India, Zaehner also distinguished four contrasting types of mysticism (1957, 1960, 1970, 1972). First, there was pan-en-henic nature mysticism when one, as it were, merged into the cosmos and had the feeling that one was one with the cosmos, and had transcended space. Zaehner gave examples of this type of mysticism from the Upaniṣads and moderns such as R.M. Bucke, Walt Whitman, and Wordsworth. Second, there was the way of isolation mysticism whereby the soul became separated from time and space and found oneness within itself. One could find *mokṣa* (release) from the world by retreat into the nakedness and isolation of the immortal soul. As Zaehner put it, 'there is a state of being which is unconditioned by time, space, causation, and the endless process of transmigration. The proof of it is in the Buddha's own Enlightenment' (1970: 94). He gave other examples from early Buddhism, Sāṅkhya-Yoga, Jainism, and others. Third, there was monistic mysticism. Here, at the level of ultimate truth, there was infinite oneness. At this level, the soul *was* the Absolute, Ātman *was* Brahman. Zaehner gave examples from the Māndūkya Upaniṣad, from 'the prince of monists Śaṅkara,' and from Eckhart's description of the 'Godhead which is beyond God' (1970: 94–6). Fourth, there was theistic mysticism. This involved loving communion of the soul with God as found in much Christian mysticism, much Sūfī mysticism, the Bhagavad Gītā, Śaiva Siddhānta, Rāmānuja, and Mahāyāna Buddhism. Here the key concepts were not oneness, emptiness, rest, and peace; but yearning, love, communion, and interaction in a world that was yet beyond time. Zaehner painted the basic contrast between monistic and theistic mysticism by using Junayd of Baghdad (1960: 173):

The journey from this world to the next is easy and simple for the believer, but to separate oneself from creatures for God's sake is hard, and the journey from self to God is exceedingly hard, and to bear patiently with God is hardest of all.

Again, it is fairly easy to criticise Zaehner's neat categories. For much of the time he was not so much analysing mystical experience, but rather opening up the logic of mystical discourse which is not the same thing. We may question the rigidities and details of his scheme; we may question his method. Nevertheless his work has made it difficult for anyone to assume that there is an essential unity and sameness of all mysticism as though this were an established fact. He has demonstrated that there are comparative differences as well as similarities between and within religions.

And so, in his technical work on Zoroastrianism and Hinduism, and in his comparative insights, Zaehner has made significant contributions to comparative religion. Parrinder describes Zaehner's commentary on the Bhagavad Gītā (1969; see *History of Religions*, Parrinder, 1976: 73) as 'perhaps the most outstanding exegetical work by any western scholar of a nonbiblical book.' However, when Zaehner strayed over into fulfilment theology he ceased to be a comparative religionist as such. 'Unless I am greatly mistaken,' he wrote, 'all the strands we have been trying to bring together in the different religions, meet only in one place, and that is in the religion of Jesus Christ' for 'Christ indeed comes to fulfil not only the law and the prophets of Israel, but also the "law and prophet" of the Aryan race' (1968: 180). Accordingly, Christ was 'the true Tao' (1970: 363), 'the fulfilment of the hope of Yudhisthīra' (1970: 363), 'the true answer to Job' (1970: 363); the Gospel is 'the fertilisation of Nirvāṇa' (1970: 359); 'Rāma and Krishna were earthly kings and both in their way prefigure Christ' (1970: 355); and 'to be a Christian, you must be both a Marxist and a Buddhist, both Confucian and Taoist, for in Christ all that has abiding value meets' (1970: 360). This is not comparative religion, it is fulfilment theology. This strain in his thought was intensified when he began to incorporate the dynamic categories of Teilhard de Chardin's evolutionary fulfilment thought into his previously more static approach. 'Perhaps Teilhard is the answer to Marx,' he wrote, 'and the only form of Christianity that may prove acceptable to modern man is perhaps the gospel according to Teilhard' (1970: 423). However, it is not the role of comparative religion to provide an answer to Marx, or to purvey fulfilment categories of any sort, whether static or dynamic. This is a legitimate task of the theologian *qua* theologian. The problem arises when the two roles become intermingled as sometimes happened in Zaehner's work.

(iii). The fifth possible theological attitude to other religions is that of universalisation theology. Within this approach, Christian theological statements are universalised to include the categories of other religions within their orbit. Roman Catholic theologians such as Karl Rahner and Raimundo Panikkar are especially important in this new development.

Their method is to take orthodox Christian theological statements such as 'Christ came to save all mankind' or 'salvation is by faith' or 'there is one God and Mediator, Jesus Christ' and then to universalise them to include others. Thus if Christ came to save all mankind, God provides the means for this to happen in most of the world through the medium of the other religious traditions (Panikkar, *The Unknown Christ of Hinduism*, 1964); faith is not so much correct answer as authentic quest, and this is found in all religions; the one God and Mediator, Jesus Christ, is not just the western *logos*, but a universal category no longer bound by the world view of the human Jesus or Greek philosophical thought. The ablest exponent of this approach is Raimundo Panikkar who is also a comparative religionist in his own right, and we shall pause briefly to consider his thought.

Raimundo Panikkar

Raimundo Panikkar is interreligious and cross-cultural by birth, his father being an Indian Hindu, and his mother a Spanish Roman Catholic; and his main, though by no means his sole, interest has been the creative interpretation of these two traditions. His three doctorates are in science, philosophy, and theology, and his interests are therefore multidisciplinary. Although a Roman Catholic priest, his concern is not solely with theology, but also with philosophy, natural science, and above all comparative religion. Like Cantwell Smith his horizon is global but he is more anchored in Christian theology than Smith; like Zaehner he is concerned with developing a creative Christian theological attitude to other religions but he is less constricted by traditional theological norms than Zaehner. It is very difficult to summarise Panikkar's thought because it is so allusive, and it covers so many different areas. He ranges from universalisation theology (*The Unknown Christ of Hinduism*, 1964), through Christian theology as such (*Christianity and World Religions*, 1969), though comparative spirituality (*The Trinity and World Religions*, 1970), and through dialogue (*The Intra-Religious Dialogue*, 1978a), to Hindu studies (*The Vedic Experience*, 1979), to integral futurology (*From Alienation to At-Oneness*, Villanova, n.d.), and to myth and hermeneutics (*Myth, Faith and Hermeneutics*, 1978b). At this point our main concern is with his universalisation theology and his comparative religion, and we shall concentrate upon them. Part of Panikkar's originality lies in his attempt to integrate theories of comparative religion and theology of religion. For him there is hardly any distinction between the two; philosophy, hermeneutics, theology, and comparative religion emerge in practice as branches within an integrated study.

It is part of the purpose of this essay to maintain that there *is* a basic distinction between theology and comparative religion. In spite of his breadth of vision and creativeness of thought, Panikkar remains basically a universalisation theologian rather than a comparative religionist as such.

Like Wilfred Cantwell Smith, Panikkar is concerned to emphasise the categories of transcendence and faith in the study of religion. Like Smith, he is therefore ready to go beyond the observable level of outward phenomena and the concerns of phenomenology (1978a: 39–52). In contrast with Smith, Panikkar is more ready to use specifically Christian theological terminology as the basis of a more universal scheme, to use faith as an existential as well as a formal category, to concern himself with spirituality, and to give content to the notion of transcendence. In our brief analysis of Panikkar we shall concentrate on his comparisons of the notions of transcendence and man's destiny, and on his comparison of trinitarian spirituality.

All religions, in the broadest sense of the term, recognise something or somebody of one type or another which or who conveys salvation, understood again in any number of possible ways: Christ, spirit, logos, *antaryāmin*, *guru*, *tathāgata*, savior, grace, doctrine, prophet, *dharma*, book, revelation, *īśvara*, message, love, service, knowledge, intuition, *tao*, faith, God, gnosis, humanity, lord, goodness, truth, etc., are different names for it, though with different connotations certainly, for which reason these expressions are by no means interchangeable. Yet, in different and not irrelevant ways, those concepts are symbols of a reality (for those who believe) which performs the religious function par excellence: that of conveying to man his salvation, of permitting him to realize his destiny, reach his goal (Panikkar 1973: 123–4).

As far as Panikkar is concerned all these names and forms, although vastly different, are equivalent from the point of view of the function they perform for those who believe. They are hermeneutically comparable in that they are all, in one way or other, mediating symbols whereby men attain salvation. In other words, Panikkar is attempting to apply comparative religious formulae not merely to observable data but also to symbols that mediate transcendence, and, to that extent, to transcendence itself.

However, he also wishes to uncover a language that will universalise what he is trying to say. The problem is that if he uses the language of a particular religious symbol system, it may be misunderstood by others whose language it is not; if he tries to invent a new language, communication will not necessarily be helped. Panikkar eventually elects to universalise Christian terms, notably 'Christ,' 'Word,' and 'Lord,' in order to attain his ends. As he puts it, he could equally well have used 'Messiah,' 'Vac,' and 'Spirit,' but this would not have aided in clarifying the situation. Panikkar is aware of the potential 'scandal of particularity' involved in using the terms 'Christ' and 'Word,' and for that reason is attracted especially to the term 'Lord' as a generic summation of the names used in the above quotation. All of these names stand for the same 'Lord,' and that 'Lord' is more than a mere name.

Panikkar applies the same process to comparative notions of the destiny of man. He writes (1973: 134):

Let us call Omega the end, the goal, the aim (or whatever other expression we may choose in order to designate the final destiny of man: Man, God, Absolute, Nothing, Knowledge, Humanity, the gods, divinised contingency, etc.). What I am saying is not that there is a 'material' agreement or correspondence between the several notions which are put forward in order to answer the question of the meaning of human life, but that there is a metaontological equivalence.

Again, all these names are functionally comparable. They stand for the same *omega*, and *omega* is more than a mere word. Panikkar is basically classifying together all the mediating symbols and all the notions of human destiny in the various religions under the terms of 'Lord' and *omega*. These happen to be western and Christian words, but their import is universal.

Two comments are in order in relation to Panikkar's theory. In the first place, he is not only attempting to extrapolate universal comparative categories concerning man and his religious apprehension, as Smith has done. Smith's four categories of faith, tradition, religious truth, and participation are basically comments about man and his religiousness seen comparatively. Panikkar is going further than this. He is extrapolating universal comparative categories concerning basic mediating symbols and ultimate transcendence. This is the proper province of theology rather than that of comparative religion, for theology in its strict sense has to do with God, with ontology, with transcendence. In regard to his subject matter Panikkar is therefore a theologian, in the widest possible sense, rather than a comparative religionist as such. In the second place, Panikkar has a dual motive in his work. On the one hand, he is eager, through his comparative categories, to promote a deeper understanding of Hinduism and all the other world religions, and also to contribute to the proper work of comparative religion. On the other hand, he is eager to deepen and renew Christian theology in order to encompass within it the spiritual universe of the other religions. Indeed, Ewert Cousins has suggested that Panikkar's greatest contribution to scholarship may be the erection of a new universalised Christian systematic theology (1977, 1978). Insofar as this may be the case, Panikkar is operating outwards from a base in Christian theology; seminal though his thought is, it is an exercise in universalisation theology rather than in comparative religion.

The same profundity and ambiguity is found in Panikkar's work on comparative spirituality. Again he takes up a Christian theological category, the trinity, but universalises it to include world religions in general; and he applies trinitarian categories to the notion of spirituality which is a central concept in his thought. He writes in *The Trinity and World Religions* (1970: 9):

One of the features that differentiates a spirituality from an established religion is that the former is far more flexible, for it is disconnected from the mass of rites, structures, etc., that are indispensable to all religions. One religion, in fact, may include several spiritualities, because spirituality is not directly bound up with any dogma or institution. It is rather an attitude of mind which one may ascribe to different religions.

In claiming, as he does, that there are three predominant and universal forms of human spirituality, Panikkar is not identifying them with particular religions but asserting that these three forms of spirituality are present in all religions. In fact, Panikkar uses terms from the Bhagavad Gītā, *karmamārga*, *bhaktimārga*, and *jñānamārga*, in naming his three forms of spirituality; and it appears at first sight as though he is universalising Hindu terms rather than Christian ones. However, he also claims that, 'the Trinity . . . may be considered as a junction where the authentic spiritual dimensions of all religions meet' (1970: 42).

Panikkar's notion of the threefold structure of human spirituality is a valuable contribution to comparative religion. Although his threefold structure does in fact correspond with the Christian trinity of Father, Son, and Holy Spirit, he asserts that it is not an *a priori* imposition but an empirical assessment of the data of spirituality. The first type of spirituality, *karmamārga*, is focussed on ritual action, icons, silence, and a transcendent Reality that is Wholly Other. This Transcendence is unknowable in itself; we can form mental images of it, but they point beyond themselves to that which we cannot comprehend. We can only obey, and stand in silence before the Absolute. We can offer the service of our *karma* (ritual works) and we can adore in silence through the icons we make to represent the ineffable Other. We approach with awe through the spirituality of *karma*. The second type of spirituality, *bhaktimārga*, is focussed on persons, love, devotion, prayer, and relationship with a personal transcendent Lord. This relationship, involving personhood on each side, is based upon mutual communication, giving, and affirmation. We can offer the service of our *bhakti* (devotion) and respond in love through a dialogue of persons. We are in the realm of personal devotion rather than that of adoration of transcendent majesty. The third type of spirituality, *jñānamārga*, is focussed on intuitive inwardness and immanence. It involves a non-duality of the self and the Absolute. It is realised through inward union. The Absolute is discovered in its own realisation when we attain to *jñāna* (knowledge) of the transcendent Reality that is within us. We are in the realm of mysticism, inward realisation, and Spirit (1970: 11–40). Although these three types of spirituality correspond in a general sense with the apophatic silence of the Buddhist, the personalism of the monotheistic religions of the Word, and the undifferentiated unionism of the *advaitin* Hindu, they are in fact common to all religions, and are outworkings of the faith that is a basic ingredient of human nature.

Our previous two comments apply equally to Panikkar's work on comparative spirituality. Although stressing the spirituality of man, he also refers repeatedly to the notion of transcendence as relevant and indeed integral to a particular structure of spirituality. In regard to subject matter, therefore, his concern is as much with God as with man, with theology as with comparative religion. More than this, he applies his threefold spirituality directly to the doctrine of the trinity so that his silent, apophatic spirituality relates to the Father, his personalistic spirituality to the Son, and his immanent spirituality to the Spirit; and the three forms of spirituality together testify to the universal apprehension of the trinitarian nature of Absolute Reality. While his work is a contribution to comparative religion, his basic starting point remains within Christian theology and his ultimate aim is the renewing and universalising of Christian theology. To this extent he is primarily a universalisation theologian.

(iv) The last two theological approaches need not detain us long. The first one, our sixth in all, is that of dialogue. Dialogue theology is eirenical but it stresses difference as well as similarity. It is because there is difference, and even tension, between religions that dialogue is possible. If religions were basically the same there would be no need for dialogue. In order to engage in dialogue it is necessary to understand the religion of one's partner in dialogue. There is the need to empathise with the other's religious position. Then, on the basis of this understanding, theological dialogue can ensue between the two positions. This dialogue may take place between individual believers, religious leaders, or even representative scholars; it may presuppose the possibility of conversion, or preclude it; it may contribute to deepening the faith, or the theology, of the participants; it may, in the persons of Kenneth Cragg, Paul Devanandan, and others, deepen our understanding of Islam, Hinduism, or other traditions (Cragg, 1956, 1959, 1964, 1971; Taylor, 1963; Thomas, 1969; Devanandan, 1963, 1964, Hallencreutz, 1977; and others). But whether dialogue theology be seen as a separate theological approach, or whether it be combined with one of the other approaches mentioned above, it is self-confessedly within the orbit of theology rather than comparative religion. It looks out from one religion in the direction of others and seeks, albeit empathetically, to gain insights for its own tradition.

Finally, there is the relativistic theological approach. This approach is eirenical by definition in that it acknowledges theologically that religions are relative not absolute in nature. According to this viewpoint, religions may be relative to the culture in which they are found, for example Islam is the main religion of the Middle East; religious truth may be relative to individual people, for example Kṛṣṇa may be the truth for one person, and Christ for another; or religions may be moving along relatively different paths towards the same ultimate goal. Exemplified after 1915 in Troeltsche's thought, theological relativism, whether it be cultural, epistemological, or teleological, remains an attempt made by a particular religion to solve its own problems in regard to the religious diversity surrounding it. It belongs therefore to the realm of theology rather than the realm of comparative religion.

3f.

Let us endeavour to sum up our discussion of the relationship between theology and comparative religion.

In the first place, it would be advantageous to rename the study of particular religious traditions so that theology (understood as the study of Christianity) became Christian studies, Muslim theology became Muslim studies, etc. Christian studies, for example, would then include theology in the sense of Christian doctrines (especially of God); it would also include Old Testament and New Testament, Church history, Christian ethics, philosophy of religion, liturgics, sociology of religion, and so on. Christian theology would then take its rightful place within a wider whole known as Christian studies. The overall effect would be the same, but the nomenclature would be more accurate. The same principles would apply in the study of other religions. Christian studies, Muslim studies, etc. would then be separate components within religious studies which would become the term for the general study of religion. The work of comparative religion in its particular and special sense would be to classify and compare the scriptures, ethics, philosophies, rituals, social concerns, and doctrines of the various particular fields of study.

In the second place, the proper realm of theology is that of the knowledge (or science) of God. Conversely, this is *not* the realm of religious studies. This is not to imply that religious studies must proceed by way of methodological atheism, or even agnosticism. Religious studies may be ready to accept that religious phenomena point beyond themselves to the intentionality and faith of those for whom they are meaningful, and that the object of intentionality and faith may be God or transcendence however experienced or viewed. The fact is that God or transcendence is not the direct concern of religious studies, it is the direct concern of theology. Insofar as the views of God held within particular religions are sometimes normative or judgmental in regard to other religions (as we saw in our analysis of the seven theological attitudes one religion can take towards others), there is the tendency on the part of theology to be normative, whereas religious studies is non-judgmental. Even were theology to attempt to be non-normative in its portrayal of the nature of transcendence, as Panikkar attempts to be, the very fact that its concentration is upon Ultimate Reality and that its context is usually particular, constitutes it as theology rather than religious studies. At the same time, theological attitudes to other religions, and theological doctrines of God in different religions, are topics for impartial comparison (see Waardenburg, 1970; Schimmel and Falaturi, 1980).

In the third place, the concern of religious studies is not directly with God but with the religious phenomena of man, and man in his religious dimension; it is not directly with transcendence, but with man's response to transcendence; it is not directly with the object of man's religiousness, but with man's religiousness itself and the phenomena whereby that is manifested. Unlike theology, religious studies is concerned with the primal, archaic, and minor religions of mankind as well as the major ones; it is concerned with myth and the gods. To this extent, religious studies is part of the humanities and it has connections with the social sciences. However, there is an implied complementarity between religious studies and theology. This is the import of the thinking of Cantwell Smith, and also of the work of Georg Schmid in his *Principles of Integral Science of Religion* (1979). As we have shown, Smith is not a theologian, but he (and Schmid) are asserting that there is a close relationship between religious studies and theology. Religious studies deals with historically demonstrable religious data, and with the religious life (or faith) that expresses itself or conceals itself in religious data. But underlying both is what Schmid calls the 'reality of religion' and what Smith calls 'God' or 'transcendence,' and these are the more direct concern of theology. Although not the same, religious studies and theology are integrally connected.

Clearly, not all scholars of religion would agree that there is such a close connection between religious studies and theology. For some, religious studies is limited to the historically demonstrable data of religion. Others would see the historically demonstrable data of religion as clues which point to the religiousness of man, and they would see religious studies as the study of man in his religious dimension. A third group would agree that religious studies is the study of man in his religious dimension but as such it is intimately associated with theology which explicates the transcendence that lies beyond man's own transcendence. At this point, the problem re-emerges that when theological content is given to the notion of transcendence this content is usually couched in the terminology of a particular religion and, to that extent, it becomes normative rather than descriptive. This appears to reintroduce the dilemma. Religious studies and comparative religion in its narrow sense are inherently plural and impartial; theology tends to be particularistic and partial. How, therefore, can they be seen to be integral?

In the fourth place, let us try to investigate a possible solution to this impasse. As we have seen, religious studies in our sense includes Christian studies, Buddhist studies, primal religious studies, etc, as separate wholes, whereas comparative religion in our sense concentrates upon the impartial comparison and classification of varied sets of religious data. Theology in our sense concentrates upon doctrines, especially doctrines of God, and insofar as they tend to arise out of particular implicit notions of revelation they usually present a normative rather than an impartial view of transcendence. Cantwell Smith avoids the issue by neglecting to give theological content to the transcendence that he claims lies behind religious studies. Panikkar takes up the issue by universalising Christian views of transcendence, thereby placing himself within the orbit of theology rather than that of religious studies. A possible solution would be to apply comparative religious categories to the notion of transcendence. This would involve accepting, as Smith does, that transcendence is ineffable; it would also involve acceptance of the fact that religious traditions have attempted to conceptualise transcendence and to that extent they have 'qualified' its ineffability. Part of the task of comparative religion is impartially to compare and classify the ways in which religions have conceptualised transcendence. Zaehner has done this by contrasting the prophetic and mystical views of transcendence and assuming that there is concordant discord between them (*Concordant Discord*, 1970); Eliade has done it in a very different way, choosing his examples mainly from primal religion, by examining various 'hierophanies' which he takes to mean 'anything which manifests the sacred' (1958a: xii); Panikkar has done it by examining functionally equivalent notions of transcendence taken from different religious systems then universalising them within Christian categories. It is not the task of comparative religion to make value judgements about concord or discord, or to universalise Christian categories, but to compare and classify the ways in which men have conceptualised and appropriated transcendence or the Sacred. At this point there is an overlap between theology and comparative religion (properly so-called).

3g. *Frederick J. Streng*

An example of this kind of approach is found in Frederick J. Streng's *Understanding Religious Man* (1969) which is the opening volume in the series *The Religious Life of Man* edited by Streng. He defines religion as 'a means of ultimate transformation' (1969: 4). For him, 'religion represents a practical technique for achieving the transformation of human life' (1969: 48). However, lying behind such a practical technique is a certain notion of ultimate reality. And as far as Streng is concerned there are four such techniques or means which are intimately bound up with four parallel notions of ultimacy. His four ways of being religious are: personally apprehending the holy; establishing the sacred through myth and sacrament; living in harmony with eternal law as preserved by seers and the learned tradition; and attaining freedom through spiritual insight. These four ways of being religious are similar to Panikkar's three forms of spirituality (see Whaling, 1979b), with the qualification that Streng does not attempt to ally them with the trinity or any particular theological expression. Like Panikkar, he is interested in the 'ultimacy' whereby religion is enabled to be a means of transformation, but he is content to analyse this ultimate reality comparatively, and he is thus engaging in comparative religion rather than universalisation theology. Like Panikkar he is also suggesting that religious traditions are not monolithic but that they can each contain different ways of being religious and therefore different notions of 'ultimacy.' He writes (1969: 48):

While each "way" is found to some extent in all the major world religions, one or two ways tend to dominate the orthodox, or most commonly accepted, expression of a particular religious tradition. By describing these different ways of being religious, we suggest that different religious traditions such as Hinduism, Buddhism, and Islam are not single monolithic entities (often identified as systems of theology or religious ideas), but a combination of a various means whereby men transform their lives.

By comparison with Smith, Zaehner and Panikkar, Streng gives examples from both major and primal religions to illustrate his four ways of being religious. Personal apprehension of the holy, for example, is to be found in the primal religious awareness of *mana*, the Jewish awareness of the Lord God of hosts, and the Vedic awareness of *Agni* (fire) and *Uśas* (dawn) as life-giving forces. It is to be found in the cosmic visions of Isaiah 6: 5, and the Bhagavad Gītā's eleventh section; it is to be found in the intense devotionalism of Wesley and St. Francis, the Hindu *bhakti* saints, and the founders of the new religions of Japan; it is to be found in the service offered by the Muslim or the Jew to an unincarnate Lord. Establishing the sacred through myth and sacrament is to be found in the mythical and sacramental response to the revelation of the sacred found in the *devas* of India and the *kami* of Japan; through the natural seasonal ritual responses of the primal and archaic religions; through ritual participation in the sacred acts of God as interpreted by Christians, Jew, and Muslims; through the ritual force of sacred words, such as 'Om,' 'Amen,' the Nembutsu, and the sayings of the Qur'ān; through *rites de passage*; and through the power of religious leaders, sacred buildings, and iconographical and aesthetic symbols, sacramentally to evoke an awareness of the sacred among people. Living in harmony with cosmic law is to be found in the Hindu (and Buddhist) following of Dharma, the Chinese following of Li (and Tao), and the Christian, Jewish, and Muslim following of the will of God as found in the Gospel, the Torah, and the Sharī'ah. Attaining freedom through spiritual insight is to be found in Hindu *yoga*, Buddhist meditation, Sūfī Islam, Christian mysticism, Taoist and Zen spiritual practice, and the various movements that can be included within the general heading of 'mysticism.'

In his impartial and comparative analysis of the four traditional modes of being religious, Streng assumes that there is a transcendent reality, that has a non-wordly and transhuman reference, lying behind the particular expressions of man's religiousness. However, he also points out that, especially in the modern Western world, there are four dimensions of human existence in which some people have found religious significance that do not point beyond themselves to transcendent reality or transhuman power. He terms them the 'aesthetic, rational, temporal-spatial and political modes of ordering existence' (1969: 83). It is not our purpose to analyse at this point Streng's notion that artistic creativity, the use of reason, the scientific world-view, and political and economic life can be *in themselves* means of ultimate transformation. We may note in passing that Zaehner sees Jungian psychology and dialectical materialism as religious expressions; Panikkar includes gnosis, humanity, goodness, and truth under the heading of things that may convey salvation; and Smith allows that the humanist orientation of nobility and force, dignity and commitment, and coherence and trust represents 'a living tradition with its own metaphysical under-pinnings, its own apprehension of or by transcendence, and ... its own type of faith' (1979: 134). The difference is that Zaehner sees Jungian archetypes and dialectical materialism as being fulfilled by Christ, and Panikkar sees gnosis, humanity, goodness, and truth as encompassed within his universalisation theology, whereas Streng and Smith are content to analyse particular apprehensions of transcendence or reality comparatively and in their own terms. This constitutes them as comparative religionists rather than theologians.

4. Comparative Religion and Phenomenological Typology

Our concern during the rest of this chapter is to investigate the different ways in which religious traditions, phenomena, themes, and patterns have been impartially compared and contrasted. One of the ways of practising this kind of comparison has been by means of phenomenological typologies.

It is not our brief, at this point, to scrutinise the phenomenological method *qua* method. This has been attempted exhaustively in a previous chapter. Our purpose is rather to examine the contribution made by phenomenological typology to comparative religion as such. However, before going on to do this, it is necessary to place phenomenological typology within a wider perspective.

4a.

The philosophical phenomenology associated with Husserl (1962, original 1913) had used phenomenology as a way of renewing philosophy. In their self-understanding of what they were attempting to do, the philosophical phenomenologists supposed that the step forward they were taking was as epoch-making as those previously taken by Descartes and Kant. Husserl wished to get back to phenomena, back to 'things in themselves.' He saw phenomena as those things that are given to consciousness, and he considered that in order to get back to naked phenomena it was necessary to employ *epoché*. By this he meant putting one's preconceptions, ideas, and beliefs into brackets in order to get back to the original phenomena. He conceived this *epoché* as unfolding in five stages. First, there was the putting into brackets of psychologism, one's personal emotions, one's likes and dislikes, in order to get back to what is given; second, there was the putting into brackets of theories and ideas in order to get back to things in themselves; third, there was the putting into brackets of all philosophy in order to isolate the phenomena that appear; fourth, having performed this threefold *epoché*, there was the further step of getting behind the externals of phenomena in order to get through to their inwardness, the technical term for this process being the exercise of *Einfühlung* (empathy); fifth, there was the final step of getting behind the accidents of phenomena in order to unfold their essence (*eidos*), the technical term for this process being 'eidetic vision.'

When the phenomenology of religion emerged in continental Europe through Kristensen's lectures from 1925 onwards (translated by John Carman as *The Meaning of Religion*, 1960), and through the publication in 1933 of van der Leeuw's book *Phänomenologie der Religion* (translated by J.E. Turner as *Religion in Manifestation and Essence*, 1938), a school began to form which adapted some of the insights of philosophical phenomenology for its own purposes. The phenomenologists of religion reacted against certain tendencies that had been present in the study of religion during the first part of the century: the evolutionism of the early anthropologists; the implied reductionism of sociologists such as Durkheim, and psychologists such as Freud; the value judgments of theologians who were depracatory of the positive in other religions; the contextual historicism of historians, such as those of the *religionsgeschichtliche Schule*, who interpreted religion in terms of historical continuities; and the isolationism of orientalists who were concerned only about the religion of their own particular region, and that often from a mainly literary viewpoint. In reacting to these tendencies, the phenomenologists implicitly applied the criteria of Husserl in two stages. In the first place, they applied *epoché* in order to avoid the value judgments of the theologians and the implied reductionism of other disciplines in regard to religion. Together with *epoché*, they applied *Einfühlung* to attempt to interpret religions empathetically by taking seriously the believer's standpoint. At this point, phenomenology was a fresh general approach to the study of religion rather than a particular method. It was a recognition of the need to put one's own convictions into brackets and to empathise with others, in order to understand others, that has become implicit in much religious research. At the second stage, the phenomenologists applied the notion of eidetic vision to the study of religion and this led them into the realm of phenomenological typology. This application of the notion of phenomenological essences to the study of religion represented a particular way of comparing religions. Phenomenological typology was now more than a merely general approach.

4b.

The debate about the meaning and importance of phenomenology of religion has been long and confused, and it is not our purpose to repeat here what has been discussed elsewhere in this volume. Again the problem is partly semantic. Phenomenology of religion can be seen as an umbrella term virtually equivalent to the general study of religion (and therefore equivalent to 'comparative religion' as an umbrella term); as a general approach that forms a basis for the whole study of religion through its emphasis upon the principles of *epoché* and *Einfühlung*; as a particular discipline radically separate from, but nevertheless linked with the history of religion, and the other branches of religious studies; or as a particular way of doing comparative religion in the narrower sense. In this chapter, we have interpreted comparative religion and theology in their narrower senses, and we feel that there is merit in applying the same process to the term phenomenology of religion. Religious studies as a synonym for the general study of religion has absorbed the phenomenological principles of *epoché* and *Einfühlung* into its ongoing methodology. Phenomenological typology is essentially part of comparative religion, and we shall treat it as such. There is therefore, according to this reasoning, less *raison d'être* for phenomenology of religion as a separate enterprise.

Clearly not all scholars will agree that *epoché* and *Einfühlung* have become basic principles of non-theological religious studies, or that the elements of the phenomenological method are more properly constituent parts of comparative religion, history of religion, and philosophy of religion. I offer this suggestion as an attempt to advance the methodological debate, and as prolegomena to our review of the varied comparative approaches to the study of religion.

4*c*.

The outstanding scholar in the investigation of phenomenological typology in recent times has been Mircea Eliade, and we shall analyse his thought as a representative example of this genre. He stands, as it were, on the shoulders of Rudolf Otto (1923, 1930, 1931, 1932), Gerardus van der Leeuw (1928, 1937, 1938, 1948), and Joachim Wach (1944, 1951, 1958, 1968), but has gone beyond them in a number of ways, not least in his concern for 'creative hermeneutics' and a non-theological approach.

Mircea Eliade

Eliade was born in Roumania in 1907, and he studied at the University of Bucharest where he received his M.A. degree in 1928 for a thesis on Italian philosophy from Ficino to Bruno. This early concern for renaissance humanism has remained an underlying motif of his thought. He studied under Surendranath Dasgupta at Calcutta University from 1928 to 1932. Indian religion has remained one of his deep interests, and his first non-Roumanian book was *Yoga. Essai sur les Origines de la Mystique Indienne* of 1936, arising out of his 1933 Ph.D. thesis. He lectured at Bucharest from 1933–40, and during the war he was at the Roumanian London Legation in 1940, and at the Lisbon Legation from 1941–45. From 1945 he taught at the École des Hautes Études of the Sorbonne in Paris, and from 1957 he has been professor of history of religions at Chicago where he has built up an impressive following (see Kitagawa and Long, 1969: 415–33).

It is difficult briefly to summarise Eliade's thought in that his interests are so wide, ranging through fiction writing, Eastern religion, shamanism, alchemy, phenomenology of religion, hermeneutics, primal religions, history of religion, and the renewal of Western man's religiousness (see Bibliography). However, central to his thought is the notion that there are certain basic comparative structures and patterns built into religion whereby man perceives the sacred. These take the form of hierophanies, symbols, and archetypes, and identifying these comparatively lies at the heart of the student of religion's task.

In his *Traité d'Histoire des Religions* (1949: *Patterns in Comparative Religion*, 1958a), Eliade lays bare some of these comparative structures. In this book he examines various hierophanies—structures which manifest the sacred. He analyses hierophanies of the sky, the sun, the moon, water, stones, the earth, vegetation and farming, as well as sacred places, sacred time, myths, and symbols. As he puts it, 'it is quite certain that anything man has ever handled, felt, come in contact with or loved *can* become a hierophany' (1958a: 11); however (1958a: 12):

> somewhere, at a given time, each human society chose for itself a certain number of things, animals, plants, gestures and so on, and turned them into hierophanies; and as this has been going on for tens of thousands of years of religious life, it seems improbable that there remains anything that has not at some time been so transfigured.

Nevertheless what matters for the student is not that anything can become a fleeting hierophany, but that hierophanies and symbols exhibit basic structures that can be recognised. Eliade's mode of comparison is to draw together all the examples he can find of the sacred manifesting itself in different types of hierophanies and symbols, and to lay bare their archetypal structure. He writes (1958a: 449):

> It is clear that we are faced with, respectively, a sky symbolism, or a symbolism of earth, of vegetation, of sun, of space, of time, and so on. We have good cause to look upon these various symbolisms as autonomous "systems" in that they manifest more clearly, more fully, and with greater coherence what the hierophanies manifest in an individual, local and successive fashion.

Comparison focusses, then, on groups of hierophanies and symbols; on their common elements taken from primal, archaic, and major religious traditions; on what Eliade terms 'the modalities of the sacred.' His concern is not with religious traditions, nor with particular historical contexts, as foci for comparison. His starting-point is the 'sacred' as 'an element in the structure of consciousness and not a stage in the history of consciousness' (1976, translated 1979: xiii), and his comparative foci are hierophanies and archetypal symbols such as the cosmic hierogamy, the cosmic tree, the mother earth, and the centre of the world.

Eliade's comparative method is basically that of phenomenological typology. He puts side by side types of religious phenomena drawn from all parts of the world in order to ascertain their fundamental structure and their archetypal significance. He admits (1958a: 461–2).

I have not tried to study religious phenomena in their historical framework, but merely as hierophanies. That is why, in order to throw light on the nature of water hierophanies, I did not scruple to place Christian Baptism side by side with the myths and rites of Oceania, America or Graeco-Oriental antiquity, ignoring the differences between them—or, in other words, history ... there is no hierophany that is not, from the date of its first becoming manifest, "historic" ... yet their structure remains the same in spite of this and it is precisely this permanence of structure that makes it possible to know them.

Although Eliade does not ignore history, as some critics have suggested, in that his latest work is a *Histoire des croyances et des idées religieuses* (vol. 1, 1976), nevertheless he considers that 'the major religious attitudes came into existence once and for all from the moment when man first became conscious of the position he stood in within the universe' (1958a: 463). When, in the first volume of his *Histoire*, he traces the growth of the religious ideas of palaeolithic man, mesolithic and neolithic man, the Mesopotamians, the Egyptians, the Megalithic civilisations, the Hittites and Canaanites, the early Jews, the Indo-Europeans, the early Indians, the early Greeks, Zarathustra, and Israel, Eliade is merely uncovering particular expressions of the fundamental unity of religious phenomena that are structurally and archetypally part of man *qua* man. For Eliade, the inexhaustible newness of religious expressions as they unfold in history is the disclosing of 'multiple variants of the same complexes of symbols ... as endless successions of "forms" which, on the different levels of dream, myth, ritual, theology, mysticism, metaphysics, etc., are trying to "realize" the archetype' (*Images and Symbols*, 1961: 120). The second (and presumably the third) volume of Eliade's *Histoire* presupposes the same pattern, the nature of which is indicated by passages in volume one such as, 'the struggle to take the place of time that characterizes the man of the modern technological societies, had already begun in the Iron Age' (1979: 55). As we have seen, for Eliade Christian baptism is 'new' in the sense that it provides an interesting and novel expression of a water hierophany; the cross is 'new' in the sense that it provides an interesting and novel expression of the archetypal symbol of the cosmic tree. Historical newness of itself is not important. What does matter is that every hierophany presupposes a system of meanings and a structure of the sacred. The more historical examples that can be examined, the better the hierophanies, symbols and archetypes will be illustrated. The historical appearances and contexts are secondary to the phenomenological typologies, for the 'dialectic of the hierophany remains one, whether in an Australian *churinga* or in the Incarnation of the Logos' (1958a: 463).

4*d*.

Clearly, Eliade's way of doing comparative religion is far more subtle and complex than we have time to illustrate in a short survey. The problems it raises for comparative religion are as follows (for descriptions and critiques of Eliade's work see: Allen, 1978; Bianchi, 1975; Dudley, 1977; Ricketts, 1973; Saliba, 1976; Smart, 1978). In the first place, there is the question of how we interpret 'history' within the history of religion. Eliade claims that religious expressions and formulations 'become "historical documents," comparable to all other cultural data, such as artistic creations, social and economic phenomena, and so forth' (1959b: 89). The problem is that 'historical documents' have a different resonance for Eliade than for the traditional historian. Historians work mainly with written documents which they use to induct historical contexts, build up historical narratives, and understand individuals and groups. Eliade's main 'historical documents' are non-written religious expressions such as myths and symbols, which stretch back in appearance far beyond the time when they are first discovered or documented; his concern is with typologies rather than historical contexts and narratives; his interest is in the structure of hierophanies and archetypal symbols rather than in the way individuals or groups interpret them. Although he does not ignore history in the sense that it is only in historical time that man can experience the sacred, Eliade's model is the *illud tempus*—the original sacred time—of the cosmogonic myth. Profane historical time is secondary to (and the antithesis of) *illud tempus* because 'what men do on their own initiative, what they do without a mythical model, belongs to the sphere of the profane: hence it is vain and illusory activity, and, in the last analysis unreal' (1959a: 97). This being the case, it is futile to expect Eliade to stress history as such, or to compare in a historical fashion. His interest in history is to examine how particular historical manifestations of hierophanies, symbols, myths, and rituals, although local, point to deeper structures of archetypal significance that have reference to the sacred. To do comparative religion, therefore, is to classify the various hierophanies, symbols, myths and rituals by their common characteristics, and to lay bare their phenomenological structures and typologies. Comparative religion is the comparison and classification of basic types and structures of religious phenomena.

In the second place, Eliade's method of comparison emphasises the importance of certain types of religious material. His primary sources of data are the primal religions, and to a lesser extent Indian religion and the archaic religions. It is significant that it is these religious expressions that stress the importance of myths, symbols, and rituals. A good example of Eliade's selection of data is to be found in *From Primitives to Zen: A Thematic Sourcebook in the History of Religions* (1967). The 1977 reprint of this work contains 88 extracts from primal religions, 93 extracts from archaic religions, and 123 extracts from the living religions most of which come from an early stage in the history of the traditions concerned. There is therefore minimum reference to contemporary major living religious traditions. Moreover, Eliade's stress upon phenomenological typology makes it difficult for him to incorporate into his approach material from the Jewish, Muslim, and Christian (especially Protestant Christian) traditions. These traditions are iconoclastic—they do not value symbols, myths, and rituals in the way that primal and Indian religions do. Eliade's concern for an archaic ontology influences his selection of data. His predilection for primal, archaic, and Indian data arises partly from his philosophical presuppositions and partly from the shape of his early career. Presumably if his early interest had been in Islam, his selection of data and his comparative theories would have been different.

In the third place, Eliade's approach minimises the importance of the religious apprehensions of particular persons or specific traditions. His emphasis is placed upon phenomena and structures rather than persons or communities. This can be a helpful way of understanding religion. For example, it may help a Christian to enlarge his understanding of the cross to know that it belongs to the hierophany of the cosmic tree, and it may help a Muslim to widen his vision of the Hajj if he is aware that it belongs to a wider structure of pilgrimage. Moreover, Eliade's approach is inherently general in its unconcern for the insights of particular traditions, and in its assumption that religious symbols and structures transcend man's consciousness and have to do more properly with the 'transconscious' part of his nature. Parochial insularity is overcome at a stroke. The problems with this approach are twofold. For most people and groups, religious or otherwise, their own self-awareness is important. They see their own religiousness in the light of their *own* religious experience, and understand aspects of their own tradition in the light of other aspects of that *same* tradition. It is a moot point, both for the scholar and the believer, whether the cross and the Hajj can be better understood within phenomenological typologies or within particular religious contexts. Perhaps the answer lies in both. The other problem is that raised by Cantwell Smith, namely that a deep knowledge and understanding of two particular traditions may lead to the recognition that authentic comparison need not necessarily follow typological lines—for example, the sacred text of one, the Qur'ān, may be equivalent to the sacred founder of another, Christ.

In the fourth place, it is clear that Eliade's way of doing comparative religion is based not so much upon objective empirical criteria but rather upon his own underlying presuppositions. We have noted some of them already: his concern to renew the desacralised West by enabling it to encounter primal and Eastern religious worldviews, his stress upon primal man as the model of religious man, his emphasis upon the 'sacred' and the hierophanies, symbols, myths, and rituals whereby it is manifested and apprehended, his penchant for structuring data into phenomenological typologies, his notion of an archaic ontology that lies behind all religions, his assumption that religious phenomena have a *sui generis* character and that they strike a chord in the 'transconsciousness' of man. Some of these presuppositions are more convincing than others, and it is not our concern to evaluate them minutely at this point. As far as comparative religion is concerned, Eliade's basic method of phenomenological typology is valuable. It is not the only way of doing comparative religion, but it is one way among others. We do not have to accept all Eliade's metaphysical underpinnings to realise that the structural grouping of religious phenomena and data can be a helpful mode of comparison and understanding. The danger comes when the claim is made that this approach or any other approach, to the study of religion in general or comparative religion in particular, is monolithic rather than complementary.

5. Jungian Psychology and Comparative Religion

5a.

Eliade's approach to comparative religion was analogous to that of other members of the Eranos Circle to which he also belonged. This circle had been dominated by the psychologist Carl Gustav Jung. It had met yearly in conference since 1933, and from 1938 on one of its dominant motifs was that of the archetype. Its members included some of the leading figures in the study of religion including Martin Buber and Gershom Scholem, D.T. Suzuki and Heinrich Zimmer, E.O. James, C.A.F. Rhys Davids and R.C. Zaehner, Raffaele Pettazzoni and Giuseppe Tucci, Mircea Eliade and Karoly Kerényi, Jean Daniélou, Friedrich Heiler and Erich Neumann, Gerardus van der Leeuw and Laurens van der Post, Joseph Campbell, Erwin Goodenough, Paul Radin and Paul Tillich. Although Eliade differed from Jung—he spoke about the transconscious rather than the unconscious, and transparent archetypes rather than unconscious archetypes—other Eranos thinkers applied Jung's psychological categories more directly to comparative religion.

Heinrich Zimmer and Joseph Campbell have been prominent in this attempt to apply Jungian concepts to comparative religion. They share with Eliade a concern for the spiritual shallowness of Western culture, a desire to understand the religion and especially the myths of other cultures, and a solicitude to renew Western culture by means of the myths and religious symbols of others which are really the myths and symbols of the 'self' of man.

5b.

Zimmer lived from 1890 to 1943, and his main works in English were completed and edited by Joseph Campbell (*Myths and Symbols in Indian Art and Civilisation*, 1946; *The King and the Corpse*, 1948; *Philosophies of India*, 1951; *The Art of Indian Asia*, 1955). As his main concern was specifically Indian, and as he died before 1945, we shall content ourselves with mentioning him and concentrate upon Joseph Campbell who has popularised Zimmer himself, and spread Jung's ideas in the sphere of comparative religion.

Campbell, an American, was born in 1907. His *magnum opus*, which is a direct attempt to apply Jung's ideas to comparative mythology, is the four-volumed *Masks of God*: *Primitive Mythology*, (1959); *Oriental Mythology*, (1962); *Occidental Mythology*, (1964); and *Creative Mythology* (1968). His method is to bring together examples of myths in their thousands and to assemble them in a structural pattern. He describes his method in another book *The Hero with a Thousand Faces* (1959: vii–viii).

It is the purpose of the present book to uncover some of the truths disguised for us under the figures of religion and mythology by bringing together a multitude of not-too-difficult examples and letting the ancient meaning become apparent of itself. The old teachers knew what they were saying. Once we have learned to read again their symbolic language, it requires no more than the talent of an anthologist to let their teaching be heard. But first we must learn the grammar of the symbols, and as a key to this mystery I know no better modern tool than psychoanalysis. Without regarding this as the last word on the subject, one can nevertheless permit it to serve as an approach. The second step will then be to bring together a host of myths and folk tales from every corner of the world, and to let the symbols speak for themselves. The parallels will be immediately apparent; and these will develop a vast and amazingly constant statement of the basic truths by which man has lived throughout the millenniums of his residence on the planet.

Campbell shows how the mythological hero does have a thousand faces by analysing hero myths from many cultures. In the beginning the hero sets out voluntarily, forcibly, or by lure, from his everyday life to the threshold of adventure. The entrance to the threshold is guarded, but the hero triumphs over or treats with the guardian (by brother-battle, dragon-battle, offering, or charm) and passes through; or alternatively he is killed by dismemberment, crucifixion, or otherwise, and passes through in death. Having crossed the threshold, the hero travels through a realm of strange forces that either hinder him with tests or help him with magical aid. At the furthest extent of his mythological journey, the hero successfully surmounts the hurdle of a supreme ordeal, and he gains a suitable reward. This may take the form of sexual union with the world mother-goddess through sacred marriage, recognition by the world father-creator through atonement, his own divinisation through apotheosis, or, if necessary, the theft of the bride, fire, or other boon he is seeking. These are symbolic of an expansion of consciousness and being through illumination, transfiguration, or freedom. The hero's final destiny is to return to the everyday world. If the strange powers of the other world have approved the hero, he returns with them as emissaries; otherwise he flees from them, overcoming obstacles in his transforming flight. Back at the threshold again, the hero leaves behind the powers of the other world, and through return or resurrection he crosses the threshold barrier to re-enter the everyday world which he restores through the elixir boon he has won.

As far as Campbell is concerned, the mythological hero and other mythological figures are not only symptoms of the unconscious 'but also controlled and intended statements of certain spiritual principles, which have remained as constant throughout the course of human history as the form and nervous structure of the human physique itself' (1949: 257).

Anticipating the obvious criticism—that religions are different and not just 'symptoms of the unconscious'—Campbell responds (1949: viii):

Perhaps it will be objected that in bringing out the correspondences I have overlooked the differences between the various Oriental and Occidental, modern, ancient, and primitive traditions. The same objection might be brought, however, against any textbook or chart of anatomy, where the physiological variations of race are disregarded in the interest of a basic general understanding of the human physique. There are of course differences between the numerous mythologies and religions of mankind, but this is a book about the similarities; and once these are understood the differences will be found to be much less great than is popularly (and politically) supposed. My hope is that a comparative elucidation may contribute to the perhaps not-quite-desperate cause of those forces that are working in the present world for unification, not in the name of some ecclesiastical or political empire, but in the sense of human mutual understanding. As we are told in the Vedas: "Truth is one, the sages speak of it by many names".

5c.

Our comments upon latter-day Jungian comparative religion vary little from those applied to Eliade's work. Eliade's phenomenological typology is more subtle and allusive. It has been erected on the basis of an ontology and dialectic of the sacred rather than upon purely Jungian premises, and its emphasis has been upon the cosmogonic myth rather than myths and folktales in general. However, there is the same un-concern for empirical history; the same stress upon data from primal, archaic, and Indian religion; the same desire to renew Western culture; the same inclination to apply prior theory to comparative religion; the same indifference to the conscious religious intentions of particular persons and particular traditions. Nevertheless the Jungian scholars have aided the work of comparative religion by their detailed research, and their general approach, although theory-bound, has stimulated general thinking about ways of comparing religions.

6. Anthropological and Sociological Approaches to Comparative Religion

6a.

As we saw earlier, most anthropological studies of religion in recent years have been particular studies of specific situations rather than comparative studies of multiple situations. The concern of anthropologists for symbols, myths, and rituals brings them close to Eliade and the Jungians in the sense that they too are dealing with primal religion, but in general anthropologists have reacted strongly against the broad schemes and hermeneutical assumptions that characterise the work of Eliade and the Jungians. In this regard, they are similar to the historians of literate religions who have voiced doubts about the validity of the cross-religious comparisons of phenomenological typologists who extract data from their appropriate contexts.

The anthropological dilemma was well summarised by Oscar Lewis in 1955 in an article entitled 'Comparisons in Cultural Anthropology.' He showed that there are two ways of approaching anthropological comparison. One is to compare societies or religious groups that share a common history, culture, or national identity. This method of comparison offers greater controls and deeper research possibilities at the grassroots level. The second is to compare societies or religious groups that are unrelated historically, culturally, or nationally in order to seek similarities in form and structure that can point to wider typologies. This method of comparison is both more exciting and less controlled. As far as Lewis is concerned, the aim of anthropological comparison is (see Lessa and Vogt, 1958: 5):

to establish general laws or regularities; to document the range of variation in the phenomena studied; to document the distribution of traits or aspects of culture; to reconstruct culture history; to test hypotheses derived from non-Western societies.

The problem facing the anthropologist wishing to compare religions is similar to that of the sociologist and the historian in that he is concerned to make the leap from a particular context to a multiple context, from a particular community or group of cummunities to (at its widest) a global community, in his search for comparative patterns. The difference is indicated in the quotation above: the anthropologist is concerned with non-Western, and mainly non-urban tribal communities; he is concerned with all aspects, not just the religious aspect, or a community; he is concerned with living communities; and he is concerned to actually live for a time in the community in question. These concerns influence the approach of the anthropologist to comparative religion.

However, the fact remains that the anthropologist who wishes to compare must also rely upon the written work of others because he cannot become expertly familiar with more than a very few societies through his own fieldwork. At that point he is reliant upon the fieldwork, the taxonomy, and the implicit viewpoint of other anthropologists (see Honko, 1979: 35–86). Indeed, he is also reliant upon his own presuppositions which are those of his own nationality, anthropological approach, and psychological disposition! There is no completely objective anthropologist or indeed historian who is also human! Within these limits, we understand the caution of those who wish to proceed slowly in the matter of anthropological comparison (see Kluckhohn, 1953; Eggan, 1954; Evans-Pritchard, 1956). Scholte makes the relevant point that the more particular inductive approach is Anglo-Saxon whereas the more formal and structural approach is French. The Anglo-Saxons, he claims, 'assume the primacy of the behavioural act, their methods are essentially quantitative and descriptive, and their problems are phrased in diachronic-causal and empirically inductive terms' (1970: 110). In complete contrast to this inductive approach is that of Lévi-Strauss to whom we now turn.

6b. *Claude Lévi-Strauss*

Lévi-Strauss was born in Brussels in 1908, and educated at the University of Paris. Early in his career he taught in the University of Sao Paulo and in New York, and his fieldwork was done in Brazil (1935–36, 1938–39). He served for a time as cultural attaché in the French Embassy in the United States. In 1950 he became *directeur d'études* at the École Pratique des Hautes Études in Paris, and from 1959 he was also professor at the Collège de France in Paris. He has become famous as the apostle of the structural method in anthropology (see Bibliography).

In 1958, Lévi-Strauss stated baldly, 'in ethnology, as much as in linguistics,... it is not comparison that founds generalisation, but the opposite' (1963a: 28). According to this viewpoint, which is common to French structuralism in general, actions and thought are derived from fundamental structures of the mind. In other words, it is not many specific examples of actions, myths, words, or religious phenomena drawn together that point us in the direction of deeper structures of the mind and linguistics. It is the fundamental structures of the mind and linguistics that point us back to particular comparative examples. Theory leads to comparison rather than comparison to theory; one deducts from the general to the particular rather than inducts from the particular to the general. To this extent, Lévi-Strauss is nearer to Eliade and the Jungians than to the more empirically concerned historians and anthropologists.

The structural approach predates Lévi-Strauss. It was introduced into linguistics by F. de Saussure at the beginning of the century, and was later adapted by other areas of thought including logic, mathematics, the social sciences, poetics, and (especially through Chomsky) modern linguistics. Vladimir Propp's work, although only translated from the Russian in 1958 as *The Morphology of the Folktale*, was important in that, way back in the 1920s, he was identifying the structural laws that could be applied from oral tradition to a wide variety of sacred or profane texts. Lévi-Strauss was therefore applying to the world of kinship, primitive classification, and myth a method that was already implicitly present in other disciplines, especially in France. As far as comparative religion is concerned, the approach has been applied to myth and to some extent to religious texts rather than to world religions in general.

Lévi-Strauss describes his general method as follows (*Totemism*, 1963b: 84):

The method we adopt, in this case as in others, consists in the following operations: (1) define the phenomenon under study as a relation between two or more terms, real or supposed; (2) construct a table of possible permutations between these terms; (3) take this table as the general object of analysis which, at this level only, can yield necessary connections, the empirical phenomenon considered at the beginning being only one possible combination among others, the complete system of which must be reconstructed beforehand.

It is only fair to state that empirical phenomena are not completely irrelevant to Lévi-Strauss. By investigating and comparing different examples of myths and religious and other phenomena, he hopes, by analysing their possible combinations and permutations, to uncover the basic structure of the human mind. However, empirical phenomena remain means rather than ends. As he puts it (*Mythologiques*, vol I, 20):

Nous ne prétendons donc pas montrer comment les hommes pensent dans les mythes mais comment les mythes se pensent dans les hommes, et à leur insu.

Underlying statements such as these is the notion that the human mind contains a universal logical structure that is most clearly evidenced in the myths of primal religion. According to this viewpoint, myths began as oral traditions connected with religious rituals, but they have come down to us transposed into modern languages divorced from the original ritual context. Nevertheless, they keep their basic structural characteristics which can be unravelled with the right modes of comparison and the correct code. Lévi-Strauss's fieldwork and a good amount of his writing relates to the myths of South America, and by analysing them he shows the rules of logic underlying the combinations and transformations between structural relationships built into these myths. Thus the relationships between humans in term of sex, status, interdependence, or enmity can be reflected directly or indirectly in the relationships between men, gods, animals, birds, or insects; in the relationships between earthly features, heavenly bodies, seasons, climates, or times; in the relationships between eating, birth, menstruation, sexual intercourse, or excretion; in the relationships between different foods and their modes of preparation; in the relationships between different sounds and silences; in the relationships between human dresses and the plants or animals connected with them; and in the relationships between different smells and tastes (see Leach, 1970: 66–7). At a more basic level, Lévi-Strauss is pointing to binary contrasts between such sets of dichotomies as male and female, wet and dry, cooked and raw, naked and dressed, sound and silence, light and darkness, sacred and profane, and so on. These are not confined to primal thought but are built into modern categories such as plus and minus—they cohere together as representing the basic structure of the human mind.

A good application of Lévi-Strauss's method is found in Marcel Detienne's *Les jardins d'Adonis* (1972). In this analysis of the structure of the different elements of Greek myth and ritual, Detienne shows how the contrast between Demeter and Persephone and Myrrha and Mintha is reflected in the contrasts between chastity and sexuality, order and disorder, marriage and incest, dryness and dampness, aromatic plants and cereals, different religious festivals, and different members of the religious pantheon. Superficially, there is a similarity to Eliade's contrasts between the cosmic polarities of right and left, high and low, day and night, life and death, and the rhythm of seasons and vegetations, and his 'human' polarities of male and female, good and evil, friend and stranger, and so on. In Eliade's case, the difference is that the complete set of polarities is subsumed within his master polarity of sacred and profane, and this introduces a 'transcendental' or 'vertical' reference that is not obviously present in the work of Lévi-Strauss.

We see certain basic factors at work in the approach of Lévi-Strauss: his lack of contextual concern, his assumption that religious man's own apprehension of his religion is secondary, his separation of myth from other integrated factors, his concentration on myth as crucial, his emphasis upon primal religion as his basic model, his depreciation of inductive history, his focus on the paradigm of language, his notion that binaries are the focus of comparative contrasts, his stress upon the innate logic of the human mind, his implicit selection of data, and his view that religion is part of a greater whole. Some of these comments can be addressed to anthropology in general, others refer more directly to Lévi-Strauss's structuralism. It is clear that there is a sense in which man *qua* man is a mytho-logical being; it is clear that Lévi-Strauss has deeply influenced the study of primitive thought; it is clear too that his particular researches are important. It remains to be seen whether Lévi-Strauss's structural theories can be applied on a universal scale to major texts and major religions. In any case, his deductive way of comparing religious phenomena must remain a complementary rather than a monolithic approach; it is one way among others of comparing religious data.

6c.

To return to the more mundane level of the inductively inclined anthropologists, we shall mention briefly some who have applied Evans-Pritchard's conception of the role of anthropology, namely to observe and describe the social life of a primal tribe, to reveal its underlying structure, and to compare the structural patterns thus revealed with patterns in other societies in order 'better to construct a typology of forms, and to determine their essential features and the reasons for their variations' (1951: 62). As we said earlier, although the theory of comparison is built into social anthropology, examples of comparative application have been relatively rare. The widespread practice of classifying dualistically in terms of right and left is demonstrated by a series of essays edited by Needham entitled *Right and Left* (1973). This is illustrated by an in-depth study of the Indian caste system by Dumont (1970) in which he views it in terms of purity and pollution, right and left. Mary Douglas (1966, 1973) illustrates the same basic theme of purity and pollution by relating it to order and disorder, moral values, and the coherence of society. G.S. Kirk, although not an anthropologist, has applied an inductive typological approach to myth in his analysis of myths in the ancient (rather than primal) world. He points out that myths can be structured according to their functions of narration, ritual repetition, or explanation (1970). Swanson (1960) analyses fifty primal and ancient societies with a view to discovering the correlation between different ideas of the supernatural and the social background of the society concerned, and he finds suggestive links between social structures and beliefs, for example between monotheism and social hierarchy, and ancestor spirits and certain kinship groups. Lewis (1971) employs a similar approach in analysing the correlation between religious ecstasy and the social structures of different societies. Lauri Honko sees the trichotomy of rites of passage, calendar rites, and crisis rites as being a 'cultural universal' (1979: 379). Victor Turner (1957, 1967, 1968, 1975) analyses in depth the universality yet differing roles of symbols.

We mention these studies fleetingly because they are referred to elsewhere in volume two. The key question would appear to be to what extent are rituals, symbols, and myths crucial and universal, and, if this is the case, to what extent can we generalise from primal religion to religion and man in general? Social anthropologists tend to be ultra-cautious in attempting relatively minor generalisations and comparisons even within primal religion. Yet implicit in much of their work is the subtle suggestion that primal man and his myths, rituals, and symbols constitute the proper basis for the study of man and his religion. The realisation is dawning that anthropological comparison tends to be somewhat static, and there is the need not only to take major religions more seriously but also to analyse more comparatively the processes of change even within primal religion itself.

6d.

Sociology too has fought shy of broad comparative models during our period. Weber remains the great name, but he was well before our era. Many of the sociological comparisons of recent times have been limited to restricted periods or areas. An obvious example is the work done on modern church/sect typology by Becker (1932), Wach, Yinger (1946, 1957), Martin (1962, 1967), and Wilson (1961, 1967, 1973). Church/sect typologies are both modern and Christian so that the comparison operates *within* a religion rather than between religions. Another example is the work done on comparing new cults as agents of social and religious change (Worsley, 1968; Cohn, 1970; Wilson, 1975). These topics have been dealt with elsewhere, and we will not spend time on them here. A further and broader example is the attempts that have been made to work out comparisons of types of religious evolution. However insofar as they belong more naturally to a discussion of historical comparison we are content to deal with them when we come to that section.

A scholar who was interested in sociological comparison and wider comparative issues is Joachim Wach, and we will pause to examine his comparative work at this point.

6e. Joachim Wach.

Wach was born in 1898 in Saxony. After two years in the army, he enrolled in 1918 in the University of Leipzig and completed his Ph.D. degree there in 1922, his dissertation topic being 'Basic Elements of a Phenomenology of the Idea of Salvation'. Wach's major area of study at this time was history of religion and his secondary areas were philosophy of religion and oriental studies. However it was the faculty of philosophy that he joined in 1924 when he became a staff member at Leipzig, and he remained there until he left Germany in 1935. From 1935 to 1945 he was professor of the history of religions at Brown University in Providence Rhode Island, a well-known liberal arts institution. His final move was to the University of Chicago where he became chairman of the history of religions programme within the federated theological faculty. Wach remained at Chicago until his death in 1955. It is interesting to note that Wach received a Th.D. degree from Heidelberg in 1930, and that towards the end of his life he received (but turned down) an invitation to occupy a chair of systematic theology at Marburg that had at one time been held by Rudolf Otto. In spite of his differences from Otto and the changes brought about by his move to America, Wach remained within the Otto tradition.

Joachim Wach's interests were wider than sociology of religion or even comparative issues. As Waardenburg puts it, 'Wach may be called one of the most universal minds in the field' (1973: 63). His only contribution to the minutiae of our knowledge of particular traditions was his small book on Mahāyāna Buddhism (1925). However, he reflected and wrote widely on hermeneutics (1968), the study of religious experience (1951), comparative religion (1958), sociology of religion (1931, 1944), particular themes in the study of religion (1922, 1925, 1932), and the general methodological problems facing the study of religion (numerous articles). It is not our purpose to investigate the total thought of Wach at this point but rather to examine his contribution to thinking about comparative, and especially sociologically comparative, issues. Nevertheless it is salutary to remember that the different facets of his thought are inter-related.

Wach's concern for sociological and comparative issues arose out of his concern for the nature and destiny of man, viewed both corporately and humanely. He recognised three basic quests of mankind that were related to three basic academic areas: ultimate reality related to theology, man himself related to anthropology, the social sciences, and the humanities, and the nature of the universe related to cosmology and science. His primary interest was in man, and he followed this through in both his sociological and comparative work.

Wach differentiated between theology and what he called the science of religion. He stated: (1944: 1)

Theology, a normative discipline, is concerned with the analysis, interpretation, and exposition of one particular faith. The general science of religion.... is essentially descriptive, aiming to understand the nature of all religions. There is thus a quantitative and qualitative difference between the approaches, methods, and goals of the two disciplines.

He considered that the general science of religion had as its province phenomenology, history, psychology, and sociology of religion. He therefore viewed the sociology of religion as part of the overall study of religion rather than as part of the overall study of theology (Troeltsch 1931, Niebuhr 1929) or as part of the overall study of sociology per se. His comparative sociological views arose out of this perspective. He wrote:

there is a third field of religious expression which is only now gaining the measure of attention it merits: religious grouping, religious fellowship and association, the individual, typological, and comparative study of which is the field of the sociology of religion. (1944: 2)

In practice, Wach did little 'individual' study in the sociology of religion. His work was essentially typological and comparative. Insofar as we are suggesting in this chapter that phenomenological typology is part of comparative religion, it is true to say that Wach's work in the sociology of religion was basically comparative through and through.

In the first place, he analysed comparatively religious groups that were naturally part of society: family cults, kinship cults, local cults, racial cults, national cults, and cult associations based on sex and age. He adduced examples from many religious traditions, primal and major, living and dead, to enforce his comparative groupings, and he pointed out that although the various groupings he mentioned are both social and religious in nature nevertheless social and religious cohesion are not equated.

In the second place, he analysed religious groupings that were not naturally part of society but which arose out of more specifically religious tendencies. In other words he compared a number of specifically founded religious groups. He pointed out that the development of founded religious groups was often promoted by a growing differentiation in sociological, political and cultural structures in more advanced societies, and by the advancing richness of religious experience in individuals and groups. Wach investigated sociologically and comparatively the nature and organisation of religious secret societies, mystery religions, the *sampradaya*-type groups found typically in Hinduism, circles of disciples that gather round a charismatic leader, religious brotherhoods, ecclesiastical-type bodies, protesting bodies that grow up within wider religious communities, and independent groups or sects that secede from a wider religious community. His illustrations are detailed and comprehensive in scope, and they draw more widely from the major living religions. Wach was concerned to erect a typology of the main founded religious groupings, as well as the main natural religious groupings that are found more normally in primal societies. He was also concerned to analyse the internal sociological structures within founded religious communities and in this way he foreshadowed some of the later work on church/sect typologies within Christianity and some of the later studies of the different branches within other religious traditions.

In the third place, Wach pointed out that social differentiation within society, for example variation of occupation, rank, and status, had its own effect upon religious attitudes and institutions. Occupational differences may have religious consequences even in primal societies, and Wach gave examples to illustrate this from Australia, the eskimos, South India, New Guinea, Melanesia, the American Indians, South Africa, West Africa, and East Africa. In higher civilisations, social differences may have more pronounced religious consequences. For example certain 'professions' such as those of warrior, merchant, and peasant have so influenced the development of religion that Wach felt justified in singling out the religion of the warrior, the religion of the merchant, and the religion of the peasant as special types. For the religion of the warrior, Wach focussed upon Mexico, Mithraism, and Zen Buddhism; for the religion of the merchant he focussed upon Vallabhacári Hinduism, the Parsis, and the Jains; and for the religion of the peasant he focussed upon West Asia.

In the fourth place, Wach made the point that there are important comparisons between religions in regard to the relationship they adopt towards the state. This problem does not normally arise in primal religions where religious and social groupings are intermingled, but it does arise with the appearance of the state and especially with the appearance of higher religions which are not normally co-extensive with the state and therefore have to formulate conceptually and act out pragmatically what their relationship towards the state should be. Wach pointed out that this relationship varies but that certain basic comparative attitudes can be extrapolated. At one extreme there is the close connection between the state and religious cults ranging from virtual identity to the intimate but not identical relationship to be found in Zoroastrian Sassanid Persia, Shinto Japan, and many Islamic nations. At the other extreme there is a radical separation between religion and state to be found for example in the secret and mystery religions. In between there are various intermediate possibilities. Wach illustrated these by analysing Confucianism which is closely tied to the state; Buddhism which in its Tibetan form dominates the state, in its Theravāda form is integrated with the state, and in its Mahāyāna form is often separate from the state but dominated by it; and Christianity which has witnessed a number of relationships between state and church, in the elucidation of which Wach anticipates the later work of Niebuhr (1956).

Finally, Wach analysed comparatively the different types of religious authority exemplified in founders, reformers, prophets, seers, magicians, diviners, saints, priests, contemplatives, and charismatic groups. It is the charisma, leadership authority, or spiritual power of these individuals or groups that have an important part to play in the founding, continuity, and transformation of religious cummunities. Again Wach illustrated this typologically with a vast range of examples from religious traditions past and present.

Although we have concentrated upon Wach's sociological religious comparisons, he was also concerned with comparison over a wider field. He took his basic point of departure from religious experience and compared the different types of religious experience under the headings of thought, action, and human fellowship. The third category, human fellowship, we have already considered in our summary of Wach's sociological comparisons. Under the heading of thought, Wach included myth and symbol, doctrines, and dogmas, and he compared especially the basic doctrines of ultimate reality, man, and the universe. Under the heading of action, Wach included worship, sacraments, sacrifice and prayer, and he began a preliminary comparison of these themes across the religious board. In some of his particular monographs he also touched upon individual comparative themes such as salvation (1922), master and disciple (1925), man (1932), and (less comparatively) death (1934).

A number of Wach's general insights have been incorporated into the work of the Chicago school, and his influence has lived on through the medium of that group. However, the sociological comparisons we have examined in this section have been less influential than might have been expected. There are basically three reasons for this and we will glance at them briefly because they raise questions of wider interest. Firstly, Wach's criterion for the sociological study of religion, 'an impartial and objective approach, with the facts studied without bias' (1944: 8) did not entirely square with his wider approach to the study of religion based upon a hermeneutical principle that sought 'a fuller vision of what religious experience can mean, what forms its expression may take, and what it might do for man' (1958: 9). Secondly, his typological method which was applied not only to religious communities but also to religious thought and religious action presupposed the decontextualising of many phenomena in the sociology of religion in order to erect the typology concerned. There was the possibility that historical and sociological contexts would be too swiftly transcended in the interests of comparative typology. Thirdly, Wach distinguished carefully between social philosophy which involved conceptualising normative theories of society and sociology of religion which he took to be descriptive. From the sociological viewpoint Wach's typologies often appeared to be more than descriptive. Moreover sociologists did not necessarily conceive their task as merely that of description. Their craft demanded analysis and the possibility of theory formation within the sociology of religion but they could see no compelling reasons why the hermeneutical principles involved should be taken from the study of religion rather than the study of sociology. The debate was and is a perennial one. Despite a certain lack of appreciation for Wach's sociological comparative religion it remains, together with Weber's work, a helpful and suggestive approach not only to sociological comparison but also to comparative religion in general.

7. Comparative Historical Approaches

7a.

As we have remarked earlier, history can mean different things to different people. To Cantwell Smith it meant cumulative tradition, to Campbell psychohistory, to Eliade the unsacralised profane. For our purposes, it can mean six things: the historical/critical method as applied to texts, the historical/critical method as applied to empirical situations, comparative views of history in different religions, the whole history of particular religions, the global history of world religions in general, and cross-historical comparisons as such. The three categories that particularly interest us are comparative views of history, the global history of world religions, and cross-historical comparisons as such.

The three topics in which we have the least concern nevertheless form the indispensable basis for our wider concerns. We can only erect a global history of religion on the basis of a knowledge of the histories of particular religions, and we can only come to a knowledge of the histories of particular religions through the critical analysis of the texts and empirical historical data of those religions. Likewise we can only set up cross-historical comparisons, on the basis of a knowledge of each religion afforded us partly by the historical method. If it be argued that the historical method is typically Western, it must be admitted that this is the case. But this only serves to raise the wider question as to whether the whole enterprise of the study of religion, including *all* the methods of studying religion, is not basically Western; it raises the question as to how the study of religion can be made genuinely global without losing the benefits its Western roots have provided.

7b. Comparative Views of History

Different religions have evolved different approaches to the question of what history and time signify. There are philosophical issues underlying this question which complicate any attempt at comparison. The question, however defined, is nevertheless basic, and there is a sense in which this topic, although separable for purposes of analysis, points beyond itself to the total Weltanschauung of the religion concerned. A comparison of the views of history in different religions shades off into a comparison of the different worldviews of religions. We shall look briefly at four writers who have dealt with this theme, namely Eliade, W.C. Smith, Brandon, and Cairns. They are representative of four contrasting approaches.

In *Cosmos and History* (1959, *Le Mythe de l'éternel retour*, 1949; *The Myth of the Eternal Return*, 1954) Eliade compares the primal, archaic, Indian, Judaeo-Christian, and modern views of history. As we saw in our discussion of Eliade, his basic paradigm of religious man is found in primal religion. For primal man it is the time before time, the *illud tempus* before history, that provides the model for living within history. Primal man can sacralise the present profane historical time by repeating the myths, celebrating the rituals, and symbolising the archetypes of that *illud tempus*. Present history, in the sense of a series of autonomous and unexpected events, is inconceivable to primal man—he makes sense of history and the suffering it brings by reference to primordial history and its models. The archaic world, however, especially the ancient Mediterranean-Mesopotamian world, connected man's sufferings and history with those of a god who gave reality and normality to history and suffering. The most representative was Tammuz whose suffering, death, and resurrection gave meaning not just to the agricultural and lunar cycle but also to human life in history. The Indian religions by contrast stressed the notions of *karma* and *saṃsāra* whereby history and its present sufferings are explained in terms of one's good and bad deeds and the rebirths that follow from them. Not only will there be final release from the round of rebirths, but history itself proceeds from a golden age through three degenerating stages to a final destruction

which will lead after a period of quiescence to a repetition of the four
ages in a continuing cyclical process. Very different were the Hebrews,
and later the Christians, who looked upon history as a theophany, as the
arena in which God revealed Himself; history therefore had significance
in itself as involving the creation, sacralisation, and consummation of
the world process under God. Finally, modern western man has secular-
ised aspects of the Judaeo-Christian view so that 'historicism'', with its
generally linear, progressive, and empirical emphases, has delivered man
into the hands of the absolutism and therefore the terror of history.

In some ways, this is the nearest Eliade comes to comparing specific
religious traditions as opposed to setting up phenomenological typologies. However he assumes the inferiority of western 'historicism' and
the primacy of 'archaic ontology'; he mentions few of the actual historical data of particular religions; and he tends to subsume all non-
secular religions, in spite of their differences, within 'the myth of the
eternal return'. Nevertheless, his classifications are valuable.

. Wilfred Cantwell Smith's *Islam in Modern History* (1957) is very different. His concern for Islam, for modern history, and for historical data
is in marked contrast with Eliade's concern for primal religion, traditional historical structures, and archetypes. Smith compares the views of
history in the Hindu, Christian, Muslim, and Marxist traditions. He
writes (p. 29):

By ignoring complexities, one might arrange representatives of these faiths in a graded
series as follows: the Hindu, for whom ultimately history is not significant; the Christian,
for whom it is significant but not decisive; the Muslim, for whom it is decisive but not
final; the Marxist, for whom it is all in all.

To substantiate his thesis, Smith gives examples from inductive
history, especially Christian and Muslim. The contrast between Christ's
worldly failure and Muhammad's worldly success is symbolic of the
more decisive emphasis given to worldly historical success in Islam. The
original model of historical success given to Islam by Muhammad and
the four early caliphs, although weakened by the fall of Baghdad in 1258,
and by the trauma of early modern Muslim weakness, has never been
fully lost, and is a partial factor in the contemporary Muslim resurgence.

The original Muslim historical model, based upon an integration of religious, cultural and wider matters, has remained vibrant. Smith's aim is to compare the basic attitudes to history that have evolved within the major religious communities and to show how these affect the present situation. He therefore ignores primal religion and concentrates upon the contemporary period.

Samuel George Frederick Brandon

S.G.F. Brandon spent much of his academic life in investigating the approach of different religions to the question of time and history. He tackled this topic in three of his books (*Time and Mankind*, 1951; *Man and His Destiny in the Great Religions*, 1962; and *History, Time and Deity*, 1965), and he was a founder member of the International Society for the Study of Time which first met in 1969. Brandon had been ordained in 1932, and had served in curacies or as an army chaplain until 1951. Although he retained an interest in Christian Studies and became widely known for his provocative views on the bearing of political matters on the life of Christ, (*The Fall of Jerusalem and the Christian Church*, 1951; *Jesus and the Zealots*, 1967; *The Trial of Jesus of Nazareth*, 1969), his appointment to the Chair of Comparative Religion at Manchester University focussed his interest upon comparative studies and from 1970 until his death in 1972 he was Secretary-General of the International Association for the History of Religions. Within the comparative field, his dominant interest remained the investigation of how men and women have responded religiously to the questions of time and history. Indeed Brandon was among the first to write what might be called 'comparative monographs'. That is to say, he took a theme, namely time and history, and compared it 'across the religious board' without any underlying hermeneutical or typological motive. As we shall see, this method of comparative religion later became more common. In effect, Brandon was using the impartial approach of *epoché* and the empathetic approach of *Einfühlung* without attempting to gain an eidetic vision into the theme of history.

In fact, Brandon's classification of views of history is not unlike Eliade's in type if not in motive. He saw five comparative ways whereby the religions of mankind have attempted to answer the problems posed by time and history. The first was that of salvation by ritual participation exemplified in the cult of Osiris in ancient Egypt. Osiris had been murdered by Seth and, resuscitated by Isis, he conquered time, became king of the dead, and became time. By repeating the appropriate rituals over mummified corpses, the Egyptians believed that they were re-enacting the death and resurrection of Osiris and obtaining for the deceased a re-awakening to life in the kingdom of the dead. The second way was that of the deification of time. This was exemplified in the Zoroastrian Zurvan, and the Kṛṣṇa of *Bhagavad Gītā* 11, who represent both the destructive and constructive aspects of death and time elevated to the rank of divinity. The third way was that of cyclical time and history. This was exemplified in the exact repetition of history envisaged in the stoic cyclical theory of the 'Great Year', in the cyclical repetition of the seasons in linear time, or in the Hindu theory of rebirth and the four *yugas*. The fourth way was that of a timeless reality beyond the circling revolutions of time and history. This was typical of mystical religion as exemplified in Plato's thought and the Buddhist *nirvāṇa*. There was the resulting paradox that the eternity beyond time could be experienced empirically within history. Finally, for prophetic religion, there was the way of God's activity in history exemplified in God's revelation to the Jews and Christ's incarnation. History was the record of God working out His purposes from creation to consummation and of man's response to the will of God.

Brandon accords with Eliade in including archaic religions in his scheme of classification. For him, by contrast with Eliade, the scheme remains simply a classification based on observation. He does not integrate the five categories into a logical scheme or an archetypal structure, and he has no prior assumption as to what time and history essentially are. In contrast to Smith, Brandon's five views of history are not separate alternatives centred in particular religious traditions. The classical Vedantic interpretation of time and history, for example, would span Brandon's second, third and fourth approaches to history, and other religions too are not necessarily limited to one approach. In this respect, his views are not dissimilar to those of Streng who had outlined four basic ways of being religious. Like Eliade, Brandon distrusts the ability of modern secularism to solve the problems of history through historicism, for 'the problem of Time abides, confronting all our seeking for significance with its chilling logic of the inevitability of decay and death' (1965: 210). However, he mounts no polemic against historicism but seeks merely to understand the nature and proportions of the problem of history through his comparative study. As we remarked earlier, his books are comparative monographs, and it was fitting that his *Festschrift*, which sadly became his memorial volume, should be a comparative study of *Man and his Salvation* (1973).

Our final example of comparative views of history is Grace Cairns' *Philosophies of History* (1963). This title intimates a recurring facet of comparative religion, namely that comparisons of a theme tend to become comparative philosophies of religion. After all, 'views of history' approximate to 'philosophies of history'. The philosopher tends to compare abstractly without regard to context, and to bring to comparative work a philosophical motive. Cairns is no exception, and a major purpose of her work is 'to show that Eastern, Western and Marxian theories of the meaning and goal of human history have much in common' (p. xv).

She stresses cyclical philosophies of history as being one of the three main philosophical approaches to the question of history. The two that she does not consider are the idea of linear progress, and the sceptical notion that history is directionless. She sees three main types of cyclical concepts of history: theories of cosmic cycles; one-cycle views of history; and culture-cycle approaches to the understanding of history. Firstly, she analyses cosmic cycles, and she begins with the origins of this view in Mesopotamia and Egypt which were related to observations of the birth-death cycle of life, the cyclical shedding of the skin by the serpent, and lunar and solar cycles. She looks, too, at the Indian mythological symbolic forms that expressed the idea of cosmic cycles, for example the dance of Śiva, the notion of the *yugas*, architectural forms, and the fire-altar ritual. She then shows how great minds developed philosophical ideas of cosmic cycles, arising out of these earlier ideas, that became the typical view of history in India, Greece, and China. Her examples include the Tibetan *maṇḍala*, the Buddhist monument of Borobudur, the yogic philosophies, Tung Chung-shu's organismic idea arising out of the *yang-yin* cycle, Taoist mysticism, Shao Yung's writings, Plato, and the Stoics. Secondly, she goes on to present some of the outstanding one-cycle patterns of cosmic and human history. She analyses the Zoroastrian, Hebrew, and Christian views of a cycle that begins with a golden age and ends with a new golden age in the kingdom of God or in paradise. This is similar to the Muslim approach. Secularists such as Condorcet converted it into a one-cycle view of progress through reason and science; Hegel developed a one-cycle-with-progress idea of history; Marx applied Hegel's dialectical scheme of history seen as Spirit to history seen as materialistic; and Aurobindo and Radhakrishnan re-interpreted the Hindu view in one-cycle terms. Finally Cairns turns to culture-cycle approaches to human history. This is more typically twen-tieth century and western, but before analysing the thought of Spengler, Sorokin and Toynbee she shows how they were anticipated by Vico and Ibn Khaldun who already saw a cyclical pattern to the rise and fall of civilisations. Her book concludes with a comparison between eastern and western cyclical patterns, and an attempt to predict the nature of the coming epoch in human history.

Cairns's work is a brave attempt to comprehend all the main views of history, eastern and western, religious and secular. Like Smith, she takes Marxism seriously; unlike him, she deals with humanists such as Condorcet. It is perhaps a weakness that she narrows down her vision from theories of cosmic cycles, through one-cycle views, to culture-cycles. Cosmic cycles span the cosmos; one-cycle views span human history; culture-cycles span small portions of human history, especially those portions that concern the modern West. It is significant that Cairns and Eliade explicitly, Smith implicitly, and Brandon indirectly, fashion their thinking to give guidance to the modern West in dealing with its contemporary problems. The question must be raised as to whether it is the task of comparative religion to solve ANY culture's problems; if the answer be affirmative, the modification may be suggested that it is global problems that are to be encompassed, not the merely parochial dilemmas of any specific portion of the globe.

7c. Global History as a basis for comparison

(i) So far we have looked at comparative views of history. Our main concern is to examine comparisons that have arisen out of the history of religion itself. The problems have been implicit in our previous discussions. How can authentic comparison be made on the foundation of inductive historical investigation? If historical contexts are viewed as primary, how can historical phenomena be lifted from their contexts to serve typological, archetypal, or other extra-historical considerations? If historical traditions have evolved in culturally bounded situations, how is comparison between traditions possible? Even if we assume that analogies or comparisons can be drawn between traditions, where do we stop the moving picture of history to make the comparisons? Are they only valid at comparable periods of history, or more universally? How do primal religions, which generally lack a recognisable history, fit into the scheme of things? Are general comparisons possible, or only comparisons involving two traditions? Is the history of religions the same thing as the history of cultures, and if not in what way does it differ, and how does this affect comparison?

The attempted answers to these questions have come under three main headings: interreligious comparison is possible in connection with overlapping historical developments which can be determined by means of a knowledge of the global history of religions; comparisons can be made of themes illustrated from the histories of many religions; and wider and more systematic comparative religious models can be built up on the basis of inductive historical foundations. We shall examine these three approaches in turn.

Attempts to conceptualise a global history of religion have been recent, but part of the implication of this endeavour has been the supposition that if different religions can be shown to have reached similar stages of development at similar periods there is a better chance of accurate comparisons between them being made. For example, Tulsi Dās can be compared more appropriately with Wesley than with St. Paul, Maimonides can be compared more appropriately with Aquinas than with Rahner.or Origen, and Aurobindo can be compared more appropriately with Iqbal than with Ghazzālī—because their historical backgrounds are more equivalent. The search for a global history of religion is an exciting endeavour because it opens up wide areas of possible mutual understanding and comparison that are not present when religions are described, however expertly, in historical isolation. Three authors, in particular namely McNeill, Bellah, and Ling, have essayed to present a global setting for the study of religion, and they will be examined now.

(ii) W.H. McNeill in *The Rise of the West* (1963) and *A World History* (1967) has surveyed the general history of the world in such a way as to bring out the importance of religions within that history. Indeed, it is almost a truism to state that, until the period of the modern West, religions have played an inherently important part in world history; before the modern period cultural and religious history have overlapped. McNeill's basic thesis is that there have been certain great breakthroughs in human history, and as a result of them, certain civilisations have become important at certain periods. The first great breakthrough (apart from the rise of man and the palaeolithic epoch which must remain vague) was the development of food production during the neolithic era. Farmers and pastoralists replaced hunters and gatherers in different parts of the world, and religious consequences followed in the wake of this change. The second great breakthrough was the rise of civilised communities in the Middle East (in Mesopotamia, Egypt, and the Indus Valley) wherein cities, writing, agricultural surpluses, and social and religious stratification became important. The Middle East remained the dominant area of the world and it influenced what later became Europe and India; in the meantime, China also emerged on the world scene. The incursions of steppe-warrior barbarians into Europe, India, and China produced interactions between the pre-existing and incoming peoples that led to the rise of these three areas to a position of rough equality with the Middle East by the sixth century BC. Around that century there was another great breakthrough in human history centred upon the rise of great religious leaders in the Middle East, Europe, India, and China, and, for the next two thousand years, these four areas developed great, parallel, equivalent, and separate civilisations. The Jewish prophets, Zarathustra, the Ionian philosophers, the Buddha, the Mahāvīra, the Upaniṣads, and Confucius were religious catalysts for these four civilisations, and the rise of Christianity within Europe and Islam in the Middle East were important new features as the two thousand year period developed. Intercultural borrowings were not negligible. For example, Buddhism spread from India into China, and Islam from the Middle East into India. But in the main the four areas were autonomous, and in a state of mutual equilibrium. The final breakthrough was the rise of the West, beginning in the sixteenth century AD with the spread of European seapower, and gaining momentum after 1750 through the scientific and technological superiority afforded to Europe by the scientific and industrial revolutions. This has led to the rise of a global community centred upon the innovations introduced by the West.

The implications of McNeill's 'secular historical' thesis for the study of religion are as follows. First, interreligious comparison works best if it is confined within his main epochs, namely the neolithic period, the period of the rise of civilised communities (c.3500–600 BC), the period of the equilibrium of the four great civilisations (c.600 BC–1500 AD), and the modern period. Second, his study places the focus upon those religions that have been at the centre of great civilisations. The consequence is that traditions that have not been so situated, such as the Jews, are underemphasised. Third, 'peripheral' regions of the world, such as Africa, America, and Australasia, are seen as backdrops to the four great Eurasian civilisations, and primal cultures and religions are undervalued. Fourth, the contemporary emergence of the Muslim Middle East, the communist world, Japan and China, and other non-Western areas, is not fully taken into account. Nevertheless, McNeill's thesis is pregnant in its importance for comparative religion and, although not specifically religious in intent, has exercised an acknowledged or unacknowledged influence upon many attempts to conceptualise a global history of religion.

A similar theory, based upon sociological rather than historical norms, is that of Robert N. Bellah. In his article on 'Religious Evolution' (1970), he outlines five key periods of religious evolution, namely the primitive (centred upon the Australian aborigines), the

archaic (centred upon Africa, Polynesian, and American primal religion, and early India, China, and the Middle East), the historic (centred
upon the emergence of the major 'world-rejecting' religions in the
historical civilisations), the early modern (centred upon the Protestant
Reformation in Europe), and the modern (centred upon contemporary
Western experience especially in America). Bellah assumes that neither
man, nor the ultimate conditions of his existence, evolve—and in this
respect, he is strikingly similar to Cantwell Smith whose constants are
man and God. What does evolve is the symbol systems of religion which
achieve, through increasing differentiation and complexity, a greater
capacity to adapt to their environment. In spite of Bellah's somewhat
simplistic analysis of the two stages of primal religion, his reliance upon
the Reformation paradigm, and his implied exaltation of the contemporary American religious situation, his scheme corresponds in essentials to McNeill's with the qualification that he has a more robust
treatment of primal religion and the contemporary period. Bellah allows
that his model is 'ideal-historical' rather than 'pragmatic-historical' in
that his stages overlap and are not inevitable. However, his stress upon
religious symbol systems, religious actions, religious organisations, and
the social implications of religious evolution, in their increasing differentiation, opens up more exact possibilities of comparison at each of
his five stages.

Trevor Ling in *A History of Religion East and West* (1968) follows a
slightly different pattern. He concentrates more directly upon the history of religion as opposed to the history of culture or civilisation. He
gives more attention to Judaism, and less attention to Chinese religion,
communism, and humanism. In the main, his history of religion is the
history of the major religions of Hinduism, Buddhism, Judaism,
Christianity, and Islam. His analysis is in seven stages. In the beginning
he looks at the early city-civilisations of Asia, early Jewish history, and
early Indian religion under the heading of 'nomads, peasants and kings.'
He is interesting, comparatively, in the claim he makes for the importance of kingship at this stage of religious development, both in its
significance for non-Hebrew religious systems, and in the growing
conjunction between Yahweh and near eastern kingship that 'was increasingly accepted within Israel, a conjunction which was to have

important consequences in the subsequent history of Western religion' (1968: 61). His second stage correlates with the sixth century BC watershed stressed by our other authors centred upon the Hebrew prophets, Zarathustra, the Buddha, the Mahāvīra, and Confucius, and he terms it the period of 'prophets and philosophers.' His third stage, entitled 'scribes, monks and priests,' lasts from c.500 BC to 70 AD, and encompasses early Buddhism, the reorientation of Judaism and Brahmanism, and the rise of Christianity. He stresses at this stage the diffusion of religious ideas across cultural boundaries. His fourth stage, headed 'creeds and conformity,' traces the emergence and spread of Christianity, Hinduism, and Mahāyāna Buddhism as religious traditions supporting and supported by great cultures. His fifth stage, under the heading of 'religion and civilisation,' is restricted to the rise of Islam and the expansion of Buddhism as 'genuinely popular, religiously inspired' cultures (1968: 256). His penultimate stage is entitled 'theologians, poets and mystics' and centres on medieval Hinduism and Christendom, the coming of age of Islam, and Buddhist civilisation in wider Asia from c.500–1500 AD; it ends with a discussion of religious contrasts and conflicts from 1500–1800 AD. His final stage, 'religion and industrial society,' brings the story up to date.

Ling's work, unlike that of McNeill and Bellah, is not the product of sustained historical or sociological analysis. It is a pioneer attempt to survey the history of religion as a whole. As Polybius remarked long ago (Book 1, 4):

He indeed who believes that by studying isolated histories he can acquire a fairly just view of history as a whole, is, it seems to me, much like one who, after having looked at the dissevered limbs of an animal once alive and beautiful, fancies he has been as good as an eyewitness of the creature itself in all its action and grace. For could any one put the creature together on the spot restoring its form and the comeliness of life and then show it to the same man, I think he would quickly avow that he was formerly very far away from truth and more like one in a dream.

In similar vein, but much later (in 1873), Max Müller commented, 'he who knows one religion knows no religion.' The problem remains, how can a scholar comprehend the whole history of religion or the whole history of mankind? He runs into the gamut of questions raised by Karl

Popper in his statement (1961: vol 2: 270):

> A concrete history of mankind, if there were any, would have to be the history of all men.
> It would have to be the history of all human hopes, struggles, and sufferings. For there is
> no one man more important than any other. Clearly, this concrete history cannot be
> written. We must make abstractions, we must neglect, select.

Clearly, this is true. But it is also true, in less intense measure, in regard
to the history of any particular man, town, nation, or religion. It is to
Ling's merit, in spite of the inadequacies of his attempt, that he has
pioneered the way for more ambitious endeavours to construct the
global history of religion. Indeed it is worthy of comment that Ling,
despite his antipathy to institutional Christianity, his partiality for
Buddhist meditation and moral striving, and his expectancy of a new
humanity as the cosmic goal for mankind, ends up with a similar
structure for the global history of religion as McNeill and Bellah. In
marked contrast is Eliade's *A History of Religious Ideas* (planned in three
volumes) which, in its author's desire to avoid reductionism by stressing
the 'unity of the spiritual history of humanity' (1976: vol 1: xvi),
succeeds in substantially divorcing religious from non-religious phenomena within global history.

(iii) However, it is not our concern to dwell upon global histories of
religion for their own sake. They are important partly because they have
opened up new directions for comparative religion. We shall now
examine a number of examples of comparative studies that have highlighted the significance of a developmentally similar historical background for comparative purposes.

(iii.1) The first example is that of ancient Egypt and Mesopotamia. A
number of scholars, notably Frankfort (ed: 1946, 1948, 1949), Brandon
(1958, 1963), Hooke (ed: 1933, 1958) and Jacobsen (1970, 1976), have
pointed out the similarities and differences between Egyptian and other
Near Eastern religions during the ancient period. Their more particular
concerns—creation legends with Brandon, the closeness of myth and
ritual with Hooke, and the mythmaking rather than philosophical
nature of ancient thought with Frankfort and Jacobsen—have all fed

into an intriguing exercise in comparative religion. Especially interesting is their analysis of kingship, myth, and ritual in ancient Egypt and Mesopotamia (and especially Babylon). Within the differences between the two areas—Egypt was better enclosed and defined geographically, more stable, more at home in the cosmos, with a more powerful and deified pharoah—common elements emerged. In both areas, the king was associated with the crops, the animals, and the people of his nation; this close association was celebrated in an annual festival wherein the security and advancement of earth, herds, and humans were ritually requested; the ritual was connected with a creation myth which retold the story of the original defeat of chaos and the emergence of the national cosmos; the king himself played a notable part in the ritual re-enactment of the creation legend. The identity of the gods concerned, the minutiae of detail, even the times of the festival, did not necessarily coincide; for example, in Egypt the myth centred upon Osiris, Isis, and Horus, and in Babylon it centred upon Marduk and Tiamat. Nevertheless, the nature of the differences, as well as the common themes—a creation myth, the dramatic death and resurrection of a god, the ritual defeat of his enemies by a god-king, the sacred marriage between a god and the land, and the triumphal procession of a god-king (see Ling, 1968: p. 7)—conspire to illuminate comparatively the religions of the two areas.

Our second example is that of Indo-European religion at a later period. This focusses more directly upon the work of a particular scholar, namely Georges Dumézil.

(iii. 2) *Georges Dumézil*

Trained by Meillet, and exposed at a formative stage to the sociology of eminent pioneers such as Durkheim and Mauss, Dumézil became professor of Indo-European civilisation in the Collège de France and was, for many years, director of studies in the Section des Sciences Religieuses of the École des Hautes Études of the Sorbonne. Dumézil is important for a number of reasons. He revivified Indo-European studies, and gave back to the field the comparative and anthropological approach it had lost in the early twentieth century. He introduced sociological and anthropological, as well as philological, insights into his discipline. He created links between Indo-European studies and the more systematic and structural side of French thought: as he said in his inaugural address at the Collège de France, '*tout, dans les représentations humaines ou du moins tout l'essential, est système*' (see Littleton, 1973: 138). Although he did not found a school of thought in the strict sense he stimulated and encouraged the work of a wide variety of students ranging from his disciples, Benveniste, Wikander, and Gerschel, to the Japanese Yoshida and the graduate programme in Indo-European studies at the University of California at Los Angeles. What has been less remarked, and yet it is of crucial importance, is the significance of Dumézil for the study of religion, notably comparative religion. His concern is with the gods as well as with men. He sees a mutual reflection between the tripartite relationship of the gods and heroes in heaven, portrayed in myths and epics, and the hierarchical social organisation of men on earth. Although not too dissimilar to Lévi-Strauss, Dumézil bases his system upon the investigation of the texts of a particular civilisation. Although not unlike Eliade, Dumézil seeks to understand the Indo-European civilisation at a reasonably defined period in time rather than erecting from it a universal and normative view of man in general. He is concerned to take seriously the different ways in which the separate Indo-European cultures appropriated their common tripartite ideology. Although ranging far and wide within Indo-European civilisation—this is what makes Dumézil an authentic comparativist—he does not attempt to extrapolate his theories from the Indo-European area into places such as Egypt, China, or the Near East. In Dumézil we have, therefore, a scholar who compared the religions and cultures of a defined civilisation at a set period in time. In over-leaping the boundaries between India and Europe, which were set to become separate civilisations, he is able to illuminate essential features of similarity and difference between the two. Dumézil makes a striking contribution to comparative religion at an interesting time in the evolution of the global history of religion.

Basic to Dumézil's thought is the correlation he sees throughout Indo-European civilisation and religion between certain kinds of gods, social organisation, and ideology. A hierarchically ordered, tripartite social organisation is represented in myth and epic by appropriate triads of gods and heroes. Thus the gods representing sovereignty are related on earth to the priestly class which is responsible for the spheres of religion and juridical sovereignty or order; the warrior gods are related on earth to the warrior class which is responsible for the spheres of physical prowess and military strength; and the fertility gods are related on earth to the class of herders and cultivators who are responsible for the sustenance and maintenance of the well-being and fertility of plants and animals. In the Indian context, Mitra and Varuṇa personify juridical and religious sovereignty, and collectively represent the Brahmin caste; the Maruts, especially Indra, represent the warrior ideal that is personified in the Kṣatriya caste; and the Aśvins and Sarasvatī represent the physical sustenance, plant maintenance and animal fertility personified in the Vaiśya caste. Elsewhere similar tripartite functions are performed, for example, by Jupiter, Mars, and Quirinius in the Roman pantheon; Hera, Athene, and Aphrodite in the judgment of Paris; different Ameśa Spentas in Zoroastrianism; Othinn and Tyr, Thorr, and Freyr and Njordr in Nordic religion.

Dumézil has made memorable contributions to our understanding of the culture and religion of particular Indo-European lands, notably in his *La religion romaine archaïque* (1966) which, as Littleton puts it, 'must certainly be ranked among the most significant scholarly achievements of our time' (1973: 140). However, our main concern is the significance for comparative religion of his theory that there is a tripartite pattern built into Indo-European society, culture, and religion. That significance manifests itself in four ways.

In the first place, there is Dumézil's stress upon the 'tripartite' nature of Indo-European religion. This is reminiscent of Panikkar's point, more universally made, that spirituality is inherently trinitarian. It is perhaps no accident that Panikkar's basic examples, in spite of the universality of his claims, are extracted from Indian and European religion; it is also the case that the Christian doctrine of the trinity, although deriving partly from Middle Eastern experience, was conceptualised in a European language. Dumézil states (*Mythe et epopée* 1968: vol. 1: 632).

Bien que les trois fonctions correspondent à trois besoins que tout groupe humain doit satisfaire pour ne pas périr, il n'y a que fort peu de peuples qui, de cette structure naturelle, ont tiré une idéologie explicite ou implicite.

In spite of attempts to show that Dumézil adapts his evidence and interpretations to fit his triadic model, it appears that his work is based upon a solid core of Indo-European evidence that is not so obviously present elsewhere.

He shows, secondly, that there is a close link between religion and language, and that a demonstrable linguistic unity necessarily implies a comparable measure of ideological unity. Thus the proto-Indo-European *Ursprache* from which Sanskrit, Avestan, Greek, Roman, and Gothic were descended was the linguistic source for the basic pattern underlying Indo-European ideology. Where the incoming Indo-European language did not prevail, as in the case of the Mitanni, the Kassites, and the Hittites, neither did the incoming ideology prevail; where the incoming language won, as in North India, Iran, and Europe, so did the accompanying ideology.

However, thirdly, Dumézil does not overstress the uniformity of Indo-European cultures. In spite of the fundamental importance of language and ideology, other factors are relevant: the level of economic and technological sophistication, the influence of neighbouring cultures, creative innovation and historical circumstances. Although parallels of ideology, language, and social order exist, and provide a similar tripartite background, they exist within comparably different milieus. For example, the Indian caste system diverged from the Roman social system, there were technical divergences between Greece and Scandinavia, and so on. There was considerable diversity within the underlying unity.

Finally, Dumézil emphasises the importance of what he terms 'ideology.' At times he makes the analogy between 'ideology' and 'theology.' For example in *L'Idéologie tripartie des Indo-Européens* (1958: 92) he argues:

tout système théologique signifie quelque chose, aide la société qui le pratique à se comprendre, à s'accepter, à être fière de son passe, confiante dans son présent et dans son avenir.

He seems to be suggesting at this point that theology forms the core of a culture. Elsewhere his intention appears to be that of subordinating theology, mythology, sacred literature, ritual, and religious organisation to ideology which is '*une conception et une appréciation des grandes forces qui animent le monde et la société, et leurs rapports* (1954: 7). Whether ideology is analogous to theology, or superior to it, it is clearly important for Dumézil. In his thought, it is virtually equivalent to 'religion.' His study of the Indo-European tripartite system is a study of the comparative religion of those Indo-European peoples which, having swept out of the steppe, provided the cultural and religious motifs of what were later to be India and Europe.

(iii. 3) Out third set of examples is taken from the forthcoming *Atlas of World Religion: From Early Man to Present Day* (edited by F. Whaling). This study includes a description of all the religious traditions of mankind, past and present, within a chronological and comparative survey of the history of religion. Although conceived in atlas form, this work gives a continuous narrative of the history of religion, the distinctive feature of which is the comparisons it opens up between different religions at particular periods. It touches upon comparisons already mentioned, namely between the early civilisations of Mesopotamia and Egypt (and the Indus Valley), and between the Indo-European civilisations. In the latter case, it traces the comparison back further than Dumézil to the early barbarian invasions out of the steppe region, and it includes in the comparison their influence upon Shang China as well as upon early Greece and Aryan India. Coming further forward in time, the *Atlas* hints at the similarities and differences between the religious breakthroughs centred upon the work of Zoroaster and the Jewish prophets in the Middle East, Confucius in China, the Ionian Philosophers in Greece, and the Buddha, the Mahāvīra, and the Upaniṣads in India. Further forward still, it compares the very different religious consequences of the hegemonies of two great empires, the Roman Empire in the West with its welter of new religious currents, and the Han Empire in China which produced the synthesis of Han Confucianism. Moving forward into the AD period, the missionary spread of Christianity into Eastern and Western Europe (from 200 to 600 AD) is compared with the contemporaneous spread of Mahāyāna

Buddhism from India into North and South China. This theme of comparative missionary spread is continued into the next period (600 to 1000 AD) which featured the very different advances of Islam throughout the Middle East, Christianity throughout northern Europe, Hinduism into parts of South East Asia, and Buddhism into the Far East. Even more striking, comparatively, is the rise, within the next epoch, of parallel religious syntheses in the Christian, Muslim, Judaic, Hindu, and Chinese worlds through the work of great philosophers such as Aquinas, Averroes (and Ghazzālī), Maimonides, Rāmānuja, and Chu Hsi. The question is raised not only of the comparison of these parallel thinkers but also of the comparison of the religious traditions that produced them. Was the process of development within these traditions so similar that it was no accident that religious syntheses should appear at that time, and if so what does this tell us about comparative religious history? After 1250 AD, the Eurasian religious picture was altered once again by the incursions of invaders from the steppe region of Asia, namely the Mongols. Again it is a matter of deep comparative interest that part of the reaction to the disintegration of old patterns produced by these invasions was the rise of important mystical movements among the Sūfīs of Islam, the Kabbalists of Judaism, the Hesychasts of Eastern Christianity, the Rhineland mystics of Western Christianity, as well as in the traditionally more 'mystical' areas further east. Once more important philosophical and historical questions are raised about religious comparison, in addition to the actual comparisons of the different mystical traditions.

The *Atlas* goes on to indicate the importance for global religious life of the rise of the West after 1500 AD. Before focussing upon this, it points out the importance comparatively of the parallel emergence of devotional vernacular movements within Protestant Christianity in Europe, the Sikh movement within the Punjab, Hindu Bhakti groups within India, Buddhist Pure Land Schools within the Far East (albeit somewhat earlier), and Shī'ite Islam within Persia (albeit to a lesser degree). This development, and the rise of the parallel religious syntheses and mystical movements mentioned earlier, is in many ways more interesting and important than later modern comparisons. The equivalence of later movements can be interpreted more readily in terms of historical diffusion. This is impossible in the case of earlier comparisons. The Protestant Reformers in Europe could have had no knowledge of equivalent Hindu Reformers such as Tulsī Dās, Kabīr, or Sūr Dās; Chu Hsi and Aquinas could not have known each other's thought.

Modern reform movements, which attempt to renew religious traditions in the light of modern conditions, are also surveyed comparatively in the *Atlas*. These renewal movements are responding to similar external factors such as the spread of modern science and technology, and similar internal self-doubts caused by the emergence of new patterns—obviously in the case of Christianity, Judaism, and Hinduism, less obviously in the case of Islam and Shinto.

Since the Second World War, the world has moved into a multireligious, global situation wherein new religious movements have arisen in many parts of the world, and the major religions have become more self-aware, more culturally conscious, and more engaged in dialogue. The contemporary situation is clearly open to interreligious historical comparison.

(iii. 4) *Ecological Comparative Religion*

A fourth example of global religious historical comparison is provided by the growing interest in ecology of religion. Although stimulated by the rising concern for ecology in the contemporary situation, its main application so far has been the analysis of the ecological background of, and the possible 'cultural stages' within, primal religion. As such, it is an attempt to compare religious groups with reference to their habitat and their response to it.

Äke Hultkrantz of Stockholm (1965, 1966, 1979) has been primarily responsible for developing this viewpoint, especially with reference to primal religion. He attributes a decisive influence to the environment in the organisation and development of religious forms. By environment he means 'the natural surroundings, topography, biotope, climate, as well as the demography and the natural resources which may be measured quantitatively in a culture' (1979: 222). Although Hultkrantz suspects that his theories may have some application to more advanced cultures, his own work has been centred upon the comparative religious effects of the environment upon primal religions. He points out that Arctic religion is characterised by basic features, such as hunting rituals, animal ceremonialism, landmark cults, sky worship, shamanism, and above-ground burials. Likewise desert nomadic groups share characteristic religious features, as do semidesert gathering groups.

By means of his approach, Hultkrantz is able to shed some light in comparative terms upon the succession of cultural stages within primal religion, and to complement the work of ethnologists, and theorists such as Bellah. This gives, so to speak, a 'historical' slant to his work. At the same time, he is also challenging the theory that historical diffusion is the necessary explanation of religious parallels. An alternative, or at any rate complementary, explanation can be found in ecological integration or convergence.

Hultkrantz's work is being subjected to searching criticisms (see Honko, 1979: 237–98) but it has opened up promising research possibilities. Research into, and comparison of, the types of religion associated with similar environments (and technologies and societies) is likely to increase.

A slightly different form of comparative ecology of religion is also beginning to emerge in the form of the comparative study of man's experience of his environment, and of his ideas of nature. This is more geared to responding to the present ecological crisis, whereas the former kind of research tends to focus disinterestedly on primal religion. It can reasonably be predicted that this concern to analyse and compare man's religious response to his environment will become more insistent in the future. But as the contemporary ecological situation is not our present concern, we shall not dwell upon the wider implications of ecology of religion at this point.

The problems of comparing religions within particular historical periods are obvious and have been hinted at in our survey: the possibility of historical (or philosophical) reductionism, the temptation to wide generalisation, the shortage of scholars with cross-cultural expertise, the problems of historical periodisation, and the differences of languages and world-views. However, the advantages of this method are great. If it be admitted that religions are comparable historically, there are clear benefits in making comparisons within particular timespans.

Other comparative approaches to the study of religion have emerged which, while not attempting cross-historical comparisons at exact periods, have acknowledged their dependence upon historical data. One approach has concentrated on the comparison of themes illustrated from history; a second has sought to classify religious traditions in such a way that they can be compared with other religious traditions; a third has erected more systematic historical models for the comparison of religions. These three approaches will now be examined in turn.

7c. Comparison of Themes using Historical Data

(i) An increasingly common way of doing comparative religion is to select a particular theme and to compare that theme 'across the religious board.' Overt value judgments are rarely built into this method, theological, typological, or otherwise. The aim is to compare objectively but sympathetically. The comparative data are taken from the histories of separate religions and grouped together. Ulterior motives of demonstrating superiority, equality, difference, or sameness are usually absent. The object of the exercise is to place side by side empirical data, taken from different religions, that illustrate the theme in question and to observe them, to 'compare' them.

Although dispassionately intended, this comparative method is not without its presuppositions. The selection of the theme, the language used in the study, the separation of the illustrative data from their historical context, and the notion that religious comparison is 'objective,' are all assumptions that are not necessarily self-evident. It is perhaps no accident that it is out of Britain, with her empirical tradition, that much of this type of comparison has emerged.

(ii) A good example of this approach to comparison is John Bowker's *Problems of Suffering in Religions of the World* (1970). Bowker immediately disarms a possible criticism by denying that there is a universally similar problem of suffering common to all religions. They all have their own problems of suffering, and as far as possible they are allowed to speak for themselves by extensive quotation. Nevertheless comparison is possible on the basis that suffering, however viewed, is a common experience of man. Indeed what religions have to say about suffering, however differently they express it, is often a clue to their view of the nature and purpose of existence.

Bowker's method is to describe and illustrate some of the main themes and ideas in connection with suffering in Judaism, Christianity, Islam, Marxism, Hinduism, Buddhism, and Dualism (Zoroastrianism, Manichaeism, and Jainism). He begins, in dealing with each tradition, by analysing the foundation of their attitude to suffering in important (often scriptural) sources, then on these foundations he traces the way in which their fundamental attitudes have developed down to the present day. He therefore draws, albeit selectively, from the history of each religion in order to compare the theme of suffering.

(iii) *Geoffrey Parrinder*

By far the most prolific contributor to this type of religious comparison is another Britisher, Geoffrey Parrinder. After taking ordination into the Methodist ministry, Parrinder spent twenty years teaching in West Africa and studying African religions. He became a founder member of the department of religious studies at Ibadan in Nigeria, and it was here that he began his monographs on African religion that were to provide a model for this later work. In the introduction to *West African Religion*, published in 1949, Parrinder pointed out that a number of authoritative works had begun to appear upon particular parts of West Africa and particular aspects of West African religion. He went on to state (1949: 1),

Often, however, the very detail of such works is a handicap to those who wish to become informed of the chief principles of African religion, and have neither the time nor the inclination to read about each group of peoples individually.

Parrinder's aim was to group the results of research in order to draw out and collate the common elements in West African religion. He saw his work as being an essential corollary to that of particular investigators who engaged in primary research within specific regions. Having successfully applied his synthetic method to four important groups in West

Africa, Parrinder went on to apply it more widely to African religion in general, so paving the way for similar efforts by young African scholars such as Mbiti (1969).

When Parrinder returned to Britain to teach comparative religion at King's College London, he extended his basic method to comparative themes embracing all the world religions. Using the research done by experts in different religious traditions, he drew together and collated their findings concerning a particular comparative theme. Employing this general approach, he dealt with such varied themes as witchcraft, religious teachings, scriptures, worship, incarnation, mysticism, and sex (see Bibliography). Parrinder's usual procedure has been to select a theme, and to trace it through each religion in turn. In following this path, he has not only broadened the approach he adopted in Africa, he has also continued the tradition of 'comparative monographs' used by his British predecessors Brandon and E.O. James, and prepared the way for the work of Bowker, Ferguson, and others.

Parrinder's method at its simplest can be seen in the four small books on 'Themes for Living' that he prepared for use in schools and colleges. These are basically source books in which he gathers together a collection of passages chosen from the great religions and civilisations to illustrate some of the major themes and principles of moral living. Altogether, within these four works, he deals with twenty-one topics: principles of right, the divine mind, nature, the nature of man, the ideal man, authority and conscience (*Man and God*, 1973); codes of behaviour, virtues, special virtues, happiness, unselfish action, wrongdoing (*Right and Wrong*, 1973); the family, society and state, race and class, force and war, freedom and responsibility (*Society*, 1973); suffering and evil, death and beyond, the goal, meditation and prayers (*Goal of Life*, 1973). With some exceptions, his selections usually follow a pattern on each topic from classical Europe, the Bible, the Qur'ān, Indian scriptures, and Chinese classics, through to modern writers. Moreover, by cross reference to lists of contents, the teachings of a particular religion and culture can be followed through.

It would be unfair to judge Parrinder's work on the basis of small books written for youngsters. He is not merely a generalist, as his work on African religion sometimes illustrates; he does not merely deal with comparative themes as his work on world religions seen as 'wholes' often demonstrates. Nevertheless one of his main contributions has certainly been to extract empirical data from specialised histories of religion, to pass them through the filter of his mind, and to present them imaginatively in comparative themes. Sometimes simply, sometimes subtly, he has used the power of his organising vision to open up new comparative topics and to hint at fresh interreligious connections. He is the most productive exponent of a thematic approach to religious comparison that is not seeking to make typological or structural or theological points. It is an approach that is proving reasonably fecund, and that is here to stay for the foreseeable future, at any rate in Britain and the United States.

(iv) The somewhat unsophisticated nature of this mode of comparison is both its strength and weakness. No one person can be master in a specialist sense of all world religions, and this thematic method of comparison is therefore a second-order activity that draws upon and complements the primary research of others. Although the exponents of this method have no methodological axe to grind, and although they use inductive historical data as illustrative material, their detaching of data from their historical context involves an implicit process of selection, if not of interpretation. Moreover the very process of detaching a theme may imply that the theme can be seen independently of the religious traditions that illustrate it. And this obstacle is compounded by the limits imposed by language. For example, to translate *duḥkha* as 'suffering' and to place it within a comparative discussion of 'suffering' may be to deflect the Buddhist meaning of *duḥkha*. On the other hand, comparison will usually be a second-order and complementary activity dependent upon the input of specialists, and an organising mentality that is sympathetic but impartial is a powerful help to thematic comparison. Insofar as this sort of comparison is impartial, the theme itself can be chosen functionally, the comparative process can be flexible, and there is little likelihood that the theme itself will develop into an 'essence,' 'structure,' or 'type' that has an independent value of its own. Particularities of language and historical context will always mean that comparison of any sort, religious or otherwise, is a sensitive enterprise, the hermeneutical complexities of which must never be underestimated.

Nevertheless, thematic comparison not only extrapolates from the language and history of separate religious traditions, with all the difficulties involved, it also feeds back suggestions into particular linguistic and historical studies thereby aiding our understanding of individual religions in particular as well as world religions in general.

7d. Classification of Religions using Historical Data

(i) The problems indicated in the last section have prompted attempts to set up comparative models based upon religious traditions rather than themes. The motivating principle of this type of comparison is no longer the choice of a theme which can then be compared, but the analysis of a religious tradition in such a way that it becomes susceptible to comparison with other religious traditions.

There have been two main approaches to this problem of describing religious traditions in terms that allow further comparison. The first has arisen mainly among historians of religion who, while nervous of the potential dangers of cross-historical comparison, have also been anxious to suggest ways of escaping the parochialism of specialist studies; the second, which we shall discuss later, has produced models rather than 'suggestions.'

The two names that come immediately to mind in connection with the first approach are those of two great scholars, Raffaele Pettazzoni and Geo Widengren. Although originating from the southern and northern extremities of Europe, Italy and Sweden, Pettazzoni and Widengren are basically similar. Their similarity derives from resemblances to be found in their academic backgrounds: in Pettazzoni's case the Italian concern for 'integral history' dating back to Croce or even to Vico, in Widengren's case the Scandinavian concern for empirical linguistic, historical, and philological research connected with the epistemological attack upon metaphysical realities and grandiose generalisations. Their concern for history, more total with Pettazzoni, more empirical with Widengren, is fundamental. Basic, too, is their suspicion of schematic structures and patterns. Comparative religion must be inducted from history not imposed upon it. Although some of their work is not too dissimilar to that of thematic comparativisits such as Parrinder, one senses in them a greater hesitancy to plunge straight into a general theme, a more urgent resolve to begin with historical particularities. The fact that their specialities lie in Greek, Middle Eastern, and monotheistic religion, rather than in Indian or Far Eastern religion enhances our point.

(ii) *Raffaele Pettazzoni*

Pettazzoni, who was born in 1883 and died in 1959, was the father of a school of Italian historians of religion, the contemporary representatives of which include Ugo Bianchi and Alessandro Bausani. He received his doctorate from the University of Bologna in 1905. After serving at the Royal Prehistorical and Ethnographical Museum in Rome and the history of religions department at Rome University, he took charge of history of religions first at Bologna, in 1914 and then at Rome in 1923. Unlike contemporaries such as Wach and Eliade, Pettazzoni professed his subject in the same country throughout the whole of his life. In 1954 he also received wide international recognition on his election to the presidency of the International Association for the History of Religions.

In a famous essay in the first edition of *Numen*, Pettazzoni reflected upon the relationship between 'history and phenomenology in the science of religion..' He concluded that they needed each other, but he entered the caveat (1954: 218).

Religious phenomena do not cease to be realities historically conditioned merely because they are grouped under this or that structure. Does not phenomenological judgement (*Verstehen*) run a risk on occasion of ascribing a like meaning to phenomena whose likeness is nothing but the illusory reflexion from a convergence of developments different in their essence; or, on the contrary, of not grasping the similar meaning of certain phenomena whose real likeness in kind is hidden under an apparent and purely external dissimilarity? The only way of escape from these dangers is to apply constantly to history.

This was essentially the same criticism of phenomenological typology that Cantwell Smith was later to elaborate. However, this did not prevent Pettazzoni (or Smith) from indulging in comparison of a more inductive sort. Unlike Smith, Pettazzoni was not afraid to include primal religion as well as major religions within his horizon of comparison.

A fascinating example of inductive historical comparison is to be found in Pettazzoni's analogy between the spread of Christianity throughout Europe and the spread of Buddhism throughout the Far East. This vast topic is wider than most inductive comparativists would dare to use—this combination of daring and care is typical of Pettazzoni—but he is judicious in restricting the analogy to two religions, and careful to stress that it is an analogy. He points out the radical differences between Christianity and Buddhism. Despite these differences, both became supranational rather than national religions, and both left the land of their birth to flourish elsewhere. The crucial spread of Christianity throughout the Roman Empire was contemporaneous with that of Buddhism throughout China, and the expansion of Buddhism into Japan coincided with the expansion of Christianity outside the confines of the Roman Empire. Pettazzoni draws out further analogies between the pre-Christian religion of wider Europe and Japanese Shinto, between the influence of Rome upon Europe and the influence of China upon Japan, and between the three European movements of the Reformation, the Renaissance, and Romanticism and the three Japanese movements of Pure Land Buddhism, neo-Confucianism, and the revival of Shinto. He alludes, too, to basic differences, such as the Buddhist tolerance of other traditions, and the Christian intolerance of paganism. In effect, this is a wider variation of the global historical type of religious comparison we examined earlier.

Pettazzoni was also interested in primal religion. This is evinced not only by his four-volume study of primal myths in the modern world (1948–63) and by his study of myth in general, but also by his analysis of monotheism and the confession of sins within the context of primal religion. Again the historical approach is important. In regard to monotheism, he states (*Essays*, 1954: 9):

We arrive at an idea of what monotheism really is, an idea which is not theological nor speculative, but purely historical, following the principle according to which the true nature of a historical fact is brought out by its formation and its development (*verum ipsum factum*).

Accordingly he opposes Schmidt's theory of 'primitive monotheism' as well as the notion that monotheism was an ideological evolution from the more rudimentary ideas of earlier times. At the same time, when historical analysis is virtually impossible, he is not afraid to investigate the mythical 'structure' of supreme gods, or the 'morphology' of confession of sins. This is not an abandonment of the historical approach but an admission that it does not work, in the normal sense, in the study of primal religion.

(iii) *Geo Widengren*

Widengren did not face the same problems as Pettazzoni in that he did not involve himself in the study of primal religion. His main areas of interest were Iranian religion, Islam, the Old Testament, Mesopotamian religion, Gnosticism, and Syrian Christianity. Although he eventually wrote on what he called 'phenomenology of religion' (1969), it took him a long time to address this topic. As we shall see, what he actually produced was not phenomenological typology but comparative suggestions and analogies arising out of inductive history.

Widengren was born in Sweden in 1907. He was educated at Stockholm, Copenhagen, and Uppsala. Like Pettazzoni he remained centred in the land of his birth. He obtained his doctorate from Uppsala in 1936, became professor of the history and psychology of religion at Uppsala in 1940, and stayed at Uppsala until his retirement. He succeeded Pettazzoni as president of the International Association for the History of Religions and held this office from 1960 to 1970.

Widengren's main concern has been to conduct thorough philological and contextual studies on the primary texts of the different religions that have engaged his interest. His comparative studies have arisen out of this prior consideration. Although engaged, through his interest in the religions of the ancient Near East, in sacral kingship theories, and although involved, through his concern to follow up Pettazzoni's work, in evolutionary theories and research into high gods, the core of his work has remained specific rather than general, descriptive rather than interpretative, historical rather than meta-historical. If borrowing, contacts, parallels, and comparative themes are to emerge they must do so as a result of the investigation of particular contexts.

It is not our brief to analyse the vast range of Widengren's painstaking studies of particular religious traditions. Our concern is with his comparative work, and the cautious nature of his comparative attempts is to be found in his contributions to *Historia Religionum*, (1969, 1971) edited by Bleeker and himself. The opening words of Widengren's introduction to the whole work are as follows:

> The History of Religion as a historical discipline is dependent on the methods elaborated since generations in other historical disciplines, above all in political history. These methods imply source-criticism which means that we have to answer *inter alia* such questions as: How do we constitute from the manuscripts the text of the source in question? How do we ascertain whether the source in question partly or in its totality is authentic or not? How do we from secondary sources work our way back to primary sources? How do we distinguish real history from legend and myth?

This statement nails Widengren's colours to the mast not only of history but also of history defined in a particular way. Nevertheless, as editors, he and Bleeker have to provide a structure for the two volumes of the book, and the overall editorial aim is to reveal (1969: vii):

> not only the individual peculiarities of the religions of the world, but also, and more particularly, the similarities in their structure, the formal parallels in their development and their most hidden interrelation and interdependence.

Accordingly each author who writes on each separate religion is asked to follow a basic pattern whereby he gives a short description of the essence of the religion, its historical development, its concept of deity, its worship (cult, ethics, myth, doctrine), its conception of man (creation, nature, destiny: path of salvation, personal and general eschatology), its subsequent influence (in the case of past religions), its present situation (in the case of living religions), a short history of its study, and a bibliography. This scheme is basically neutral and functional, it presupposes no conclusions or generalisations, and it depends upon the predilection of each separate author. The same comment may be applied to Widengren's own *Religionsphänomenologie* (1969, reelaboration of

Religionens Värld, 1953), with the qualification that it is a one-author work arranged around topics rather than religions. The topics are selected according to considerations that are empirical rather than meta-physical, arbitrary rather than structured, classificatory rather than syn-thetic. It is perhaps no accident that the vast majority of the contributors to *Historia Religionum* are European scholars, for it is from the continent of Europe, and especially from Scandinavia and Italy, that comparative religion as inducted from history has mainly emerged.

7e. *More Systematic Historical Models of Comparative Religion*

(i) In the wake of the somewhat tentative classifications we have just analysed more ambitious systematic historical models have come into being. These models have attempted to achieve two aims. On the one hand, they have sought to analyse religious traditions in such a way that the method of analysis led to a better understanding of the religion concerned; on the other hand, they have opened up new possibilities of comparison upon thematic lines. At the same time, these models have retained their grounding within historical data, yet they have not allowed historical considerations to place obstacles in the way of res-ponsible comparison. They have aimed, in other words, to keep the best features associated with thematic comparison, the comparison of religious traditions, and historical impartiality.

(ii) *Ninian Smart*

One of the best-known of these models has appeared in the anglo-saxon world in the work of Ninian Smart. The model that he has produced has become known as a 'dimensional' model, and we shall analyse it now.

Ninian Smart was born in 1927, and was educated at Glasgow Academy and Oxford University. His interest in non-Western religion was aroused during his army service in the British Intelligence Corps. His teaching experience has been in four related yet distinct areas. He taught philosophy at the University College of Wales, Aberystwyth from 1952 to 1955, history and philosophy of religion at King's College London from 1956 to 1961, theology at Birmingham from 1961 to 1966, and from 1967 he set up a new programme in religious studies at Lancaster. Latterly he has spent six months of each year at the University of California, Santa Barbara, and six months at Lancaster. It may well be that intercontinental teaching of comparative religion, as practised by Smart, Panikkar (formerly of Banaras and Harvard), Annemarie Schimmel (Bonn and Harvard), and John Hick (Birmingham and Claremont), will become a trend of the future. Smart has recently developed an interest in the problems associated with teaching religious education in schools, and in the contribution that television can make to the understanding of religion. He has also made important interventions in the general methodological debate concerning religion which he sums up elsewhere in this book. We shall concentrate now upon his comparative model.

Smart's basic model of what a religion is can be found in his book *The Religious Experience of Mankind*. He states (1969: 16–17):

It is a six-dimensional organism, typically containing doctrines, myths, ethical teachings, rituals, and social institutions, and animated by religious experiences of various kinds. . . . This general account of religion which we have given depends on comparing religions as we find them in the world. Comparisons, though, need to be handled carefully. . . . We are confronted by *religions*. And each religion has its own style, its own inner dynamic, its own special meanings, its uniqueness. Each religion is an organism, and has to be understood in terms of the interrelation of its different parts. Thus, though there are resemblances between religions or between parts of religions, these must not be seen too crudely.

This model, later refined by Smart, is useful both for understanding a particular religion and for comparing religions among themselves. His basic way of conveying what a religious tradition is remains historical. His notion of each religious tradition being a six-dimensional organism is inducted from the history of the religion concerned. His model is parasitic on history, not imposed upon it. Nevertheless it is a model more firm in structure than the suggestions offered by scholars such as Widengren.

Smart is careful to stress that his dimensions, although they represent yardsticks for comparison, must be viewed flexibly, not simplistically or typologically. His ritual dimension includes worship, prayers, and offerings, both inward and outward; it also includes contemplation and mysticism. His mythological dimension includes the myths, images, and stories whereby religious traditions symbolise the invisible world, and these may include 'historical' events, such as the Passover, that function as myths. His doctrinal dimension centres upon the doctrinal concepts that give system, clarity, and intellectual formulation to the basic ideas underlying a religious tradition. His ethical dimension focusses upon the ethical teachings of religions as they refer to the standards of behaviour expected of the individuals and groups concerned. His social dimension emphasises the fact that religious traditions are organisations with communal and social significance. Underlying the previous five dimensions is the final dimension of experience. Smart stresses the experiential dimension as being vital and gives to his book the title of *The Religious Experience of Mankind*. These six dimensions are interconnected within the total organism of a religious tradition. Nevertheless, they are also separable for the purposes of analysis and comparison. Their flexibility gives them strength as a descriptive model of comparison.

As is the fate of models, Smart's does not command universal agreement. Any model based upon a concept of 'religions' as organisms must parry the thrust of Cantwell Smith's claim that they are reifications without truth or meaning in themselves. The notion of a religion as an organism may be a liberating concept, it may also be an imprisoning one; the idea that religions have six dimensions may be emancipating, it may also be limiting. Moreover not everyone will agree that the six dimensions suggested by Smart are the most helpful, and this comment applies especially to his experiential dimension. Nonetheless, no model can be perfect. The test of a model lies in its usefulness. Measured by this test Smart's model, as it continues to be refined, is proving to be a successful descriptive and comparative tool, and Smart is emerging as a major figure in the contemporary study of religion.

(iii) Alternative systematic models for the comparative study of religion are those of two other British scholars, Michael Pye and Frank Whaling. In *Comparative Religion: Introduction through Source Materials* (1972), Pye isolates four elements as being essential to the understanding of any religious tradition. Unlike Smart, he does not apply his model to religious traditions as such. He organises his elements thematically. But by implication they can be seen as constitutive dimensions within separate religions. It is therefore appropriate to consider his work at this point.

Unlike the thematic comparativists such as Parrinder whom we looked at earlier, Pye is methodologically sophisticated in his explanation of why his four elements are vital to the discussion of any religion. The four aspects that he stresses are: religious action, religious groups, religious states of mind, and religious concepts. These are subdivided into thirty sub-themes, and are followed by eleven more complex comparisons which criss-cross in a complicated fashion between the four aspects.

Like Smart, Pye insists upon the historical grounding of his work. A comparative model, he states, is (1972: 22):

an attempt to begin with data from the history of religions and to go beyond the constraints of the immediate context in order to construct a more generally useful frame of understanding. But on the other hand it is the servant of history and, as a theoretical construct, it always leads back to the attempt to understand particular further cases of religion.

This is a good summary of the dialectical relationship between comparative models and the historical data of religion.

For Pye, the comparative method, phenomenologically conceived, is THE method of studying religion, and it contains the four approaches or aspects mentioned above. The study of religious concepts involves the examination of the doctrines, creeds, scriptural contents, myths, symbols and ideas of a religious tradition, and this implies the need to understand what a religion means to its practitioners. The study of religious action involves the examination of the festivals, liturgies, meditational exercises, and ethical actions of a religious tradition. Religious concepts and religious actions are partly the products of groups, and Pye's third focus of attention is the religious group. Religious concepts and religious actions also raise questions about the states of mind of those involved, and Pye's fourth focus of attention is religious states of mind. He stresses that equal attention should be given to his four main aspects, and that all are essential to his model. He emphasises also that the study of religious groups and religious states of mind involves sociological and psychological factors that are wider than the believer's awareness of his own religious experience, important as that is.

The sub-divisions within Pye's four elements are interesting in that they open up many initial points of comparability between religious traditions. Within the theme of religious action he groups: special places, times and objects; the use of the body; ritual cleansing; sacrifice, offering and worship; rehearsal of the significant past or myth; meditation and prayer; seeking specific benefits; occasional rites; ethics and society; and propagation. Within the theme of religious groups he deals with: simple group religion, civil religion, folk religion, minor group religion, and specialists in religion. Within the theme of religious states of mind he groups: alienation and conversion; self-giving; experience of power and presence; mystical states; and possession, automatism and special powers. Within the theme of religious concepts he groups: fundamental ideas; myth; legend and hagiography; symbols and systems; crudity and subtlety in religious language; creating religious concepts; authority and tradition; reinterpretations; syncretisms; and religious theories of religion.

Pye's model opens up innumerable avenues of research into particular comparative topics as well as a wider interpretation of what comparative religion basically is. The fact that he does not apply it to particular religious traditions is not an obstacle to this being done, and to this extent it is an extension of Smart's model.

Our final example of a comparative religious model is taken from the work of a third British scholar, Frank Whaling (1977, 1979a). Like Smart and Pye, he insists that his model is dialectically linked to historical data; like Smart, he is willing to apply his model to religious traditions; like Pye, he opens up a number of new comparative possibilities.

According to Whaling, there are eight inter-linked elements within religious traditions viewed as historically dynamic organisms: the elements of community, ritual, ethics, social involvement, scripture/myth, concept, aesthetics, and spirituality. There is some overlap between Smart's six dimensions, Pye's four aspects, and Whaling's eight elements. By comparison with Smart, Whaling divides the social element within a religious tradition into two: the religious community according to its inward organisation, and the social (and political) involvement of a religious tradition in wider society. He also stresses the role of scripture within the major traditions as correlative to that of myth in the primal traditions. An original feature of his scheme is the importance he gives to aesthetics. By this he refers to the role played by music, painting, architecture, dance, general literature and iconography within the theory and practice of religion. Finally, he emphasises spirituality rather than religious experience as an inter-linked rather than dominant element within a religious tradition.

Whaling is careful to stress the point that although all religious traditions contain the eight elements of community, ritual, ethics, social involvement, scripture/myth, concept, aesthetics, and spirituality, these elements are present in separate traditions with different weights and emphases. A combination of the twin truths, that all religions have these elements yet have them in different measure, provides the possibility of, and the countless variations within, the process of comparative religion. It also safeguards the model from the criticism of Pettazzoni and Smith whereby the same phenomenon is seen differently within separate traditions.

Whaling's model contains three other mentionable features. He concedes that lying behind each religious tradition there is a view of transcendent reality. He makes no value judgments concerning this, but shows that it can hardly be ignored. He also points out that there is usually a dominant religious symbol within a religious tradition whereby transcendent reality, which is ineffable, is communicated to man. Although comparable, because they are dominant symbols, Christ, the Torah, the Qur'ān, Dharma, and so on, are functionally rather than typologically similar. Thirdly, Whaling shows that, underlying every religious tradition, there is the intentionality of the people concerned. It is not just the community, ritual, ethics, social involvement, scripture/myth, concept, aesthetics, and spirituality of a religious tradition that are being described and compared, but what they mean to those

for whom they are significant. This does not mean that religious traditions are reduced to the individual intentions of those involved in them,
but it does mean that the component of human intentionality that
inherits and changes a dynamic continuum of inter-linked elements is
not lost from sight.

Although the three models we have summarised are helpful in the
description and comparison of all religious traditions, insofar as they are
historically based they have more practical significance in relation to the
major religions whose history is known.

It may be anticipated that models such as we have described, and
refinements on them, will find continuous use in comparative religious
work during the years to come.

7g. Comparisons of Two Religious Traditions

(i) To round off our discussion of contemporary comparative approaches to the study of religion, we will look finally at comparisons of two
religious traditions, and then at limited comparisons of particular
themes. The methodological principles behind these kinds of comparison have already been analysed in other connections, therefore we
will proceed quickly and by way of illustration.

Comparisons of two traditions have been fairly numerous, although
less numerous than might have been expected. In theory it is less difficult
to attempt a comparison of two traditions than it is to set up models of
comparison that can apply to many traditions. In practice it is sometimes
more difficult. For while it is clear that no one can have the expert
knowledge to compare many traditions in depth, it is possible, though
unusual to know enough to attempt an in-depth comparison of two
traditions. This type of comparison is both sensitive and difficult. For
the comparison of two traditions involves the scholar in three inter-
linked tasks: the description-cum-interpretation of tradition A, the
description-cum-interpretation of tradition B, and the comparison between the two. Even if he has an equal expertise in both traditions,
which is not common, he may be loathe to make the leap of comparison.

Another less-acknowledged problem rests in the fact that the majority of comparisons of two religions tend to include Christianity as one of the partners in comparison. The reason for this is quite simply that the practitioners of religious studies have been largely Westerners whose expertise began with, or contained, some knowledge of the religious tradition of their own culture, namely Christianity. But comparing one's own religious tradition with another, whether one's own tradition be so by personal commitment or cultural inheritance, requires sensitivity as well as methodological knowhow.

This difficulty, if it be such, is slowly disappearing as comparisons between two religious traditions other than Christianity become more common. In any case, as we shall briefly observe in the four examples that follow, the methods involved in comparing two religions are similar to those involved in comparing many.

(ii) Our first example is N.K. Devaraja's *Hinduism and Christianity* (1969). This book exemplifies a 'theological' approach used against Christianity. Devaraja is empathetic towards the Hindu tradition but exercises value-judgments in regard to the Christian tradition which he interprets in the light of the Hindu tradition. Indeed he approaches both Christianity and Hinduism from the standpoint of a particular Hindu philosophical viewpoint which leads him to say (1969: 119):

I do not envisage an easy and secure future for such faith-centred creeds as Christianity and Vaishnavism. The only religions that seem to me to have a future are such rational creeds as Buddhism and philosophic Hinduism.

Such a theological statement may find its justification within a theological setting, it is hardly appropriate within comparative religion which looks for a degree of impartiality in its approach.

Our second example is Julia Ching's *Confucianism and Christianity. A Comparative Study*. This study is both comparative and theological. On the one hand, it is 'a study of Confucianism in the light of certain perspectives borrowed from Christianity' (1977: xviii); on the other hand, there is no intention to judge Confucianism (or Christianity) 'according to any predetermined, hierarchically oriented, system of values' (1977: xix). It is a helpful and pioneering work in both comparative religion and dialogue theology. It makes no attempt to pass value judgments on Confucianism, offers illuminating insights into the Confucian tradition, and opens up interesting comparative issues between the Confucian and Christian traditions.

The problem is that Ching does not analyse the Confucian and Christian traditions and then, in the light of her findings, engage in comparison. Her comparative perspectives are confessedly borrowed from Christianity. Although her analysis of the Confucian tradition is empathetic, she does not conceptualise it or compare it in the light of its own data but in the light of data brought in from elsewhere. We therefore end up with the comparison of Confucianism in the light of Christianity rather than the comparison of both in the light of each other.

Our third example is Winston King's comparison of Christianity and Theravāda Buddhism (1962). King's treatment differs from those of Devaraja and Ching in two respects. His method is more phenomenological in that he attempts to see the two traditions he is comparing through the combined spectacles of *epoché* and *Einfühlung*. He also concentrates upon Theravada Buddhism rather than attempting to refer to Buddhism as a whole. Even so, his task is enormous. Inevitably he ends up by comparing certain aspects of Christianity and Theravada Buddhism, namely their concepts, ethics, and spirituality. Nevertheless, he does this in an interesting way.

King points out the similarities and the differences between Christ and the Buddha; he alludes to the joint attack of the Christian and Buddhist traditions upon selfishness, but shows how the Buddhist *anātman* notion questions the very concept of the 'self;' he stresses the Buddhist practice of meditation in its similarity to and its difference from the more relational mode of Christian prayer; he indicates the primacy of love within Christian ethics and the primacy of equanimity within Buddhist ethics; he notes the motive of Buddhist striving as the attainment of Nirvāṇa through escape from rebirth and the motive of Christian striving as the attainment of God through escape from sin; he compares the Buddhist stress upon merit with the Christian stress upon faith.

Subtle points are disclosed within the shorthand whereby, inevitably,

King has to unfold his wide comparisons. His work is a good illustration of a knowledgeable, dispassionate and *ad hoc* comparison between two traditions. It suffers slightly perhaps from the lack of a model underlying its framework. Lying behind this is a general reluctance to visualise the Christian tradition as a 'religious tradition' that can be studied impartially yet empathetically by Christians and others. As this reluctance fades, and as models become refined, this type of comparison is likely to become more important.

Our fourth example is Wilfred Cantwell Smith's comparison of Islam and the Christian tradition (1959). As we saw earlier, he insists upon a deep linguistic knowledge as essential for comparative work. It is only through an intimate acquaintance with the history and data of two religions that knowledgeable comparison is possible, and he applies these principles in his own work. Thus a thorough understanding of the Christian and Muslim traditions shows that the real focus of inter-comparison should not be Christ and Muhammad, because Christ is seen by Christians to be divine whereas Muhammad is not divine in Muslim eyes. A more accurate in-depth comparison exists between Christ and the Qur'ān which are both interpreted as being the Word of God. Muhammad is more equivalent to St. Paul, the main preacher and organiser of the early Christians, and the Bible is equivalent not so much to the Qur'ān but the *ḥadīth* in that both are the record of the revelation of God rather than the Revelation itself. Smith points out that Christian theology has the importance for Christians that the *sharī'ah* has for Muslims, whereas Muslim Theology is less weighty in Muslim eyes and more equivalent to Christian philosophy of religion. Philosophy of religion, by contrast, has been of minimal significance in Muslim history, and the philosophers have operated at the periphery of Islam, rather like sects within the Christian tradition. Smith points out that the Muslims have no sacraments as such, but that reciting the Qur'ān is their functional equivalent of the Christian eucharist. Likewise the Muslim mosque is equivalent not so much to the Roman Catholic church building but to the Protestant chapel which, like the mosque, is basically a meeting place rather than a consecrated 'holy place.'

Smith's approach is valuable. He emphasises in-depth comparison rather than superficial comparison; he stresses the need for a knowledge of the history, language and tradition of the two religions that are being compared; he underlines the importance, in any comparison, of taking seriously the faith of believers. However, while it is likely that more people will adopt his method of comparison, and that fascinating insights will surface as a result, this does not mean that thematic, classificatory, or modular comparison are thereby invalidated. Smith's objection is to comparative themes becoming types or structures. This need not happen. Comparative themes, although seemingly 'superficial,' can, if used flexibly, enhance rather than obscure in-depth comparison.

7h. Comparisons of More Limited Topics

(i) Our final task is to survey briefly comparisons of more limited topics. This is a more restricted form of comparison than those we have looked at previously. This type of comparison is usually not typological, archetypal, or structural—these approaches are concerned with 'groups' of phenomena spanning many religious boundaries, and tend to focus on generality rather than particularity. Nor does limited comparison concern itself with the total comparison of two religions, it is more likely to isolate one topic and compare that between two religions. It may arise out of thematic comparison or systematic models of historical comparison, but if so it will be more specific in scope. The likelihood is that limited comparison will have a historical base, or that it will be closely associated with a particular discipline, for example, philosophy in the case of comparative religious philosophy.
(ii) Particularly interesting are limited comparisons which, because of their specificity, open up creative new insights. An example of this is Whaling's study of Rāma, Kṛṣṇa, and Christ (1980). Hitherto, Rāma and Kṛṣṇa had been compared together as Hindu *avatāras* over against Christ the Christian incarnation. Whaling points out that detailed research reveals that Rāma is in some ways more similar to Christ than he is to Kṛṣṇa. They are both examples to their followers in a way that Kṛṣṇa is not; at key times in his life, Rāma chooses the way of suffering as the

right path for him to tread, whereas Kṛṣṇa knows very little suffering; devotional attitudes to Rāma and Christ tend to stress service, awe, and friendship, and to downplay the approaches to the deity as child or erotic lover that are prominent in Kṛṣṇa devotion; the stories of Rāma and Christ are set at the beginning in the *Rāmāyaṇa* and the New Testament, whereas Kṛṣṇa's life details emerge over a long period of time. In other ways, Kṛṣṇa is closer to Christ. For example, they are both teachers, whereas Rāma is not. Yet again, in other ways Rāma and Kṛṣṇa are more similar to each other than they are to Christ. Inductive comparisons of specific topics are potentially very productive in that they open up new patterns of research.

(iii) At the other extreme, inductive comparative research can create new interest in fields that have already been widely investigated. An obvious example is the whole field of mysticism. This area of study abounds in general theories that can only be substantiated or otherwise by reference to particular studies. Such studies, as they emerge, create a dialectic between theories of mysticism and practical instances of mysticism. A particular comparison by Otto of Śaṅkara and Eckhart (1937) did much to increase interest in the topic earlier in the century. A specific comparison by Suzuki of Zen Buddhism and Eckhart (1957) performed a similar function for a later generation. Joseph Politella (1965) also focussed comparatively on Eckhart in his *Meister Eckhart and Eastern Wisdom*. A series of other comparative studies have dealt with particular topics such as: Theravādin and Ignatian meditation (Corless 1972), Zen and Christian mysticism (Johnston 1967), Russian and Eastern mysticism (Chari 1952), the bootstrap theory of quantum physics and Taoism (Capra 1975), and so on. Of outstanding interest is the comparison by T. Izutsu of Ibn ʾArabī on the one hand, and Lao-Tsu and Chuang-Tsu on the other. This is one of the few instances of a comparison of two non-Western mystical systems, namely Sufism and Taoism. Although motivated by a desire to increase global understanding through philosophical dialogue (1966: vol 2: 191–6), Izutsu analyses Ibn ʾArabī in his own right and goes on to draw comparisons with the Taoist thinkers not by manipulating their thought but because he feels that a genuine correspondence can be demonstrated between the two mystical worldviews. Staal, by contrast, is sceptical about the benefits of mental comparisons, and argues for an end to speculation and a start of 'real investigation' (1975: 186).

This sentiment is echoed, albeit phenomenologically rather than existentially, by Steven Katz in his symposium entitled *Mysticism and Philosophical Analysis* (1978). He states:

there is a great deal more "technical" work to be done on the mystical material itself, i.e. in the understanding of texts, linguistic researches, editions of material, "form-criticism" of sources, etc.; and secondly, there are philosophical issues which are essential to an accurate and complete understanding of mysticism which need either to be further refined or to be rethought *in toto*.

Mystical theory has become a minefield of conflicting interpretations, at Katz intimates. For the *philosophia perennis* school, associated with Coomaraswamy, Schuon, Huxley, Guénon (and Izutsu), there is an underlying mystical truth common to most, if not all, the major religions, therefore mystical truth is equated with true religion. Others, such as W.T. Stace (1961), would not go so far as to state that mysticism is the whole of religion, but they would suggest that the mysticism which is part of religion is basically the same although interpreted differently. Ninian Smart (1962, 1965) would agree that phenomenologically it may be difficult to distinguish different kinds of mysticism but in practice mystical experiences acquire a 'flavour' imparted by the mystic's own background, a position expounded even more firmly by Scholem in his classical statement, 'there is no mysticism as such, there is only the mysticism of a particular religious system, Christian, Islamic, Jewish mysticism and so on' (1961: 6). Zaehner, as we saw earlier, would claim that the four different types of mysticism he describes, pan-en-henic, isolationist, monistic, and theistic, are not even phenomenologically similar, they are basically as well as hermeneutically different. Katz is even more pluralistic in arguing for 'a wide variety of mystical experiences which are, at least in respect of some determinative aspects, culturally and ideologically grounded' (1978: 66). This spectrum of possibilities, ranging from mysticism being the same to mysticism being contextually different, is influenced by a further consideration as to whether each possibility is viewed rationally or experientially (or, in the case of Frits Staal, both rationally and by having (1975: 186) 'contemplation under the guidance of a guru'!).

Amidst such a welter of differing theories, inductive comparative research is important and will become increasingly so. General theories need substantiation and modification by case studies to be convincing; case studies need comparative investigation to avoid contextual isolation. As we have said before, and as Collingwood (1946) and others have shown, even historical case studies involve not only historical data but also some element of interpretation. The problem of hermeneutics cannot be avoided—it is a question of whether the degree of interpretation required is greater or less. As we remarked in discussing comparisons between two religions, greater skill in interpretation is necessary than in the case where only one is under observation. To a lesser degree the same point applies to the discussion of a limited topic such as mysticism when it is compared between two religions as opposed to being observed in one. Inductive comparisons of this sort form a bridge between particular contexts and general theories and, as such, their value is obvious.

(iv) The same method of inductive comparison can, of course, be applied to many topics. It is especially valuable in testing and refining classifications such as those of Pettazzoni and Widengren, and models such as those of Smart and Whaling. Insofar as these are based on history, they can be modified by history. This particular process of verification is less easy in respect of typological, archetypal, or structural models which lay more stress upon deducting from premises than upon inducting from particulars. Nevertheless these types of models too are not independent of comparative inductive research. An analysis of *Philosophy East and West* from 1950 to 1975 reveals 75 comparative studies of topics that fall mainly within the orbit of comparative philosophy although some stray over into comparative ethics, comparative aesthetics, and comparative spirituality. This particular journal since 1975, and other journals before and after 1975, have produced many more articles that focus upon particular comparisons in these and other areas. Inductive comparative research remains a fruitful mode of study within comparative religion, and its significance is almost certainly destined to increase rather than decrease.

8. Summary, Conclusion and 'New-Style'
Comparative Religion

By contrast with most of the other chapters in this book, the focus of concern in this present chapter is not that of an academic discipline. The basic common denominator is the comparative method as such. Comparative approaches have emerged out of a number of different disciplines that constitute religious studies. But the fundamental nature of comparative religion as such is the fact of comparison. Different disciplines feed into it, but it is dominated by none. Comparative religion assumes a complementarity of disciplines that together illustrate the essentially comparative nature of religious studies. To this extent, comparative religion may be seen as part of the cement holding together the separate bricks of the religious studies building.

Part of the former hesitation felt in using the term 'comparative religion' lay in the fear that it was a normative enterprise intended to grade religions in some theological, evolutionary, or other scale. Comparative religion, in the sense that I am giving to it in this chapter, is the very opposite of normative. The disciplines that feed into it may have their own strong hermeneutical presuppositions but their comparative insights are accepted impartially by comparative religion. Nevertheless, comparative religion is greater than the sum of its parts. Although not a discipline in the normal sense, the classifications, comparisons, and models it uses to make sense of the myriads of comparative data fed into it by different disciplines enable it to contribute to a deeper understanding of religious traditions, religious man, and the disciplines concerned.

To this extent it is likely that comparative religion will take over at least part of the role played in past years by the phenomenology of religion. As we saw earlier, the general phenomenological concerns of *epoché* and *Einfühlung* have been fairly widely accepted as underlying principles of religious studies in general and comparative religion in particular. At the same time, phenomenological typology, derived implicitly from the concern for eidetic vision of the philosophical phenomenologists, has emerged as one well-defined way of doing comparative religion based upon the grouping together into types of the phenomena of different religions. For example, in the work of Mircea Eliade, phenomenological typology seeks to uncover the basic types of hierophanies and symbols in order to reveal their fundamental structure and archetypal significance. However, this is merely *one* way of doing comparative religion, and, as a part but not a whole, it fits into the wider framework of 'new-style' comparative religion.

The comparative religion of the future will continue to remain diversified in approach. There is indicated in the appropriate places in this chapter an estimate of what might be the likely prospects for particular approaches. Overarching these separate developments, one may anticipate that there will be a growing interest in what we have called 'new-style' comparative religion. Within this integral enterprise, each approach sees itself as part of a wider whole, and mutual understanding is the order of the day between the parts that constitute the whole. Limited comparisons of a theme feed into and are modified by general comparisons of the same theme, and these in turn feed into and are modified by structural or typological comparisons that touch upon the theme in question. Likewise, limited comparisons of two religious traditions feed into and are modified by wider comparisons of the two traditions, and these in turn feed into and are modified by general comparisons of all traditions. Furthermore, as has been said, classifications of primal and major religions influence each other; comparisons of particular themes are interwined with comparisons of other themes; comparisons of themes are interwined with comparisons of religions; comparisons of spiritualities, ways of being religious, and so on, are linked to comparisons of both themes and traditions. A balance is held between the bias towards similarity found in comparisons that result from implied definitions of 'religion' as a structural element in man, and the bias towards difference found in comparisons that result from implied definitions of 'religion' as religions. Cross-historical comparisons at particular periods lend insights to and borrow ideas from wider models and from similar comparisons at other periods.

As was remarked earlier, comparative religion is a web, albeit not a seamless one. It is supportive of, but not subordinate to, the approaches that feed into it; it is neither superior nor inferior to them. It is not reduced to any of the methods that service it, whether they be strongly hermeneutical or spartanly empirical. It is in the process of building up more sophisticated yet flexible models of its own, and it is inevitable that these will become more refined. It is this gathering, weighing, classifying, and modelling of different kinds and different degrees of evidence that lies at the heart of the task of comparative religion. To that extent it is perhaps the focal point of religious studies. Yet, it is not an end in itself. Its function is to coordinate and direct the overall comparative enterprise, but this is a means to the end of understanding religious traditions and religious man.

It is likely that comparative religion will grow in importance not only in its separate approaches but also in its holistic task that we have briefly outlined. It has a growing significance as a branch within the wider whole of religious studies. It is a connecting branch, probably the main connecting branch, within the study of religion. As such, it may acquire an importance that is not intrinsically its due. However, its main function is comparison. This function, in part and in whole, seems destined to become enhanced. Whether 'new-style' comparative religion develops other roles due to a vacuum of unifying ideas elsewhere in religious studies remains to be seen. If it does develop such roles it will cease to be 'comparative religion' in the sense we have outlined here. In either case, we may anticipate increasing research in this area.

Bibliography

Adam, D.S. (1921), 'Theology' in *Hastings*, Vol. 12, 293–300.
Adams, Charles J., ed. (1977), *A Reader's Guide to the Great Religions*. New York: Free Press.
Allen, D. (1978), *Structure and Creativity in Religion. Hermeneutics in Mircea Eliade's Phenomenology and New Directions*. The Hague: Mouton.

Baaren, Th. P. van and Drijvers, H.J.W. (1973), *Religion, Culture and Methodology*. The Hague: Mouton.

Barth, Karl (1959), *God, Grace and Gospel* (Scottish Journal of Theology Occasional Monograph 8). Edinburgh: Oliver and Boyd.

Becker, Howard (1932), *Systematic Sociology on the Basis of the Beẕeichuungslehre and Gebidelehre of Leopold von Wiese*. New York: J. Wylie & Sons.

Bellah, Robert N. (1970), 'Religious Evolution', in *Beyond Belief*, 20–50. New York: Harper and Row.

Bleeker, C.J. (1959), 'The Phenomenological Method', *Numen* 6: 96–111.

Bleeker, C.J. (1960), 'The Future Task of the History of Religions', *Numen* 7: 221–34.

Bleeker, C.J. (1963), *The Sacred Bridge. Researches into the Nature and Structure of Religion.* Leiden: E.J. Brill.

Bleeker, C.J. (1971), 'Comparing the Religio-Historical and Theological Method', *Numen* 18: 9–29.

Bleeker, C.J. (1975), *The History of Religions 1950–1975.* Monograph produced for the Lancaster IAHR Congress 1975.

Bleeker, C.J. (1975), 'Looking Backward and Forward' in *Proceedings* of IAHR Stockholm Congress, 23–32. Leiden: E.J. Brill.

Bleeker, C.J. (1978), 'Die Bedeutung der religionsgeschichtlichen und religionsphänomenologischen Forschung Friedrich Heilers', *Numen* 25: 2–13.

Bleeker, C.J. and Widengren, G. eds. (1969, 1971), *Historia Religionum. Handbook for the History of Religions*, 2 vols. Leiden: E.J. Brill.

Bolle, Kees W. (1967), 'History of Religions with a Hermeneutic Oriented toward Christian Theology?' in *Kitagawa*, 1967, 89–118.

Bonhoeffer, Dietrich (1954), *Prisoners for God.* New York: Macmillan.

Bouquet, A.C. (1942), *Comparative Religion.* Harmondsworth: Penguin.

Bowker, John (1970), *Problems of Suffering in Religions of the World.* Cambridge: Cambridge University Press.

Brandon, Samuel George Frederick (1951), *The Fall of Jerusalem and the Christian Church.* London: SPCK.

Brandon, S.G.F. (1951), *Time and Mankind.* London: Hutchinson.

Brandon, S.G.F. (1958), 'The Myth and Ritual Position Critically Considered' in Hooke, 1958.

Brandon, S.G.F. (1962), *Man and His Destiny in the Great Religions.* Manchester University Press.

Brandon, S.G.F. (1963), *Creation Legends of the Ancient Near East.* London: Hodder and Stoughton.

Brandon, S.G.F. (1965), *History, Time and Deity.* Manchester University Press.

Brandon, S.G.F. (1967), *Jesus and the Zealots.* Manchester University Press.

Brandon, S.G.F. (1969), *The Trial of Jesus of Nazareth.* New York: Stein and Day.

Brandon, S.G.F., ed. (1970), *A Dictionary of Comparative Religion.* London: Wiedenfeld and Nicolson.

Buren, Paul van (1963), *The Secular Meaning of the Gospel.* New York: Macmillan.

Cairns, Grace (1963), *Philosophies of History.* London: Peter Owen.

Campbell, Joseph (1949), *The Hero with a Thousand Faces*. Bollingen Series 17. Princeton: Princeton University Press.

Campbell, J. (1959, 1962, 1964, 1968), *The Masks of God* (Primitive Mythology, Oriental Mythology, Occidental Mythology, Creative Mythology). New York: Viking.

Capra, Fritjof (1975), *The Tao of Physics*. London: Wildwood House.

Carman, John (1966), 'The Theology of a Phenomenologist. An Introduction to the Theology of Gerhardus van der Leeuw', *Harvard Divinity Bulletin* 29(3): 13–42.

Chardin, Pierre Teilhard de (1959), *The Phenomenon of Man*. London: Collins. (Orig: *Le Phenomène Humain*, Paris: Editions du Seuil, 1955).

Chari, C.T.K. (1952), 'Russian and Indian Mysticism in East/West Synthesis', in *Philosophy East & West* 2(2): 226–37.

Ching, Julia (1977), *Confucianism and Christianity. A Comparative Study*. Tokyo: Kodansha.

Cohn, Norman (1970), *The Pursuit of the Millennium*, rev. ed., New York: Oxford University Press.

Collingwood, R.G. (1946), *The Idea of History*. Oxford: Clarendon.

Corless, R.J. (1972), 'The Function of Recollection in Theravadin and Ignatian Ascesis', *Monastic Studies* 8: 159–69.

Cousins, Ewert (1960), 'The Trinity and World Religions', *Journal of Ecumenical Studies* 7: 476–98.

Cousins, E. (1977), 'La Pluralisation de l'Hermeneutique', in *Instituto di Studi Filosofici* (Rome), 205–17.

Cousins, E. (1978), *Bonaventure and the Coincidence of Opposites*. Chicago: Franciscan Herald Press.

Cox, Harvey (1965), *The Secular City*. London: SCM.

Cragg, Kenneth (1956), *The Call of the Minaret*. New York: Oxford.

Cragg, K. (1959), *Sandals at the Mosque. Christian Presence Amid Islam*. London: SCM.

Cragg, K. (1964), *The Dome and the Rock. Jerusalem Studies in Islam*. London: Allenson.

Cragg, K. (1969, 1975). *The House of Islam*. Belmont: Dickenson.

Cragg, K. (1971), *The Event of the Qur'ān*. London: Allen & Unwin.

Davis, Charles (1974), 'The Reconvergence of Theology and Religious Studies', *Sciences Religieuses* 4: 205–21.

Desroche, H. & Séguy, J., eds. (1970), *Introduction aux Sciences Humaines des Religions*. Paris: Cujas.

Detienne, Marcel (1972), *Les Jardins d'Adonis*. Paris: Gallimard.

Devanandan, Paul D. (1963), *I will Lift Up Mine Eyes Unto the Hills* (edited by Nalini Devanandan and S.J. Samartha). Bangalore: CISRS.

Devanandan, P.D. (1964), *Preparation for Dialogue* (edited by Nalini Devanandan and M.M. Thomas). Bangalore: CISRS.

Devaraja, Nand Kishore (1969), *Hinduism and Christianity*. Bombay: Asia Publishing House.

Dhavamony, M. (1973), *Phenomenology of Religion*. Rome: Gregoriana.

Douglas, Mary (1966), *Purity and Danger*. London: Routledge and Kegan Paul.

Douglas, M., ed. (1973), *Rules and Meanings*. Harmondsworth: Penguin.

Drijvers, H.J.W. (1973), 'Theory Formation in Science of Religion and the Study of the History of Religions', in Baaren and Drijvers, 57–77.

Dudley III, Guilford (1977), *Religion on Trial. Mircea Eliade and His Critics*. Philadelphia: Temple University Press.

Dumézil, Georges (1952), *Les dieux des Indo-Européens*. Paris: Presses Universitaires de France.

Dumézil, G. (1954), 'Rituels indoeuropéennes à Rome', in *Études et Commentaires* 19. Paris: Klincksieck.

Dumézil, G. (1958), *L'idéologie tripartie des Indo-Européens*. Brussels; Latomus.

Dumézil, G. (1966), *La religion romaine archaique*. Paris: Payot (translated as *Archaic Roman Religion* by P. Krapp, University of Chicago, 1970).

Dumézil, G. (1968–73), *Myth et épopee*, vols. 1–3. Paris: Gallimard.

Dumont, Louis (1970), *Homo Hierarchicus*, Chicago: University of Chicago Press.

Earhart, H.B. (1969), *Japanese Religion: Unity and Diversity*. Belmont: Dickenson.

Earhart, H.B. (1974), *Religion in the Japanese Experience: Sources and Interpretations*. Belmont: Dickenson.

Eggan, Fred (1954), 'Social Anthropology and the Method of Controlled Comparison', in *American Anthropologist* 56: 143–63.

Eliade, Mircea (1955), *The Myth of the Eternal Return*. New York: Routledge and Kegan Paul (translated by Willard R. Trask) (Orig: *Le mythe de l'éternel retour*, Paris: Gallimard, 1949). Later *Cosmos and History*. New York: Harper, 1959.

Eliade, M. (1958a), *Patterns in Comparative Religion*. London and New York: Sheed and Ward (translated by Rosemary Sheed) (Orig. *Traité d'histoire des religions*, Paris: Payot, 1949).

Eliade, M. (1958b), *Yoga, Immortality and Freedom*. New York and London: Routledge and Kegan Paul (translated by Willard R. Trask) (Orig.: *Yoga. Essai sur les origines de la mystique indienne*, Paris: Librairie Orientaliste Geuthner, 1936; *Le Yoga. Immortalité et Liberté*. Paris: Payot, 1954).

Eliade, M. (1959a), *The Sacred and the Profane. The Nature of Religion*. New York: Harcourt, Brace & Co. (translated by Willard R. Trask) (Orig.: *Le sacré et le profane*, Paris: Gallimard, later edition 1965).

Eliade, M. (1959b), 'Methodological Remarks on the Study of Religious Symbolism', in *Eliade & Kitagawa* 1959, 86–107.

Eliade, M. (1961), *Images and Symbols. Studies in Religious Symbolism*. New York: Sheed and Ward; London: Harvill Press (translated by Phillip Mairet) (Orig.: *Images et symboles*, Paris: Gallimard, 1952).

Eliade, M. (1977), *From Primitives to Zen. A Thematic Sourcebook on the History of Religions*. London: Collins; New York: Harper and Row, reprint, 1977.

Eliade, M. (1979), *A History of Religious Ideas*, vol. 1, London; Collins (translated by Willard R. Trask) (Orig.: *Histoire des croyances et des idées religieuses*, vols. 1, 2. Paris: Payot, 1976, 1978).

Eliade, M. and Kitagawa, J.M., eds. (1959), *The History of Religions. Essays in Methodology*. Chicago: University of Chicago Press.

Evans-Pritchard, E.E. (1956), *The Institutions of Primitive Society*. Oxford: Clarendon.

Evans-Pritchard, E.E. (1965), *Theories of Primitive Religion*. London: Oxford University Press.

Ferguson, John (1977), *War and Peace in the World's Religions*. London: Sheldon.

Frankfort, Henri (1946), *Adventure of Ancient Man: An Essay on Speculative Thought in the Ancient Near East*. Chicago University Press.

Frankfort, H. (1948), *Kingship and the Gods: A Study of Ancient Near Eastern Religion as the Integration of Society and Nature*. London: Oxford University Press.

Frankfort, H. (1949), *Ancient Egyptian Religion. An Interpretation*. New York: Columbia University Press.

Geering, Lloyd (1980), *Faith's New Age*. London: Collins.

Geyl, Pieter (1955), *Debates with Historians*. London: Collins.

Glock, Charles Y. and Bellah, Robert N. (1976), *The New Religious Consciousness*. Berkeley, Los Angeles, London: California University Press.

Gualtieri, A.R. (1972), 'Confessional Theology in the Context of the History of Religions', in *Sciences Religieuses* 1: 347–60.

Hallencreutz, Carl F. (1966), *Kraemer Towards Tambaram*. Uppsala: Gleerup.

Hallencreutz, C.F. (1977), *Dialogue and Community. Ecumenical Issues in Inter-religious Relationships*. Uppsala: Swedish Institute of Missionary Research.

Hardy, Alister (1979), *The Spiritual Nature of Man. A Study of Contemporary Spiritual Experience*. Oxford University Press.

Hastings, James, ed. (1908–1926), *Encyclopaedia of Religion and Ethics*, 13 vols. (vol. 12, 1913). Edinburgh: T. and T. Clark.

Heelas, P. (1978), 'Some Problems with Religious Studies' in *Religion* 8: 1–4.

Heiler, F. (1960), 'The History of Religions as a Way to Unity of Religions', in *Proceedings of the Tokyo IAHR Congress*, 7–22.

Hick, John (1973), *God and the Universe of Faiths*. London: Macmillan.

Hick, John & Hebblethwaite, B., eds. (1980), *Selected Readings. Christianity and Other Religions*. London: Collins.

Honko, L., ed. (1979), *Science of Religion. Studies in Methodology*. The Hague: Mouton.

Hooke, Samuel H., ed. (1933), *Myth and Ritual: Essays on the Myth and Ritual of the Hebrews*. London: Oxford University Press.

Hooke, S.H., ed. (1958), *Myth, Ritual and Kingship: Essays on the Theory and Practice of Kingship in the Ancient Near East and in Israel*. Oxford: Clarendon.

Hopkins, T.J. (1971), *The Hindu Religious Tradition*. Belmont: Dickenson.

Hultkrantz, Åke (1965), 'Type of Religion in the Arctic Hunting Cultures: A Religio-Ecological Approach' in *Hvarfner*, ed., 265–318.
Hultkrantz, A. (1966), 'An Ecological Approach to Religion', *Ethnos* 31: 131–50.
Hultkrantz, A. (1970), 'The Phenomenology of Religion: Aims and Methods', *Temenos* 6: 68–88.
Hultkrantz, A. (1979), 'Ecology of Religion: Its Scope and Method', in *Honko*, 221–36.
Husserl, Edmund (1962), *Ideas. General Introduction to Pure Phenomenology*. London: Collier-Macmillan (translated by W.R. Boyce Gibson) (Orig.: *Ideen zu einer reinen Phänomenologie und Phänomenologischer Philosophie*, 1913).
Hutchinson, John A. (1969), *Paths of Faith*. New York: McGraw-Hill.
Huxley, Aldous (1946), *The Perennial Philosophy*. London: Chatto and Windus.
Hvarfner, H., ed. (1965), *Hunting and Fishing*. Lulea: Norrbottens Museum.

Isambert, F.A. (1970), 'La phénomenologie religieuse', in *Desroche & Seguy*, 217–40.
Izutsu, Toshihiko (1966), *A Comparative Study of the Key Philosophical Concepts in Sufism and Taoism in Ibn Arabi and Lao-Tzu, Chuang-Tzu*, 2 vols., Tokyo: Keio Institute of Cultural and Linguistic Studies.

Jacobsen, Thorkild (1970), *Toward the Image of Tammuz*. Cambridge: Harvard University Press.
Jacobsen, T. (1976), *The Treasures of Darkness: A History of Mesopotamian Religion*. New Haven: Yale University Press.
Johnston, W. (1967), 'Zen and Christian Mysticism: A Comparison in Psychological Structure', *International Philosophical Quarterly* 7: 441–69.
Jurji, Edward J., ed. (1947). *The Great Religions of the Modern World*. Princeton University Press.
Jurji, E.J., ed. (1963), *The Phenomenology of Religion*. Philadelphia: Westminster.
Jurji, E.J., ed. (1969), *Religious Pluralism and World Community. Interfaith and Intercultural Communication*. Leiden: E.J. Brill.

Kahler, Erich (1964), *The Meaning of History*. New York: Braziller.
Katz, Steven T., ed. (1978), *Mysticism in Philosophical Analysis*. London: Sheldon.
King, Winston (1962), *Buddhism and Christianity*. Philadelphia: Westminster.
Kirk, G.S. (1970), *Myth*. Cambridge University Press.
Kitagawa, Joseph M. (1957), 'The Nature and Program of the History of Religion Field', *Chicago Divinity School News*, Nov. 1957: 13–25.
Kitagawa, J.M., Eliade, M. and Long, C., eds. (1967), *The History of Religion. Essays on the Problem of Understanding*. Chicago University Press.
Kitagawa, J.M. & Long, C., eds. (1969), *Myths and Symbols. Studies in Honor of Mircea Eliade*. Chicago: University of Chicago Press.
Klostermaier, K. (1976), 'From Phenomenology to Metascience: Reflections on the Study of Religion', *Sciences Religieuses* 6: 551–64.

Kluckhohn, Clyde (1953), 'Universal Categories of Culture' in *Anthropology Today: An Encyclopedic Inventory* (prepared by A.L. Kroeber). Chicago: University of Chicago Press.

Kraemer, Hendrick (1938), *The Christian Message in a Non-Christian World.* London: Edinburgh House Press.

Kraemer, H. (1956), *Religion and the Christian Faith.* London: Butterworth; Philadelphia: Westminster.

Kraemer, H. (1960), *World Cultures and World Religions.* London: Butterworth.

Kristensen, W. Brede (1960), *The Meaning of Religion.* The Hague: Nijhoff (translated by J.B. Carman).

Lanczkowski, G. (1978), *Einführung in die Religionsphänomenologie.* Darmstadt: Wissenschaffliche Buchgesellschaft.

Leach, Edmund (1970), *Lévi-Strauss.* London: Collins.

Leeuw, G. van der (1928), *La structure de la mentalité primitive.* Paris: Alcon.

Leeuw, G. van der (1937), *De primitive mensch en de religie. Anthropologische studie.* Groningen-Batavia: J.B. Wolters.

Leeuw, G. van der (1938), *Religion in Manifestation and Essence: A Study in Phenomenology.* London: Allen and Unwin (translated by J.E. Turner). (Orig.: *Phänomenologie der Religion,* Tübingen: Mohr, 1933).

Leeuwen, Arend Th. van (1964), *Christianity in World History.* New York: Scribner.

Lessa, William A. and Vogt, Evan Z., eds. (1958), *Reader in Comparative Religion.* New York: Harper and Row.

Lévi-Strauss, Claude (1963a). *Structural Anthropology.* New York: Basic Books (Orig.: *Anthropologie structurale.* Paris: Plon, 1958).

Lévi-Strauss, C. (1963b), *Totemism.* Boston: Beacon Press (translated by Rodney Needham) (Orig.: *Le totémisme aujourd'hui.* Paris: Presses Universitaires de France).

Lévi-Strauss, C. (1964), *Tristes Tropiques. An Anthropological Study of Primitive Societies in Brazil.* New York: Atheneum (Orig.: *Tristes tropiques.* Paris: Plon, 1955).

Lévi-Strauss, C. (1966), *The Savage Mind.* London: Weidenfeld and Nicolson (Orig.: *La pensée sauvage,* Paris: Plon, 1962).

Lévi-Strauss, C. (1969), *The Raw and the Cooked.* New York: Harper (translated by J. and D. Weightman) (Orig.: *Le cru et le cuit,* Paris: Plon, 1964).

Lewis, I. (1971), *Ecstatic Religion.* Harmondsworth: Penguin.

Lewis, Oscar (1955), 'Comparisons in Cultural Anthropology', in *Yearbook of Anthropology* (edited by W.L. Thomas). New York: Wenner-Gren Foundation.

Lienhardt, G. (1964), *Social Anthropology.* London: Oxford University Press.

Lindbech, G., Deutsch, K. and Glazer, N., eds. (1976), *University Divinity Schools: A Report on Ecclesiastically Independent Theological Education.* Rockefeller Foundation.

Ling, Trevor (1968), *A History of Religion East and West.* London: Macmillan.

Littleton, C. Scott (1973), *The New Comparative Mythology.* California University Press.

McNeill, William H. (1963), *The Rise of the West*. Chicago: University of Chicago Press.
McNeill, W.H. (1967), *A World History*. New York: Oxford University Press.
MacQuarrie, John (1963), *Twentieth Century Religious Thought*. London: SCM.
MacQuarrie, J. (1966), *Principles of Christian Theology*. New York: Scribner.
Mann, U., Ed. (1973), *Theologie und Religionswissenschaft*. Darmstadt. Wissenschafflliche Buchgesellschaft.
Martin, David (1962), 'The Denomination', *British Journal of Sociology*, 12(1): 1–14.
Martin, D. (1967), *A Sociology of English Religion*. London: Heinemann.
Mbiti, John S. (1969), *African Religions and Philosophy*. London: Heinemann.
Mensching, G. (1976), *Structures and Patterns of Religion*. Delhi: Matilal Banarsidass.
Moore, George Foot (1920), *History of Religions*, 2 vols. Edinburgh: T. and T. Clark.
Müller, Max (1873), 'The Comparative Study of Religions', in *Introduction to the Science of Religion*. London: Longman Green.
Murray, J., ed. (1919), *A New English Dictionary*. Oxford: Clarendon.

Nakamura, Hajime (1975), *Parallel Developments: A Comparative History of Ideas*. Tokyo: Kodansha.
Needham, Rodney, ed. (1973), *Right and Left*. Chicago: University of Chicago Press.
Needleman, Jacob and Lewis, Dennis, eds. (1975), *Sacred Tradition and Present Need*. New York: Viking.
Neumann, Erich (1955), *The Great Mother. An Analysis of the Archetype*. Princeton: Princeton University Press (translated by R. Manheim) (Orig: *Die grosze Mutter. Der Archetyp des groszen Weiblichen*. Zurich: Rhein Verlag, 1956 later edition).
Neusner, Jacob, ed. (1968), *Religions in Antiquity; Essays in memory of Erwin Ramsdell Goodenough*. Leiden: Brill.
Neusner, Jacob (1970, 1974), *The Way of the Torah: An Introduction to Judaism*. Belmont: Dickenson.
Niebuhr, H.R. (1951, 1956 paper), *Christ and Culture*. New York: Harper and Row.
Niebuhr, H.R. (1929), *The Social Sources of Denominationalism*. New York: Holt.
Noss, John B. (1956), *Man's Religions*. New York: Macmillan.

Ogden, Schubert M. (1978), 'Theology and Religious Studies: Their Difference and the Difference it Makes', *Journal of the American Academy of Religion* 46: 3–17.
Otto, Rudolf (1923), *The Idea of the Holy*. London: Oxford University Press (translated by J.W. Harvey). (Orig.: *Das Heilige*, Munchen: Breslau, 1917).
Otto, R. (1930), *India's Religion of Grace and Christianity Compared and Contrasted*. New York: Macmillan (translated by F.H. Foster). (Orig.: *Die Graden religion Indiens und das Christentum*, Munchen 1930).
Otto, R. (1931), *Religious Essays: A Supplement to the Idea of the Holy*. London: Oxford University Press (translated by B. Lunn).
Otto, R. (1932), *Mysticism East and West*. New York: Macmillan (translated by B.L.

Bracey and R.C. Payne) (Orig.: *West östliche Mystik*, Gotha 1926).

Oxtoby, Willard (1968), 'Religionswissenschaft Revisited', in *Neusner* (ed), 590–608.

Oxtoby, Willard, ed. (1976), *Religious Diversity. Essays by W.C. Smith*. New York: Harper and Row.

Panikkar, Raimundo (1964), *The Unknown Christ of Hinduism*. London: Darton, Longman and Todd.

Panikkar, R. (1969), 'Christianity and World Religions', in *Christianity*. Patiala: University of the Punjab.

Panikkar, R. (1970), *The Trinity and World Religions*. Madras: C.L.S.

Panikkar, R. (1973), 'The Category of Growth in Comparative Religion: A Critical Self-Examination', *Harvard Theological Review* 66: 113–40.

Panikkar, R. (1978), *The Intra-Religious Dialogue*. New York: Paulist.

Panikkar, R. (1978), *Myth, Faith and Hermeneutics*. New York: Paulist.

Panikkar, R. (1979), *The Vedic Experience*. London: Darton, Longman and Todd.

Panikkar, R. (n.d.) *From Alienation to At-Oneness*. Villanova.

Pannenberg, W. (1973), *Wissenschaftstheorie und Theologie*. Frankfurt: Suhrkamp.

Parrinder, Geoffrey (1949), *West African Religion*. London: Epworth.

Parrinder, G. (1954), *African Traditional Religion*. London: Hutchinson's University Library.

Parrinder, G. (1963), *Witchcraft, European and African*. London: Faber and Faber.

Parrinder, G. (1961), *Worship in the World's Religions*. London: Faber and Faber.

Parrinder, G. (1962), *Comparative Religion*. London: Allen and Unwin.

Parrinder, G. (1963), *What World Religions Teach*. London: Harrap.

Parrinder, G. (1964), *The World's Living Religions*. London: Pan Piper.

Parrinder, G. (1962), *Upanishads, Gītā and Bible*. London: Faber and Faber.

Parrinder, G. (1970), *Avatar and Incarnation*. London: Faber and Faber.

Parrinder, G. (1973), *Themes for Living (Man and God, Right and Wrong, Society, Goal of Life)*. Amersham: Hulton Educational Publications.

Parrinder, G. (1976), 'Robert Charles Zaehner' in *History of Religion*, 66–74.

Parrinder, G. (1976), *Mysticism in the World's Religions*. London: Sheldon.

Parrinder, G. (1980), *Sex in the World's Religions*. London: Sheldon.

Penner, H.H. (1970), 'Is Phenomenology a Method for the Study of Religion?', *Bucknell Review* 18: 29–51.

Penner, H.H. (1976), 'The Fall and Rise of Methodology: A Retrospective Review' *Religious Studies Review* 2: 11–16.

Pettazzoni, Raffaele (1922), *Dio: Formazione e sviluppo del monoteismo nella storia delle religioni*. vol. 1: *L'Essere celeste nelle credenze dei popoli primitivi*. Rome: Anthenaeum.

Pettazzoni, R. (1929–1936), *La confessione dei peccati*. 3 vols. Bologna: Zanichelli.

Pettazzoni, R., ed. (1948–1963), *Miti e leggende*. 4 vols. (Africa-Australia, Oceania, America settentrionale, America centrale e meridionale). Torino: Unione Tipografico-Editrice Torinese.

Pettazzoni, R. (1954), *Essays on the History of Religions*. Leiden: E.J. Brill (translated by H.J. Rose).

Pettazzoni, R. (1956), *The All-Knowing God: Researcches into Early Religion and Culture*. London: Methuen (translated by H.J. Rose) (Orig.: *L'onniscienza di Dio*. Torino: Einaudi).

Plott, John, C. (1969), *Sarva Darsana Sangraha. A Bibliographical Guide to the Global History of Religion*. Leiden: E.J. Brill.

Plott, J.C. (1977–1980), *Global History of Philosophy*. 3 vols. so far. Delhi: Motilal Banarsidass.

Politella, Joseph (1965), 'Meister Eckhart and Eastern Wisdom', P.E.W. 15(2): 117–34.

Popper, Karl (1961), *The Open Society and its Enemies*. 2 vols. Princeton. (Orig.: London: Routledge 1945).

Propp, Vladimir (1958), *Morphology of the Folktale* (ed. s. Pirkova-Jakobson, translated by L. Scott). Bloomington: Indiana University Press.

Puech, Henri-Charles, ed. (1970, 1972, 1976), *Histoire des Religions*. Paris: Gallimard.

Pummer, R. (1972), 'Religionswissenschaft or Religiology?', *Numen* 19: 91–127.

Pummer, R. (1975), 'Recent Publications on the Methodology of the Science of Religion', *Numen* 22: 161–182.

Pye, Michael (1972), *Comparative Religion. An Introduction Through Source Material*. Newton Abbot: David and Charles.

Ramsey, P. & Wilson, J.F., eds. (1970), *The Study of Religion in Colleges and Universities*. Princeton University Press.

Ricketts, M.L. (1973), 'In Defence of Eliade. Toward Bridging the Communication Gap between Anthropology and the History of Religions', *Religion* 3: 13–34.

Ringgren, H. and Ström, A.V., eds. (1967), *Religions of Mankind Today and Yesterday*. Philadelphia: Fortress (translated by N.L. Jensen) (Orig.: *Religionerna i historia och nutid*. 3rd ed. Stockholm: Svenska Kyrkans Diakonistyrelses Bokförlag, 1964).

Reynolds, S. (1973), *The Christian Religious Tradition*. Belmont: Dickenson.

Robinson, R.H. (1970), *The Buddhist Religion*. Belmont: Dickenson.

Robinson, R.H. and Johnson, W.L. (1977), *The Buddhist Religion*. Belmont: Dickenson.

Rudolph, K. (1971), 'Religionsgeschichte und Religionsphänomenologie', *Theologische Literaturzeitung* 96: 241–50.

Rudolph, K. (1973), 'Historia Religionum. Bemerkungen zu einigen neueren Handbuchern der Religionsgeschichte, *Theologische Literaturzeitung* 98: 401–18.

Rudolph, K. (1979), 'Religionswissenschaft auf alten und neuen Wegen. Bemerkungen zu einigen Neuerscheinungen', *Theologische Literaturzeitung* 104: 11–34.

Saliba, J.A. (1976), *Homo Religiosus in Mircea Eliade*. Leiden: E.J. Brill.

Schimmel, A. and Falaturi, eds. (1980), *We Believe in One God: Experience of God in Christianity and Islam*. London: Burns and Oates.

Scholem, Gershom G. (1961), *Major Trends in Jewish Mysticism*. New York: Schocken.

Scholte, R. (1970), 'Epistemic Paradigms: Some Problems in Cross-Cultural Research on Social Anthropological History and Theory' in *Claude Lévi-Strauss: The Anthropologist as Hero* (edited by E. Nelson and T. Hayes) Cambridge: MIT Press.

Schmidt, G. (1979), *Principles of Integral Science of Religion*: The Hague: Mouton.

Schröder, C.M., ed. (1961-present), *Die Religionen der Menschheit*. 42 vols. planned. Stuttgart: Kohlhammer.

Sharma, A. (1975), 'An Inquiry into the Nature of the Distinction between the History of Religion and the Phenomenology of Religion', *Numen* 12: 81–96.

Sharpe, Eric & Hinnells, John R., eds. (1973), *Man and His Salvation. Studies in Memory of S.G.F. Brandon*. Manchester University Press.

Sharpe, Eric (1975), *Comparative Religion. A History*. London: Duckworth.

Sharpe, E. (1977), *Faith Meets Faith*. London: SCM.

Sierksma, F. (1952), *Phaenomenologie der religie en complexe psychologie. Freud, Jung en de religie*. Assen: Van Gorcum.

Smart, Ninian (1962), 'Mystical Experience', in *Sophia*, 19–25.

Smart, N. (1965), 'Interpretation and Mystical Experience', in *Religious Studies*, 75–87.

Smart, N. (1969), *The Religious Experience of Mankind*. New York: Scribner.

Smart, N. (1973), *The Phenomenon of Religion*. London: Macmillan.

Smart, N. (1973), *The Science of Religion and the Sociology of Knowledge*. Princeton: Princeton University Press.

Smart, N. (1978), 'Beyond Eliade: The Future of Theory in Religion', *Numen* 25: 171–183.

Smith, Huston (1958), *The Religions of Man*. New York: Harper and Row.

Smith, Ronald Gregor (1956), *The New Man*. New York: Harper and Row.

Smith, Wilfred Cantwell (1957), *Islam in Modern History*. Princeton: Princeton University Press.

Smith, W.C. (1959), 'Comparative Religion: Whither and Why?', in *Eliade & Kitagawa*, 31–58.

Smith, W.C. (1959), 'Some Similarities and Differences between Christianity and Islam: An Essay in Comparative Religion' in J. Kritzeck and R. Bayly Winder, eds., *The World of Islam: Studies in Honour of Philip K. Hitti*, London: Macmillan; New York: St. Martin's, 47–59.

Smith, W.C. (1964), *The Meaning and End of Religion*. New York: New American Library, Mentor.

Smith, W.C. (1965), *The Faith of Other Men*. New York: New American Library, Mentor.

Smith, W.C. (1967), *Questions of Religious Truth*. New York: Scribner.

Smith, W.C. (1967), 'The Teaching of Religion: Academic Rigour and Personal Involvement' MS, Harvard.

Smith, W.C. (1976), *Religious Diversity* (ed. Willard Oxtoby). New York: Harper and Row.

Smith, W.C. (1977), *Belief and History*. Charlottesville: University of Virginia Press.

Smith, W.C. (1979), *Faith and Belief*. Princeton: Princeton University Press.

Smith, W.C. (1981), *Towards a World Theology*. Philadelphia: Westminster.
Staal, Frits (1975), *Exploring Mysticism*. Harmondsworth: Penguin.
Stace, W.T. (1961), *Mysticism and Philosophy*. London: Macmillan.
Streng, F.J. (1969), *Understanding Religious Man*. Belmont: Dickenson.
Suzuki, D.T. (1957), *Mysticism Christian and Buddhist*. London: Allen and Unwin.
Swanson, Guy (1960), *The Birth of the Gods*. Ann Arbor: University of Michigan Press.

Taylor, John (1963), *The Primal Vision*. London: SCM.
Thomas, M.M. (1969), *The Acknowledged Christ of the Indian Renaissance*. London: SCM.
Thomas, Owen C. (1969), *Attitudes Towards Other Religions: Some Christian Interpretations*. New York: Harper and Row.
Thompson, L.G. (1969, 1975), *Chinese Religion: An Introduction*. Belmont: Dickenson.
Toynbee, Arnold (1934–1961), *A Study of History*. 12 Vols. London: Oxford University Press.
Toynbee, A. (1976), *Mankind and Mother Earth*. New York: Oxford University Press.
Troeltsch, E. (1931), *The Social Teaching of the Christian Churches* (2 vols., translated by Olive Wyon). London: Allen and Unwin.
Turner, Victor (1957), *Schism and Continuity in African Society*. Manchester University Press.
Turner, V. (1967), *The Forest of Symbols*. Ithaca: Cornell University Press.
Turner, V. (1968), *The Drums of Affliction*. Oxford: Oxford University Press.
Turner, V. (1975), 'Symbolic Studies', in *Annual Review of Anthropology*.

Voegelin, Eric (1956–1974), *Order and History*. 4 Vols. Baton Rouge: Louisiana State University Press.

Waardenburg, Jacques (1970), *L'Islam dans le miroir de l'occident*. 3rd ed. The Hague: Mouton.
Waardenburg, J. (1973), *Classical Approaches to the Study of Religion*. 2 vols. The Hague: Mouton.
Waardenburg, J. (1973), 'Research and Meaning in Religion', in *Baaren and Drijvers*, 109–36.
Waardenburg, J. (1975), 'Religionswissenschaft in Continental Europe', *Religion*, Aug 1975: 27–54.
Waardenburg, J. (1976), 'Religionswissenschaft in Continental Europe excluding Scandinavia. Some Factual Data' *Numen* 23: 219–39.
Waardenburg, J. (1978), *Reflections on the Study of Religion*. The Hague: Mouton.
Waardenburg, J. (1978), 'Religionswissenschaft New Style. Some Thoughts and Afterthoughts' in *Annual Review of the Social Sciences of Religion* 2, 189–220.
Waardenburg, J. (1979), 'The Language of Religion and the Study of Religions as Sign Systems', in *Honko*, 441–57.
Wach, J. (1922), *Der Erlösungsgedanke und seine Deutung*. Leipzig: J.C. Hinrichs.

Wach, J. (1925), *Mahayana, besonders im Hinblick auf das Saddharma-Pundarika-Sutra: eine Untersuchung über die religionsgeschichtliche Bedeutung eines heiligen Textes der Buddhisten.* München-Neubiberg: Schloss.

Wach, J. (1931), *Einführung in die Religionssoziologie.* Tübingen: J.C.B. Mohr.

Wach, J. (1932), *Typen religiöser Anthropologie: ein Vergleich der Lehre vom Menschen im religionsphilosophischen Denken von Orient und Okzident.* Tübingen: J.C.B. Mohr.

Wach, J. (1934), *Das Problem des Todes in der Philosophie unserer Zeit.* Tübingen: J.C.B. Mohr.

Wach, Joachim (1944), *Sociology of Religion.* Chicago University Press.

Wach, J. (1951), *Types of Religious Experience. Christian and Non-Christian.* Chicago: University of Chicago Press.

Wach, J. (1958), *The Comparative Study of Religions.* New York: Columbia University Press.

Wach, J. (1968), *Understanding and Believing: Essays.* (edited by J.M. Kitagawa) New York: Harper and Row.

Warfield, B.B. (1951), *The Inspiration and Authority of the Bible.* London: Marshall, Morgan and Scott.

Welch, Claude (1971), *Graduate Education in Religion. A Critical Appraisal.* Missoula: University of Montana Press.

Werblowski, Zwi (1960), 'Marburg and After?', *Numen* 7: 215–20.

Werblowski, Z. (1976), *Beyond Tradition and Modernity.* London: Athlone Press.

Whaling, Frank (1966), *An Approach to Dialogue: Hinduism and Christianity.* Lucknow: Lucknow Publishing House.

Whaling, F. (1977), 'Teaching Christianity as a World Religion', in *Education in Religion*, 1–17.

Whaling, F. (1979), 'Śankara and Buddhism', *Indian Journal of Philosophy* 7: 1–42.

Whaling, F. (1979), 'The Trinity and the Structure of Religious Life', *Scottish Journal of Theology* 32: 359–69.

Whaling, F. (1979), 'Śrī Aurobindo. A Critique', *The Journal of Religious Studies* 7(2): 66–103.

Whaling, F. (1979), 'Christianity as a World Religion', in *SHAP Bulletin*, 5–15.

Whaling, F. (1980), *The Rise of the Religious Significance of Rāma.* Delhi: Motilal Banarsidass.

Whaling, F. (1981), 'The Development of the Word Theology', *Scottish Journal of Theology* (34): 289–312.

Whaling, F., ed. (projected 1986), *An Atlas of World Religion From Early Man to Present Day.* Edinburgh: J. Bartholomew and T. and T. Clark.

Widengren, Geo. (1961), *Iranische Geisteswelt. Von den Anfangen bis zum Islam.* Baden-Baden: Holle Verlag.

Widengren, G. (1968), 'Some Remarks on the Methods of the Phenomenology of Religion', *Acta Universitatis Upsaliensis* 17: 250–60.

Widengren, G. (1969), *Religionsphänomenologie.* Berlin: De Gruyter (enlargement of

Religionens värld, 2nd ed., Stockholm: Svenska Kyrkans Diakonistyrelses Bokförlag, 1953).

Widengren, G. (1975), *Religious Syncretism in Antiquity: Essays in Conversation with Geo. Widengren* (ed. by Birger A. Pearson). Missoula: Scholars Press.

Wiebe, D. (1979), 'The Role of Belief in the Study of Religion. A Response to W.C. Smith', *Numen* 26: 234–49.

Wilson, B.R. (1961), *Sects and Society*. London: Heinemann.

Wilson, B.R., ed. (1967), *Patterns of Sectarianism*, London: Heinemann.

Wilson, B.R. (1973), *Magic and the Millennium*. London: Heinemann.

Wilson, B.R. (1975), *The Noble Savage*. Berkeley: University of California Press.

Worsley, B.R. (1968), *The Trumpet Shall Sound*. London: MacGibbon and Kee.

Yinger, J.M. (1946), *Religion in the Struggle for Power*. Durham: Duke University Press.

Yinger, J.M. (1957), *Religion, Society and the Individual*. New York: Macmillan.

Zaehner, Robert Charles (1955), *Zurvan: A Zoroastrian Dilemma*. Oxford. Clarendon.

Zaehner, R.C. (1956), *Teachings of the Magi: A Compendium of Zoroastrian Beliefs*. London: Allen and Unwin; New York: Macmillan.

Zaehner, R.C. (1957), *Mysticism Sacred and Profane*. Oxford: Clarendon.

Zaehner, R.C. (1958), *At Sundry Times: An Essay in the Comparison of Religions*. London: Faber and Faber (later *The Comparison of Religions*, Boston, 1968).

Zaehner, R.C. (1960), *Hindu and Muslim Mysticism*. London: Athlone Press.

Zaehner, R.C. (1961), *The Dawn and Twilight of Zoroastrianism*. London: Weidenfeld and Nicolson.

Zaehner, R.C. (1962), *Hinduism*. London: Oxford University Press.

Zaehner, R.C. (1963), *The Convergent Spirit: Towards a Dialectics of Religion*. London: Routledge and Kegan Paul.

Zaehner, R.C. (1966), *Hindu Scriptures*. London: Oxford University Press.

Zaehner, R.C., ed, (1968). *Concise Encyclopaedia of Living Faiths*. Boston: Beacon Press.

Zaehner, R.C. (1969), *The Bhagavad Gītā*. Oxford: Clarendon.

Zaehner, R.C. (1970), *Concordant Discord*. Oxford: Clarendon.

Zaehner, R.C. (1971), *Evolution in Religion*. Oxford: Clarendon.

Zaehner, R.C. (1972), *Drugs, Mysticism and Make Believe*. London: Collins.

Zaehner, R.C. (1974), *Our Savage God*. London: Collins.

Zimmer, Heinrich (1946), *Myths and Symbols in Indian Art and Civilisation*. New York: Pantheon.

Zimmer, H. (1948), *The King and the Corpse*. New York: Pantheon.

Zimmer, H. (1951), *Philosophies of India*. New York: Pantheon.

Zimmer, H. (1955), *The Art of Indian Asia*. New York: Pantheon.

4

Myths and Other Religious Texts

KEES BOLLE

Los Angeles

1. Myth and Mythology within the Study of Religion

The terms 'myth' and 'mythology' evoke more problems and un-
certainities in the general study of religion than they should. It is true
that the word 'mythology' is ambiguous, but this ambiguity is quite
transparent and is not disturbing. Mythology can refer to the entire body
of myths in a given tradition, or to the study of myths. A discussion on
our subject, if it is clear enough in itself, can hardly be impaired by the
two meanings of 'mythology.'

The term 'myth' continues to raise uncertainties in the best of intellectual circles, and it would be in order to clarify it as much as possible at
the outset. For the historian of religions myth *never* means 'mere myth,'
'fable,' or 'made-up story.' On the contrary, myth is the word or speech
that communicates validity and meaning in a religious tradition. A ritual
can be performed periodically, or the office of a priest may be highly
esteemed, but it is only the myth that illumines these customs and
institutions; and only myth accounts for their endurance, for it is
through myth that one generation instructs the next. As such, myth,
μῦθος, is the word of authoritative and sufficient communication and is
distinct from logos, λόγος, the word of calculation, of mental analysis, of
evaluation, disputation, and reflection. (Nestle 1942: Krappe 1930: 11;
Baumann 1959: 1; Otto 1955: 263.)

Every discussion of scholarly methods and specialization in the study of religion relates to the question: What is religion? Naturally, the answers presented or suggested by psychologists of religion, sociologists of religion, specialists in church history, Islam or Buddhism, or by philosophers of religion will vary and illuminate different aspects in particular. Whatever those answers may be, the general historian of religions is concerned with the *evidence* of religion as a universal phenomenon; and of all the evident forms in which religion is expressed, myth has the first claim to our attention.

Religion would not be available to the historian if it were not for the process of symbolization which provides us with documents of the sacred in human existence. The sacred *as such* is not a topic of lengthy discussion for the historian of religions. The expressions of the sacred, however, are. These expressions are by nature symbolic; they join the 'absolute,' 'ungraspable,' 'altogether other,' the 'real reality' of the sacred with a specific form accessible to man (Van der Leeuw 1963: chap. 107). These symbolic expressions of the sacred are either things (sacred trees, holy places, amulets—in short, *symbols*), or acts (rituals, rites, liturgies, sacred dances—in short, *cults* or cultic behavior), or verbal communication (in one word, *myth*).

I have said before that myth has the major claim to the historian of religions' attention, and it will now be clear why this is the case. The aim of the historian of religions is to interpret the phenomenon of religion, and it stands to reason that he turns to that element in the world of religion that itself interprets the sacred, communicating it from man to man, from generation to generation: myth.

2. Trends since the Second World War

Has progress been made in the study of myth and religious texts in general in the past thirty or forty years? Certainly, much work has been done. Many texts from classical India, China, from the entire world, from all periods of history as well as from present day 'primitive' religions have been edited and translated. But that does not answer the question. We do not intend here to compile the many bibliographies relevant to the subject. (Among them are Adams 1977, Lurker 1968ff., IBHR 1952ff., Thompson 1966, Grimal 1965, as well as many more specialized indices.)

Our discussion concerns *trends* in recent times, and the question whether progress can be recorded deserves an answer that goes beyond references to quantities of materials alone. One of the most significant books on mythology written in the last decade (Feldman and Richardson 1972) demonstrates that the recent study of myth is less novel than we may think. The book demonstrates this with excerpts from scholarly treatises published between 1680 and 1860! Our own century's concern with myth, even in the most recent past, is part of a much broader movement that began before the end of the Renaissance (Feldman and Richardson vol. XIX). Explanations of myth by means of naturalistic, or astral, psychological and diffusionist hypotheses, as well as new versions of Euhemerism and allegorical theories, all have had their adherents. Paging through the collection, it is hard to avoid the even more dizzying impression that whatever has been proposed since the seventeenth century is itself more often than not a variation on the eruditions of antiquity.

I believe that there is every reason to speak of recent progress cautiously. The history of religions is part of the historical and humanistic studies in which the term 'progress' functions principally in the application for research grants. In most of the remaining usages it expresses wishful thinking. Only occasionally may it be a means to envision sense and meaning in the discussion of our materials. Though some might want to write off even this last usage as mere poetry, it is the only one possible in discussing recent trends in the study of myth.

The most often quoted treatise on the state of mythological studies comes to my aid through its own cautiousness. It is Paul Ehrenreich's *Die allgemeine Mythologie und ihre ethnologischen Grundlagen*, published in 1910. Even if one does not share all his feelings, it is easy to muster some imaginative understanding and empathy for Ehrenreich's opening phrase: '*Allgemein mythologische Untersuchungen gehören bekanntlich zu den undankbarsten Aufgaben.*' (Ehrenreich 1910: iii) ['We know that general mythological researches are among the most thankless tasks.'] And truly it is not in order to insult great scholars of today that we repeat literally what he then said '*Autoritäten gibt es zudem auf diesem Gebiete überhaupt noch nicht.* ['Besides, we still have no authorities at all in this area.']

Just like Ehrenreich, however, we too must struggle with the question of what we should consider worthwhile in our field, and what we should regard as achievement. Ehrenreich conveniently enumerates features that in his opinion should characterize the general study of myth. Three of those features have definitely been dropped since his day. It may be useful at the outset to list these changes, so pronounced in the post-war orientation; perhaps they indicate real progress.

Ehrenreich regarded an evolution of the human mind as obvious, and in his view the supremacy of myth, once extending over the entire world, was destined to give way to conceptual thought expressing a scientific worldview (Ehrenreich 1910: 3). This idea, widespread as it was then, and long-lingering as it has been, even in intellectual circles (e.g., in Cassirer 1953), has met resistance among prehistorians (e.g., K.J. Narr 1964) and ethnologists (e.g., A.E. Jensen 1963) in their endeavors to be just to their materials. The unavoidable, related practice of viewing 'primitive' cultures in the contemporary world as 'leftovers,' living fossils of the supposed mythological past, had already lost most of its appeal for specialized anthropologists well before the war (e.g., Paul Radin). In fact there are two related but distinct ideas here, propounded in Ehrenreich's time, that are no longer ours. One is the general certainty of the evolution of the human mind, in perfect analogy to Darwin's evolution of the species. The second is the certainty that myth precedes reason. The second was perhaps the more tenacious assumption, slow to die; witness not only Cassirer, but also Gusdorf (1948), one of the most inspiring philosophers of religion in the post-war era.

I hasten to state that I do not mean to discredit Cassirer or Gusdorf or anyone else. Rather, in the years immediately after the war, these philosophers in developing their own thought relied on general views held in the study of myth. At the time, only some anthropologists and historians had articulated the necessary changes from generally held evolutionistic theories.

The third idea in Ehrenreich that has definitely been discarded, except by some folklorists, is that fairy tales and myths could be mentioned in one breath. It is above all the merit of Hermann Baumann, in addition to his extensive ethnological work, to have specified types of folk literature and to have refined the category of myth (Baumann 1959).

The three outmoded features we have noted in Ehrenreich's work are helpful in setting the scene of recent enquiries. However, there are numerous other changes that can be described in the sort of research done, in the sort of questions asked, in short, in the nature of mythological study. For our survey it will be best to focus on several select topics in order to identify dominant themes, schools, and tendencies.

a. *The carry-over of neo-romanticism*

Art historians or literary critics might not be altogether pleased with my use of the word 'neo-romanticism.' However, I need the term to describe a mood rather than a precisely labelled style. It is a certain emotional attitude to be found after the second world war. It obviously continued pre-war trends and was to quite an extent found in the same people, simply having grown older. For better or worse, with this mood, even the most shocking events of the wars seem to leave little or no noticeable marks even on studies of the most sensitive matter of human existence: religious orientation. I have never stopped wondering about the publication of Rudolf Otto's *Das Heilige*, no doubt the single most influential work in the history of religions, in the year 1917, during the first world war. Similarly, the second world war was not a watershed in scholarly fashions.

In what I choose to call neo-romanticism, the continuity is astonishing. I do not propose to explain it on these pages, although I wish I could, but I do think it is the first topic we should attend to. Neo-romanticism blossoms in Europe between the two world wars. It is a time in which some of the most widely read novelists and poets deal with man's spiritual loneliness, his quest for peace and happiness, and sometimes evoke a nostalgia bordering on sentimentality (especially in the stories telling us of the childhood and growth of the protagonist). Knut Hamsun (1859–1952) attains international fame and is awarded the Nobel prize for literature in 1920. Hermann Hesse (1877–1962) wins the hearts of his devotees between the two wars and wins the Nobel prize in 1946. The famous Indian poet Rabindranath Tagore (1861–1941) becomes one of the darlings of the European reading public. (He had already won the Nobel prize in 1913). Thomas Mann (Nobel prize 1929) and many others could be mentioned.

It is impossible to see the work of a good number of historians of religions separate from the 'feeling of life' expressed in literature. Of course, the literary world was not homogeneous. There were many variations and conflicts in the neo-romantic assemblage. The rise of Nazism and the war saw many in opposing camps, nationally, politically, ideologically. As it was among the men of letters (one might think of Ezra Pound, working for the Italian radio during Mussolini's reign, and of T.S. Eliot, lecturing before a BBC microphone), so it was among historians of religions.

What characterizes the neo-romantic mood among historians of religions? It is the fascination with perfect beginnings, as in the genesis of the human race, or the origin of a nation, or in the creation myths of a tradition. It is also a nostalgia for everything that expresses a *totality*, distinct from and much more than the fragmented and finite profane world. In all this, we find elaborated, time and again, the idea that primitive man is somehow the total man, who lives as we all did before the fall—the old idea of the noble savage, but now presented with great historical and textual detail.

I am thinking here of some of the greatest scholars, and personally, I would rather be placed in their camp than in the emaciated, positivistic sciences they were at odds with all their lives. Among these scholars, the first who comes to mind is Walter F. Otto. In an article, 'Der Mythos,' published in 1955, he says:

Je mehr ... das Rationale den Mythos zurückdrängt und die Welt entheiligt wird, musz sich das ursprüngliche Wissen vom Göttlichen in das Gefühl, in die Herzensinnigkeit zurückziehen. Das

Profane tritt neben das Religiöse und nimmt bald den weitaus gröszeren Raum ein. (W.F. Otto 1955: 265)

[The more ... the realm of reason represses myth and the more the world is desanctified, the more the original knowledge about the divine has to retreat into the emotion, into the inner life. The profane appears next to the religious and soon occupies a larger place.]

Otto is a classicist limiting his work to Greek mythology. His statements are balanced and philosophically accounted for. Yet they are militant. In one sense, they fight a very outdated battle. They suggest that the entire history of myth is a process of decay. In another sense, they proclaim the significance of a 'higher' word in a world of increasing, self-proclaimed secularity. That significance can never be completely extinguished, even if it is forced back into the innermost heart of man.

Paraphrasing the great romantic poet Hölderlin, Otto exclaims that the divine sounds forth in *names* (W.F. Otto 1955: 265). All religions, he asserts, receive their essence in a revelation of divine forms, and myth is diminished only through the development of unbelief. To be sure, religion does not disappear from the face of the earth, but unbelief brings about a repression of religion to inner experiences. In other words, religion turns from an experience and certainty shared by all to a matter of mysticism in those few who are gifted with religious genius. Next to Hölderlin, the romantic philosopher Schelling is a source of inspiration for Otto. The renewal of romanticism in the study of myth which is so evident here has its kinship with Rudolf Otto's *The Idea of the Holy* and his stress on religious *experience* as crucial in our understanding of religious documents.

Walter Otto is also convinced that not all myths are of the same quality or weight. Such a conviction may be quite common, but Otto adds that the quality of any myth depends on the closeness of its relationship to the *Urmythos*, or primordial myth expressing the divine form fully (W.F. Otto 1955: 264).

The majority of students might not feel inspired by all these neo-romantic statements, or might voice immediate criticisms. Yet we must realize that these statements are not mere poetic hyperbole. With a much more down-to-earth appearance, ideas of a similar kind occur in the ethnologist A.E. Jensen, who is best known for his publications concerning the culture of the *Urpflanzer*, 'primordial planters' or rootcroppers (Jensen 1939, 1963). Rootcroppers are found in various tropical regions of the world and exhibit certain similar features not only in their means of life—the cultivation of bulbous fruits and roots—but apparently also in their mythology. The most intensively studied myths come from Eastern Indonesia (Ceram) and Southern Irian (New-Guinea). In all of them the central figure is a more-than-ordinary human being who was killed in primordial times and whose death brought about vegetation, the 'normal' life and death cycle of existence, and all that is needed for truly human life. This figure is known as the *dema*, the name used by the Marind-anim of Irian (Wirz 1922: vol. II, 6–23; Van Baal 1966).

In terms of their occupation with roots and bulbs, the peoples under discussion seem to form an intermediary stage between the hunters and gatherers of prehistory and the rice-and-grain-based civilizations of protohistory and history. Jensen was quite aware of his own interpretations as a critical extension of the earlier work by F. Graebner and W. Schmidt on 'stages' of cultural evolution, each with its own type of myths and cults. Moreover, the intermediary rootcroppers seem to play a special role, as if designed to improve our understanding of all mythical and cultic structures. Particularly, the mythical killing of the *dema*-deity is ritually enacted and—according to Jensen—functions to embody quite positively the meaning of life and death (Jensen 1950; De Vries 1977: chap. 23). An important corollary to this interpretation is that later sacrificial procedures, viz. those in the early empires built on grain-cultivation, lost their real significance. Jensen uses the expressions *Ausdruck* (expression) and *Anwendung* (application). Supposedly, the original myth expressed its meaning adequately, in a manner experienced by the people. In later times, the application of the myth in life and ritual becomes mere repetitiousness. As a result, sacrifices can even become acts of senseless cruelty, such as the slaughter of human beings by the Aztec (De Vries 1977: 198, 208). In other words, the history of myth is subject to a 'semantic depletion' (Jensen 1963: 76–79).

I do not intend to discuss Jensen—himself a pupil of Frobenius—and the valuable contributions to anthropology by himself and his school (the school of Frankfurt). I only want to take note of Jensen's guiding ideas in the study of myth: the theory of depletion; of expression and application; of an originally fully understood and experienced mythology. These ideas fit entirely into the neo-romantic tradition.

The 'phenomenology of religion' designed by G. van der Leeuw (1890–1950) deserves a special discussion outside this section, and yet it would be impossible to overlook its impetus in the neo-romantic mood. The empathy (*Einfühlung*) Van der Leeuw urges the historian of religions to practise in the understanding of the phenomena (Van der Leeuw 1963: chap. 107; 1948b: 72–73) is not merely a technique.

Quite a number of other students of myth who deserve to be discussed under other headings may nevertheless be mentioned here as well. In various ways the practice of empathy is advocated by many scholars, and most of these belong among the neo-romantics (e.g., F. Heiler, W.B. Kristensen, C.J. Bleeker).

Related to Van der Leeuw and others in this section, yet distinct from them, is Mircea Eliade (born 1907). It is true that he is not obsessed with the idea of a unilinear semantic depletion of religious practice (nor does he sing the praises of *Einfühlung*), but he does exhibit a paramount interest in the 'cosmic religion' of 'archaic man.' Even though archaic man in some of his writings is more a 'real man' who exists beneath appearances in all people, he is more clearly visible among Australian tribal hunters or in prehistoric shamanism (Eliade 1964, 1973) than in the modern West. The notion of *illud tempus* which Eliade employs to understand the time in which mythical events occur has an unmistakable resemblance to romantic philosophemes since Schelling. Much of his work concerns man's urge to escape time, and his nostalgia for paradise.

It should go without saying that the mythological material itself demands treatment of the cosmogony-before-all-time and of paradisal imageries. It is striking that occasionally in Eliade's writings the line between mythical time and a historical long ago is vague. Should historical developments and mythical motifs not be separated? Isn't it perhaps inappropriate to make *illud tempus* seem more accessible by making it look like the time of our recollection or experience? I am only asking this question, and I realize that the answer, whether negative or positive, cannot be prescribed for anyone.

I register two examples of a neo-ramantic slant in Eliade. First, he asserts that in an earlier stage, all human beings had easy communication with the world of the gods, while later, only shamans could ascend to the sky; and likewise, the shamanic experience, pure and natural at first, later would be induced by narcotics. Where does history end and myth begin? Both changes, the diminishing contact with the gods and the decay of shamanism, seem related, and Eliade reminds the reader explicitly of a myth concerning an early golden age, as if this would somehow prove the transformation of general experiences to personal shamanic experiences (Eliade 1964: 265, 401, and *passim*). Second example: Eliade delights in concurring with the prehistorian J. Maringer that universally attested ideas concerning mythical ancestors and a life of abundance in a dim past somehow preserve the recollection of an ice age in which man lived in a hunter's paradise (Eliade 1976: 43).

One would hesitate to call Eliade a neo-romantic without a great deal of qualification. Like other creative and thought-provoking giants in our field, such as Van der Leeuw and Pettazzoni, he cannot be pigeonholed, but we do hope to show some important aspects by stating that Eliade's work, especially in the treatment of myth, has a romantic root. When the general discussion of a mythical theme polarizes into the choice between an economic or sociological explanation and an interpretation revealing man's lasting religious urges, the latter is Eliade's preference. Thus in the problem of cargo-cults and millenarianism in general, Eliade pays little attention to economic and other needs triggering a messianic movement, but sees clear evidence of man's undying desire to make a clear break with historical vicissitudes and re-enter a paradisal state (Eliade 1965: 125–159; Segal 1978).

In a survey of neo-romantic features in the study of myth in recent years, the names of Henri Frankfort and Thorkild Jacobsen cannot be omitted. *The Intellectual Adventure of Ancient Man*, published by them along with H.A. Frankfort and John A. Wilson shortly after the war, became almost a manifesto in the study of the ancient Near East (Frankfort et alia 1946). The work was renamed *Before Philosophy* and reprinted a number of times. The scholars took a firm stand against the persistent opinion that myth was a matter of mere amusement or resembled fairy tales, and, by implication, against the paternal idea that myths were products of minds that had not reached our modern development. In the defense of myth, they introduced the notion of a 'mytho-poeic age.'

This age, as its name implies, created myths, such as the myth of Marduk and his victory over the powers of chaos. The myth of Marduk is poetry, yet more than poetry, proclaiming a truth celebrated at the New Year's Festival, creating the world anew and creating man's relationship with nature.

The application of this interpretation went beyond the world of Mesopotamia, Egypt, and Greece, to which the authors confined themselves. Its influence touched numerous students, just as it had itself been influenced, if not determined, by the neo-romantic mood of the time. It certainly was of supreme importance that certain specialists saved their materials from the 'primitivism' that had come close to declaring them subhuman. Obviously, the antipositivistic stance of the 'mytho-poeicists' is akin to the tradition of Rudolf Otto, to whom Thorkild Jacobsen in particular likes to refer (1976: 3).

Violet MacDermot has dealt comparably with a more recent period of history, in a fascinating book about the seers and the visionary and ecstatic experiences in late antiquity and early Christianity (MacDermot 1971). Although she has some interest in the physiological causes of the visions, her major interest lies in the reality of the experiences. Hence her work is akin to that of Frankfort and Jacobsen.

The one inevitable question concerning a 'mytho-poeic,' highly visionary age is this: just when might it have occurred? The problem is not simply, for instance, that the Coptic and Syriac texts are at considerable distance in time from the glory of Babylon and Egypt, but that the suggestion of a myth-creating age itself seems unconvincing. The suggestion of certain creative periods suffers from the same weakness as do loose references to geography in reference to supposed differences between the Eastern and Western mind.

I repeat that I am far from disparaging the neo-romantic efforts, which have done so much to preserve mythological materials when dry specialization devoid of vision seemed ready to vitiate the study of myth altogether. Nevertheless, the myth of a golden age, when it begins to resemble a datable epoch on scholarly pages, may need some correction.

b. *Texts and manuals. Specialization*

A mountain of specialized work in specific religious traditions and subjects has been amassed—so enormous as to prevent us from making a bibliographical dent in it here. The study of Indian culture, including mythology in the major traditions of Hinduism as well as the village and tribal cults, has grown enormously in philology, sociology, and anthropology. Special subjects, such as the myths and cults of late antiquity and gnosticism, have reached new heights. The establishment of area study centers, for the Near East, India, the Far East, Southeast Asia, and Latin America, has stimulated specialized study programs. We can do no more here than refer to some recent manuals and the bibliographies therein (Bleeker and Widengren 1969, Schröder 1960 ff., Spuler 1959 ff. especially vol. VIII, Hermann 1959, Pritchard 1954).

There has been, in this scholarship, a remarkable will to specialize. It is something quite distinct from the endeavor toward a systematic understanding, and we might even suspect in it a conscious opposition to the neo-romantic trends I described.

The crowning example of the trend toward specialization is the third edition of the famous handbook *Die Religion in Geschichte und Gegenwart*, published in six volumes (RGG 3, 1957–1962). Even a cursory comparison with the preceding edition, in five volumes (RGG 2, 1927–1931), reveals differences. The most striking feature is not the increase in size, but the altogether different shape of many crucial articles, such as those on myth and mythology. In the preceding edition, many entries were attempts to present a comprehensive, systematic view of their subject. In the newer edition we find instead compilations of facts and opinions and booklists. The ideal of completing the facts has replaced the desire for systematic understanding.

The inclination toward exhaustiveness in specialization is not without its difficulties. Tabulations of facts and views often conceal one or more theoretical biases. The conceptual and psychological article on 'Mythos und Mythologie' in RGG 3 (by J. Sløk) beings by positing that myth is formally a type of story, but goes on to distinguish it sharply from saga, fairy tale, and fable. Thus the general assumptions of many folklorists are quietly discarded. The article stresses that the action narrated in myths has its own time, viz. a time before and beyond ordinary historical time. This is the view emphatically expounded by M. Eliade. Further on, the article states that the primordial time of myth can only become historical when the narrated events are re-enacted, as happens in cultic practice. This view is one to which many myth-ritualists—with whom Eliade is not associated—would adhere. (The myth-ritual school will occupy us below.) The second (religio-historical) part of the article under discussion, by another author (J. Haekel), summarizes some altogether different definitions of myth by various scholars, and then proceeds to state not the author's own view, but a program of things to be done in order to arrive at a fuller understanding. What we need, according to the author, are more thorough analyses and comparisons of the various religious expressions of peoples. Above all, it is suggested, we ought to pay attention to what myths may mean from the point of view of the culture in which they function. And as in ethnology or anthropology, such a study should make use of all possible methods: psychology, history, functionalism, and structuralism.

These fragments—which I hasten to add do not render the contributions in their entirety—express many of the feelings of the growing group of specialists at work since the second world war. An explicit sympathy is stated for the practice, in anthropology, of following many paths. In wide circles of specialists anthropology became an appealing model because of its manifold approaches, and its certainty of knowledge in limited areas, such as fieldworker-specialists have been after ever since Franz Boas.

The tendency toward specialization has done much good as an antidote to wild and presumptuous hypotheses. At the same time, it must be added that in the growth of specialization necessary critical questions have often received short shrift. Obviously, the reduction of meaning in myth to its function in its own culture, no matter how important, cannot be the end of all study. Myth's claim to truth demands more than sheer relativism, even in an admittedly manifold world.

c. *Myth-Ritualism*

Myth-ritualism as a school is particularly associated with the name of the British scholar S.H. Hooke, and most especially with the book *Myth and Ritual,* which he edited and published in 1933. Of course, myth in connection with ritual is not a far-fetched focus of attention. Even earlier, several scholars had turned to the subject in a more than casual way. Among them were Sir James Frazer, Hermann Gunkel (1862–1932), and Sigmund Mowinckel (1921–24, 1954, 1962).

To Gunkel we owe the term '*Sitz im Leben,*' for it was he who first studied the meaning of certain biblical texts within the religious context in which they might have *functioned.* Mowinckel is known for his study of the psalms and his convincing interpretation of a number of them as owing their life to some cultic setting, such as the New Year's festival, or the enthronement of the king, ceremonial dialogues between God and a priest, performed in the midst of the people.

After biblical scholarship, the entire area of ancient Near Eastern studies has been most concerned with myth and ritual. Among anthropologists, we should mention particularly V. Grønbech, the Danish scholar famous for his study of Germanic culture and customs (1954), and A.M. Hocart (1969), the indefatigable inquirer into the meaning of 'primitive' religion. Hocart was among the contributors to the second book on myth and ritual edited by Hooke (1935).

There are several reasons why in the post-war years myth-ritualism came to be considered a school, and not merely an obvious topic worth investigating. An external and obvious reason is that most supporters of myth-ritualism have carried on their debates, almost exclusively in Britain and Scandinavia, around the ideas of a few influential, local scholars. They did so with vigor. Indeed, it seemed to some in England that the clamor of myth-ritualism had come to fill the world. Only a few years ago the Cambridge classicist G.S. Kirk referred to the myth-and-ritual theory as universal, (although he did so only in order to proceed to demonstrate its errors [Kirk 1974: 224]). There also has been in myth-ritualism a noteworthy similarity of specific, factual interests in several of the scholarly essays involved, and a desire for greater simplicity in the interpretation of texts. The 'school' has been predominantly occupied with ancient Near Eastern materials, (although it has also included some with an anthropological bent). The inclination immediately after the second world war, as we have already noted, was to deal with 'hard facts.' The philology needed for Sumerian, Akkadian, Ugaritic,

Hebrew, and Egyptian documents strengthened the impression of dependable, factual knowledge. S.H. Hooke himself quite consciously saw his work as a reaction to the vagueness of more comparative, non-historical approaches (Hooke 1933: 1; 1958: 4), and, defending against criticism, he stressed that the myth and ritual patterns were revealed through careful study of texts in the original cuneiform (Hooke 1958: 3-4). As to what constitutes the key in mythical problems, although there was no consensus in this 'school,' the general tendency was to give cult the priority.

No one could seriously doubt the existence of ties between certain rituals and certain myths. At the same time, placing this relationship in the forefront seems almost arbitrary if one considers the variety of options available in the search for focal points of interpretation: in the realm of economic and cultural existence; in social stratification; in politics; in existential necessity; in human creative imagination; perhaps even in the experience of the holy which a generation of scholars had been talking about. In addition, there are many instances in which a cult or a myth is known to have originated in some one individual's vision or dreams. Joseph Fontenrose, the indefatigable critic of all generalizations, devoted a helpful small book to the criticism of this theory giving cult priority in the understanding of myth (1971). To be sure, the majority of myth-ritualists have not been extremists, and the importance of their work is precisely that it focused on texts on which they were experts. As to the validity of the myth-ritual pattern, the 1958 collection *Myth, Ritual and Kingship* itself voices reservations in several chapters. The greatest significance for the development of the study of myth lies perhaps in the clarity with which these specialists have shown that more than philological expertise is needed to arrive at valid interpretations of myth (as well as ritual)—whether they have shown this intentionally or not.

Even if the hypotheses of myth-ritualism were often narrow, a number of scholars associated with it explored specific mythological topics in a remarkable way, precisely because of their specialization, and thus enlarged our knowledge. I. Engnell is known for his inquiries into kingship in the ancient Near East (1943), though he certainly did not satisfy all his fellow experts. Geo Widengren, although he moved in a wide, indeed universal area of religio-historical study and even tried his hand at a phenomenology of religion (1969), has done his best work in specific philological and historical studies, in which the focus on myth and ritual is evident (e.g., Widengren 1938, 1958).

A rather independent figure in the scholarship of myth and ritual is Theodor H. Gaster. His independence borders on the admirable obstinacy that sometimes accompanies specialization. Gaster's studies cover many subjects, yet concentrate on the literary documents of the ancient Near East and, within those, on specific questions. He is well-known for his updated and annotated editions of Sir James Frazer (Frazer 1959, Gaster 1969), and it is probably most accurate to see the peculiar independence of Gaster precisely in the tradition of Frazer, at the same time old-fashioned in its stress on certain ideas (such as 'fertility' and 'primitive thought') and astounding in its forceful and wide scholarship of ancient literary texts and folkloric materials. Gaster's insistence on the crucial importance of ritual for our understanding of myth is not dogmatically one-sided. He shows his interest in a wider cultural and aesthetic world in which human civilizations have their being. The subtitle of his principal work, *Thespis*, is *Ritual, Myth and Drama in the Ancient Near East* (Gaster 1961). Gaster sees the dramatic element of human existence in the ancient and universal new year ceremonies meant at the same time to renew life and to revitalize fertility and human moral force. He does not regard the question of whether myth or ritual 'came first' as important. The two are always found together, and Gaster understands myth as an aspect of ritual, calling it basically consubstantial with ritual (Gaster 1954: 187).

d. *The history of science and Neo-Panbabylonism*

The history of science (and technology) has made great strides in recent decades. Alexandre Koyré (1968) gave a much firmer historical footing to investigation of scientific development in the Western renaissance centuries. Lynn White (1978) and several other scholars have furnished fascinating new insights in the history of Western science. Joseph Needham (1961 and ff.) has attained fame through his gigantic work on science and technology in China. Otto Neugebauer (1962) devoted his entire life to the study of mathematics and astronomy in ancient Mesopotamia, fully aware of the precision of the scientific data, the subject contrasting to the amorphous questions and answers of humanistic historians. In recent years David Pingree has done a good deal of the basic work in sorting out the astronomical documents of ancient India (1963, 1967–68, 1971). Most startling of all have been the discoveries and interpretations of prehistoric data by Alexander Marshack (1972). Much prehistoric, upperpalaeolithic and early neolithic material turns out to reveal precise and consistent calendrical notations.

The worldviews of peoples affected by precise observation of heavenly bodies and corresponding mathematical calculations of course concern the historian of religions. Even if religious and scientific data are not always transparent in their mutual relationship, the era in which they were considered mutually exclusive is definitely over. If any one generalization is valid, it is that the sum total of the superb recent historical scholarship devoted to science reveals the intricate interwovenness of religious and scientific views and persuasions everywhere and at all times. As a matter of fact, the distinction between religion and science, though it is still easily made today, is inapplicable in most cases. Man experiences both as one in their origin in the endeavor to orient himself. No wonder that historians of religions have made a grateful use of the works by recent historians of science (see especially Eliade 1976, 1978 and ff.; as well as H. Smith 1976).

There is another side, however, to the interest in scientific history, and it is this side that evokes the term neo-Panbabylonism. It will be recalled that earlier in this century the name Panbabylonism was given to scholarship which suggested that the entire mythology of the world had diffused from astronomical observations made in the ancient Near East (see De Vries 1977: chap. 14). It is impossible not to remember this in reading the work by some recent scholars who are certain they have decoded man's mythological imagination.

Giorgio de Santillana searched for the links between science and myth quite consciously, and together with another notable historian, Hertha von Dechend, he published a sizable tome presenting the key (de Santillana and von Dechend 1969). Like the earlier Panbabylonists, the authors attribute the greatest importance to the ancient Near East, for there, in their estimation, the first understanding of the world in terms of number, measure, and weight was formulated (de Santillana and von Dechend 1969: 132). The work proposes to explain myth as a repository of that scientific understanding. To be sure, the authors have not met with much scholarly approval, and it is true that they ignored some of the most obvious questions. How exactly does myth become the repository of mathematics and astronomy? Why is so much literary garment needed for relatively simple scientific facts? The questions remain unanswered, and, to make matters worse, the authors act as if no mythological interpretation had been offered by such men as Jensen, Jung, Lévi-Strauss, or Eliade.

Any explanation of myth built on one narrow foundation, no matter how scientifically designed, seems doomed. Strangely, any one-sided explanation, if only it is eloquently proposed, seems to gain devotees almost immediately. Freudian depth-psychology (Bettelheim 1954, 1976), Jungian depth-psychology (Neumann 1954, 1955), the discovery of intoxicating uses of mushrooms, or, to be more precise, the fly-agaric (Wasson 1968, Allegro 1970), all have found their serious and not-so-serious defenders as the key to all mythology. The current craving for scientific explanations, or rather, for explanations on the basis of one scientific positive discipline as taught in a modern college textbook, is part of this same trend. A recent eloquent title is *The Myth of Invariance, the Origin of the Gods, Mathematics and Music from the Rgveda to Plato* (McClain 1976).

There are a good many endeavors that seem to connect the study of myths with science. Often they have a monistic theological signature, and I believe they are only tangential to our subject. Most famous in this area is Teilhard de Chardin (1959, 1964, 1965), scientist and theologian in one, who has set many minds and pens in motion. For our purposes, his work is not extremely relevant, for the simple reason that he does not touch immediately on myths. The relationship Teilhard de Chardin described so lyrically is that between the revelation and purpose of God on the one side, and the structure and purpose of the scientifically explorable world on the other. The central problem is not religio-historical, but theological; it is the ancient issue of natural theology, which has been explicitly discussed again by Alister Hardy in his Gifford Lectures (Hardy 1965, 1966) and in *The Biology of God, a Scientist's Study of Man, the Religious Animal* (Hardy 1976). Hardy is convinced that man is religious by nature, and that ultimately man's scientific pursuits also cannot be otherwise, and thus theology and other disciplines of learning somehow coalesce. He makes a straightforward case for natural theology, borrowing freely from Bergson's and Whitehead's process philosophies, and referring with sympathy to Tillich's terminology.

No matter what strong convictions the historian of religions may have about the religious nature of man, the study of myths, and religion in general, he does not profit a great deal by the notion of a natural theology. The very idea presumes to build a bridge between what is and what should be, or between the describable world and the God of faith and revelation. Just as a natural theology is not very useful for actual church life, cannot function in the care of souls, and cannot begin to comfort people in distress by speaking of God as 'the ground of being' or 'being itself,' so the understanding of specific myths is not furthered by a general process philosophy, whether from a Whiteheadian or Bergsonian source, or for that matter, from Śrī Aurobindo's devotees, or from anywhere else. The lesson that the actual religious life of man is too varied, too specific, and in each instance too unique to be covered by a conception resembling natural theology should already have been learned in the eighteenth century (Hamann 1962, Hume 1947, O'Flaherty 1967, Jansen Schoonhoven 1945). That lesson, though primarily addressed to philosophy, is still valid for specific scientific inquiries, including the study of myth in the history of religions.

Glossing over the line between the realm of scientific questions in specific disciplines dealing with specific objects and that other realm where norms are discussed and all of reality in its ultimate coherence is the issue—glossing over that line, or even worse, pretending to have wiped it out or suggesting that it does not exist: this is the most elementary mistake that can be made, and once it is made, knowledge becomes illusory. Perhaps the most conspicuous mistakes of this type have been made by theologians all too eager to show the relevance of their doctrines. But in recent years we have had our share of self-styled scientists who explained all mythology in one fell swoop. Thus, the

Egyptian darkness has no meaning except as a curious record of planetary catastrophies. A Buddhist description of the human experience of *duḥka*, torn out of its context, becomes another illustration of the same. The factual mistakes made by Velikovsky are negligible compared to the wide-spread ignorance of elementary rules in the order of knowledge. Is it necessary to mention the curious popularity, even among people who should know better, of Von Däniken? Again: thoughtless jumping from supposed facts to an ultimate explanation of religious documents. We should remember, however, that the danger for our work is not the influence of extravagant examples, but the continual temptation to impose some scientific discipline on the entire territory of philosophy.

We have a great deal to learn from scientific approaches. For instance, in the study of the Purāṇas we meet with cosmogonic and cosmological accounts that mention specific large numbers of years. Until the work by Pingree no one had taken the trouble to relate these numbers to astronomical and calendrical calculations. As a result, one had no recourse but to attribute these matters to a rather fantastic myth-making creativity or a 'primitive mentality,' or to look for explanations even more mysterious than the facts offered in the myths. The history of science obviously had to set us right. It is supremely important, however, to realize clearly that our problems did not reside in the myths themselves, but in the custom in our universities of splitting the sciences from the humanities.

It should also be noted that serious historians of science do not pretend to discover the ultimate truth of the universe when they publish their findings. If students of myth feel stimulated by scientific facts in their documents, they had better preserve the same modesty. If they do not, they should be even more modest, and first brush up on elementary astronomy.

e. *Associations with existentialist moods*

A few words should be said about existentialism. I do not propose to summarize the philosophies of Heidegger, Sartre, or Jaspers, but I do want to make mention of the *mood* of existentialism that affected many people outside the existentialist schools.

In 1950 Maurice Leenhardt presented a paper to the International Association for the History of Religions touching on the subject of myth and ritual. However, he did not engage in the old debate as to which of the two came first. Instead, his paper took a stance against rational, merely chronological scholarly habits of thought by speaking of real myth as being in origin a matter of *expérience vécue*, lived experience, in which the separation of myth and ritual behavior would be artificial and nonsensical. He argued that the living of a myth somehow should be seen as taking priority over its narration.

One cannot say that this manner of dealing with myth 'caught on,' but I believe it was the most forthright statement of an idea that affected other students of myth as well. Jensen and Eliade occupied themselves at about the same time with the actual function, the lived experience of myth, Jensen in his studies of Ceramese culture, Eliade especially in his work on shamanism. The idea of myth as an experience, no matter how it may be explained in its details, naturally is akin to the older theory that mysticism and religious experience are crucial to our understanding of religion (Rudolf Otto 1946; Joachim Wach 1924, 1951).

It may seem curious to call one post-war strain in the study of myth existentialist when it fits so well in what I called the neo-romantic mood—curious because existentialism is commonly thought of as a reaction to philosophies of the romantic era (especially Hegel). Again, I cannot venture into the intricacies of the history of European thought, yet I do register the coalescence of scholarly moods associated with existentialism and neo-romanticism. Wach, whose relation to the entire romantic tradition is beyond doubt (see Kitagawa 1963; 1968; Wach 1951: especially on Otto, 209–227), at the same time finds support for his discussion of religion in Tillich's existentialist notion of 'ultimate reality.' (Wach 1951: 32) In passing, *via negativa*, one might well note that scholars such as the Italians Pettazzoni (1954), Brelich (1966), Bianchi (1975: 171–176), or Lanternari, who did not give a great deal of credence to Rudolf Otto's ideas, are at the same time impervious to ideas affected by existentialism. Some ideas travel freely, others seem to observe national or cultural borders. Obviously, the original *expérience vécue* of a myth is a matter of theory, and just as with Rudolf Otto's *numinosum*, there is never clear evidence in any specific social environment or historical setting. Those scholarly traditions where sociological and historical studies prevailed were least affected by reflections on existentialist hypotheses.

Maurice Leenhardt published a fascinating book about religion in Melanesia, *Do Kamo* in 1947 (Leenhardt 1971), summing up his findings on the culture and religion of New Caledonia, where he spent many years. Having learned much from Lucien Lévy-Bruhl, Leenhardt was in the habit of philosophizing on all that related to 'primitive' culture. The relationship of reason and myth attracted his full attention. Rather than contrasting the two, he understood them as complementary modes of consciousness (see preface by M.I. Pereira de Queiroz in Leenhardt 1971: 34). In the analysis of conceptions of the body, life and death, the experience of time, and so on (is it only a coincidence that these topics are so dear too to existentialist thinkers?), he tends to assign the greatest importance to myth. Again, remembering some of Walter Otto's statements, it seems natural to mark an association with the neo-romantics. An important element in Leenhardt's views is the idea that myth is not in the first place associated with the past or with primitive peoples. It is a mode of thought of all people in all times. Here Leenhardt clearly goes beyond the earlier works of his mentor Lévy-Bruhl and enters a new era with the later works of Van der Leeuw. This new era—need it be said?—does not bring with it universal agreement.

f. *Phenomenology and morphology of religion*

The phenomenology of religion, though practised by many, is principally the design of Gerardus van der Leeuw. The morphology of religion (Eliade's term) is not really distinguishable from it in its major outline, and it is exactly the same in its treatment of myth. Therefore it will be best to deal with both of them together.

The phenomenology of religion by Van der Leeuw (1963) does not owe very much to Husserl, in spite of the name 'phenomemology.' The *Epilegomena* of the work spell out a theoretical framework, and the figure of far more significance to it is Wilhelm Dilthey. Moreover, Van der Leeuw acknowledges his debt to students of religion before him who developed ideas on which he elaborated. The most significant and earliest historian of religions who designed a phenomenology of religious forms was P.D. Chantepie de la Saussaye. (The philosophical endeavor by Hegel falls outside our scope here.) Chantepie added a 'phenomenological part' to the first edition of his *Lehrbuch* (Chantepie de la Saussaye 1887: 48–170). There he presented a number of religious forms that occur universally and in all periods, such as gods, magic and divination, sacrifice and prayer. One section dealt explicitly with mythology.

As in the case of Chantepie's work, we have to think of Van der Leeuw's endeavor in the first place as a matter of common sense. After all, it is common sense to try to gain as firm an awareness as possible of terms and their applicability in any specific religio-historical research. There is a second point to consider, however, and that is the specific task of *understanding*, which Van der Leeuw considers central to his discipline. What myths and other religious forms *really* are is the issue, and Van der Leeuw makes the first task of the phenomenology of religion the very assignment of names, such as 'myth' (Van der Leeuw 1963: vol. II, 688). Although Van der Leeuw himself seems to avoid the word 'essence' as much as possible, others influenced by him do use it (Heiler 1961).

It is only natural to ask why we should need an additional discipline to search for meaning, thereby to become truly objective in understanding, and to give appropriate names. Does not the existing discipline of history do that? This criticism has been forcefully stated by Pettazzoni (1954: 215–219).

It would not be necessary to touch on the nature of the phenomenology of religion if the subject had no bearing on the fundamentals of the study of myth. As far as I can see, there are at present only three truly serious methods in the interpretation of myths, and the phenomenology of religion is certainly one of them, next to comprehensive historical study and structuralism.

Part of the legacy of Dilthey in the phenomenology of religion seems close to exhausted by now. It is the very emphasis on understanding (*Verstehen*) as distinct from explanation (see the marvelous study by Sierksma, 1951; for a concise discussion of understanding and meaning in Dilthey, see Rickman in Dilthey 1962: 37–43). All human documents are by nature meaningful, Dilthey argues, and the principal scholarly way to deal with them is 'to rediscover the I in the Thou,' for that is what understanding amounts to. It is distinct from the process of explaining, in the sense of pointing out causes, which is the method of the natural sciences. The obvious danger here—but not so obvious during Dilthey's lifetime (1833–1911)—is a rather inappropriate bipartition in the world of learning. The application of Dilthey's ideas has no doubt contributed a great deal to the isolation of the historical and humanistic studies from the sciences, which I noted before (section *d* above). Certainly it would be difficult to find scientists at the present time who would consider their method principally one of establishing causes by means of respectable laboratory tests. Historians today would be quite as aware as Dilthey that the French revolution, or, for that matter, the birth of a myth, could never be identically reproduced; yet they would not belittle the notion of causes. The theory of knowledge may have grown more complex in our day, but it also has brought greater unity, or an increased awareness of *common* problems (K. Popper 1957; Löwith 1949; Michael Polanyi 1962; Radnitzky 1973; and others).

What does the phenomenological method contribute to the study of myth? The pages Van der Leeuw wrote on the subject are among the most brilliant in his works, and—this is not a secret—they are not really augmented by Eliade's elaborations.

Van der Leeuw's statements about myth are made with great sensitivity, a wide grasp, and a subtle sense of balance. Some of them quite clearly fit into the neo-romantic tradition. Just like Walter Otto, Van der Leeuw likes to identify the work of the poet with that of the myth-maker (Van der Leeuw 1948a: part 3, chap. I; especially p. 122 in the English translation). Some of his statements reveal his reflection on specialized studies. Not in the last place, Van der Leeuw is quite aware of the problems in the philosophy of history, and of philosophical problems in man's experience of time, and as a result he articulates clearly the distinction between myth and other verbal communication. The uniqueness of myth is given in its identity with the word itself. It is the powerful, spoken word, hence the basis of all human existence, new whenever it is spoken, accompanying the sacred action. We should not be misled by the fact that so many myths have come to us—as have especially the Greek myths—through literary adaptations. Myth when truly functioning as myth not merely accompanies a celebration but is itself a celebration. It does not generalize in the manner of scientific laws and abstractions. On the contrary, myth makes even the elements of what we call 'nature' into a unique event; that is why repeated narration of myth must occur; the myth's life consists in its uniqueness or novelty (Van der Leeuw 1963: vol. II, 413–414). The time in which mythical actions proceed differs radically from ordinary or measurable time; thus Van der Leeuw describes what Eliade will call *illud tempus*, that peculiar time all-by-itself of which myth speaks (Eliade 1958: chap. 12). In one of his last essays Van der Leeuw dealt elaborately with myths of creation and eschatological myths (Van der Leeuw 1957). He shows myth as a universal and continuing basic element in human orientation (see also his earlier works—Van der Leeuw 1941: especially chap. XIII; and 1937). The beauty of the essay on myths of creation and eschatology is especially that he nowhere polemicizes. He quotes and makes use of various scholarly works representing very different points of view. It is true that Van der Leeuw's conception of 'primitive' man remained one derived at the same time from older evolutionistic and from neo-romantic theories, but in the late forties these ideas were shared by many without much of an inner conflict.

The idea of myth as principally an account of the world's birth, set forth by Van der Leeuw, is elaborated by Eliade. The cosmogony is basic to all other myths, and functions significantly in times of crises or disease to reconstitute reality. Even eschatological myths, speaking of a return to paradise or a total renewal of the world, are variations on the cosmogonic account. In the final analysis, modern political movements and ideas governing human conceptions of history are comprehensible only through the study of myths (Eliade 1963; 1958: chaps. XI and XII). Just like Van der Leeuw, Eliade sees the fundamental structure of man's religious forms, including myths, revealed in 'primitive' or, in terms he prefers, 'pre-Socratic' and 'pre-Mosaic' documents. Hence Eliade also discusses subjects such as the decadence of myths, and survivals and camouflages of myths (Eliade 1963: chaps. VIII and IX).

The phenomenology of religion has been criticized in various quarters, perhaps most explicitly by Pettazzoni (1954: chap. XIX). The criticism, levelled at Van der Leeuw, is directed particularly against the supposed un-historical nature of phenomenology. By slighting history, does one not run the risk of placing side by side in the phenomenological scheme items with altogether different roots and functions? It seems of great significance to me that Eliade, who could as well be an object of the same criticism, is in the process of fulfilling a promise he made in his *Traité d'histoire des religions* in 1948 regarding the possibility of laying the foundation for a history of religions (see Eliade 1958: xiii). The two volumes published so far of his most recent work present a wealth of ideas which may well contribute to a more spacious yet more unified understanding of myths than the conflict between history and phenomenology has suggested (Eliade 1976: 1978 and ff.). In this context it may be useful to remember that Eliade's preference for the word 'morphology' rather than 'phenomenology' of religion is more than a mere matter of taste. 'Morphology,' as used in scientific pursuits, biology, linguistics, etc., reveals an empirical orientation (see author's foreword in Eliade 1958). Whether this choice will be sufficient in the long run to avoid philosophical discussions of the sort in which Van der Leeuw became engaged is perhaps not so certain.

Under the heading of 'phenomenology of religion' one more name should be mentioned, to show especially that this school—if we can call it that—has many facets. W. Brede Kristensen is older than Van der Leeuw and Eliade; he hardly touched on philosophical problems in any obvious manner at all, and he limited his studies by and large to the ancient religions of the Mediterranean world, Egypt, Rome, and Greece, with occasional references to ancient Iran. He quite consciously dealt with materials of which he had first-hand knowledge through his own language studies. One could argue that he never even raised the matter of myth as a problem in religion. However, all his writings dealt with mythical themes and topics (Kristensen 1947, 1954, 1955, 1960). The theme which occupied him above all was that of the spontaneity of life arising from death in Egyptian, Roman, and Greek documents (Kristensen 1926). Kristensen's work is characterized by his abstention from theoretical controversies. His influence is clear among a multitude of ardent admirers. The amazing thing is that these pupils followed very different paths themselves and hardly ever seem to have seen eye to eye on any issue, except their admiration for Kristensen. Kristensen was not only one of Van der Leeuw's teachers, but also one of the most revered masters of Hendrik Kraemer. Kraemer was an expert on Islam, an actively involved church leader, who, after some years as professor in Leiden for the history of modern religions and the phenomenology of religion, became the first director of the Ecumenical Institute of Bossey. K.A.H. Hidding, altogether different from Kraemer in scholarly and religious persuasions and style, was appointed in Kraemer's chair and shared with him an unflagging reverence for Kristensen. The theologian K.H. Miskotte counted Kristensen among those from whom he had learned the most. Of all Kristensen's admirers, only A. de Buck was a full-time Egyptologist. Barthians, liberal Christians, people with altogether different goals and careers all spoke with enthusiasm of Kristensen as their teacher. Hidding emphatically stated that Kristensen rather than Van der Leeuw deserved the title of 'initiator of the phenomenological school' (Hidding 1974: 211). For all his pupils and admirers, Kristensen was the supreme practitioner of empathy, and therefore the perfect interpreter of myths.

There is one useful moral in all this. The fear Pettazzoni held that the phenomenology of religion was somehow a camouflaged theology (North 1975, and bibliography there in footnote 2) would seem to be groundless. Real schools in the study of religion are very few and far between—Pettazzoni's own school is perhaps the only true one—and the phenomenology of religion is obviously not monolithic, theologically or otherwise.

Van der Leeuw's work did not create a school, no matter how many were stimulated and inspired by his teachings. The most gifted and prolific pupil of Van der Leeuw, F. Sierksma (1917–1977), wrote several important works, yet his major theoretical roots are in Freud rather than in Van der Leeuw (Sierksma 1951, 1956, 1960, 1961, 1964).

The Netherlands have taken the lion's share in this discussion, because in fact the phenomenology of religion has flourished there more than anywhere else. I have already mentioned the Swede Widengren (under *c.* above), but, as I suggested, his phenomenological work is not his most striking contribution. Mensching could also be mentioned, but his ideas, especially with respect to myth, are not startlingly original (Mensching 1949: 98–100). Something similar might be said of the heavy volume by Friedrich Heiler (Heiler 1961) and a good many other works. Joachim Wach, like Van der Leeuw strongly established in the scholarly tradition of Rudolf Otto, is of the greatest importance for the phenomenology of religion, yet his part in the study of myth is negligible (Bolle 1968: 4–5).

g. *About structuralism*

The word structuralism has been used in so many ways as to make us nearly forget that in principle its meaning is clear. It means that below the surface of things we can find certain patterns or consistencies; or, more accurately, structuralism is the assumption that we can do so, in mythology and a great many other fields of inquiry.

As a method, structuralism is simpler than any species of phenomenology, even though the latter is also interested in establishing coherencies. It is simpler in that the structures structuralism thinks it can discover are supposed to be present in the material studied, whereas the phenomenological method, exemplified in Van der Leeuw, deals at length with the process of understanding itself and is more concerned with the interaction between the (knowing) subject and the (known) object. One might as well say that structuralism as practised by most structuralists is philosophically far more naive, if not downright uncritically positivistic. Even Eliade, who does not elaborate on the philosophical foundations of his work, begins his *Traité d'histoire des religions* by quoting Henri Poincaré, reminding his readers that it is the scale that makes the phenomenon (Eliade 1958: xi), and with that he places himself squarely in the camp of the phenomenologists and their concern for the process of understanding.

A most decisive difference between the phenomenologists and the structuralists is the distance they observe toward Rudolf Otto. All phenomenologists of religion are somehow pupils of Otto. Among structuralists, of whatever persuasion (and they show as wide a spectrum as do the phenomenologists), the notion of the sacred, crucial in Otto, either does not function at all (as in Lévi-Strauss) or else has a much reduced significance (as in the school of De Josselin de Jong). Here again it is quite clear that Eliade is situated among the phenomenologists. He attaches great importance to the distinction between sacred and profane, and does so with reference to Otto's *Idea of the Holy* more than to Durkheim's *Formes élémentaires* (Eliade 1959: 8–10). With reference to the subject of 'myth and reality,' it is actually myth which *conveys* reality; it presents what *really* happened (Eliade 1963: 6), or the divine model (Eliade 1954: 21).

The word structure has enjoyed a special vogue in linguistics, in the important work done in that science in the last fifty years by Trubetzkoy, Roman Jacobsen, Zelling Harris, A. Noam Chomsky (although the structuralism of Chomsky is perhaps better defined as a type of formalism), and others (see especially Lyons 1970). These men took up again ideas of earlier students of language, Wilhelm von Humboldt (1767–1835) and Ferdinand de Saussure (1857–1913), and certainly my designation 'philosophically naive' does not pertain to this tradition. Also, the general idea of precise structures discernible in phonetics, grammar, syntax, (no matter how recent as the subject of a mature, fullblown science), would not strike any layman among us as foreign.

But what of mythology? At first sight, the attempt to find a linguistics-inspired set of structures in myth does not seem far-fetched. Myth after all is a matter of speech, a crucial form of speech in the transmission of religion and culture, and it would seem to stand to reason that its linguistic structures, once they are ascertained, would light up our understanding of all civilization.

Yet might not these suggestions be anthropologists' day-dreams, entertained to keep alive the hope for a truly scientific, truly defensible foundation in their field? It is interesting in this respect to consider the international fame achieved by Claude Lévi-Strauss; he has even been playfully called the pope of anthropology in France. Is it possible that Lévi-Strauss's ascendancy to anthropological and mythological prominence is due primarily to a certain scientific *crise de conscience*? Anthropology, which was so certain of its scientific foundations at the time of Tylor and Frazer, finally had to catch up with the twentieth century. The modern practitioners of the profession were not as well trained historically and philologically as the early masters, and, even more significantly, they had few defensible ideas at their disposal to support their claim to scientific respectability. (None of this can detract from particular accomplishments, such as the marvelous linguistic feats of Boas's pupils.) A year's fieldwork in a remote village with a difficult language, a description of whatever one observed there, together with a bit of theory concerning cultural stages of development, a bit of Freudianism, some scraps from Weber and Durkheim's sociological certainties, plus some vague ideas about how religion 'functions' with respect to the supposed facts of economics and society (a Malinowskian misunderstanding of Marcel Mauss)—all this together does not add up to a science in most instances.

Claude Lévi-Strauss appeared at the right moment to restore confidence in a scientific understanding of man and his mythology. Fieldworkers who had retreated into specialized descriptions of one or two small tribes suddenly saw new vistas on a world-wide scale, and those who were aware of their lack of philosophical foundation were encouraged by a complete scientific system, up-to-date and-—triumph of the modern age!—suitable for use in computers. The multiple heritage of anthropology was systematized as never before.

More than a century ago, E.B. Tylor expressed his conviction that myth was open to scientific investigation, by which he meant that laws could be established as they were in the positivistic and evolutionistic sciences of his day. He spoke of 'the evident regularity of mental law' applicable to myths of different regions, and he believed that myth might be 'more uniform than history' (Tylor 1958: 282). Lévi-Strauss could have used a number of Tylor's expressions to proclaim his new system (Maranda 1972: 8).

Lévi-Strauss's point of departure is the notion that 'any classification is superior to chaos' (1966a: 15). Granted that many of his statements seem to be made for their oratorical effect, this particular one comes back in various ways; and every time the theme is struck, Lévi-Strauss seems to delight in its double meaning. The idea that any classification is preferable to chaos, even if the classification does little or no justice to our sense impressions, is in the first place meant as a description of myth's function. At the same time, it is a militant rationalism that asserts the systematizing function of the human mind today as in bygone days, among us as well as among remote South American tribes, as the ultimate authority. It is this latter meaning that makes Lévi-Strauss the evangelist of 'primitive' myths, crossing swords with such intellectual heroes of the modern world as Jean Paul Sartre. A special appeal in Lévi-Strauss's work is precisely the rejection of theories that lead to an existential despair or to a gloomy recognition that ultimate meanings escape us. Ultimate meanings, to the extent one can talk about such things at all, must be rational meanings clear to any reasonable mind.

Lévi-Strauss baffled many of his readers by his assertion that somehow the structures of the human mind and of matter conform to each other (1966a: 269). He distinguishes two ways in which knowledge comes about, but in the end—one can only say: through Lévi-Strauss—even these two come together. The first method of knowledge was perfected in the neolithic; it is characterized by an extremely well-developed sense for the concrete, and *The Savage Mind* begins by elaborating on the extensive classificatory schemes preserved in 'primitive' societies. The other method of knowledge was perfected only in our modern scientific world; it is characterized by a developed sense for abstract reasoning. However, both types are evidence of the basic conformity of the reality known—matter—and the structure of the mind itself. In our own world, as I have said, it has finally become possible for the two paths of knowledge to cross.

Any brief summary of Lévi-Strauss sounds a bit like a dream, and in fact his writings, in spite of his confessed preference for clarity, are marked by associations as much as by reasonings. Associations not only play a role in his general manner of writing, but are built into the organization of his materials, for instance in his comparison of mythology with music (Lévi-Strauss 1969). The actual evidence of similarity seems to reside only in the necessity in both music and mythology to repeat themes rather than just to state them once. The reader who takes the time to read leisurely will reflect that even this similarity is not sameness, but a poetic association that one might well extend from myth to meditative texts, or poetry, or even to the lines in painting. But all this, no matter how puzzling, may add to the popular appeal of this structuralism.

Throughout his studies of myth, Lévi-Strauss seems preoccupied with the conflict between empiricism (associated with 'the concrete') and rationalism (associated with the 'abstractions' of modern science) (see especially 'Overture' in Lévi-Strauss 1969); it is the old contrast between Locke and Descartes. One might well wonder whether the core of Lévi-Strauss's mythology is not really the dream of a Western philosopher: the ultimate reconciliation of thought and reality. Not more than a dream? I am convinced that the phenomenological method is right precisely in its realization that the student of a far-away religious system should not act as if he could forget his own; real recognition is built on the realities of two parties. At the same time, it is mandatory that one broach one's own cultural problems cautiously, and furthermore, one should be aware that formulations other than one's own might serve one equally well. What would have happened if Lévi-Strauss had studied the pre-Socratics instead of occupying himself with our conflict between empirical and mental structures? Or suppose he had engrossed himself in Nāgārjuna's philosophy? I do not think questions of this type are outrageous, for anthropology is a discipline designed to overcome cultural provincialism. Or do we have to conclude that in the end provincialism is insuperable? Must we superimpose our philosophical categorization on myths?

What worries me more is Claude Lévi-Strauss's aversion to religious forms themselves. His most beautiful book is *Tristes Tropiques* (Lévi-Strauss 1964). Although it can be read as an anthropological study of tribes in Brazil, it is primarily an account full of autobiographical reflections. If anywhere, here it becomes quite clear that Lévi-Strauss's scientific studies of man cannot be seen in splendidly objective isolation. Somewhere he recounts his astonishment over the ease with which the Bororo move back and forth between the religious sphere and the sphere of ordinary, profane life. It reminds him of other examples of 'artless religiosity' he has observed, for instance in Southeast Asia, where he saw bonzes who slept and lived in the same room where religious services were held and who at times caressed their pupils. Then, with admirable honesty, he tells us how his mind turns to 'the only contact with religion' he has had in his own life. It was in his childhood, when, he says, 'I was already an unbeliever.' (Lévi-Strauss 1964: 215). He lived with his grandfather, who was the rabbi of Versailles, and whose house was linked with the synagogue by a corridor; Lévi-Strauss recalls how this corridor was 'an impassable frontier' between the profane and the sacred. This impassibility he remembers together with a mass of rules and customs.

It is rare to find an anthropologist or any other student of myths who allows us such views of his upbringing, conditionings, or inner motivations. The 'case' of Lévi-Strauss nevertheless is not exceptional. His religious upbringing, just like the religious upbringing of so many in the modern and scientific world, came to a halt in childhood. Afterwards, like most, he learned about mathematics, physics, biology, history, and literature, while his knowledge of religion never developed into anything mature. Hence, perhaps, the puzzle of religious customs and myths demanded in him a responsible explanation of the same clarity as the clarity of the sciences he had acquired. The resentment toward his early religious environment—again, such a common element among intellectuals in our age—only stimulated his urge for rational explanation. The experience is disturbingly common, and the formula, though hardly ever as honestly revealed as in *Tristes Tropiques*, is transparent: one's own religious origin and environment are to be diminished in some way, and the other, distant culture put on a pedestal and explained in supposedly perfectly scientific terms. But can any wisdom, as cultivated among adults in the one tradition or in the other, ever be approached in this manner? I cannot believe it. Lévi-Strauss's popularity in anthropology runs parallel to the dwindling significance of the term 'wisdom' in the study of history. His importance is principally the felicitous systematization of ideas many intellectuals desire to espouse in order to get a handle on the study of man.

In the structuralism of this school, myths are made transparent by their translation into computer language. Various forms of myths must be collected. Each myth must be divided into episodes, sections, mythemes, and so on. Such division and subdivision in order to arrive at a scientific comprehension had already been proposed by Vladimir Propp in the twenties (see brief description in Maranda 1972: 139–150), except that Propp paid more attention to historical changes by asking what was basic and what was derived in any myth.

In the last few years the critique on Claude Lévi-Strauss has been mounting. Even the most severe critics would not deny that myths do combine the empirical manifoldness of the world with a search for meaning, but apart from this, much is open to debate (Harris 1968: 464–513, Korn 1973, Pettit 1975, Strutynski 1977, Goody 1977). Against Lévi-Strauss, many would hold that myths are poly-interpretable, and that the logical slice he selects is only one of the possibilities. Isn't logic itself, like mathematics, to which it is adjacent, and like all other scientific pursuits, most fascinating when it has the courage to examine its own foundations? This critical and rhetorical question is one way of implying that in the history of science we may be ultimately led back to myth as the cornerstone of the entire scientific edifice.

Binarism is essential to Lévi-Strauss's theories. It is taken from linguistics, or to be more precise, from phonology, and he considers it fundamental to the workings of the human mind (Pettit 1975: 75), and therefore to myth as well. Thus his theories swarm with assumptions about which even the most sympathetic readers may have their doubts (Leach 1970: 53).

The most serious criticism, as usual, is philosophical in nature. There is no doubt that Lévi-Strauss has explained many mythical themes, but so have other systems of interpretation. Philosophical objections are raised against the very manner of his argumentation (Polanyi and Prosch 1975: chap. 9; also Ricoeur 1974: 27–61 and *passim*).

It is not the first time that a student of a particular branch of learning prematurely drew his science close to philosophy or even identified the pursuits of the two. Durkheim did it in his sociology by suggesting that he had somehow solved the problem of human consciousness; the particulars of a describable society were supposed to yield the clue to the human mind. Structurally comparable, Tylor thought he had found in his animism evidence of the real natural religion of all mankind. Thus a transcendental question seemed answerable through some limited, particular, empirical enquiry. And Lévi-Strauss follows an analogous course. He presents a particular analysis of consciousness as definitive, while his philosophical critics are weary of such definitiveness and would rather see some openness-in-principle instead. If some positive science (in this case anthropology) posits consciousness as objectifiable, all things, including myths, suddenly seem manageable. But the philosophical objection remains.

Structuralism of this type is still strongly oriented toward the wording of myths, using the computer and feeding it sections of the texts. In other words, it is still literature-oriented and does not meet the criticism other students of myth had already levelled at earlier schools. For instance, where and how does ritual enter in? What do sacrifices mean? What makes a Muslim story relate to a symbol such as the Ka'bah, or a Christian tradition to the Vatican? The variety of myths seems to be as great as the variety of religious symbolisms. Hence, there is every reason to be wary of improper limitations if we establish divisions and categories as basic to all myths. The wideness of the world in which myths are told cannot possibly be ignored. Here, I believe, is the reason for mentioning another school of structuralism.

It is the school of J.P.B. de Josselin de Jong (1886–1964), anthropologist in Leiden. Although he did not use the term 'structure,' he did speak of 'the system of a culture' (Van Baal 1971: 185), and I think that his preference for that term indicates a significantly wider scope of interest, in spite of a certain similarity of the two terms. He developed his theories on dualism well before Lévi-Strauss (De Josselin de Jong 1913, 1929), and his dualism shows a certain kinship to Lévi-Strauss's binary opposites. He discussed mythological complementary opposites such as the double image of benefactor and fool in one and the same figure, the trickster of American Indians, and Hermes in Greek myths. Although he expressed appreciation for Lévi-Strauss's ideas on kinship systems (De Josselin de Jong 1952), he did not live to see Lévi-Strauss's elaborations on myth (Lévi-Strauss 1964; 1966b; 1968). One can only speculate that his appreciation concerned works pertaining to the social setting in which myths function. He was not a prolific writer, but none of his publications, even when linguistically oriented, ever lost sight of wider cultural, social, and historical contexts, and the same is true for his pupils. G.W. Locher (1932) studied the Kwakiutl; G.J. Held (1935) wrote on the gambling theme in the Mahābhārata. In both works the importance of two parties, or complementary opposites, or moieties in a clan, is clearly visible. The most important scholars in this tradition are J. Van Baal and Hans Schärer. The former wrote an elaborate work on the Marind-anim culture of South New Guinea (Van Baal 1966). The study of New Guinea occupied him for many years, and from 1953 to 1958 he served as governor of what was then Netherlands New Guinea.

Myths are crucial in his study, which for that very reason is entitled
Dema (the same type of mythic being studied by A.E. Jensen). At the
same time, his work is striking because of its insistence on taking into
account all parts and aspects of life: language, ritual, culture, social
organization, law, and so on. To Van Baal we also owe a general work,
Symbols for Communication (1971). One detail worth mentioning in our
context is Van Baal's guarded admiration for Lévi-Strauss's structuralism. His reservation is precisely the awareness he shares with the other
Dutch structuralists that no simple and pure conceptualization such as
dualism ever takes on a real manifest and living form in human society or
behavior (Van Baal 1971: 193–194). A related reservation concerns the
division between the conscious and the unconscious in their relevance to
forms of culture (among which myths are counted).

   The second great contribution of 'Dutch structuralism' was by the
Swiss Hans Schärer, and was in fact made even earlier. The study of
myth and of religion in general suffered a great loss with his premature
death in 1947. We owe to him a compact work on the Ngaju Dayak of
Borneo or Kalimantan (1963) and a lengthy collection and study of the
Ngaju Dayak funeral cult and mythology (1966). Without giving a
detailed analysis here, or listing the influences on Schärer of other
authors whose scholarship could not be ignored in the years immediately following the war, I want to underline the importance of his
work as a work of structuralism, (even though Schärer, like De Josselin
de Jong, did not use the term). It seems to me that, as in the case of Van
Baal's work, the paramount significance is the endeavor to be truly
exhaustive and to realize continually that even the profoundest conceptions in a religious tradition find novel expressions and unanticipated
forms. Diverging from the custom of most fieldworkers until this day,
Schärer did not rely on the knowledge which the 'average man' had of
his tradition, but searched out specialists among the Ngaju Dayak who
could inform him authoritatively about legal customs, specific ritual
forms, particular myths, etc. (see author's own account in the introduction of Schärer 1966, vol. I). Myths are too important to be analyzed
with the help of only one or even a few ideas, no matter how well
structured, or on the basis of data given by a number of random
informants, or even by reliance on the best possible account of only one

moment in history. Various trustworthy sources together are needed for a structuralism worthy of the name—if a name is indeed needed for this difficult task. Schärer has been able perhaps more than others in this school to demonstrate that one coherent cluster of symbolism reveals itself to the student willing to devote his energy to the complex expressions of a tradition.

h. *Historical methods*

A number of scholars of mythology and religious texts can conveniently be grouped together as 'historians.' This is not to say that they all agree in method. However, they do have one thing in common that we cannot miss after having reviewed so many systems that invited one-sidedness or exaggeration: they all seem to resist fads, and instead give their attention to the documents. I repeat that they do not form a monolithic organization at all. Some men whom I already mentioned, such as W. Brede Kristensen, might well be mentioned here again, and there are more of these 'historians' than I will list in this section.

The actual man-hours of these scholars are given to historical texts, and even if they do not abstain from controversy altogether, they usually spend more time correcting their own already accomplished work than on the discussion of new systems of interpretation. They provide a breathing-spell in the swirl of passionately presented and usually short-lived theories of myth.

Even the most unshakable historians are of course children of their time, and in our century this means that, depending on their environment and decade, they too have occasionally taken for granted the validity of evolutionistic, animistic, neo-romantic, diffusionistic, or other dominant ideas. But even then, the involvement in historical texts can actually be so concentrated as to make of those ideas no more than ripples on the surface.

Concentration on original documents, most typical of this group, almost always implies some amount of specialization. Werner Jaeger is a classicist, although the range of his works on the Greek ideal of culture and education (see Jaeger 1939–1944), on its transformation in early

Christianity (1961), and on the mythical world reflected in the pre-Socratic philosophers (1947) is obviously wider than that of most classicists. Gerhart Ladner is a church historian, but one who has made it his task to trace crucial ideas through an astounding variety of documents (Ladner 1959), including those of religio-symbolic and artistic value (Ladner 1965). Gershom G. Sholem is rightly one of the most famous scholars of the post-war era in the study of religion, because of his disciplined study of Judaism and its gnostic and mystical expressions (Scholem 1941, 1949, 1965, 1971, 1974). He is one of those scholars whose work will be remembered when many present controversies on method have ceased. Henri Corbin, an expert on Sūfism, has shed light on the continuations and transformations of mythical themes in ancient Iranian Zoroastrianism through Islamic philosophy and mysticism (Corbin 1946, 1957, 1960a, 1960b, 1969, 1971). Martin P. Nilsson's work, thorough and self-critical in the best historical tradition (especially Nilsson 1955–61), is mandatory material for any serious student of Greek myths. Of specific value in Indian mythology is Stella Kramrisch's essay on goddesses in ancient India (Kramrisch 1975).

Historical approaches to myth, like other approaches in history, are geared primarily toward the problem of change. Form and contents of myths change, and changes are apparent in social, cultural and economic environments. This point may seem self-evident, yet it is useful to remember that the modern study of myth is largely indebted to the work of anthropologists, and among anthropologists the discovery of change is a very recent matter. Th.P. van Baaren brought out a timely reminder on the flexibility of myth. He argues that in non-literate societies, which for a long time were considered static, changes in myths occur more easily than they do in literate societies (Van Baaren 1972). A related problem, perhaps not explored sufficiently, is that of religious expressions and secularization, which are not at all the antithetical entities most theoreticians have considered them to be. In the history of myths the two belong together, as sanctification and secularization are two sides of the same historical process (Bolle 1970).

There is more than one way to demonstrate the importance of historical scholarship; and I am aware that the scholars I have already mentioned might locate its importance differently than I do. There is really only one basic reason why I think we are entitled to speak of some historical approaches as belonging together. It is the sense as well as the practice of this historical scholarship to establish the meaning of human documents with reference to the flux in which they are created. Although there are a great many, some very important, theoretical writings about historical scholarship, the actual work of historians remains the laboring over documents in the full practical knowledge that only recorded changes in the course of time will reveal the meanings of the documents at hand.

It is true, for instance, that Claude Lévi-Strauss touched occasionally on the problem of history, but it is also true that he had only one publicly known confrontation on the subject: his discussion with Sartre (see Lévi-Strauss 1966: chap. IX). And that could only be called an easy way out. It was a marvelous skirmish between two brilliant rationalists, or, if one prefers to say it otherwise, a battle between two modern Cartesians with different temperaments. Lévi-Strauss made no secret of the anti-historical sentiments in his theories. And as to the equally theoretically inclined Sartre, how could one ever explain to a historian the possibility of writing a book on Judaism and anti-Semitism without a single sentence concerning Moses or the Torah? (Sartre 1948) Such a procedure would seem as far-fetched to a historian as the endeavor to view the Iliad as a document proving that human consciousness had not yet dawned (Jaynes 1976), or the endeavor to prove that religion originated with the intoxication by mushrooms (Allegro 1970).

Historical practice discloses continually and ever anew that meanings reside *in* history. In fact, serious linguists, as distinct from those who know theoretical schemes but not languages, are also familiar with this experience, for semasiology begins only by establishing the meanings of words *in time*, i.e., in the process of their changes.

The paramount example of historical scholarship in the area of myth is Raffaele Pettazzoni (1883–1959). The best collection of myths we have we owe to him. If comprises the entire world: vol. I, Africa and Australia; vol. II, Oceania, published posthumously and completely by Vittorio Lanternari; vol. III, North America; vol. IV, Central and South America, published shortly after Pettazzoni's death, but completed with the collaboration of Tullio Tentori (Pettazzoni 1948–1959).

The work presents virtually all available myths of 'primitive' societies in the modern world (exceptions being made only for certain pre-Columbian American traditions). In the preface to the first volume, Pettazzoni refers to the Pawnee tradition (recorded by Dorsey 1906: 10; 13, 141, 428) distinguishing true stories from false ones. The former are limited in number; they are the myths functioning in human traditions. The latter can be 'made up;' therefore there is no limit to their number. Pettazzoni considers the distinction basic for our understanding and refers to it elsewhere again (Pettazzoni 1947–48, 1950, 1954a: 11–23).

Pettazzoni is a paradigm in historical scholarship in two respects. First, he had the courage to deal with topics of enormous scope. In principle, all students of myth would admit that extensive work is needed; yet doing this work is a different matter. It is much more tempting, even for devoted followers of a historical method, to look for safety in a small area where it is easier to deal with questions raised by equally specialized colleagues. Nevertheless, mythical themes can only be fathomed adequately by disciplined and wide-ranging comparisons and contrasts, (without ever doing violence to the specificity of any tradition). The courage to deal with topics enormous in size as well as importance is the first standard Pettazzoni demonstrated. Second, throughout his work—and in this respect his work is equally paradigmatic—he was continually engaged in correcting his findings.

Each one of his works shows the courage to deal with great topics: his books on the confession of sins as a universal religious phenomenon (Pettazzoni 1929–36) and his studies on the mythical structure of supreme gods engaged him all his life (Pettazzoni 1922, 1925, 1930, 1931, 1935, 1956).

Clearly, with such gigantic subjects no investigator can claim firsthand knowledge of all the documents. However, Pettazzoni saw his work as combining the phenomenology of religion with history properly so called, for, in fact, the two were one in his opinion (Pettazzoni 1954b), and this one science he considered essential for all accurate historical interpretation. Two examples will clarify this at once.

The rise of monotheism had never been well studied, and, when stated as a problem, suffered from an overdose of theoretical assumptions.

Evolutionistic biases assumed that a monotheistic conception of divinity had to be a late product in the world's religious development. New evidence collected by Andrew Lang (1844–1912) showed that, contrary to theory, culturally least advanced peoples of the world had clear mythological accounts of a supreme deity. The new evidence was accepted by Wilhelm Schmidt (1868–1954) and somehow associated with the much older Christian theological hypothesis that the original (paradisal) revelation might still be visible in distorted ways in pagan traditions. Neither theologically inclined theories nor general assumptions about the development of human consciousness seemed to have any clear connection with the known facts. Pettazzoni was the first to point to the specific historical contexts in which forms of monotheism first occurred; they are only those contexts where myths tell us how among many gods one becomes *primus inter pares*, and the cultural background is typically pastoral (see, e.g., Pettazzoni 1954a: 1–10, 1922).

The second example is from Pettazzoni's work on the religion of ancient Greece (Pettazzoni 1953, 1954a: 68–80). Certainly, here he had access to all the sources and he had the advantages of the specialist in the narrow sense of that term. Nevertheless, his work owes its appeal largely to the vistas in which the particular facts are pointed out. Greek religion arose out of two cultures, one of them Mediterranean, the other Indo-European and superimposed in the first. Furthermore, we gain a profounder understanding and a more adequate measure of the unique details of this culture by viewing it side by side with coalescing civilizations elsewhere: Egypt, Anatolia, Mesopotamia, India, and pre-Columbian America. Far from providing reductionistic simplifications or evaporating generalizations, Pettazzoni describes the meetings of peasants and pastoral peoples, of more or less matriarchal traditions with militantly organized conquerors, and the resulting amalgamations, in order to find the original elements. In other words, the method employed seems especially suited to counteract the dangers of phenomenology and structuralism.

In our survey it is not possible to describe every development, but it is worth noting that Pettazzoni in one of the exceptional figures in the history of religions who founded a school and has influenced many scholars. Among his outstanding pupils is his successor in Rome, Angelo Brelich, well-known for his study of heroes in Greek mythology (1958), and for a number of other specific studies characterized by a disciplined comparative historical method (e.g., Brelich 1949, 1955, 1960, 1962, 1966, 1976). Vittorio Lanternari has become known through his book on messianic cults in recent times (1963). He is fascinated by the interaction of religious traditions with their newer expressions under the impact of political and economic pressures. Some of his generalizations are perhaps too easy, as when he explains Christianity as a reaction to the Jewish priesthood and the Roman empire (1963: 247), and interprets the message of millenarian cults as escapism. Part of the moral is no doubt that it is truly difficult to be and continue to be a self-correcting historian of religions; fatigue can set in and make one a victim of theoretical short-cuts. Ernesto de Martino, who, like others in this circle, prefers the name 'historical ethnology' for his inquiries, has written several books whose scope is wide not only in terms of material covered (De Martino 1948), but also in terms of the integration of various disciplines into one intellectual pursuit: sociology, history, folklore, music, anthropology, psychology (De Martino 1961).

Historical approaches to myth are of course not a novelty. Many years ago P.D. Chantepie de la Saussaye said in his famous *Lehrbuch*: 'The explanation of a myth cannot be anything else ... but its history' (Chantepie 1887: 157). He said even more that could well serve today to warn us against structuralist or depth-psychological methods of un-covering the supposedly hidden, unconscious meanings in myths: 'It is not our task to find a rational nucleus in irrational stories, but to describe the origin and the development of a myth.' And he underlined even at that time that we should not expect to find one simple key to the puzzle.

What makes the Italian group I have tried to describe so distinct is precisely their insistence on history as a complex of various strands, and it is especially the availability of 'primitive' materials that has made the large scope of their work and the integration of various 'keys' possible.

One more thing is worth mentioning here. It is no accident that Italy produced a remarkable group of prominent historians of religions and so many contributions to mythology. Behind the figures of Pettazzoni, De Martino, and others is the influential philosopher of history Croce, and further back the great eighteenth century thinker Giambattista Vico. With whatever variations, the theme of seeing history as a totality, with religion not an external appendage, but part and parcel of the texture of human life, is central to these modern Italians. This tradition also explains why none of the members of this group has much appreciation for the work of Rudolf Otto, and why they refuse to see the phenomenology of religion as an independent discipline.

There is another name that should not be omitted in this survey of historians: Georges Dumézil. He has not founded a school in the manner of Pettazzoni, and in a sense his work is more specialized. Nevertheless, his ideas and theories have had repercussions in many places. Certainly no one would deny that his studies have infused new life into the almost fossilized study of ancient Indo-European languages. This renewal began before the second world war, but the steady flow of Dumézil's publications has continued ever since (see Bibliography) and their influence is certainly an important factor in the post-war era. Dumézil did not take up the same historical linguistics for which F. Max Müller has been criticized so severely. The bulk of Dumézil's work concerns mythical configurations which occur in ancient Rome and India, Germanic and Irish traditions, and other parts of the early Indo-European world. Dumézil's principal ideas are widely accessible through his own clear summary of the tripartite ideology (Dumézil 1958), and have been hailed as a method profitable for anthropology (Littleton 1973).

As in the case of so many French scholars, it is difficult to read Dumézil without perceiving at once the overtones of Emile Durkheim's and Marcel Mauss's sociological interests. Dumézil's central and well-known thesis is that in ancient Indo-European literature we find tripartition of society: the first group is that of the spiritual leaders (the *brahmans* in ancient India); the second, the warriors or nobility, whose function is the defense of society (the *kṣatriyas* in India); the third, the peasants and other wealth-producing people on whose functions the well-being of the whole nation depends (the Indian *vaiśyas*). The myths, sagas, and epics also show a heavenly counterpart to the tripartite establishment on earth; or rather, the heavenly tripartition is the model for man. The Indian traditions in many old texts portray Mitra and

Varuṇa on the highest level, that of sovereignty; Indra the divine warrior-king on the second; and the Aśvins, the divine twins with their beneficence and health-restoring power, on the third.

The danger, especially for many non-Frenchmen, is that they are inclined to understand Dumézil's notion of 'functions' and 'classes' as if they were clear empirical factors in society. The essential "heavenly" model in the myths, however, should explain sufficiently why Dumézil prefers to call the entire structure an *idéologie*. He could as well have said: religion.

Dumézil's renown in the study of myth should be attributed to the fact that his painstakingly precise textual analyses in a great variety of documents have shown an amazing coherency. It is true that he has met with criticism from some specialists, but the core of his contribution has not been affected by it. It seems certain that especially in the area of Roman mythology his work will be gratefully preserved. 'Historical' accounts in Latin sources, especially the early books of Livy, had never been satisfactorily explained until Dumézil showed them to be 'historicized' versions of Indo-European myths which he had uncovered in his comparative studies (Dumézil 1970; see also Bayet 1957: chap. II).

i. *Some special contributions*

The eight rubrics I have listed so far cover the major tendencies in the study of myth since the second world war. Still, they are not exhaustive. A number of individuals, although some of them have been referred to already or could well be added under the headings I gave, should be mentioned briefly because of their special contributions.

Among students of 'primitive' religion, some have been instrumental in bringing about a move from the old-established theories on 'primitive thought' to a new and positive appreciation of myth outside the major religions of the world. A number of scholars have had direct influence on this change of mind; Lévi-Strauss, Jensen, Kristensen, and others could be mentioned again. Two more names however seem of special significance to me in the history of scholarship. Placied Tempels, Belgian missionary in the Congo, published a work on Bantu philosophy, which was soon translated into French and English (Tempels 1946). The title *Bantu Philosophy* is eloquent and marks a new chapter in Western attitudes. Tempels passionately turned against the traditional scholarly methods that had made it virtually impossible to understand 'primitive' peoples and that instead contributed to a spiritual degeneration among the nations studied or converted. The second scholar is the French anthropologist Marcel Griaule, whose fame rests on his conversations with the Dogon sage Ogotemmêli (Griaule 1965). The story behind his book, told by Germaine Dieterlen in the introduction, reveals dramatically the same change in approach. Griaule had made his field-trips to the Dogon for seventeen years, beginning in 1931. In 1947, some Dogon elders and priests decided that this steady visitor deserved to be told what their tradition was really about. They appointed Ogotemmêli as his instructor. This event and the resulting book are another landmark in the transformation of Western scholarly attitudes. Tempels' and Griaule's works, even if they did not change the climate by themselves, are indicative of a new and encouraging perspective. A recent thought-provoking work on ethnophilosophy by Wilhelm Dupré is an impressive example to consider (Dupré 1974). The term 'ethnophilosophy' itself characterizes the new mood. The work is difficult to read, but its insistence on relating mythology and philosophy, in terms of precise intentions and formulations in both, makes it significant and invites further study.

The German Africanist Hermann Baumann clarified the functions of myth and the terminology surrounding it (Baumann 1959). He first distinguished myth from other forms, such as fairy tale, folktale, and saga (see above p. 301). In terms of our discussion it might be most accurate to say that Baumann went on to elaborate on Pettazzoni's theme, 'the truth of myth.' Myth can be all sorts of things, as students of man have pointed out, sociologically and emotionally, educationally and in rare cases even morally, yet none of these exhausts the function of myth. Baumann quotes many examples, and, without arriving at a precise definition—which would be another unwarranted reductionism—he touches on a number of essentials. The narrative character of myths makes all simple explanations impossible, e.g., in terms of social functions or economic necessities. Furthermore,

Baumann emphasizes the immoral episodes found in innumerable myths, especially in myths of culturally undeveloped peoples. He seems to approximate Eliade's position when he stresses the events of the cosmogony and the creative power of myth as essential in any mythology.

Certainly Baumann did not try to refute more sociologically inclined anthropologists. Functionalism of the type associated with Malinowski (Malinowski 1936, 1948) has continued to attract many students. It is only proper to add that several influential anthropologists dealing with myth have not taken Baumann's cautious expositions seriously, and prefer to look upon myths only as justifications for patterns of behavior. They have certainly ignored the attention given to indigenous philosophies by men such as Griaule. In works by E.E. Evans-Pritchard (1937, 1956) myths do not form a significant subject. Religious 'ideas' or 'beliefs' and 'practices' are referred to in order to understand their function in (ordinary) life, and with respect to social and personal relations to God; authoritative pronouncements within the traditions studied are scarce in his books. Similarly in Mary Douglas's interesting writings we find the author fascinated with the 'ordinariness' of religion, and it is concepts (pollution, powers, magic, miracles, etc.) rather than myths which provide the material (Douglas 1963, 1966, 1970). Godfrey Lienhardt, by contrast, in his study of the Dinka makes a full use of myths (1961) and seems to combine an interest in social and other 'ordinary' facts and functions with an interest in the given, yet hard to define authority of myths. I believe it is quite encouraging for the study of mythology to see the same combination of the down-to-earth and extraordinary functions of myth in studies by John Middleton (1960, 1965, 1967, 1970), Rodney Needham (1962, 1972, 1973), and other anthropologists in recent years.

Very slowly, Western philosophers have paved the way for a positive understanding of myth and have begun to abandon the custom of relegating the subject altogether to a supposed stage before the origin of real thought. Ernst Cassirer (1874–1945), well-known philosopher in the Kantian tradition, tried to interpret the subject in various writings (Cassirer 1944, 1946a, 1946b, 1953). See also the influential expansion of his ideas by Susanne Langer, 1942, 1953, 1967–72), without being able to rid himself well enough-from the point of view of a student of myth-from then-dominant evolutionistic ideas. Georges Gusdorf seems far more relevant to our subject, most of all through some of his general works of great historical and epistemological clarity (Gusdorf 1956, 1960, 1966), but to some degree also for his explicit ideas on myth (Gusdorf 1948, 1953). He sees that myth functions to make human life possible (Gusdorf 1953: 18). He characteristically points to such things as the knowledge of death, which always and everywhere 'already' exists and precedes all rational thought in some mythical form. His sympathy with the philosophy of Schelling is quite clear. By way of footnote: even if one gratefully accepts many of the ideas articulated by these philosophers, it is always a bit disturbing for students of mythology to observe that no struggle with specific myths is ever in evidence; no single myth is ever quoted.

The fact that philosophers pay so little attention to actual mythical statements, even if they discuss myth, should not deter us. I hope to have made the importance of philosophy for the mythologist clear in this essay. If I had my wishes fulfilled, philosophical awareness among mythologists would be a reality. The following is a statement of all of us by a foremost twentieth century philosopher: 'Philosophy is an attitude of mind toward doctrines ignorantly entertained' (Whitehead 1938: 233). The implications and exhortations of philosophers, including recent ones, are often as important to us as their explicit observations on myth. For our field is saturated with doctrines ignorantly entertained.

In the present category of special contributions, there are further names and trends to be mentioned. Next to Cassirer and Gusdorf (in his later works, rather than his earlier work on the topic of sacrifice), I should mention Michael Polanyi once more, because in a clearer way than anyone else he has placed the subject of myth squarely within the arena of all intellectual activity (Polanyi and Prosch 1975: chap. 9). Perhaps Wittgenstein also can prove an inspiration to some mythologists (see Long 1969). Certainly, the work by Merleau-Ponty (1908–1961) has set many minds in motion (Kwant 1962). It is of obvious value to a mythologist who has just discovered the truth of myth to discover in Merleau-Ponty's philosophy good reasons for rejecting notions of 'the absolute.' Merleau-Ponty's critical essay on sociology is equally relevant to the study of myth (1960). The mythologist must reflect on the notion that no facts are 'objective.' He must be aware that it is an illusion to think that facts exist apart from a theory. In these elementary but highly necessary reflections, Merleau-Ponty is an excellent guide, (and as clear as the great William James). Finally, the name of Enrico Castelli must be mentioned. Under his sponsorship a number of discussions have taken place among participants of theological as well as philosophical learning. Of the resulting books, often dealing with topics touching on mythology, the volume on myth and faith should be mentioned (Castelli 1966; see also 1967 and 1974).

Specific subjects or themes in mythology have been given special attention since the end of the second world war. A few examples should suffice here. The subject of myth and ritual, often together with kingship, has been a central focus for many; some of this we have already noted. Ugo Bianchi published a special work on dualistic motifs in myth (Bianchi 1958); and generally, the subject of gnosticism has kept several excellent students occupied (see Grant, 1961, 1966; Jonas 1963; Quispel 1972; Puech 1949, 1952, 1953–57). Millenarianism, a mythology directed toward the end of time rather than the beginning of time, has attracted many students. The flux of cargo-cults after the second world war provided a strong motivation, but the topic is of course much wider. Mention should be made of Norman Cohn's excellent historical study of millenarianism in the West (1970). Of special importance is the wide range of the book edited by Sylvia Thrupp, *Millennial Dreams in Action*, which is comparative in its design (1962). A related work, even wider in scope and with some additional philosophical, literary, and political reflections, is a collection on the idea of utopia by Frank Manuel (1967). There is no lack of works in this area of myth. Personally, I consider the study Sierksma devoted to the subject of millenarianism the best of his many works (Sierksma 1961).

Psychological studies have dealt with symbolism extensively, but much less with myth. Carl Gustav Jung's merit is primarily in his central role in the *Eranos* meetings, where many scholars have discussed topics that are relevant to myth. Publications of the *Eranos Jahrbücher* began in 1933.) The so-called 'individuation process,' the integration of the person, which interested Jung clinically, inspired Joseph Campbell in a study of mythical and legendary heroes and their quests (Campbell 1949). Under the same inspiration, yet more independently, and with great literary flair, he published four volumes on myth encompassing the entire world (Campbell 1959, 1962, 1964, 1968), and edited a volume on myths, dreams and religion by a number of scholars (1970). Of special interest is the *Introduction to a Science of Mythology*, which Jung himself wrote together with Karl Kerényi. Not only did Kerényi lucidly discuss some mythological themes of Greek antiquity, but he clarified the notion *archē* implied in 'archetype.' The ἀρχαί the earlier Greek philosophers talked about are 'beginnings' or 'first principles,' not mere causes, but rather 'primary states' fundamental to the specific images that occur in myths, but not themselves images (Jung and Kerényi 1949: 6–9).

The correction is helpful even today for mythologists with a historical inclination who feel a bit irked by the timelessness of Jung's 'collective unconscious' and its 'archetypes.' It is an even more important correction if one is aware that Jung's idea of the collective unconscious rested to quite an extent on Lévy-Bruhl's assumption of the *participation mystique*, i.e., precisely the assumption which anthropologists had rejected (Jung 1958: 50–51; Eliade 1969: 16).

Under the aegis of Freud, several interesting attempts have been made. Sometimes they are of importance to mythology even if they do not envisage the subject directly. Bruno Bettelheim has given us specimens of applied Freudianism (Bettelheim 1954, 1976). His explanation of fairy tales is so like a caricature of Freud that few mythologists with an awareness of historical contexts would look upon it as a model for their own subject. Among the most original rediscoverers of Freud is the classicist Norman O. Brown. We already owed an important monograph on myth to him before his rediscovery of Freud (Brown 1947). The work for which he is best known, *Life against Death*, owes part of its inspiration to Geza Roheim, who, especially in the thirties, integrated Freudian ideas with anthropological and historical insights. If one important strand may be singled out in Brown, it is the sustained effort to analyze the unconscious as the impelling force of all human achievements, including the most creative. In the same context the name of Sierksma may be mentioned again (Sierksma 1956, 1959, 1966).

Finally, repercussions in the study of myth are likely for readers of Ira Progoff's *Death and Rebirth of Psychology* (Progoff 1956), if they see myth as a continuous component of human existence. This work tries no less than to grasp the spiritual significance of the entire depth-psychological movement.

3 Future Prospects

Every historian, including historians of myth, would like to be something of a prophet. Speaking of 'future prospects' in the study of myth, I have to make every effort to resist the temptation. However, I cannot repress my hopes for the future.

I am not under the illusion that I have kept my own opinions on my topic a secret. Any endeavor to delineate myth or to approximate a definition betrays a student's hopes and wishes, as well as his reasonings. Nonetheless, in my view myth is the cornerstone of religion, and its priority in the study of religion seems to me indisputable. This view may not be exceptional, but it is rather novel in our discipline. Recent general works on the history of religions (Ringgren and Ström 1967, Bleeker and Widengren 1969–1971) pay no special attention to it. On the whole, the subject of myth, whenever touched at all, has been treated cavalierly. Our survey gives me every hope that this situation will no longer prevail; things are bound to improve rapidly.

The sloppily posited antithesis of 'conscious' and 'unconscious' is an embarrassment from which the study of religion has suffered a great deal. In whatever manner scholars have made the dichotomy, its application has not often helped interpretation. Among the many assumptions made at the beginning of our century was the assumption that myths were formed *unconsciously* (Ehrenreich 1910: 21). The idea, although already old at the beginning of the century, has come up in innumerable variations and among scholars who would never seem to see eye to eye on anything. Freud, Jung and Kerényi, Durkheim, and, since the War, Lévi-Strauss and many others, myth-ritualists and mytho-poeicists and diffusionists alike, specialists and generalists, all were of the opinion that myths in the form in which we had them needed to be looked through in order to yield their real meaning, which presumably was not consciously apprehended by their own narrators. The real meaning, though unconscious in its own tradition, could be understood by the scientist employing the proper theory of analysis, sociologically, psychologically, or logically. I think that the dichotomy 'conscious/unconscious' will not be made so glibly in the future. If it were to survive, it could only jeopardize the progress made by various experts who, each in his own manner, have shown that we cannot profitably separate myth-making, 'primitive' man from ourselves.

My personal preferences turn to the historical methods as most effective in the study of myth. This is not to say that others cannot serve the purpose. The multiform enemy—a sloppy distinction of 'conscious/unconscious'—can be defeated on many fronts, in various disciplines and specializations. Why indeed should a myth be beautiful and elaborate if it can be 'looked through' and its meaning summarized ('made conscious') in an easy formula? A recent study, popular in literary circles, proposes the human tendency toward violence as the principal building block of myths and religious behavior (Girard 1972). Even if violence is significant, how many myths can one really read from beginning to end while seriously entertaining this hypothesis? An interpretive theory that in effect declares the literary and poetic garb superfluous cannot be accepted as valid. Myth a libretto for a ritual? Myth a classificatory system for kinship relations? Myth a mysterious, roundabout way to express mankind's concealed logic? Every endeavor that opposes a given myth with a real meaning clear only to the modern interpreter seems suspect to me. They are all variations, no matter how subtle and appealing, on the theme of conscious and unconscious. Worse, even in their recent echoes, they remind me of that one loudest variation, the colonialist finale opposing a conscious Western élite, fully in control of the world, called to that task, to the teeming masses of natives, unable to think for themselves, or to think at all. Ideas of this sort may have been understandable (although hardly ever defensible) in the days of E.B. Tylor and the young Freud, but they do not meet the prime criterion of all sensible explanation of human documents. Explanations of a myth must be capable of being presented to the

narrators and not merely to scientific colleagues. In all methods employed, the scientific imagination should be strong enough to extend
research to that point. This very practical goal is possible, even if the
people whose documents we study belong to a dim past. If this is a
'vision,' it certainly is a modest one, within the scope òf ordinary human
communication and experience. It is reasonable to hope that various
disciplines of study will meet the criterion, not merely because such is
my wish, but because the political development of the world leaves no
viable alternative. After all, when our subject is another man's fundamental orientation in the world, what else can we do but take him
seriously?

Work in linguistics, in archaeology, in the history of science, and in all
other disciplines bearing on mythological documents will be even more
needed than in the past. We need not merely to know 'the context'—all
too reminiscent of *the* real, ferreted out, conscious meaning—but to
study the entire fabric of contexts in which our texts exist.

Somewhat more cautiously, I would like to express my hope for a
continuing philosophical watchfulness. We need to be reminded, constantly, that the thirst for 'reality' in all its variations links us in our efforts
to the people whose myths we have before us. When we feel tempted to
view ourselves as distinct from 'the others,' 'tribals,' 'non-literates,' or
'ancients,' we might do well to bring to mind one of Michael Polanyi's
illustrations. When modern science deals with frogs, and wishes to make
precise observations and classifications and to establish laws about them,
it nevertheless always starts out already knowing what a frog is.

Is what we 'already know' something 'prescientific?' No doubt it is.
But it is this sort of prescientific knowledge that links us with the people
whose religious documents we look at. Far more, it is the knowledge
without which neither science nor anything else human can be complete.

I enjoy the distance that separates us from a statement by a famous
scholar only half a century ago. Lehmann began a discussion on myth in
1925 as follows: 'It is a mark of decay of the higher religions when the
mythical element surfaces again in their beliefs and teachings' (Lehmann
1925). One does not have to sympathize with any of the neo-romantics
to appreciate their reaction to the impoverishment of science evident in
such statements.

I cannot prevent myself from uttering one wish of a practical nature. Perhaps the wish is not only my own, and in that case merely stating it may help lead to its fulfillment. It is the wish for more discussion and teamwork in our endeavors. A little reflection shows that cooperative effort would not be a luxury for us.

If one characteristic stood out clearly among the neo-romantics, it was their eagerness to present the sublimity of religious experience. By contrast, the ordinary world received scant attention. The general discussions, the many parties involved in the debates of the last thirty years, should make it clear by now that sublime symbolic communication in its most poetic garb has consequences in, and is presupposed by, the most profane expressions in economics, society, politics. The many levels of mythological reverberation invite more discussion. Perhaps we should say 'demand' rather than 'invite.' The many levels, if we are willing to take them into account, should put an end to fruitless, arrogant, or improper types of specialization. The present lack of real discussion is itself caused to quite an extent by the growth of specialization and not by the subject matter. At the present time, the study of myth can be served no better than by a new willingness to listen to other specialists and to address their questions as well as those that arise in one's own area. Hence more teamwork would be a desideratum, not for the compilation of specialized treatises on a dissected subject, but as a disciplined endeavor to discuss the topic. Thus teamwork could be of the highest importance not for mythological study alone, but for the urgent necessity of a new intellectual integration in our age.

Bibliography

Adams, Charles J., ed. (1977), *A Reader's Guide to the Great Religions*, second ed. New York: Free Press.

Allegro, John M. (1970), *The Sacred Mushroom and the Cross. A Study of the Nature and Origins of Christianity within the Fertility Cults of the Ancient Near East*. London: Hodder and Stoughton.

Baal, J. van (1966), *Dema. Description and Analysis of Marind-anim Culture (South New Guinea)*. The Hague: Nijhoff.

— (1971), *Symbols for Communication. An Introduction to the Anthropological Study of Religion*. Assen: Van Gorcum.

Baaren, Th. P. van (1972), 'The Flexibility of Myth,' in C. J. Bleeker et al. eds, *Ex Orbe Religionum. Studia Geo Widengren*, vol. 2, 199–206. Leiden: Brill.

Barth, Karl (1957), *Theologische Fragen und Antworten*. Zürich: Evangelischer Zollikon.

Baumann, H. (1959), 'Mythos in ethnologischer Sicht,' in 2 parts. *Studium Generale* 12: 1–17; 583–597.

Bayet, Jean (1957), *Histoire politique et psychologique de la religion romaine*. Paris: Payot.

Bettelheim, Bruno (1954), *Symbolic Wounds. Puberty Rites and the Envious Male*. Glencoe: Free Press.

— (1976), *The Uses of Enchantment: The Meaning and Importance of Fairy Tales*. New York: Knopf.

Bianchi, Ugo (1958), *Il dualismo religioso*. Rome: 'L'Erma' di Bretschneider.

— (1975), *The History of Religions*. Transl. by G. Castellani. Leiden: Brill. (Orig. *Storia delle religioni*. 6th ed. Torino, 1970.)

Bleeker, C. J. (1970), 'The conception of Man in the Phenomenology of Religion,' *Studia Missionalia* 19: 13–38.

Bleeker, C. Jouco, and Widengren, Geo, eds. (1969–1971), *Historia Religionum. Handbook for the History of Religions*. 2 vol. Leiden: Brill.

Bolle, Kees W. (1968), *The Freedom of Man in Myth*. Nashville: Vanderbilt University Press.

— (1970), 'Secularization as a Problem for the History of Religions,' *Comparative Studies in Society and History* 12: 242–259.

Brelich, Angelo (1949), *Vesta*. Transl. from the Italian by V. von Gonzenbach. Zürich: Rhein.

— (1955), *Tre variazioni romane sul toma delle origine*. Rome: Edizioni dell' Ateneo.

— (1958), *Gli eroi greci, un problema sotrico-religioso*. Rome: Edizioni dell' Ateneo.

— (1960), *Der Polytheismus*, in Numen 7: 123–136.

— (1962), *Le iniziazioni*. Rome: Edizioni dell' Ateneo.

— (1966), *Introduzione alla storia delle religioni*. Rome: Edizioni: dell' Ateneo.

— (1976), 'Nascita di miti,' *Religioni e civiltà* (Studi e Materiali di Storia delle Religioni 42, 1973–76, N.S.) 2.

Brown, Norman O. (1947), *Hermes the Thief. The Evolution of a Myth*. Madison: University of Wisconsin Press.

— (1959), *Life against Death. The Psychoanalytical Meaning of History*. Middletown: Wesleyan University Press.

Buber, Martin (1952), *Eclipse of God*. New York: Harper.

Buren, Paul M. van (1965), *The Secular Meaning of the Gospel*. London: SCM.

Campbell, Joseph (1949), *The Hero with a Thousand Faces*. New York: Pantheon.

— (1959), *The Masks of God: Primitive Mythology*. New York: Viking.

— (1962), *The Masks of God: Oriental Mythology*. New York: Viking.
— (1964), *The Masks of God: Occidental Mythology*. New York: Viking.
— (1968), *The Masks of God: Creative Mythology*. New York: Viking.
— (ed.) (1970), *Myths, Dreams and Religion*. New York: Dutton.
Cassirer, Ernst (1944), *An Essay on Man*. New Haven: Yale University Press.
— (1946a), *Language and Myth*. New York and London: Harper.
— (1946b), *The Myth of the State*. New Haven: Yale University Press.
— (1953), *The Philosophy of Symbolic Forms. Vol. II: Mythical Thought*. New Haven: Yale University Press.
Castelli, Enrico (ed.) (1966), *Mythe et Foi*. Paris: Aubier.
— (1967), *Le mythe de la peine*. Paris: Aubier.
— (1974), *Le Sacré*. Paris: Aubier.
Chantepie de la Saussaye, P.D. (1887), *Lehrbuch der Religionsgeschichte* I. Freiburg: Mohr.
Cohn, Norman (1970), *In Pursuit of the Millennium*. Rev. and expanded ed. New York: Oxford University Press.
Corbin, Henri (1946), *Les motifs zoroastriens dans la philosophie de Sohrawardi*. Teheran: Bibliote que Tranienne.
— (1957), 'Cyclical Time in Mazdaism and Ismailism,' in Joseph Campbell (ed.), *Man and Time, Papers from the Eranos Yearbooks*. New York: Pantheon. Bollingen Series XXX (3): 115–172. Transl. by Ralph Manheim (orig. 1951).
— (1960a), *Terre céleste et Corps de résurrection: de l'Iran mazdéen à l'Iran Shī'ite*. Paris: Buchet Chastel.
— (1960b), *Avicenna and the Visionary Recital*. Transl. by Willard R. Trask. New York: Bollingen LXVII. Orig. *Avicenne et le récit visionnaire*, 2 vols. Teheran and Paris, 1952, 1954: Bibliotheque Iranienne 4–5.
— (1969), *Creative Imagination in the Ṣūfism of Ibn 'Arabī*. Transl. by Ralph Manheim. Princeton: Princeton University Press (Bollingen Series XCI).
— (1971), *L'homme de lumière dans le soufisme iranien*. Chambery: Editions Présence.
Croce, Benedetto (1929), 'Christianity for Our Time: an Argument against Historical Materialism,' transl. by Claudio Delitala, in *The Drift of Civilization*, 59–66. New York: Simon and Schuster.

Dijksterhuis, E.J. (1961), *The Mechanization of the World Picture*. Transl. by C. Dikshoorn. London, Oxford, New York: Oxford University Press.
Dilthey, Wilhelm (1962), *Pattern and Meaning in History. Thoughts on History and Society*. Edited and introduced by H.P. Rickman. New York: Harper.
Dorsey, G.A. (1906), *The Pawnee: Mythology*, Part I. Washington: Carnegie Institution.
Dorson, Richard M. (1968), 'Theories of Myth and the Folklorist,' in *Murray*, 76–89.
Douglas, Mary (1963), *The Lele of the Kasai*. London: Oxford University Press.
— (1966), *Purity and Danger. An Analysis of Concepts of Pollution and Taboo*. London: Routledge and Kegan Paul.
— (1970), *Natural Symbols. Explorations in Cosmology*. New York: Pantheon.

Dumézil, Georges (1934), *Ouranos-Varuṇa, étude de mythologie comparée indo-européenne.* Paris: Adrien Maisonneuve.

— (1941), *Jupiter Mars Quirinus, essai sur la conception indo-européenne de la société et sur les origines de Rome.* Paris: Gallimard.

— (1944), *Naissance de Rome (Jupiter Mars Quirinus II).* Paris: Gallimard.

— (1945), *Naissance d'Archanges, essai sur la formation de la théologie zoroastrienne* (Jupiter Mars Quirinus III). Paris: Gallimard.

— (1948), *Jupiter Mars Quirinus, IV, explication de textes.* Paris: Presses Universitaires de France.

— (1952), *Les dieux des Indo-Européens.* Paris: Presses Universitaires de France.

— (1953), *La saga de Hadingus.* Paris: Presses Universitaires de France.

— (1958), *L'idéologie tripartie des Indo-Européens.* Bruxelles: Collection Latomus, Vol. XXXI.

— (1968–73), *Mythe et épopée*, vols. 1–3. Paris: Gallimard.

— (1970a), *Archaic Roman Religion, with an Appendix on the Religion of the Etruscans*, 2 vols., transl. by Philipp Krapp. Chicago: University of Chicago Press. (Orig.: *La religion romaine archaique suivi d'un appendice sur la religion des Etrusques.* Paris: Payot, 1966.)

— (1970b), *The destiny of the Warrior*, transl. by Alf Hiltebeitel. Chicago: University of Chicago Press. (Orig.: *Heur et malheur du guerrier: Aspects mythiques de la fonction guerrière chez les Indo-Européens.* Paris: Presses Universitaires de France, 1969.)

— (1973a), *From Myth to Fiction. The Saga of Hadingus.* Transl. by Derek Coltman. Chicago and London: University of Chicago Press. (Orig.: *Du mythe au roman: La saga de Hadingus et autres essais.* Paris: Presses Universitaires de France, 1970.)

— (1973b), *Gods of the Ancient Northmen.* Ed. by Emar Haugen, intr. by C. Scott Littleton and Udo Strutynski. (Orig.: *Les dieux des Germains.* Paris: Presses Universitaires de France, 1959.)

Dupré, Wilhelm (1974), *Religion in Primitive Cultures. A Study in Ethnophilosophy.* The Hague: Mouton.

Ehrenreich, Paul (1910), *Die allgemeine Mythologie und ihre ethnologischen Grundlagen.* Leipzig: Hinrichs.

Eliade, Mircea (1954), *The Myth of the Eternal Return.* Transl. by Willard R. Trask. New York: Bollingen. (Orig.: *Le mythe de l'éternel retour: archétypes et répétition.* Paris: Gallimard, 1949.)

— (1958), *Patterns in Comparative Religion.* London and New York: Sheed and Ward. (Orig.: *Traité d'histoire des religions.* Paris: Payot, 1948.)

— (1959), *The Sacred and the Profane.* Transl. by William R. Trask. New York: Harcourt.

— (1963), *Myth and Reality.* Transl. by William R. Trask. New York: Harper.

— (1964), *Shamanism. Archaic Techniques of Ecstasy.* New York: Pantheon.

— (1965), *The Two and the One.* New York: Harper.

— (1969), *The Quest. History and Meaning in Religion.* Chicago and London: University of Chicago Press.

— (1973), *Australian Religions. An Introduction.* Ithaca and London: Cornell University Press.

— (1976, 1978), *Histoire des croyances et des idées religieuses.* 2 vols so far. Paris: Payot.

Engnell, I (1943), *Studies in Divine Kingship in the Ancient Near East.* Uppsala: Almquist.

Eranos (1933–), *Eranos-Jahrbuch.* Zürich: Rhein, 1933–1969. Leiden: Brill, 1970–.

Evans-Pritchard, E.E. (1937), *Witchcraft, Oracles, and Magic among the Azande.* London: Oxford University Press.

— (1956), *Nuer Religion.* London: Oxford University Press.

Farber, Marvin (1967), *The Foundation of Phenomenology. Edmund Husserl and the Quest for a Rigorous Science of Philosophy.* Rev. 3rd ed. Albany: State University of New York Press.

Feldman, Burton, and Richardson, Robert D. (1972), *The Rise of Modern Mythology 1680–1860.* Bloomington, London: Indiana University Press.

Fontenrose, Joseph (1971), *The Ritual Theory of Myth.* Berkeley, Los Angeles, London: University of California Press.

Frankfort, Henri (1948), *Kingship and the Gods.* Chicago: University of Chicago Press.

Frankfort, Henri, et al. (1946), *The Intellectual Adventure of Ancient Man.* Chicago: University of Chicago Press. Republished as *Before Philosophy.* Harmondsworth: Penguin, 1949.

Frazer, Sir James George (1959), *The New Golden Bough.* Edited, and with notes and foreword by Theodor Gaster. New York: Criterion Books.

Gaster, Theodor (1954), 'Myth and Story,' *Numen,* 1: 184–212.

— (1961), *Thespis. Ritual, Myth and Drama in the Ancient Near East.* Garden City: Anchor.

— (1969), *Myth, Legend, and Custom in the Old Testament. A* Comparative Study with Chapters from Sir James G. Frazer's 'Folklore in the Old Testament.' New York: Harper.

Girard, René (1972), *La violence et le sacré.* Paris: Grasset.

Goody, Jack (1977), *The Domestication of the Savage Mind.* Cambridge: Harvard University Press.

Grant, Robert (1961), *Gnosticism. A Source Book of Heretical Writings from the Early Christian Period.* New York: Harper.

— (1966), *Gnosticism and Early Christianity.* New York: Columbia University Press.

Griaule, Marcel (1965), *Conversations with Ogotemmêli, an Introduction to Dogon Religious Ideas.* London: Oxford University Press. (Orig.: *Dieu d'eau: Entretiens avec Ogotemmêli.* Paris: Fayard, n.d.)

Grimal, Pierre (ed.) (1965), *Larousse World Mythology.* Transl. by Patricia Beardsworth. New York: Putnam.

Grönbech, Wilhelm (1954), *Kultur und Religion der Germanen.* 2 vols. Übertragen von Ellen Hoffmayer. Stuttgart: Kohlhammer. Orig. Danish: *Vor Folkeaet i Oldtiden.*

Copenhagen, 1909–1912. Eng. expanded edition: *The Culture of the Teutons*. London, Copenhagen, 1931.

Gunkel, Hermann (1968), *Die Psalmen, übersetzt und erklärt*. 5th ed. Reprint. Göttingen: Vandenhoeck und Ruprecht.

Gusdorf, Georges (1948), *L'expérience humaine du sacrifice*. Paris: Presses Universitaires de France.

— (1953), *Mythe et métaphysique, introduction à la philosophie*. Paris: Flammarion.

— (1956), *Traité de métaphysique*. Paris: Librairie Armand Colin.

— (1960), *Introduction aux Sciences Humaines*. Paris: Les Belles Lettres.

— (1965), *Speaking*. Transl., with an introduction by Paul T. Brockelman. Evanston: Northwestern University Press. (Orig.: *La Parole*. Paris: Presses Universitaires de France, 1953.)

— (1966), *Les Sciences Humaines et la pensée occidentale*. Vol. I: *De l'histoire des sciences à l'histoire de la pensée*. Paris: Payot.

Guthrie, W.K.C. (1950), *The Greeks and Their Gods*. Boston: Beacon Press.

Hamann, Johann Georg (1962), *Mysterienschriften*. Ed. and annotated by E. Jansen Schoonhoven and Martin Seils. Gütersloh: Mohn.

Hardy, Alister (1965), *The Living Stream*. Gifford Lectures I. London: Collins.

— (1966), *The Divine Flame*. Gifford Lectures II. London: Collins.

— (1976), *The Biology of God. A Scientist's Study of Man the Religious Animal*. New York: Taplinger.

Harris, Marvin (1968), *The Rise of Anthropological Theory*. New York: Thomas Y. Crowell.

Harris, Zellig S. (1951), *Structural Linguistics* (Same as *Methods in Structural Linguistics*). Chicago: University of Chicago Press.

Heiler, Friedrich (1961), *Erscheinungsformen und Wesen der Religion*. Stuttgart: Kohlhammer.

Held, G.J. (1935), *The Mahabharata. An Ethnological Study*. Amsterdam: Uitgeversmy.

Hermann, Ferdinand (ed.) (1959–1967), *Symbolik der Religionen*. 12 vols. Stuttgart: Hiersemann.

Hidding, K.A.H. (1974), 'Godsdienstfenomenologie en culturele anthropologie,' *Nederlands Theologisch Tijdschrift* 28: 201–214.

Hocart, A.M. (1969), *The Life-Giving Myth and Other Essays*. With an Introduction by Rodney Needham. London: Methuen.

Hooke, S.H. (ed.) (1933), *Myth and Ritual*. London: Oxford University Press.

— (1935), *The Labyrinth*. New York: MacMillan.

— (1958), *Myth, Ritual, and Kingship. Essays on the Theory and Practice of Kingship in the Ancient Near East and in Israel*. London: Oxford University Press.

— (1963), *Babylonian and Assyrian Religion*. Norman: University of Oklahoma Press.

Hume, David (1947), *Dialogues Concerning Natural Religion* (first published in 1779). Ed. Norman Kemp Smith. London: Thomas Nelson.

I.B.H.R. (1952–), *International Bibliography of the History of Religions*. Leiden: Brill.

Jacobsen, Thorkild (1976), *The Treasures of Darkness. A History of Mesopotamian Religion*. New Haven and London: Yale University Press.

Jaeger, Werner (1939–1944), *Paideia. The Ideals of Greek Culture*. 3 vols. (2nd ed. vol. 1, 1945). Transl. by Gilbert Highet. New York: Oxford University Press.

— (1947), *The Theology of the Early Greek Philosophers*. Oxford: Clarendon Press.

— (1961), *Early Christianity and Greek Paideia*. Cambridge: Harvard University Press.

Jansen, Schoonhoven. E. (1945), *Natuur en Genade bij J.G. Hamann, den Magus van het Noorden 1730–1788*. Nijkerk: Callenbach.

Jaspers, Karl (1964), *Nikolaus Cusanus*. München: Piper.

Jaspers, Karl and Bultman, Rudolf (1958), *Myth and Christianity. An Inquiry into the Possibility of Religion without Myth*. Transl. by H. Wolff. New York: Noonday Press. (Orig.: *Die Frage der Entmythologisierung*.)

Jaynes, Julian (1976), *The Origin of Consciousness in the Breakdown of the Bicameral Mind*. Boston: Houghton Mifflin.

Jensen, A.E. (1939), *Hainuwele. Volkserzählungen von der Molukken-Insel Ceram*. Frankfurt: Klostermann.

— (1950), 'Über das Töten als kulturgeschichtliche Erscheinung,' in *Paideuma*, 23–38. Bamberg: Meisenbach.

— (1963), *Myth and Cult among Primitive Peoples*. Transl. by M.T. Choldin and W. Weissleder. Chicago: University of Chicago Press. (Orig.: *Mythos und Kult bei Naturvölkern*. Wiesbaden: Steiner, 1951.)

Johnson, Roger A (1974), *The Origins of Demythologizing*. Leiden: Brill.

Jonas, Hans (1963), *The Gnostic Religion. The Message of the Alien God and the Beginnings of Christianity*. 2nd ed. Boston: Beacon Press.

Josselin de Jong, J.P.B. de (1913), *De waardeeringsonderscheiding van 'levend' en 'levenloos' in het Indogermaansch vergeleken met hetzelfde verschijnsel in enkele Algonkin-talen. Ethno-psychologische studie*. Leiden: Van der Hoek.

— (1929), 'De oorsprong van den goddelijken bedrieger.' *Mededeelingen der Koninklijke Akademie van Wetenschappen*, Afd. Letterkunde, deel 68, serie B, no. 1, Amsterdam.

— (1952), 'Lévi-Strauss's Theory on Kinship and Marriage.' *Mededeelingen Rijksmuseum voor Volkenkunde*, deel 10. Leiden: Brill.

Jung, C.G. (1958). *Psychology and Religion: West and East*. Transl. by R.F.C. Hull. Number 11 of the Collected Works. New York: Bollingen, Pantheon.

Jung, C.G. and Kerényi, C. (1949), *Essays on a Science of Mythology. The Myths of the Divine Child and the Divine Maiden*. Transl. by R.F.C. Hull. New York: Pantheon. (Orig.: *Einführung in das Wesen der Mythologie*. Zürich, 1941.)

Kirk, G.S. (1971), *Myth. Its Meaning and Functions in Ancient and Other Cultures*. London, Berkeley, Los Angeles: Cambridge University Press, University of California Press.

— (1974), *The Nature of Greek Myths*. Harmondsworth: Penguin.

Kitagawa, Joseph M. (1963), *Gibt es ein Verstehen fremder Religionen?* Leiden: Brill.
— (1968), 'Introduction' in Joachim Wach, *Understanding and Believing*. New York: Harper.
Korn, Francis (1973), *Elementary Structures Reconsidered. Lévi-Strauss on Kinship.* Berkeley and Los Angeles: University of California Press.
Koyré, Alexandre (1968), *From the Closed World to the Infinite Universe*. Baltimore: Johns Hopkins University Press.
Kramer, Samuel Noah (ed.) (1961), *Mythologies of the Ancient World*. Garden City, New York: Doubleday.
Kramisch, Stella (1975), 'The Indian Great Goddess,' *History of Religions* 14: 235–265.
Krappe, Alexandre H. (1930), *Mythologie Universelle*. Paris: Payot.
Kristensen, W. Brede (1926), *Het leven uit den dood. Studiën over Egyptischen en oud-Griekschen godsdienst*. Haarlem: Bohn.
— (1947), *Verzamelde bijdragen tot kennis der antieke godsdiensten*. Amsterdam: North-Holland.
— (1954), *Symbool en werkelijkheid, een bundel godsdiensthistorische studiën*. Arnhem: Van Loghum Slaterus.
— (1955), *Inleiding tot de godsdienstgeschiedenis*. Transl. by J. Kristensen-Heldring. Arnhem: Van Loghum Slaterus.
— (1960), *The Meaning of Religion. Lectures in the Phenomenology of Religion*. Transl. by John B. Carman. The Hague: Nijhoff.
Kwant, R.C. (1962), *De fenomenologie van Merleau-Ponty*. Utrecht-Antwerpen: Het Spectrum.

Ladner, Gerhart B. (1959), *The Idea of Reform. Its Impact on Christian Thought and Action in the Age of the Fathers*. Cambridge: Harvard University Press.
— (1965). *Ad Imaginem Dei. The Image of Man in Mediaeval Art*. Latrobe, Pa.: Archabbey Press.
Langer, Suzanne (1942), *Philosophy in a New Key*. Cambridge: Harvard University Press.
— (1953), *Feeling and Form. A Theory of Art*. New York: Scribner.
— (1967–72), Mind. *An Essay on Human Feeling*, 2 vols. Baltimore: Johns Hopkins Press.
Lanternari, Vittorio (1963), *The Religions of the Oppressed. A Study of Modern Messianic Cults*. Transl. by Lisa Sergio. New York: Knopf. (Orig.: *Movimenti religiosi di libertà e di salvezza dei popoli oppressi*, 1960.)
Leach, Edmund (1970), *Claude Lévi-Strauss*. New York: Viking Press.
Leenhardt, M. (1951), 'Mythe mode de connaissance,' in *Proceedings of the Seventh Congress for the History of Religions*, 89–91. Amsterdam: North-Holland.
— (1971), *Do Kamo. La personne et le mythe dans le monde mélanésien*. Préface de Maria Isaura Pereira de Queiroz. Paris: Gallimard. Transl. by B.M. Gulati, with Introd. by V. Crapanzano, as *Do Kamo. Person and Myth in the Melanesian World*. Chicago: University

of Chicago Press.

Leeuw, G. van der (1937), *De Primitieve mensch en de religie. Anthropologische studie.* Groningen, Djakarta: J.B. Wolters. French transl.: *L'homme primitif et la religion.* Paris, 1940.

— (1941), *Der Mensch und die Religion.* Basel: Zum Falken.

— (1948a), *Wegen en grenzen.* 2nd ed. Amsterdam. Paris. English transl. (from the German transl.) by David E. Green: *Sacred and Profane Beauty: the Holy in Art.* Nashville, New York: Abingdon, 1963.

— (1948b), *Inleiding tot de theologie.* Amsterdam. Paris.

— (1954), 'Confession scientifique,' in *Numen* I.

— (1957), 'Primordial Time and Final Time,' transl. by Ralph Manheim, in Joseph Campbell (ed.), *Man and Time. Papers from the Eranos Yearbooks.* New York: Bollingen, 324–350. (Orig.: in *Eranos Jahrbuch* 17. Zürich: Rhein, 1949.)

— (1963), *Religion in Essence and Manifestation,* 2 vols. Transl. by J.E. Turner. New York: Harper. (Orig.: *Phänomenologie der Religion.* Tübingen, 1933.)

Lehmann, Edvard (1925), 'Erscheinungs- und Ideenwelt der Religion,' in Alfred Bertholet and Edvard Lehmann, *Lehrbuch der Religionsgeschichte* I. Tübingen: Mohr.

Lévinas, Emmanuel (1971), *Totalité et infini. Essai sur l'extériorité.* 4th ed. The Hague: Nijhoff. (There is an inadequate English translation by A. Lingis, *Totality and Infinity. An Essay on Exteriority.* Pittsburgh: Duquesne University Press, 1969.)

Lévi-Strauss, Claude (1958), *Anthropologie structurale.* Paris: Plon.

— (1963a), *Totemism.* Transl. by Rodney Needham. Boston: Beacon Press. (Orig.: *Le totémisme aujourd'hui.* Paris: Presses Universitaires de France.)

— (1963b), 'The Bear and the Barber,' *Journal of the Royal Anthropological Society,* vol. 93.

— (1964), *Tristes Tropiques. An Anthropological Study of Primitive Societies in Brazil.* Transl. by John Russell. New York: Atheneum, 1964. (Orig.: *Tristes Tropiques.* Paris: Plon, 1955.)

— (1966a), *The Savage Mind.* Transl. from the French. London: Weidenfeld and Nicolson. Chicago: University of Chicago Press. (Orig.: *La pensée sauvage.* Paris: Plon, 1962.)

— (1966b), *From Honey to Ashes.* New York: Harper. (Vol. 2 of *Introduction to a Science of Mythology.*)

— (1968), *L'origine des manières de table.* Paris: Plon. (Vol. 3 of *Introduction to a Science of Mythology.*)

— (1969), *The Raw and the Cooked.* New York: Harper. (Vol. 1 of *Introduction to a Science of Mythology.*) Transl. by John and Doreen Weightman. (Orig.: *Le cru et le cuit.* Paris: Plon, 1964.)

— (1971), *L'homme nu.* Paris: Plon. (Vol. 4 of *Introduction to a Science of Mythology.*)

Lienhardt, Godfrey (1961), *Divinity and Experience. The Religion of the Dinka.* London: Oxford University Press.

Littleton, C. Scott (1973), *The New Comparative Mythology.* 2nd ed. Berkeley and Los

Angeles: University of California Press.

Locher, G.W. (1932), *The Serpent in Kwakiutl Religion. A Study in Primitive Culture.* Leiden: Brill.

Long, Charles H. (1969), 'Silence and Signification. A Note on Religion and Modernity,' in *Myths and Symbols, Studies in Honor of Mircea Eliade,* ed. by J.M. Kitagawa and Charles H. Long, 141–150. Chicago: University of Chicago Press.

Löwith, Karl (1949), *Meaning in History.* Chicago: University of Chicago Press.

Lurker, Manfred (1968–), *Bibliographie zur Symbolik, Ikonographie und Mythologie.* Baden-Baden: Koerner.

Lyons, John (1970), *Noam Chomsky.* New York: Viking Press.

MacDermot, Violet (1971), *The Cult of the Seer in the Ancient Middle East. A Contribution to Current Research on Hallucinations. Drawn from Coptic and Other Texts.* 2 vols. Berkeley and Los Angeles: University of California Press.

Malinowski, B. (1936), *The Foundation of Faith and Morals.* New York.

— (1948), *Magic, Science and Religion.* Boston: Beacon Press.

Manuel, Frank, (ed.) (1967), *Utopias and Utopian Thought.* Boston: Beacon Press.

Maranda, Pierre, (ed.) (1972), *Mythology. Selected Readings.* Harmondsworth: Penguin.

Maranda, Pierre and Maranda, Elli Köngäs, (eds.) (1971), *Structural Analysis of Oral Tradition.* Philadelphia: University of Pennsylvania Press.

Maringer, Johannes (1977), 'Priests and Priestesses in Prehistoric Europe,' *History of Religions* 17: 101–120.

Marshack, Alexander (1972), *The Roots of Civilization. The Cognitive Beginnings of Man's First Art, Symbol and Notation.* New York: McGraw-Hill.

Martino, Ernesto de (1948), *Il Mondo Magico.* Turin.

— (1961), *La terra del rimorso. Contributo a una storia religiosa del Sud.* Milano: Il Saggiatore.

McClain, Ernest G. (1976), *The Myth of Invariance. The Origin of the Gods, Mathematics and Music from the Rgveda to Plato.* New York: Nicolas Hays.

Mensching, Gustav (1949), *Vergleichende Religionswissenschaft.* 2. neubearbeitete Auflauge. Heidelberg: Quelle and Meyer.

Merleau-Ponty, Maurice (1960), 'Le philosophe et la sociologie,' in *Signes,* 123–142. Paris: Gallimard.

Middleton, John (1960), *Lugbara Religion; Ritual and Authority among an East African People.* London: Oxford University Press.

— (1965), *The Lugbara of Uganda.* New York: Holt, Rinehart and Winston.

— (ed.) (1967), *Myth and Cosmos. Readings in Mythology and Symbolism.* Garden City, New York: Natural History Press.

— (1970), *The Study of the Lugbara. Expectation and Paradox in Anthropological Research.* New York: Holt, Rinehart and Winston.

Molé, Marijan (1963), *Culte, mythe et cosmologie dans l'Iran ancien. Le problème zoroastrien et la tradition mazdéenne*. Paris: Presses Universitaires de France.

Mowinckel, S. (1921–1924), *Psalmenstudien*, 6 vols. Kristiania: Dybwad.

— (1954), *He That Cometh*. Transl. by G.W. Anderson. New York, Nashville: Abingdon. (Orig.: *Han son kommer*. Copenhagen: Gad, 1951.)

— (1962), *The Psalms in Israel's Worship*. Transl. by D.R. Ap-Thomas. Oxford: Blackwell.

Murray, Henry A., (ed.) (1968), *Myth and Mythmaking*. Boston: Beacon Press.

Mylonas, George E. (1961), *Eleusis and the Eleusinian Mysteries*. Princeton: Princeton University Press.

Narr, Karl J. (1964), 'Approaches to the Religion of Early Paleolithic Man,' *History of Religions* 4.

N.E.B. (1976), *New English Bible* with the *Apocrypha*. New York: Oxford University Press.

Needham, Joseph (1961–), *Science and Civilization in China*. Cambridge: Cambridge University Press.

Needham, Rodney (1962), *Structure and Sentiment. A Test Case in Social Anthropology*. Chicago: University of Chicago Press.

— (1972), *Belief, Language, and Experience*. Oxford: Blackwell.

— (ed.) (1973), *Right and Left. Essays on Dual Symbolic Classification*. Chicago: University of Chicago Press.

Nestle, Wilhelm (1942), *Vom Mythos zum Logos. Die Selbstentfaltung des griechischen Denkens von Homer bis auf die Sophistik und Sokrates*. Stuttgart: Alfred Kroner.

Neugebauer, Otto (1962), *The Exact Sciences in Antiquity*. 2nd ed. New York: Dover.

Neumann, Erich (1954), *The Origin and History of Consciousness*. Transl. by R.F.C. Hull. New York: Bollingen.

— (1955), *The Great Mother. An Analysis of the Archetype*. Transl. by Ralph Manheim. Princeton: Princeton University Press. (Orig.: *Die grosze Mutter. Der Archetyp des groszen Weiblichen*. Zürich: Rhein, 1956.)

— (1955–61), *Geschichte der griechischen Religion*, 2 vols., 2nd ed. München: C.H. Beck'sche Verlagbuchhandlung.

North, Patricia A. (1975), 'Gerardus van der Leeuw's Phenomenology of Religion,' in *Epoche: History of Religions at UCLA Newsletter* 3: 12–18.

O'Flaherty, James C. (1967), *Hamann's Socratic Memorabilia. A Translation and Commentary*. Baltimore: Johns Hopkins University Press.

Otto, Walter F. (1954), *The Homeric Gods. The Spiritual Significance of Greek Religion*. Transl. by Moses Hadas. London: Thames and Hudson. (Orig.: *Die Götter Griechenlands. Das Bild des Göttlichen im Spiegel des griechischen Gesistes*. Frankfurt, 1929.)

— (1955), 'Der Mythos,' *Studium Generale* 8: 263–68.

— (1965), *Dionysus. Myth and Cult*. Translated with an introduction by Robert B. Palmer.

Bloomington, London: Indiana University Press. (Orig.: *Dionysos*. Frankfurt, 1933.)
Otto, Rudolf (1946), *The Idea of the Holy*. Transl. by J.W. Harvey. London: Oxford
University Press. (Orig.: *Das Heilige*, 1st ed. Breslau, 1917.)

Pettazzoni, Raffaele (1922), *Dio: Formazione e sviluppo del monoteismo nella storia delle
religioni*. Vol. I (the only one published): *L'Essere celeste nelle credenze dei popoli primitivi*.
Rome:
— (1925), 'Ahura Mazda, the Knowing Lord,' in *Indo-Iranian Studies in Honour of Dastur
Darab Peshotan Sanjana*. London and Leipzig:
— (1929–36), *La confessione dei peccati*. 3 vols. Bologna. French transl.: *La confession des
péchés*. 2 vols. Paris, 1931–32.)
— (1930), 'L'omniscience de Dieu,' in *Actes du Ve Congrès International d'Histoire des
Religions* (1929). Lund.
— (1931), 'Allwissende höchste Wesen bei primitivsten Völkern,' *Archiv für
Religionswissenschaft* XXIX.
— (1935), *Studi e Materiali di Storia della Religioni*, vol. XI 215–17.
— (1947–48), 'Verita del mito,' *Studi e materiali di storia delle religioni*, 104–16.
— (1948–59), *Miti e leggende*. 4 vols. Torino: Unione Tipografico-Editrice Torinese.
— (1950), 'Die Wahrheit des Mythos,' *Paideuma*, Vol. IV, 1–10.
— (1953), *La religion dans la Grèce antique des origines à Alexandre le Grand*. Traduction de
Jean Gouillard. Paris: Payot.
— (1954a), *Essays on the History of Religions*. Transl. by H.J. Rose. Leiden: Brill.
— (1954b), 'Aperçu introductif,' *Numen* I. Translated as 'History and Phenomenology
in the Science of Religion,' chap. XIX in Pettazzoni 1954a.
— (1956), *The All-Knowing God. Researches into Early Religion and Culture*. Translated by
H.J. Rose. London: Methuen.
Pettit, Philip (1975), *The Concept of Structuralism; a Critical Analysis*. Berkeley and Los
Angeles: University of California Press.
Pingree, David (1963), 'Astronomy and Astrology in India and Iran,' *ISIS* 54: 229–46.
— (1967–68), 'The Paitāmahasiddhānta of the Viṣṇudharmottarapurāṇa,' *Brahmavidyā*
31–32: 472–510.
— (1971), 'On the Greek Origin of the Indian Planetary Model employing a Double
Epicycle,' *Journal for the History of Astronomy* 2: 80–85.
Polanyi, Michael (1962), *Personal Knowledge. Toward a Post-Critical Philosophy*. Rev. ed.
London: Routledge and Kegan Paul.
Polanyi, Michael, and Prosch, Harry (1975), *Meaning*. Chicago: University of Chicago
Press.
Popper, K. (1957), *The Poverty of Historicism*. London: Routledge and Kegan Paul.
Boston: Beacon Press.
Pritchard, J.B., (ed) (1954), *Ancient Near Eastern Texts Relating to the Old Testament*.
Princeton: Princeton University Press.
Progoff, Ira (1956), *The Death and Rebirth of Psychology*. New York: The Julian Press.

Puech, H. -Ch. (1949), *Le manichéisme, son fondateur, sa doctrine*. Paris: Musée Guimet.
— (1953–57), 'Phénoménologie de la gnose,' in *Annuaire du Collège de France* 53–57.
— (1952), 'La gnose et le temps,' *Eranos-Jahrbuch*, vol. XX, 57–113.
Puhvel, Jaan, (ed.) (1970), *Myth and Law among the Indo-Europeans*. Berkeley, Los Angeles, London: University of California Press.

Quispel, Gilles (1972), *Gnosis als Weltreligion. Die Bedeutung der Gnosis in der Antike*. 2nd ed. Zürich: Origo.

Radnitzky, Gerard (1973), *Contemporary Schools of Metascience*. 3rd enlarged ed. Chicago: Regnery.
Reill, Peter Hanns (1976), 'Philology, Culture, and Politics in Early 19th-Century Germany,' in Supplement to *Romance Philology*, vol. 30 (Friedrich Diez Centennial Lectures, Center for Medieval and Renaissance Studies Contributions 9: 18–29.)
RGG 2 (1927–1321), *Die Religion in Geschichte und Gegenwart*. 5 vols. 2nd ed. Tübingen: Mohr.
RGG 3 (1957–1962), *Die Religion in Geschichte und Gegenwart*. 6 vols. 3rd ed. Tübingen: Mohr.
Ricoeur, Paul (1965), *History and Truth*. Transl., with an Introduction by Charles A. Kelbley. Evanston: Northwestern University Press. (Orig.: *Histoire et vérité*. Paris: Editions du Seuil, 1955.)
— (1974), *The Conflict of Interpretations. Essays in Hermeneutics*. Ed. Don Ihde. Evanston: Northwestern University Press. (Orig.: *Le conflit des interprétations: Essais d'herméneutique*. Paris: Editions du Seuil, 1969.)
Ringgren, Helmer, and Ström, Åke V. (1967), *Religions of Mankind. Today and Yesterday*. Ed. J.C.G. Greig. Transl. by Niels L. Jensen. Philadelphia: Fortress Press. (Orig.: *Religionerna i historia och nutid*. 3rd ed. Stockholm: Svenska Kyrkans Diakonistyrelses Bokförlag 1964.)
Rowley, H.H. (1951), *The Old Testament and Modern Study. A Generation of Discovery and Research*. London: Oxford University Press.

Santillana, Giorgio de, and Dechend, Hertha von (1969), *Hamlet's Mill. An Essay on Myth and the Frame of Time*. Boston: Gambit.
Sartre, Jean Paul (1948), *Anti-Semite and Jew*. Transl. by George J. Becker. New York: Schocken. (Orig.: *Réflexions sur la question juive*. Paris: Morihien, 1947.)
Schärer, Hans (1963), *Ngaju Religion. The Conception of God among a South Borneo People*. Transl. by Rodney Needham. The Hague: Nijhoff. (Orig.: *Die Gottesidee der Ngadju Dajak in Süd-Borneo*. Leiden: Brill, 1946.)
— (1966), *Der Totenkult der Ngadju Dajak in Süd-Borneo*, 2 vols. The Hague: Nijhoff.
Scholem, Gershom (1941), *Major Trends in Jewish Mysticism*. Jerusalem: Schocken.
— (1949), *Zohar. The Book of Splendor*. New York: Schocken.
— (1965), *On the Kabbalah and Its Symbolism*. Transl. by Ralph Manheim. New York:

Schocken. (Orig.: *Zur Kabbala und ihrer Symbolik.* Zürich: Rhein, 1960.)
— (1971), *The Messianic Idea in Judaism, and Other Essays on Jewish Spirituality.* New York: Schocken.
— (1974), *Kabbalah.* Jerusalem: Keter.
Schröder, Christel Matthias, (ed.) (1960–), *Die Religionen der Menschheit.* 36 vols. Stuttgart: Kohlhammer.
Sebeok, Thomas E., (ed.), 1958, *Myth, a Symposium.* Bloomington and London: Indiana University Press.
Segal, Robert A. (1978), 'Eliade's Theory of Millenarianism,' in *Religious Studies* 14: 159–173.
Sierksma, F. (1951), *Freud, Jung en de religie.* Assen: Van Gorcum.
— (1956), *De religieuze projectie, een anthropologische en psychologische studie over de projectieverschijnselen in de godsdiensten.* Delft: Gaade.
Sierksma, F. (1960), *The Gods as We Shape Them.* Transl. by G.E. van Baaren-Pape. London: Routledge and Kegan Paul. (Orig.: *De mens en zijn goden.* Amsterdam: De Brug-Djambatan, 1959.)
— (1961), *Een nieuwe hemel en een nieuwe aarde; messianistische en eschatologische bewegingen en voorstellingen bij primitieve volken.* 's Gravenhage: Mouton.
— (1964), *Profiel van een incarnatie. Het leven en de conflicten van een Tibetaanse geestelijke in Tibet en Europa.* Amsterdam: Van Oorschot.
— (1966), *Tibet's Terrifying Deities. Sex and Aggression in Religious Acculturation.* The Hague: Mouton.
Smith, Huston (1976), *Forgotten Truth. The Primordial Tradition.* New York: Harper.
Spuler, B. (ed.) (1959–), *Handbuch der Orientalistik.* ('... in Heften verschiedenen Umfangs in zwangloser Folge ...'). Leiden, Köln: Brill.
Strutynski, Udo (1977), 'Claude Lévi-Strauss and the Study of Religion. A Reaction to *The Savage Mind,' Epoche, History of Religions at UCLA Newsletter* 5: 40–46.

Teilhard de Chardin, Pierre (1959), *The Phenomenon of Man.* Transl. by Bernard Wall. London, New York: Collins, Harper. (Orig.: *Le phénomène humain.* Paris: Editions du Seuil, 1955.)
— (1964), *The Future of Man.* Transl. by Norman Denny. London, New York: Collins, Harper. (Orig.: *L'avenir de l'homme.* Paris: Editions du Seuil, 1959.)
— (1965), *Hymn of the Universe.* Transl. by Simon Bartholomew. (Orig.: *Hymne de l' univers.* Paris: Editions du Seuil, 1961.)
Tempels, O.F.M., P. Placied (1946), *Bantoe-filosofie.* Antwerpen: De Sikkel.
Thompson, Stith (1966), *Motif-Index of Folk-Literature.* 6 vols. Revised and enlarged edition. Bloomington: Indiana University Press.
— (1958), 'Myth and Folktales,' in Thomas E. Sebeok (1958), 169–180.
— (1977), *The Folktale.* Berkeley, Los Angeles, London: University of California Press.
Thrupp, Sylvia L. (ed.) (1962), *Millennial Dreams in Action. Essays in Comparative Study.* The Hague: Mouton.

Tylor, Sir Edward Burnett (1958), *Primitive Culture*. I. *The Origins of Culture*; II. *Religion in Primitive Culture*. New York: Harper. (Orig.: London: Murray, 1871.)

Vries, J. de (1977), *Perspectives in the History of Religions*. Transl. by Kees W. Bolle. Berkeley, Los Angeles, London: University of California Press. (Orig.: *Godsdienstgeschiedenis in vogelvlucht*. Utrecht: Het Spectrum, 1961.)

Wach, Joachim (1924), *Religionswissenschaft*. Leipzig: Hinrichs.
— (1951), *Types of Religious Experience, Christian and Non-Christian*. Chicago: University of Chicago Press.
Wasson, Robert Gordon (1968), *Soma, Divine Mushroom of Immortality*. New York: Harcourt.
Whitehead, A.N. (1927), *Science and the Modern World*. Cambridge: Cambridge University Press.
White Jr., Lynn (1978), *Medieval Religion and Technology. Collected Essays*. Berkeley, Los Angeles, London: University of California Press.
Widengren, Geo (1938), *Hochgottglaube im alten Iran*. Uppsala and Leipzig.
— (1958), 'Early Hebrew Myths and Their Interpretation,' in Hooke 149–203.
— (1969), *Religionsphänomenologie*. Berlin: De Gruyter. Enlarged edition of the 2nd Swedish edition *Religionens värld*. Stockholm: Svenska Kyrkans Diakonistyrelses Bokförlag, 1953.
Wirz, Paul (1922), *Die Marind-anim von Holländisch-Süd-Neu-Guinea*. Hamburg: L. Friederichsen.

5

The Scientific Study of Religion in its Plurality

NINIAN SMART

Lancaster and *Santa Barbara*

There has been since World War II, and in particular since the mid-1960s, a great flowering of the study of religion. There has been great growth in institutions offering courses in religion in the English-speaking world; while in Continental Europe and Scandinavia there has, in the period since 1945, not only been a restoration to vigour of the faculties of theology, but also a modest but significant advance in the history of religions, partly in the context of a widened interest in non-European cultures. At the same time, work in the social sciences has increasingly converged, in matters related to religion, upon the work of comparative religionists.

But though we may live during a period when old-fashioned rationalism is declining, and when the importance of the study of religion is more widely recognized, there is not always much clarity in the assumptions brought to bear upon it. Or at least there is much divergence of aim and method in the way in which it is approached.

This is partly because the subject is considerably shaped by the institutions in which it is embedded. Thus the existence of faculties of Christian theology imposes certain categories upon scholarship—for instance the division into such branches of enquiry as New Testament, patristics, church history, systematic theology, philosophy of religion, comparative religion (or history of religions). This builds into the subject already an asymmetry in the way in which Christianity is treated as compared with other religious traditions. This of course reflects the history of scholarship and the fact that classically the study of religion has been tied for the most part to the training of clergy and other specialists; and so the modern universities of Europe and America in some degree inherit the cultural assumption that Christianity should have a privileged place in the curriculum. Conversely, worry about such an arrangement sometimes leads to the exclusion of theology from the secular university. It is not my task here to enter into the controversies surrounding this matter: but rather to look to the way in which the history of the subject affects approaches to it. Undoubtedly for many scholars there remains the assumption that their task is to be understood in the light of Christian (or Jewish or other) truth: that is, in one way or another commitment is relevant to study. We can in respect of all this point to a number of differing models.

First, there is the full-fledged model of what may be called constructive traditionalism. That is, there is the approach to the study of religion from the perspective of a given tradition—most frequently Christianity, and in particular some variety of it (Lutheranism, Roman Catholicism, etc.). Ultimately here the exploration of tests, the undertaking of a critical evaluation of them, the processes of hermeneutics, the systematic exploration of doctrines and so on are geared to the constructive presentation of the tradition as expressing spiritual and intellectual truth. Ultimately the task is one of expressing rather than describing. Thus the work of such figures as Barth, Küng, Bultmann, Käsemann, Tillich, and John Robinson—to put together a variegated selection of recent theological and Biblical scholars—is in the last analysis concerned with working out Christian truth, rather than simply doing history or even debating on both sides of the question (as might happen in the context of the philosophy of religion).

Second, there may be an attitude of seeing the study of religion as primarily concerned with issues in philosophical theology—that is, with the questions arising concerning the nature and existence of God (or of the Ultimate, to use a wider-reaching term) as perceived in the light of the history of religion, etc. This orientation may be called pluralistic theology. The accent is primarily on questions of truth in religion rather than on truths concerning religion.

Third, the theological tradition may be treated positivistically: that is the essential task of the theologian is to explore and describe the history of the faith independently of truth judgments about the content of faith. Still, it is naturally the case that such an approach has its agenda set by some implicit evaluations—for instance, about the importance of particular periods and aspects of Christian, or other, history. We may call this approach theological positivism. The fact of positivism does not preclude such an approach from being critical, and making use of the various tools of modern critical historiography.

It is clear that looked at from a planetary point of view there are questions arising about such models of theology. For one thing, the very word 'theology' is a western one. What does one use for Buddhism? Should we talk of the Buddhologian? Moreover, not all traditions are as hospitable either to pluralism or to critical positivism as is the modern western tradition. Nevertheless, historians of religion have opened up critical questions about the various traditions. I do not wish to argue the point here, but it seems to me clear that every tradition will inevitably have to come to terms with such scrutiny. It matters, of course, less in some faiths than others. For instance, Buddhism is not quite so tightly wedded to history as is Christianity or Judaism, while the facts of early Islam are less in doubt than those of these other religions. But naturally the critical positivist questions necessarily raise issues of truth in the context of what we have dubbed pluralistic theology and thus are liable to generate new approaches within the various forms of constructive traditionalism. Thus neo-Hindu theologies (such as those of Vivekananda and Radhakrishnan) can be seen as ways of coming to terms not merely with western culture but also with modern methods of scholarship, concerning India's deep past.

The modern period has of course seen the opening up more richly than in the past of contacts and conversations between religious traditions. The exchange of insights between faiths has come to have the name of dialogue. It is true that dialogue could simply be a method of exchanging information and so just be a tool of historical research: but more pregnantly it has been a particular style of pluralistic theology, a kind of cooperative spiritual exploration of truth. Because however it does differ in style and tradition it may be useful to have a different name for it. I shall call it constructive dialogue.

But none of all this so far is what may be thought of as the scientific study of religion. It is quite true that sometimes so-called scientific studies of religion (say in sociology) conceal value- or truth- assumptions which are of an essentially theological or philosophical nature (e.g., projectionism makes certain assumptions about the truth of religious belief, typically). It is quite true also that pluralistic theology, constructive traditionalism and so forth may in fact use scientific methods in the course of their enquiries. Certainly, such great theologians as Karl Barth made use of much plain historical material and critical method. But the main thrust of their concerns was not descriptive and scientific but expressive, proclamatory, philosophical: presenting a faith-stance or a worldview.

It may be thought that there is a 'science of God.' In a sense perhaps there is (and to that sense I shall later come). But I think in a more obvious way the idea that there is a 'science of God,' a kind of theological science, uses the term in a Pickwickian way. Belief in God is highly debatable, only indirectly (at best) testable, a question of reaction and commitment, much bound up with value questions. Since the alternative views of the Ultimate are so various, and even include the view that there is no Ultimate, it would be rash to define a theological science by postulating to start with a personal God. At best we might think about a 'science of the Ultimate.' Now it is clear that some men claim to experience the Ultimate, and it would be wrong to neglect such experience. But because of the vagaries and strangenesses of issues about interpretation it would be better in the first instance to confine the use of the word 'scientific' to the relatively neutral investigation of phenomena, including those comprised by religious experience. In brief, then, I think it is reasonable to say that the various models I have listed above (constructive traditionalism through to constructive dialogue) do not fall, essentially, within the purview of what may be called the scientific study of religion, though they may overlap with it.

Those overlaps actually are important. How can one really get the feel of a faith except by mingling among its adherents? A religion is more than texts, and the past: it is living history. This being so, a kind of dialogue with people is necessarily part of the fabric of enquiry into religion, whether scientific or otherwise.

Again, the philosophical skills which are fashioned in the philosophy of religion are important in the empirical investigation of religion. For one thing, descriptions have to be scrutinized for assumptions. Often our categories come not in utter nakedness but trailing clouds of theory, often inappropriate theory. Again, philosophy is much bound up with questions of verification and method. Moreover the whole enterprise of hermeneutical enquiry is one which requires philosophical debate. So it is idle to think one can simply do the history of religions, or the sociology of religion, or whatever, without in fact bumping up against philosophical and conceptual problems.

Moreover, the processes of critical history concerning, for example, Christian origins, vital in the task of constructive Christian theology, are relevant to other areas of religio-historical enquiry.

In brief, there is an overlap between the value-laden models for the study of religion and the relatively value-free scientific study of religion.

One has, however, to be clear about this notion of the relatively value-free. It is sometimes said that it is not possible (or even desirable) to be perfectly value-free, perfectly 'objective.' The term 'objective' is an unfortunate one, because actually all science and all unravelling of the world involves a kind of interplay, a struggle even, between the inquirers and that which they are concerned to understand. Nature is mean about her secrets. The right questions have to be posed: and she is a great slaughterer of theories. Objectivity is important only in two ways—one being that by being relatively free of prejudice the inquirer may show imagination in developing new questions to pose to nature; and secondly objectivity implies the acceptance of the possible death of one's pet ideas. One should be adventurous and sagacious, but also stoical in defeat. When we come to the human sciences, however, there is a difference of a profound kind: for it is no longer a mute nature that addresses us, but living and communicative beings. Empathy becomes important. And that means somehow adopting the American Indian proverb: 'Never judge a man till you have walked a mile in his moccasins.' Or rather: 'Never describe a man until you have walked a mile in his moccasins.' The term 'objectivity' is not usually taken to include much in the way of feeling or empathy.

So though the scientific study of religion should be relatively value-free, it has got to enter somehow into the world of values. This is part of what has come to be called the phenomenological method, as practised by for instance Kristensen and van der Leeuw. However, it happens that partly because of its particular philosophical origins in the tradition of Husserl, phenomenology of religion has also come to be bound up greatly with the search for essences: that is, with describing types of religious phenomena, and classifying them. This is to be seen in *Religion in Essence and Manifestation* and in Widengren's phenomenological work, and represents part of the whole enterprise known as the comparative study of religion. It is thus probably useful for the sake of clarity to distinguish between what I have referred to above as the phenomenological method, which involves 'entering in' to the thought world of the believer, and typological phenomenology, which is an attempt to anatomize the forms of religion in a comparative manner.

The use of the term 'phenomenology' implies, as it is usually employed, a suspension of belief, a prescinding from the worldview which the investigator may happen to hold, except in so far as he may think that the investigation of religious phenomena is important, which may imply something about a worldview, though at a higher logical level. (It is in general important to pay attention to levels: thus to say that we should use empathy to enter into people's various positions is a position about positions, i.e., it belongs to a higher level.) This sometimes obscures the fact that structures are important as well as empathy. That is, since the believer views his activity against the background, (or should we say from within the background?), of a whole web of beliefs and resonances, the person who wishes to understand the meaning of his action needs to unravel that structure or web. For instance, what are we to make of the Buddhist laying a flower before the statue of a Buddha in Sri Lanka? To understand her it is necessary to understand her understanding of the world, and that constitutes quite a complex structure. So empathy has to be more than imaginative feeling: it has to include a delineation of structures. So there is a certain tension between the phenomenological method or structured empathy, and typological phenomenology, which tends to try to cut through the organic particularities of a given cultural milieu.

This tension is something which runs deeply through the territory of the history of religions. For while some of the scholars in the field are more concerned with the comparative study of religion (a phrase which comes in and out of vogue—out of vogue in so far as comparisons could be thought to be odious, and redolent of whiffs of western imperialism and Christian superiority, the phrase falls on evil days; yet in vogue in so far as we wish the study of religions to make use of the opportunities for comparison and contrast, opportunities which are useful in testing various hypotheses about religion)—others again are concerned more with the history of a given tradition or culture. Thus the study of religion contains among other things the histories of various traditions, which may or may not be at one time or another in mutual historical interaction; but it also contains attempts at comparative treatment, which is necessarily cross-cultural. It is at different times important to stress uniquenesses of historical development and similarities of phenomena and elements in differing cultures. The danger of separate histories is that each may fail to see certain aspects of the dynamics of religion which can be gleaned from cross-cultural comparison. The danger of the comparative study of religion is that it may crassly bulldoze the particularities of the traditions.

Basically the comparative study of religion as it is practised tends to comprise first an attempt at a world history of religions; and second various kinds of typological phenomenology (for instance the comparative study of mysticism, sacrifice, worship and so on). To complicate matters, it has become usual to substitute the phrase history of religions for the comparative study of religion. Sometimes, as in the work of Eliade, such history of religions includes a special scheme of typological phenomenology. Actually Eliade's scheme has been remarkably fruitful, especially in raising issues about the religious and human meaning of space and time. But in addition Eliade's work, like Otto's and Wach's— to name two important forerunners—includes a general theory of existence: a kind of philosophy, one might say, compounded out of various sources including Eliade's own historical experience. Thus his typological phenomenology, especially in regard to views of history, is in part determined by a kind of philosophical theology. This does not mean that we have to discard the typology, but it does mean that we have to be aware, critically, of assumptions open to question and lying behind the more empirical presentations of the data. It would perhaps be ironic if having escaped from theological dogmatism as inappropriate for the scientific study of religion we met it in new and more heavily disguised form in a philosophy of existence unquestioned behind the shamanism. The point is that the science of religion should welcome imaginative ways of looking at the data, including Eliadean ones, Marxist ones and so on; but that is not to say that what counts as the scientific study of religion should be determined and defined by any one theory. For each theory should be testable in relation to the data in the field. Assuming any one theory to define the field destroys its true testability and gives it a spurious authority.

Because of the institutional evolution of the subject the comparative study of religion has not always existed in close relationship to such scientific or social-scientific disciplines as the sociology of religion, anthropology of religion and psychology of religion. True, in the late nineteenth century especially the influence of anthropology was very considerable, partly because it was fashionable to speculate about the origins and evolution of religion and 'primitive' cultures were thought of also as somehow primeval and so containing clues to the earliest phases of human culture and spirituality. Actually there seems no intrinsic reason why the history of religions and the sociology and anthropology of religion should not be treated as a single investigatory enterprise. The divergences are somewhat fortuitous. Thus the difference between sociology and anthropology represents a crude division between large- and small-scale societies, a difference of style of founding fathers and gurus, and a certain distinctness of methodological emphasis. But as for the scale question, this is hardly in the last resort relevant to overall theorizing about society; as to the styles, well, they add up to differing and often competing theories which have to be tested in the same empirical marketplace; and as for methods, differences are to do with feasibilities—cancer research may employ different techniques from research into the brain, but we do not thus artifically divide human functioning. Further, though obviously the concern of the social scientists is primarily with social relationships and dynamics, this is after all a major aspect of a religion and its cultural expression and milieu, so that there is in principle no absolute divide between history of religions and the social sciences of religion.

Similarly one may see history of religions as somewhat like economic history: the latter is history with the accent on economic aspects of existence, and the former is history with the accent on religious aspects of existence. It would be as artificial to deal with the economic history of 1979 without mentioning Khomeini as it would be to treat of the religious history of the Amish without dealing with the economics of small-scale agriculture.

It may be noted also that some of the major figures in the sociology of religion have also been concerned with typology. To take two examples: Weber and his theories of the relationship between religious and socio-economic development; and Bryan Wilson and his attempt to classify various sects and new religious movements. This work is relevant to the often neglected point that one can have a typology of historical changes—e.g., what happens in cases of culture contact.

Though one might consider, reasonably, that the difference between the various disciplines (history, sociology, anthropology of religion) is somewhat artificial, it does create one advantage, in that the institution-alization of differing approaches leads to effective intellectual lobbies against the neglect of certain areas. Thus it is easy to do the history of religions in a rather textual and 'unliving' way. The social scientists pressure us to restore balance here. A result is the renewed modern interest in the sociology of early Christianity, the attempt to look at Buddhism from the perspective of modern Asian societies, the need to analyse rites of passage in context and so on. The same can be said about some recent and rather adventitious developments. Thus in North America especially the advent of women's political activism has resulted in a burgeoning of women's studies and with that a renewed interest in the female in religion; likewise recent concerns about Blacks, Chicanos, and Native Americans have led to something of a revival in the study of the religions of these people.

One major methodological issue arises especially in regard to the sociology of religion, and in a differing form regarding the psychology of religion. The tendency in these fields is for theories to be developed which are in general projectionist. Thus God and the Ultimate and the lesser entities and symbols of religious belief tend to be seen as uncon-scious or social projections, which then act reflexively upon society and individuals. Thus a highly sophisticated modern form of projection theory is to be found in Peter Berger's *The Sacred Canopy* (British title: *The Social Reality of Religion*), in which he claims to espouse 'methodological atheism.' It is taken as axiomatic that a scientific approach to religion cannot accept the existence of God. But the non-acceptance of the existence of God is not equivalent to the acceptance of the non-existence of God. What should be used in approaching religion is not so much the principle of methodological atheism as the principle of methodological agnosticism. It is not useful for the investigator of religion to begin by imposing assumptions drawn from his own worldview upon the subject matter. Thus the suspension of belief here required is a kind of higher-order agnosticism. Thus God or the Ultimate need neither be affirmed nor denied, but seen as something present in human experience and belief, wherever it is so present. It is only in this sense that there is a 'science of God.' It is important that the power of religious experience and belief and the way God serves as a focus of human activity and feeling should be recognized as factors in history and society and in individual psychology. Often the power of the Ultimate-as-experienced is underestimated by modern rationalist historians and social scientists. How important it is is not a question of validity of experience, but a matter of empirical impact. Conversely it may be that on occasions religionists have overestimated the actual impact of the Ultimate-as-experienced. So though there is not a science of God there is a sort of science of God-as-experienced. This is the advantage of speaking of religion as a phenomenon.

Since impacts are in principle measurable it is not surprising that much attention has been paid by some social scientists to statistical data: we can see one manifestation of this approach in the *Journal for the Scientific Study of Religion*. One of the problems arises from the way in which a suitable wedding between this and more impressionistic but empathetic phenomenology can be achieved. We see a like chasm in the psychology of religion between much of the interesting work being done in typological phenomenology, e.g., over the classification of mysticism and other forms of religious experience, and the measurement of attitudes, etc., which occupies much of psychology-oriented psychology of religion. Frits Staal's sketch on how to deal with mysticism in his *Exploring Mysticism* goes some way towards achieving a synthesis;

but there remain important philosophical problems not fully resolved either by him or by others in regard to the ways to classify inner experiences—an issue much bound up with the important, but vexed, question of the relationship between experience and interpretation. Considerable conceptual problems enter into this discussion, which has recently been carried on in the context of philosophical analysis. Lack of concern with the problem has vitiated some influential works on religious experience, e.g., by Stace and Zaehner.

For various reasons, the interplay between anthropology, depth psychology and history of religions has proved fruitful in the variety of ways myth and symbolism can be approached. There are certain congruences between structuralism, Eliade, and Jung, which suggest that the analysis of religion may be a vital ingredient in any theory of human psychology. And this in turn raises an important question as to what the comparative and phenomenological study of religion ultimately aims at. Though it may be methodologically unsound to try to define the study of religion in terms of some theory within the field, and the data should be so far as possible presented in a way which is not theory-laden—for this would lead too easily and cheaply to 'confirmation' of the theory by the data,— yet it may remain important for the history of religions to supply material which can be used theoretically. Thus the following are important, though difficult areas for speculation and research: Are there in fact archetypal symbols which are liable to appear independently in different cultures? If so, what kind of explanation of this would be in order? What kinds of patterns can be found in the processes of syncretism and the creation of new religious movements in the third world (as the many thousand in Africa) and in parts of the western world? If the mythic mode of expressing existential relationships to the cosmos and to society has been widespread among peoples in the past and to some extent in the present, what other changes are liable to accompany the erosion of this style of thinking? To what extent do non-religious ideologies function in similar ways to traditional religious belief-systems? Can any form of projection theory be empirically confirmed? Most importantly, the confluence of anthropological and religio-historical approaches may be vital in giving us a better modern understanding of human symbolic behaviour.

Curiously, though religions obviously have a vital interest in the arts and music, there has been relative neglect of the visual, musical, and literary dimensions of religious consciousness. This is perhaps in part due to the kind of training typical of western scholars—concerned often with texts as evidences, and fascinated often by doctrinal and intellectual aspects of faith. An interesting methodological question arises in regard to literature, in that novelists especially are devoted to a kind of fictional 'structured empathy' such as I described earlier. They bring out the feel of what it is like to be a given person looking at the world and at others in a certain way (consider, for instance the divergent expressions of attitude delineated by Dostoievsky in the case of the brothers Karamazov). To what degree would new forms of literary presentation be relevant to the task of phenomenology? One thinks here of the novels of Eliade and Sartre as cases where more abstract analyses are clothed in particular flesh.

One can discover, in the evolution of the study of religion, a series of stages. One stage is represented by the discovery and decipherment of other cultures (I look here at the matter inevitably from the standpoint of the western culture which gave rise to the modern study of religion). This process is still going on. There are still large numbers of important texts not yet edited and understood, and the recording of oral traditions is still only very partial. Access to the records of differing religious traditions made possible the process of comparison. Classificatory comparisons form ideally the second stage in the study of religion as a human phenomenon. The third stage is where theories whether sociological (e.g., Weber), anthropological (e.g., Tylor) or psychological (e.g., Jung) can be formulated. We remain at a rather early stage in the development of theorizing about religion. Perhaps also we are at the beginning of a harvest, in which the many fruits of the extensive expansion of research since World War II can be gathered, and when the history of religions— and in a more general way the study of religion—may enter a period of greater influence, in the broader world of learning.

So far we have looked at the scientific study of religion as being plural in scope, for it concerns the many traditions and the plethora of forms of religion to be discovered on the planet and in history; and as being multidisciplinary—for it must include not just the techniques and processes of structured empathy and typological phenomenology, but also methods drawn from history, sociology, anthropology, iconography, and so on. But there remain problems concerning the boundaries of the field. Notoriously an agreed and useful definition of religion is hard or impossible to find. Yet at the same time often scholars seem unnaturally confident as to what they mean by the study of religion. It is a real question as to whether the subject should consider the symbolic systems usually held in the West to lie beyond religion proper—e.g., nationalism, forms of Marxism, and so on. There does seem an incongruity in treating the Taiping rebellion (or revolution) in the category of the history of religions and Maoism in another quite separate category of political history. After all, both movements were trying to resolve much the same problem of China's national identity in a time of crisis, and they have many other properties in common. It is interesting to note that in the account of one of the discussions at the History of Religions Study Conference in Turku Finland (see Lauri Honko, editor, *Science of Religion Studies in Methodology*, (1979: 30) the following passage occurs:

Similarly picking up van Baaren's remark, he—sc. Zwi Werblowsky—suggested (not facetiously) that comparative religion ought also to look at the current process of formation of secular canons, e.g., the works of Chairman Mao.

What is interesting is the disclaimer 'not facetiously.' For it is a result of perhaps an ideological rather than a scientific divide that we put traditional religions in one basket and secular ideologies in another. My own plenary paper, 'From the Tao to Mao,' at the Lancaster Congress of the IAHR in 1975, was itself a protest against the rigid division between traditional and modern secular worldviews. It is after all ultimately an empirical matter to discover if theories worked out in regard to traditional religions also work in the case of their secular counterparts.

Thus there is an argument for saying that the scientific study of religion is non-finite—that is, there is no clear boundary which we can draw around it. It simply has to be discovered in practice how far theorizing goes beyond the traditional faiths. Incidentally it is quite clear that the methods of structured empathy are as necessary in the exploration of secular worldviews as in the case of religions proper.

Though there is increasing reason to hold that the scientific study of religion should be so far as possible value-free, save in so far as in the nature of the case it has to evoke values, via the processes of empathy and phenomenology, there is little doubt that it has a reflexive effect *upon* values. For one thing, the historical approach to scriptures is bound to (and has) affected attitudes to their authority, and can nibble at their contents. Similarly knowledge of other religious traditions is bound to affect attitudes to one's own tradition. Thus a lot of ink has been spilled on the question of the uniqueness of Christianity, since from the perspective of certain theologies there is a motive to stress the difference between Christianity and other faiths; while there is something of the opposite from the perspective of modern Hinduism. The question of Christianity's likeness or unlikeness to other traditions in this or that respect is strictly an empirical question (though it may remain a debatable one). In this way empirical theses may have evaluative consequences.

The fact that the scientific study of religion can have such effects is one reason why it takes a special kind of temperament to be devoted to its pursuit—a kind of passion for evocative dispassion. It is, though, one of the noblest of human enterprises to try to enter imaginatively into the feelings and thoughts of others. This is an ingredient in religious methodology which has many lessons to teach in the modern world and the multicultural ambience of the planet. This is one among a number of reasons why the study of religion and religions should play a widening part in the educated person's understanding of the world. Eliade is right to call for a creative role for the history of religions. Better, this role should be played not just by the history of religions, but more widely by the whole set of disciplines which in interplay make up the study of religion. All this is only perhaps a second-order way of saying that religious sentiments, ideas, and institutions remain a pervasive aspect of the human world. That so often the wider study of religion—what I have called the scientific study of religion—has been suspected from the side of faith and neglected from the side of reason has contributed to the lopsidedness of the human sciences.

Additional Note on Philosophy of Science and the Study of Religion

FRANK WHALING

Edinburgh

Recent changes in the philosophy of science have important implications for the study of religion. It was the rise of modern science in the West that paved the way for the scientific, industrial and technological revolutions that produced the 'global village' in which we now live. The increasing transport facilities, communications, and educational innovations resulting from those revolutions changed the face of our globe and rapidly increased our accumulated store of religious data as well as our interreligious contact. Lying behind the practical achievements of modern science were certain theories about scientific method. These theories had an influence outside the realm of the natural sciences, and had some effect upon approaches to the study of religion. Now that these theories are changing due to advances in the philosophy of science it is important that there should be analysis of the implications of these changes for the study of religion.

Our first task is to examine briefly some former presuppositions about the nature of the scientific method; we shall then summarise some recent developments in the philosophy of science; finally, we shall attempt to estimate the import of these developments for contemporary approaches to the study of religion.

Our aim in accomplishing this task is to complement the fine pieces by Ninian Smart and Ursula King on the science of religion by going behind the complicated discussions as to whether or in what way the study of religion is a science in order to investigate the changing view of science within science itself. This is a necessary accompaniment to the wider discussion. It is a sobering thought that when A. J. Ayer wrote

Language, Truth and Logic in 1936 which led to the advance of 'scientific' positivism within philosophy, the short-comings of positivism had already been pointed out within the scientific world by thinkers such as Popper (1935) and Bachelard (1934). There is the same danger of introducing or perpetuating within the study of religion views of science that are outmoded among scientists.

The positivist and empiricist views of science that held sway until recently, and are still purveyed in books such as Nagel's *The Structure of Science* (1961), considered certain assumptions to be axiomatic, namely: there is an external world; we can describe that world fully in scientific language; that language stands in one-to-one relationship to factual data; these data are ascertained by observation and experiment; scientific observation and experiment are based upon what our senses can reveal; scientific theories are built up through our induction of factual data; this induction and this theorizing is 'objective' and not reliant upon personal predilections; the scientific knowledge that results is proven knowledge of the world as it objectively is. A number of drawbacks were found by the philosophy of science in this viewpoint. It was pointed out that the inductive principle is not necessarily upheld by an appeal to logic and experience—induction cannot be used to justify induction! (Stove 1973, Lakatos 1968, Duhem 1962) Moreover the principle of observation with which science starts and which is supposed to provide its base turns out to need the support of prior theory (Hanson 1958, Popper 1968, 1972, Scheffler 1967, Droscher 1971). In addition to this, the empirical and positivist view no longer delivered the goods. As Chalmers puts it (1978: 33):

The main reason why I think inductivism should be abandoned is that, compared with rival and more modern approaches, it has increasingly failed to throw new and interesting light on the nature of science.

Therefore any attempt to base the study of religion upon methods centred upon empirical or positivist criteria must face these same objections.

An alternative view of scientific methodology was introduced by the falsificationists, notably Karl Popper (1968, 1969, 1972), and Peter

Medawar (1969). The falsificationists admitted the point that observation is preceded and guided by prior theory, and conceded that observational evidence alone does not establish the truth of scientific theories. For them, theories were not proven or true in themselves but the best available constructs produced by creative human minds to advance the scientific process, and to improve upon past theories that had not stood the test of time. The falsificationists insisted that theories should be tested by experiment and observation, and if they failed these tests, if they were falsified by them, they must give way to other theories. They demanded that scientific hypotheses must be falsifiable otherwise they were scientifically worthless, and the more falsifiable and therefore scientifically informative a theory was, the more valuable it became. The falsification of a theory was not a disaster but a growing-point whereby a bolder, more novel, and more falsifiable theory could emerge to pave the way for further advances. Popper pointed out that the dialectical materialistic view of history and the Freudian view of psychoanalysis were not falsifiable and therefore, according to his view of science, not scientific. In the light of Popper's theory, any approach to the study of religion that is not falsifiable is likewise not scientific. This would apply for instance, to projectionist theories, whether psychological, sociological, or Marxist, and to ontological theories such as Eliade's notion of the sacred.

The problem is that there are limits to falsificationism itself in that observation statements remain theory-dependent and fallible, and therefore they cannot conclusively be falsified. Furthermore, if falsificationism had been applied rigorously within historical situations, Newton's theory of gravitation, Bohr's theory of the atom, and the Copernican Revolution itself would never have got off the ground in that there was some contemporary observational evidence against them as well as for them!

A third development emerged within the philosophy of science which considered both the inductionist theory of the empiricists *and* the falsification theory too piecemeal to account adequately for the complexities of a Newton, a Bohr, or a Copernicus. Centred in the work of scholars such as Lakatos (1974; see also Koertge 1971, Bloor 1971, Musgrave 1974), emphasis came to be placed upon theories as structured wholes.

Because observation is dependent upon theory, and because the coherently structured theories of the historical giants of science had given a precise meaning to scientific concepts that had enabled science to grow, therefore the need was felt for open-ended modern structures that would perform the same function through the medium of well-articulated research programmes. In his 'Falsification and the Methodology of Scientific Research Programmes' (1974) Imre Lakatos gave an account of the way in which such research programmes might operate. He stipulated, on the one hand, that research programmes should include a set of basic assumptions and very general hypotheses that would form the 'hard core' of the programme in question, and he suggested that this hard core should not be rejected or modified by, so to speak, a methodological fiat. He stipulated, on the other hand, that surrounding the hard core there should be a protective belt of auxiliary hypotheses and initial conditions that *could* be falsified and that therefore could be modified and rejected, after independent testing, without violating the hard core. The hard core gave the stability on the basis of which the programme could develop; the protective belt provided the more changeable, positive, and falsifiable part of the operation. Lakatos felt that this scheme provided sound guidelines for research in that it provided both coherence and the possibility of the discovery of novel phenomena. He pointed out that the work of Marx and Freud satisfied the criterion of coherence but did not enable novel phenomena to be discovered, and modern sociological theory enabled novel phenomena to be discovered but did not satisfy the criterion of coherence. His scheme had the merit of allowing research programmes to prove themselves by being progressive, if they became consistently regressive they could be dropped. What was not allowable was any violation of the hard core, and any taking up of hypotheses that were not independently testable; therefore any incoherent programme or untestable hypotheses were ruled out.

As Dr. King has stated, Dudley has attempted to apply Lakatos's research programme to religious studies by suggesting that Eliade's work should provide the basis for such a research structure. It is fair to say that Eliade's programme is a reasonably well-articulated total structure, and as has been stated in different parts of this book there is the need for holistic theories that can take an overview of the total work of the study of religion. Indeed, the chapters by Kees Bolle, Ninian Smart, Frank Whaling, and (to a lesser extent) Ursula King feel for and gently imply fuller structures for wide areas in the study of religion. The problem posed by Lakatos is twofold. He provides no criteria for deciding whether one research programme is better than another except by the hindsight verification principle of progression or degeneration. According to this principle, it may be asked whether the historical and phenomenological models that have dominated research until recently have not outlived their usefulness in their present form, but, if it be assumed that this is the case, Lakatos gives no clear guidelines as to what should succeed them. The case for suggesting Eliade's programme depends, in effect, upon the conscious decision of a number of scholars to follow Eliade's programme rather than upon generally agreed criteria whereby it is clear that his is the best programme to follow. What tends to happen is that the groupings of scholars following particular research programmes congregate in particular institutions so that there arises a Chicago school, a Harvard school, a Lancaster school, and so on, around key scholars who have structured research programmes. These programmes are proving helpful and, insofar as they abide by the kind of principles suggested by Lakatos, they are likely to bear fruit in advancing the study of religion. But by what standards are we to evaluate them?

An alternative view that scientific theory is a complex structure was developed by Thomas Kuhn in *The Structure of Scientific Revolutions* (1962). When Kuhn turned from physics to the history of science he found his ideas about science became fundamentally changed, and like Lakatos he realised that inductivist and falsificationist accounts of science did not square with the historical evidence. Kuhn stressed the revolutionary nature of scientific progress whereby a revolution involves the abandonment of one theoretical structure in favour of another, incompatible one. He emphasised too the importance of historical contexts and the importance of the sociological characteristics of scientific communities. He saw science progressing from a disorganised situation to a normal situation when a single 'paradigm' becomes normative for a community of scientists. After successful use and adaptation the paradigm eventually begins to break down. This leads to a crisis situation, and out of the crisis a new paradigm emerges through a scientific revolution. Kuhn considered that mature science is governed by a single paradigm, for example Newtonian mechanics, wave optics, or classical electromagnetism. The paradigm will usually be imprecise and open-ended, it will use explicitly stated laws and theoretical assumptions, it will build up standard ways of applying laws to situations, it will admit the possibility of anomalies, it will see itself as a puzzle-solving activity using instrumental techniques according to general metaphysical principles. The crisis for a paradigm will become serious when anomalies persist in time, multiply in number, and coincide with pressing social needs, and therefore cause professional insecurity among those who had formerly seen the paradigm as being normal.

It is interesting and instructive to apply Kuhn's theories to the study of religion. It is doubtful whether religious studies has ever been governed by one single paradigm such as that of a Newton or an Einstein. It is by no means clear that any of the early giants mentioned in Waardenburg's volume (1973), such as Müller, Durkheim, Jung, etc, dominated the field through a single paradigm; it is equally clear that the scholars singled out by Whaling as being contemporaneously prominent, like Smith, Panikkar, Zaehner, Lévi-Strauss, Brandon, Dumézil, Eliade, Parrinder, Smart, Widengren, and Pettazzoni, have produced no single paradigm that commands universal acceptance. In the light of Kuhn's theory this can be interpreted in two ways: either religious studies is at the stage of pre-science and has yet to reach the stage of being a 'normal science' governed by a single paradigm, or it has reached a possible crisis state wherein it is ripe for a revolution to produce a strong paradigm out of a weaker historical/phenomenological one.

However, not all scientific theories give such a special status to science. An extreme example of non-conformity in the philosophy of science is Paul Feyerabend (1968: 75). He denies that there is one objective and authentic scientific method that is the cause of the high veneration for science in the modern world. His view is that science is revered because it is taught in schools as if its claims should be taken for granted rather than being a matter of choice or open to debate. Science, he argues, is admired for institutional reasons, not because it has a cast-iron methodology. In fact, he claims, it has no particular methodology and no particular theoretical structure. Its methods and theories are plural. For 'there is only *one* principle that can be defended under *all* circumstances and in *all* stages of human development. It is the principle: anything goes' (1975: 14). Less anarchistic than Feyerabend, but also moving in a relativistic and pluralistic direction are Rescher (1979) and Hesse (1980). They contend that natural science should be integrated into a wider framework embracing the humanities as well, and that scientific theories are not 'true' but that they are social creations along with comprehensive theories in the humanities. At this point, their work converges with the work of some continental scholars who see a relationship between views of science, anthropology, and social practice. There is a similarity between their work and the communication theory associated with the Frankfurt school of sociology and Jurgen Habermas, (see Habermas 1963, 1968, 1973; Gadamer 1960; Apel 1980). Although Rescher and Hesse begin with science, and Habermas begins with social theory, their wider concerns are to establish possibilities for universal agreement concerning truth, and norms for collective responsibility.

The type of philosophy of science exemplified in the work of scholars such as Hesse has implications for the study of religion in three ways. First, the apparent failure to set up an ideal, true, conceptual framework for religious theory can be viewed in more positive terms when it is seen that the same position may exist in relation to contemporary scientific theory. As Hesse writes: (1980: xxiv):

... there are no defences except the pragmatic criterion against the relativity of scientific theories, and ... the pragmatic criterion permits a permanent plurality of conceptual frameworks ... no important philosophical or scientific positions are given away if we abandon the ungrounded assumption that there is an ideal, true conceptual framework for scientific theory.

The study of religion may, and we have suggested should, seek for a philosophical overview of and an integrated framework for its theory and methods. But when this holistic aim is pursued it is in response to promptings from within the study of religion itself; it is no longer motivated by a desire to follow the natural sciences which increasingly see the search for a universal conceptual framework as an unrealisable hope.

Second, scholars such as Hesse view the relationship between the natural sciences and the humanities in the form of a continuum rather than in the form of a dichotomy. The two former notions—that the natural sciences amounted to empiricism with its stress upon natural facts independent of the observer and of theory, natural laws directly related to external relations, scientific language that was exact, universalisable and univocal, and scientific concepts that were meaningful independently of their application—and that the humanities amounted to hermeneutic with its stress upon the constitutive importance of human meaning and intentionality, the holistic and internally related nature of theoretical interpretation, and the metaphorical and dynamically adaptable nature of the language of interpretation—are now seen to be in continuity rather than schism. Fact and interpretation belong together in both the sciences and the humanities. However, the natural sciences and the humanities have different interests as well as overlapping concerns. The natural sciences retain a technical interest in external instrumental control, whereas the humanities have a communicative interest in interpretative understanding, social functions, and so on. In the former case, the criterion of pragmatism with its concern for prediction and control enables evaluative ideologies to be filtered out historically within the natural sciences leaving a deposit of pragmatic or instrumental truth. In the case of the humanities, there is no *a priori* guarantee of the success of the pragmatic criterion, therefore their goals are other than those of prediction or control. To put it in simpler terms, the natural sciences are dealing with nature and the humanities are dealing with man: and this diversity in regard to data rather than considerations centering upon empiricism and hermeneutic focuses the difference. This distinction is important also for the study of religion. Discussion has tended to focus upon the difference between empirical and hermeneutical study as though the establishment of the study of religion as an empirical rather than hermeneutical endeavour would constitute it as an authentically scientific area of scholarship. It now appears that neither the study of science nor the study of religion can avoid hermeneutics, but that the study of religion can never be a 'science' in the predictive or controlling sense because its subject matter is basically man rather than nature. Thus history, which has exercised an important role within the study of religion, must be viewed hermeneutically as well as empirically, and it has no predictive or controlling function insofar as it deals with man rather than nature. History may and almost certainly will remain central within the study of religion, but this will be on grounds other than those of scientific empiricism.

Third, philosophers of science such as Hesse claim that the natural sciences must be seen in a wider framework. In the case of Hesse, the wider framework envelops the philosophy of social science, the realm of hermeneutics, the sociology of knowledge and, to a lesser extent, theology. Therefore within this approach, which again overlaps with the work of continental thinkers such as Habermas and Gadamer, the wider framework within which science is conceptualised includes empirical, hermeneutical, critical, and ethical elements, all of which interact together. The study of religion always *has* viewed itself within a wide framework, and the chapters of this book bear witness to this. Ideally the different elements within the framework of the study of religion *do* interact together. However, two interesting lessons, relevant to this point, brought by the philosophy of science to the study of religion are: first, that ethics and evaluation are included within the wider framework of the study of science, whereas ethical and other value-judgments are suspected by many scholars of religion and, second, that science is not afraid to see the *whole* scientific enterprise within a wider framework, whereas the study of religion has been more prone to confine its interest to matters relating to itself.

A trend last to be mentioned within the philosophy of science would go in an opposite direction from that taken by Hesse, Rescher, Feyerabend, and those scholars with epistemological interests. This mainly Anglo-American movement of metaphysical scientific realism would neglect epistemology in favour of analysing the ontology of theories on the assumption that contemporary science has come close to the 'truth'. There is taken to be an intelligibility inherent in the universe that intelligent people many grasp if they 'know' properly. There is assumed to be an intrinsic rationality in the field of science and, by implication, in other fields, and there is therefore the need to be open to the intrinsic intelligibility of reality within science and fields other than science. Underlying this approach there is the implicit notion that there is still a normative, true and unified theory of science, and that there can be such a theory for other areas of knowledge. Accordingly the construction of theories and the search for conceptual revolutions is subordinate to the task of bringing our present understanding of science and other fields into greater coherence with 'the way things are.' The work of Michael Polanyi (1964) is relevant in this respect. This type of thought has not been applied directly to the field of the study of religion, partly because there is no firm consensus nor longstanding tradition as to what the contemporary study of religion basically *is*. However, it is interesting that scientists such as Polanyi have talked in terms of ontology and transcendence, and Polanyi has pointed us to an 'ontology of mind,' an 'ontology of commitment,' and the 'ontological principles of stratified entities' (*Science, Faith and Society*, 1946: 10). His notion is that for science to be science it operates with 'a transcendent reality,' irreducibly given, over which we have no control (*The Logic of Liberty*, (1951: 40ff). The question that is obviously raised is: if the natural sciences can produce eminent men who talk in terms of 'transcendent reality' why is it that the study of religion should find it problematical so to do?

To explore more fully the relationship between the philosophy of science and the study of religion would require more space than is available here. We have briefly looked at: the inadequacy within present scientific thought of naively inductive, empirical, positivistic views of science; the falsification notion of Popper and Medawar; the methodology of scientific research programmes of Lakatos; the research structures of Kuhn; the more relativistic and pluralistic trends of Feyerabend, Rescher, and Hesse; and the metaphysical scientific realism of Polanyi. A few conclusions impose themselves. Empirical positivism is on the retreat; there is not just one but there are many theories of science; there are a variety of views concerning methodology in science; approaches to theory vary from the metaphysical scientific realism of Polanyi to the relativism of Feyerabend; science is no longer seen to be monolithic in itself nor necessarily superior in regard to other disciplines; its primary concern is for nature rather than man. As far as the study of religion is concerned, the following comments may be made. First, attempts to model the study of religion upon outmoded views of science based upon empirical positivism are fighting a rearguard action in that empirical positivism is being superseded in scientific theory. Second, the study of religion focusses mainly upon man in connection with whom the pragmatic criteria of prediction and control are less relevant and reliable than when they are applied to nature which is the proper concern of the natural sciences. Third, as the rise of a variety of approaches to the study of science is neither a handicap nor a brake to progress, so also the variety of approaches within the study of religion is evidence of life and not a sign of backwardness. Fourth, there are parallels to most of the main approaches adopted by the philosophy of science within the study of religion. The inductive approach is favoured by social anthropologists who insist upon fieldwork studies of the groups they are researching; the empirical approach is favoured by many historians who stress the importance of critical studies of texts; the falsificationist approach is emphasised by Ninian Smart and others who point out that religious data, like scientific data, must be amenable to falsification and that a hermeneutic too divorced from reference to data is unhelpful; the Lakatos methodology of research programmes is adopted implicitly by a number of scholars of religion such as Eliade, Lévi-Strauss, and Dumézil, who commit themselves and their students to a research structure based upon a hermeneutical hard core surrounded by protective hypotheses; the Kuhn notion of a single paradigm resulting from a theoretical revolution provides a stimulus to the study of religion to seek for such a paradigm as an extension of, rather than a revolution against, the historical/phenomenological approach which, although dominant, has not provided the study of religion with such a paradigm; the Hesse-type approach is paradigmatic of the complementarity of methods within the study of religion, and the need for the study of religion to see itself in a wider framework; and the metaphysical scientific realism of Polanyi is reminiscent of phenomenological or hermeneutical attempts to postulate an ontology of the sacred, a religious dimension within man, or a transcendent reality as pre-given. Fifth, the study of religion follows the philosophy of science in recognising that there is a dialectic between the establishing of data and hermeneutics, and that both are necessary, but it also recognises that data must not become too divorced from hermeneutics. Sixth, there is a sense that the field of religion is intrinsically wider than that of science including as it does the worldviews of men and a transcendent reference; as a corollary there is the realisation that thinking on theory and methods is less advanced within the study of religion even though its field is wider than that of science. Seventh, there is a sense of challenge: to emulation, within the study of religion as a whole and within the particular branches of that study, of the vibrant energy to be found within the philosophy of science and the different branches of science; to greater cooperation between the philosophy of the study of science and the philosophy of the study of religion; and to a more creative endeavour on the part of the study of religion to contribute, as science has done, to the advancement of scholarship on a global basis.

(The bibliography for Frank Whaling's Additional Note on Philosophy of Science and the Study of Religion is amalgamated with the bibliography for chapter 6, The Study of Religion in a Global Context, and appears at the end of chapter 6).

6

The Study of Religion in a Global Context

FRANK WHALING

Edinburgh

This is not the sort of book from which any one straightforward conclusion can emerge. It would be strange if this were to be the case, granted that a number of contributors have written in detail and in depth about practically the whole gamut of the study of religion. This chapter will not attempt to arrive at normative and definitive conclusions.

Instead we will complete this study by examining the implications for the study of religion of our present global context—this involves breaking new ground as well as treading ground that has already been covered.

The term 'global context' can mean a number of different things. At an obvious level, it can mean simply 'worldwide,' implying that the study of religion should involve the study of *all* religions, not just those of a particular part of the globe. Although anthropology of religion tends to focus upon primal religion, and sociology of religion and psychology of religion tend to focus upon western religion, there are historical reasons for these limitations of subject matter. These limitations are not necessarily inherent within these disciplines and, as we have seen, they are certainly not inherent within the other approaches to the study of religion, the overall context of which is implicitly planetary.

At another level the notion of 'global context' implies the need to take seriously insights and scholarship from other parts of the globe so that the study of religion may become global rather than 'western' in outlook. The reader, in working through this book, may perhaps have become aware that the contributors, the approaches they have described, the scholars they have mentioned, and the concepts they have used, have been primarily western. Unease at the seeming western monopoly of the study of religion has been growing throughout our period. A recent book by a non-westerner, Edward W. Said (1978), dramatically, if somewhat one-sidedly, highlights a similar point in regard to the study of Orientalism. However, it is part of the purpose of this chapter to make the point that non-Christians in the West such as Buber, and non-westerners such as Coomaraswamy, Radhakrishnan, Suzuki, Mbiti, Nasr, and Wing-Tsit Chan, have already made significant contributions to the study of religion from the perspectives of their own cultures. Advances in knowledge and understanding have emerged not merely from western studies of and contact with other religious traditions, but also from the work of scholars of other traditions who have studied their own culture and reflected upon their contact with the West. Indeed signs are already beginning to emerge of non-westerners (such as Izutsu) studying other non-western religions, and therefore by-passing the West as an omnipresent factor in the study of religion. The process whereby other religious traditions are studying themselves and others, as well as being studied by the West, is being hastened on by religious developments such as the renewal of the other major religious traditions and by extra-religious developments such as the emergence of independent countries, the oil crisis, the rise of communist nations, and so on.

Indeed at another level, the study of science and the study of religion are part of a greater whole. As we survey the 'global context' since 1945 it is clear that during that period the world has become one in a way that was not so evident before. The growth of world population, the spread of nuclear weapons, increasing pollution, the problem of world poverty, and the diminishing of non-renewable energy resources affect the whole planet. What Toffler has called the 'Third Wave' (1980), the new technological revolution centred upon space exploration, the development of the riches of the sea, the increasing use of micro-technology, and the extension of the genetic sciences has consequences for the whole globe. And these consequences are not merely scientific. As Ervin Laszlo puts it, 'The dominant consensus in Western societies is that such problems are mainly physical and ecological in nature, and that they can be overcome by more and higher technology' (1979: 1). He points out, however, that, 'The root causes even of physical and ecological problems are the inner constraints on our vision and values' (1979: 3). In other words, there is a growing awareness of the interconnectedness of our global problems. They are not only physical and scientific, they are also human and cultural. They have to do with the vision, values, the worldview of men, and to that extent they have to do with 'religion.'

One of the important themes in this book has been that of the interrelationship between the different approaches to the study of religion. Implicit in our discussion has been the question as to whether the various methods of studying religion are complementary or opposed. We have suggested in general that the approaches we have outlined are interconnected parts of a wider whole. We have suggested that anthropology of religion, sociology of religion, psychology of religion, history and phenomenology of religion, comparative religion, the study of myths and texts, and the scientific study of religion are all elements within the wider study of religion, and that apparent clashes between the different methods are provisional rather than final. However, any serious grappling with our global context must involve us in a wider discussion centred not only upon the relationship between the different approaches within the study of religion but also upon the relationship between the study of religion and the study of other fields.

In western intellectual history, three dominant educational models have emerged. The Graeco-Roman model was that of *humanitas*, what we would call the humanities, and its main stress was upon literature and man; the medieval European model was that of *theologia*, what we could call theology, and its main stress was upon theology and God; the modern model has until recently been that of the natural sciences, with its main stress upon the analysis of nature, and with its penchant for minute specialisation. The impingement upon scholarship of the modern global context has opened the way for an intensified discussion about the very nature of science, the humanities, and theology, and the relationship between them. There is a growing awareness of the need to redefine areas of human knowledge both for the sake of the disciplines concerned and for the sake of gaining a more integral view of human knowledge with a view to coping more adequately with our global problems. The major part of this book has attempted to summarise the contemporary position in religious studies in order to aid this field of knowledge in its own self-awareness. In this chapter we shall glance briefly at the wider question of the place of religious studies within the whole spectrum of human knowledge. How does it fit into the three areas that have been predominant in western thought? Is religious studies complementary with other areas of knowledge, and, if so, in what way? Has religious studies any part to play in the search for a wider integration within the total academic enterprise?

Clearly all the questions we have raised under the heading of 'the study of religion in a global context' are important. Limitations of space prevent us from dealing with them at length. Insofar as these questions are attempting to chart partly unexplored territory there remains an element of prophecy about them. In ten years time it will be easier to exercise a mature judgment in regard to them. Nevertheless to ignore them completely would be unwise. They represent possible growing-points for the field of religious studies. Insofar as they are so basic, one may reasonably predict that the response made to them (whether it be active or passive, creative or negative) will be significant for the future development of religious studies, and possibly for wider scholarship as well.

In the first place, then, we shall look briefly at the work of certain influential non-Christian or non-western scholars of religion, and attempt to estimate their impact upon the study of religion. A related and important topic concerns the effect of non-western studies upon the field of religious studies: do they relativise or fragment an area of study formerly united by its western provenance, or does it remain a recognisable but perhaps transformed area? Second, we shall place the study of religion within a wider academic spectrum, and attempt to understand its nature by reference to its differences from and its relationship to other academic fields.

We may usefully begin our examination of non-western studies of religion by reflecting upon the implications of Edward W. Said's *Orientalism* (1978). This book is a study of the genesis, growth, and continuation of a western (mainly French and British) tradition of knowledge concerning the Orient (mainly the Arabo-Islamic world). According to Said there was a convergence between Orientalism and western imperialism whereby the western scholars of the Orient, wittingly or unwittingly, aided and abetted the European colonial advance throughout the Orient. As Said puts it:

Orientalism came to signify: a systematic discipline of accumulation. And far from this being exclusively an intellectual or theoretical feature, it made Orientalism fatally tend towards the systematic accumulation of human beings and territories. To reconstruct a dead or lost Oriental language meant ultimately to reconstruct a dead or neglected Orient; it also meant that reconstructive precision, science, even imagination could prepare the way for what armies, administrators, and bureaucracies would later do on the ground in the Orient (1978: 123).

Although he traces this process back into the eighteenth century, Said also mentions respected modern scholars such as Louis Massignon and Sir Hamilton Gibb as exponents of French and British Orientalism. Indeed, in his final chapter, 'Orientalism Now,' Said analyses the supposed role of American Orientalism in influencing or implementing American government policy, and in aiding international business interests. Perhaps Said gets to the heart of the matter in his comment:

The real issue is whether there can be a true representation of anything, or whether any and all representations, because they are representations, are embedded in the language and then in the culture, institutions, and political ambience of the representor (1978: 273).

The implication is that the notion that a university is an academic community committed to the unbiased and disinterested pursuit of knowledge as an end in itself is a chimera. According to Said, western academics, consciously or unconsciously, created an image of the Orient that served the interests not of pure scholarship but of western culture.

Said's thesis is so important in its possible implications that we must first offer a brief critique of it before going on to investigate its ramifications in regard to the study of religion. In the first place, Said's thesis is limited in its terms of reference to Orientalism. This term, as interpreted either by Said or western orientalists, is both wider and narrower than the study of eastern religions—wider because it comprehends the study of the language, literature, and total culture of the area concerned, narrower because it tends to see religion as a facet of the total culture rather than as significant in its own right. Orientalism is therefore both related to and different from the study of eastern religions. In the second place, Said's notion of the Orient refers in practice to Islam rather than to the whole eastern world, indeed it refers in particular to the eastern part of the Arabo-Muslim world. It is difficult, if not hazardous, to draw general conclusions about western studies of the whole world east of Suez from studies of such a specific nature. In the third place, Said's references are mainly to French and British Orientalism. He says relatively little about the work of scholars from other European countries and American scholars who also played key roles in oriental studies. In the fourth place, Said is ambivalent about what should be the approach of one culture towards another. Was the rise of Orientalism inevitable because the West could not avoid seeing other cultures in the light of its own interests, or should the West have known better? Now that the Orient is becoming economically and politically more powerful, does this mean that scholars within resurgent Muslim countries, Japan, China, India, Israel and so on must inevitably view other cultures in the light of their own interests? Or is this not merely a form of political and cultural reductionism? In the fifth place, although Said does not ignore historical data, his method is basically synchronic and structural, and his approach is reminiscent of that of Michel Foucault (1971, 1976). Orientalism as it developed historically was far more diverse, complex, multifaceted, and dynamic that Said gives it credit. For example, early British Orientalists in India such as William Jones, Charles Wilkins, Colebrooke, and H.H. Wilson helped Hindus to reconstruct their own past by researching the Veda, the six systems of Indian philosophy, the Vedānta, and the *smṛti* texts; and it was the Orientalists who *opposed* the cultural arrogance of Macaulay and the Christian imperialism of Grant, and helped to pave the way for the Indian renaissance.

It is easy to analyse the drawbacks in Said's thesis. It is evident also that he is saying something important. Said claims that he has written to help contemporary students of the Orient 'to criticise—with the hope of stirring discussion—the often unquestioned assumptions on which their work for the most part depends' (1978: 24). In this respect his advice is valuable not only for Orientalists but also for students of religion. Western scholarship may have freed itself from excesses of cultural arrogance, yet it is sometimes betrayed by its own presuppositions. For example, the *Journal of the History of Ideas* for 1979 contains forty-five papers: forty-three deal with the history of ideas in the West, one deals with medieval Jewish literature (in the West), and one with the confluence of Chinese and western intellectual history. Has the history of ideas really been centred so exclusively upon the West?

In addition to pointing to the presuppositions underlying western studies of eastern cultures, Said asks a further important question: 'Can one divide human reality, as human reality seems to be genuinely divided, into clearly different cultures, histories, traditions, societies, even races, and survive the consequences humanly?' (1978: 45). His implicit plea is that firstly we should recognise, conceptualise, and genuinely realise the self-awareness of different cultures, histories, traditions, societies, races, and religions but that secondly we should situate them within the one human reality. This summarises in a nutshell the problem put to religious studies by the present global context. How can western scholars and scholars from other cultures authentically represent and transmit a mutually verified knowledge of the various religions of the world in their difference while at the same time recognising that they are part of a wider whole, namely humanity? The first step is to free or allow other cultures and religions to free themselves from western stereotypes; the second step is to see and academically conceptualise the global unity lying behind the religious diversity. In former times the global unity was imposed by the western stereotypes; in the present context it must be interculturally conceptualised by academic colloquia no longer constrained by western sovereignty.

In fact, a number of non-western scholars have already made noteworthy contributions to the study of religion. We shall analyse the work of seven such scholars now before attempting to estimate the implications of their work.

Ananda Coomaraswamy

Coomaraswamy was born in 1877 in Colombo, the son of a Sinhalese father and a British mother. Ananda was only two years old when his father Sir Mutu Coomaraswamy died, and he was educated in Britain at Wycliffe Hall and University College London. He was a Doctor of Science by the time he was thirty, his thesis being centred upon the geology of Ceylon, but during his scientific research in Ceylon and India he became intensely aware of the aesthetic and religious values of those areas and he was destined to spend the rest of his life researching, expounding, and defending those values.

Most of his productive work was done when he was researcher or curator at the Boston Museum of Fine Arts, a period that lasted for thirty years. When he died in 1947, he left behind a wealth of correspondence, books, and notes. Roger Lipsey has recently published two large volumes of papers by Coomaraswamy on traditional art and symbolism and on metaphysics, together with a volume on his life and work (1977), and although it is true to say that Coomaraswamy lived mainly before our period the fact remains that his influence has been more recent.

In his *Modern Indian Thought: A Philosophical Survey*, V.S. Naravane lists Coomaraswamy along with Ram Mohun Roy and his followers, Ramakrishna, Vivekananda, Tagore, Gandhi, Aurobindo, Radhakrishnan, and Iqbal as exemplars of modern Indian thought. Most of these thinkers would rank as advocates for rather than scholars of Indian religion. Coomaraswamy, although he never held a university post in the study of religion, can be classed primarily as a student of Indian art and religion, and his researches in this wide area were both comprehensive and minute—comprehensive in the sense that they covered a wide range of art, metaphysics, religion, and symbolism comparatively as well as regionally, narrow in the sense that he was willing and anxious to tackle particular philological points, as in his comments on entries in the Pali Text Society Dictionary such as *vyānjanā*, and in his essay on *saṃvega* in connection with Buddhist art (Rykwert 1979).

For our purposes, Coomaraswamy's work is important for three reasons. In the first place, he was concerned to reflect, academically, culturally and religiously, upon the Indian experience. He did so both as a scholar and as one who had made 'an unspecified but formal gesture of allegiance to Hinduism' (Rykwert (1979: 107). His reflection upon the Indian experience was neither narrowly Hindu nor narrowly Indian. He had a deep interest in the Buddhist tradition; he wrote on Mughal art showing how it integrally fused Persian and Indian motifs; he wrote on the art and culture of wider India, for example Indonesia; and he traced also the continuity between pre-Aryan, Vedic and Buddhist India. Romain Rolland claims, in his preface to Coomaraswamy's *Dance of Shiva* (1957) that the author's purpose in that book is:

to show the power of the Indian soul, to show all the riches that it holds stored up.... The vast and tranquil metaphysic of India is unfolded: her conception of the Universe, her social organisation ... the magnificent revelation of her art. The whole vast soul of India proclaims from end to end of its crowded and well-ordered edifice the same domination of a sovereign synthesis.

In his small book on *Hinduism and Buddhism* (1943, 1971) Coomaraswamy examines again the main categories of those traditions, claiming that western scholarship had not fully grasped the meaning of the Veda, *karma*, *māyā*, reincarnation, and the six philosophical systems of the Hindu tradition, nor the Buddha's message within the Buddhist tradition. As he puts it, 'few indeed are the translations of Indian books into European languages that can yet come up to the standards set for themselves by the Tibetan and Chinese Buddhists' (1971: 49). Our concern is not to examine the minutiae of Coomaraswamy's analysis of Indian religion, but to point out that, even before our period began, he was stating for an academic and indeed western audience:

The heart and essence of Indian experience is to be found in a constant intuition of the unity of all life, and the instinctive, ineradicable conviction that the recognition of this unity is the highest good and the uttermost freedom (*Dance of Shiva*, 1957: 22).

Coomaraswamy, secondly, while examining and interpreting Indian religion from his own viewpoint saw it as part of a perennial philosophy embodying universal truths exclusive to no one tradition or period. He writes:

Who that has breathed the pure mountain air of the Upanishads, of Samkara and Kabir, of Rumi and Lao Tse and Jesus—to mention Asiatic prophets—can be alien to those who have sat at the feet of Plato, Kant, Tauler, Ruysbroeck, Whitman, Nietzsche, Blake? (*Dance of Shiva*, 1957: 152).

Religious traditions may therefore be extrinsically different and unique, intrinsically the essential spiritual language of their perennial philosophy remains the same. Coomaraswamy surmised that, due to the problems associated with the rise of industrialisation, the West had partially broken away from the moorings of its own perennial philosophy (see Schmitt 1966) and was in danger of leading the rest of the world in the same direction. And so, before the appearance of Aldous Huxley's well-known book *Perennial Philosophy* in 1946, and before the rise of the 'school' of Philosophia Perennis, an eastern thinker was already uttering these thoughts, and unlike his western contemporary, Guénon, he was unwilling to surrender the tools of scholarship to 'esotericism' in so doing (see Eliade 1979).

In the third place, Coomaraswamy stressed the role and importance of art in Indian religion and life as a support to contemplation, as an evocation of religious archetypes, and as an aid to deeper understanding. The art that he had in mind was not naturalistic presentation, individualistic assertion, 'art for art's sake,' or art for enjoyment's sake, but the significant and liberating art of those 'who in their performances are celebrating God ... in both of his natures, immanent and transcendent' (1977: vol. 1, 40). In many of his works, Coomaraswamy worked out his theories about the aesthetic and religious value of such art. In books such as *Christian and Oriental Philosophy of Art*, he applied his theories comparatively. For him, true works of art are religious icons rather than merely useful objects and they direct the attention of the receptive observer away from outward things to the inward realisation of what he *is*.

Coomaraswamy has been criticised on a number of counts. As Rykwert points out (1979: 104) there were contradictions within his own life between the 'traditional' philosophy and religion he stressed and his own western life-style. The dichotomy he saw between the fragmented life of the industrial West and the integrated pattern of life in the East was too simplistically conceived. It is not clear that the picture he draws of Indian metaphysics and aesthetics can be verified within the actual life-experience of Indian villages. Moreover, his notion of a Philosophia Perennis is a hermeneutical presupposition rather than a verifiable principle. Nevertheless it is clear that, even before the Second

World War, here was an eastern thinker who was ready academically to reconceive the nature of eastern religion without denying the authenticity of other religious traditions. To return to Said's thesis, Coomaraswamy was not willing to accept the western academic stereotype (as he saw it) of Indian religion. He produced an alternative to it, or perhaps we should say an extension of it, and in so doing introduced an eastern dimension into the study of religion.

Sarvepalli Radhakrishnan

Our second non-western scholar, Radhakrishnan, is both similar to and different from Coomaraswamy. By comparison with Coomaraswamy, Radhakrishnan was more interested in philosophy than art, more deeply involved in university concerns, more engaged in Indian national and political life, more concerned with inter-religious relationships than with 'perennial philosophy,' and just as academically engrossed in reinterpreting for the present the Indian (and other) traditions as in recovering and recapitulating their past. Like Coomaraswamy, Radhakrishnan was responsible, because of his intellectual calibre, for the academic promotion of an Indian view of the nature of Indian religion; like Coomaraswamy he was at the same time both a genuine scholar and a committed Hindu.

Radhakrishnan was born in 1888 at Tirutani in South India and (unlike Coomaraswamy) he was brought up in India within a Hindu family. His education at Christian institutions, notably Madras Christian College, influenced him both positively and negatively. A critical study of Hindu ideas was forced upon him but the need for philosophy that arose when his faith in tradition was shaken served only to fuel an interest in both philosophy and Indian religion that became a life-long concern. From 1909 to 1926 Radhakrishnan lectured at Madras, Mysore, and Calcutta. He returned to India briefly to be Vice-Chancellor of Andhra University after a spell as professor of comparative religion from 1929 at Manchester College Oxford, but went back to Oxford in 1936 to take up the Spalding professorship of Eastern religions and ethics. By the time R.C. Zaehner succeeded him in the Spalding chair,

Radhakrishnan was launched upon a more political career that was to culminate in his being President of India from 1962 until 1967.

A number of Radhakrishnan's writings became and continue to be influential, and the impact of their clarity of thought was enhanced by the beauty of their style. In relation to Said's thesis, they constitute, to use one of Professor Joad's terms, a counter-attack from the East. Indeed the writings of Radhakrishnan and Coomaraswamy reassert academically the importance and role of the Indian tradition, and they perform at the academic level the task accomplished in different ways by figures such as Ram Mohun Roy, Sen, the Tagores, Saraswati, Ramakrishna, Vivekananda, Gandhi, and Aurobindo.

Radhakrishnan's serious writing career began in 1918 with his book on the *Philosophy of Rabindranath Tagore*. His treatment of Tagore, by whom he was influenced, in whom he saw a Upanishadic concern for the unity of things rather than Tagore's equal stress on Vaishnavite theism, and through whom his concern for modern India and philosophy were strengthened, fore-shadowed a number of his future interests. His *Reign of Religion in Contemporary Philosophy* (1920) proved to be a temporary aberration in the development of his basic approach. In this book he tried to separate the roles of religion and philosophy. He argued that religious systems should not govern philosophy which was an independent activity in no way dominated by religion. In retrospect this book may be seen as the parting of the ways for Radhakrishnan. Had he continued down the path indicated in this work it is likely that his academic stance would have been more western. In fact much of his later work endeavoured to show not only the close interrelationship between philosophy and religion in India but also their close connections elsewhere. His *Indian Philosophy* (1923, 1927) became an academic classic, combining as it did a lucid style, a historical overview of Indian philosophy, and a penetrating (if neo-Vedāntist) insight into the nature of the Indian religious and philosophical tradition. Radhakrishnan's next two works, *Hindu View of Life* (1927) and *Kalki* (1929) veered towards an implicit apologetic of Hinduism over against the West. He attempted to summarise the positive aspects of Hindu thought in order to portray Hinduism within the wider context of Indian values as a worldview based upon tolerance and spiritual vision; at the same time he warned against the long-term implications of technological growth and material progress unaccompanied by religious idealism. *An Idealist View of Life* (1932) was the culmination of Radhakrishnan's earliest period of writing. In it he was not afraid to express his own commitment to an idealist view of life. Although his outlook was clearly eastern he also wrote comparatively about western philosophy and western idealism, and he claimed that idealism, broadly conceived, had an important part to play in modern thought. It contended, he wrote (1932: 15):

that the universe has meaning, has value. Ideal values are dynamic forces; they are the driving power of the universe. The world is only intelligible as a system of ends. Such a view has nothing to do with the problem whether a thing is only a particular image or a general relation.

Radhakrishnan wrote a great deal after 1932, but there is a sense in which the main themes of his work were set by then and his later writings merely widened patterns that were already there. He continued to write on Indian religion, and became especially interested in the role of Buddhism as part of the total development of the Indian tradition; he continued to write comparatively on the integral relationship between religion and philosophy; he continued to write on Indian cultural renewal; and he continued to write upon the contribution religion can make to heal the problems of the modern world (see Bibliography for references).

Radhakrishnan is especially interesting, in the context of our present discussion, for three reasons. In the first place, he represents, even more clearly than Coomaraswamy, a 'counter-attack from the East.' Not only was he not content passively to continue western patterns of scholarship in regard to Indian religion, he also brought into the bloodstream of western scholarship an Indian outlook in regard to the study of religion. He approached religion from the viewpoint of philosophy in contrast to the classical western approaches which had been more inclined to stress anthropology, history, sociology, psychology, or phenomenology. In this he is not untypical, scholars such as T.R.V. Murti (1955) would follow him in this, and even today religion is studied mainly within the philosophy departments of Indian universities (only the Punjabi

University at Patiala has a religious studies department in its own right).
Moreover, he had a wide view of philosophy which made him unable to
restrict it to epistemological or parochial issues. As Naravane puts it
(1964: 242):

> Radhakrishnan expects of philosophy that it should be dynamic and practical, that it
> should broadly accept the wholeness of reality and the unity of the different aspects of the
> universe, and that it should help in the recognition, conservation and furtherance of
> value.

In short, he had both a broad notion of the nature of philosophy and a
conviction that religion and philosophy were integral rather than separate studies. In addition to this, he had an Indian insight into the way
philosophy operates. He saw the world as mysterious as well as rational,
as graspable by intuition as well as intellect. But he regarded intuition as
being a way of knowledge rather than an alternative to it, he accepted it
as being a form of thought rather than a flight from thought. In all this,
his approach was clearly Indian.

In the second place, Radhakrishnan was not afraid to lay bare his own
religious commitment. He was unashamedly an idealist, and therefore
not a naturalist, a scientific materialist, a doctrinaire nationalist, or a
humanist. Within idealism, his predilection was towards Śaṅkara's
school of Advaita Vedānta, although his allegiance to Śaṅkara was by no
means uncritical. This meant that one of his main concerns was to
enquire into the nature of ultimate reality which he saw as 'the Beyond
who cannot be comprehended by our concepts or recognised by our
understanding.... He can only be described negatively, or through
seemingly contradictory descriptions' (1939: 298). He states (Schilpp
1952: 671):

> It is my opinion that systems which play the game of philosophy fairly and squarely, with
> freedom from presuppositions and with religious neutrality, end in Absolute Idealism.

In spite of his use of the words 'freedom from presuppositions' and
'religious neutrality,' his approach is not the phenomenological one of
using *epoché* and *Einfühlung* in order to describe and understand the

position of others. His approach is predetermined and his commitment undisguised. Although he asserted that students of religion should 'treat all religions in a spirit of absolute detachment and impartiality' (1933: 16), his own notion of impartiality arose from his partiality for a philosophical approach to religion derived from his Indian background.

Thirdly, and in contrast to Coomaraswamy, Radhakrishnan had a keen interest in the dynamics of the present global religious situation. He was not content, with Coomaraswamy, to attempt to recapture and conceptualise the perennial philosophy of·religions that the modern world was in danger of losing (although his search for the continuity and centrality of idealism approximated to this), his concern was also for the present-day dialogue of religions. This concern revealed itself in two ways. As far as Indian religion was concerned, Radhakrishnan was keen to describe and interpret it in such a fashion as to make it relevant to the contemporary world, and to make it contribute to dialogue. An example of this was his continuing attempt to reinterpret the concept of *māyā*. On the wider scene, he saw the dialogue of world religions as an important element in the building up of a new world culture. He wrote (in Rouner 1966: 296):

The different religions are to be used as building stones for the development of a human culture in which the adherents of the different religions may be fraternally united as children of one Supreme. All religions convey to their followers a message of abiding hope. The world will give birth to a new faith which will be but the old faith in another form, the faith of the ages, the potential divinity of man which will work for the supreme purpose written in our hearts and souls, the unity of all mankind.

Sentiments such as these were contrary to the more historically oriented tendencies of the western study of religion. It seemed to western scholars that the academic status of the study of religion was being subordinated to the laudable, humanitarian, but not directly academic aim of building up world peace and harmony. Moreover, Radhakrishnan's work fed into a movement towards dialogue that was beginning to become manifest within Christian theology, and which was equally suspicious to western scholars of religion. However, the point is that Radhakrishnan's work represented a distinctively non-western contribution to the study of religion which brought into prominence not only an Indian view of the study of Indian religion but also an Indian view concerning the general study of religion. Before the imperial age was over, Radhakrishnan's work was already begun, and the tradition he represents has continued in being right up to the present day.

D.T. Suzuki

Our third non-western scholar, Suzuki, brought a Buddhist and Japanese perspective to the study of religion. His influence upon that study was exercised within his own culture and in the United States rather than in Europe. Although he ranks as a genuine scholar, Suzuki also bears some of the attributes of a guru. Indeed he is similar in certain respects to Radhakrishnan in that he combined a concern for the renewal and defence of his own tradition, a concern for scholarship, and an ability to represent his own tradition with the authority of an academically respected 'father-figure.' He differs from Radhakrishnan by virtue of his relative lack of interest in philosophy, and by virtue of his relatively greater interest in his own religion and indeed his own language.

Suzuki died in 1966 aged ninety-five, and his career divides naturally into three periods. Up to the mid-1920s, he was involved in the defence and presentation of the Buddhist tradition in the West, and in the reformulation and renewal of the Buddhist tradition in the East. From the mid-1920s to about 1949, he was engaged in the more specifically academic task of translating and exegeting Buddhist texts from India, Japan, and China. From 1949 to 1966, Suzuki continued to reinterpret the Buddhist tradition but at the same time he was called upon to represent the views of Buddhism upon various contemporary issues, especially in the United States where his influence led to an increasing interest in Buddhist studies.

Suzuki's first major work, *Outlines of Mahāyāna Buddhism*, appeared in 1907. His assumption was that the Buddhist tradition was a living organism arising out of the Buddha's experience of enlightenment and growing ever since. Although interested in the whole Buddhist tradition, both academically and ecumenically, his main concern was to interpret Chinese and Japanese Mahāyāna Buddhism. In this early work his concern was for Mahāyāna Buddhism in general, later he would become more directly interested in Pure Land and Zen Buddhism in particular. Already there were premonitions of his later ideas. He saw Mahāyāna Buddhism as an integral part of the Buddhist whole, and he saw religious experience as important in the understanding of religion as a whole. He wrote in an eastern ahistorical vein (1907: 15):

Mahāyānism is not an object of historical curiosity. Its vitality and activity concern us in our daily life. It is a great spiritual organism; its moral and religious forces are still exercising an enormous power over millions of souls; and its further development is sure to be a very valuable contribution to the world-progress of the religious consciousness. What does it matter, then, whether or not Mahāyanism is the genuine teaching of the Buddha?

Suzuki sought an ecumenical reconciliation within Buddhism between the moral disciplines of Theravāda and the more speculative disciplines of Mahāyāna, but he stressed within Mahāyāna the priority of mystical intuition in contrast to merely philosophical speculation. He wrote (1914: 272–3):

Vidya must now give way to *dhyana* or *prajna*; that is, intellection must become intuition, which is after all the ultimate form of all religious discipline. Mysticism is the life of religion. Without it religion loses her reason of existence; all her warm vitality departs, all her inexpressible charm vanishes, and there remains nothing but the crumbling bones and cold ashes of death.

It is not our concern to examine in detail the writings of Suzuki which have been collected in over thirty volumes (1969). In addition to his works in Japanese, his technical writings on Indian, Japanese and Chinese Buddhist texts, and his interpretative writings upon Buddhism in general and Mahāyāna Buddhism in particular, he gave his special attention to two other themes. Firstly, he was fascinated by the topic of mysticism. In a Japanese work of 1916 *Zen no taehiba kara* (see *Works*, Vol xiv) he wrote on 'Zen and Mysticism,' 'Tauler's Zen,' and 'Kabir's Zen.' These titles indicated that his interest in mysticism was comparative as well as parochially Buddhist, and this was born out in his *Mysticism: Christian and Buddhist*, which appeared in 1957, in which he compared Meister Eckhart as a representative Christian mystic with some Zen masters and some Pure Land *myōkōnin*, notably Asahara Saichi. Suzuki recognised five common factors in mysticism: intuitive inner experience, a new kind of inner life flowing out of that experience, paradoxical linguistic description of mystical experience, necessarily negative conceptualisations of essentially positive experience, and realistic symbolism. He noted four classifications of the forms of mysticism: the mysticism of faith, including much Christian, Muslim, Hindu, and Pure Land Buddhist mysticism; contemplative mysticism, including Christian prayer, Hindu *yoga*, and Buddhist *dhyāna*; intellectual mysticism, including neo-Platonic and German Christian mysticism, Vedānta Hinduism, the Taoist mysticism of Lao-tze and Chuang-tze, and Mahāyāna Buddhist mysticism; and superstitious mysticism (Hiroshi 1977). Suzuki was more interested in mystical experience and the inner life resulting from it than in the systematic expression of mystical doctrines, and this is evidenced in his treatment of Christian, Zen, and Pure Land mysticism which are outwardly and doctrinally different but 'can be grouped together as belonging to the great school of mysticism' (1957: xix).

Suzuki is remembered secondly for his researches into, and his renewal of, Zen Buddhism. As Dornish comments 'the present vitality of Zen and Western interest in it demonstrate how well he argued his case' (1970: 60). Again his aim was not logically to reconstruct the Zen system or to develop the concept of Emptiness lying at its heart in any thorough-going way. As Shimomura Toratarō points out, Nishida Kitarō and Tanabe Hajime did this far better than Suzuki. His concern was rather with the religious psychology of Zen experience, and although he admired the work of William James and Jung, and was indeed a member of Jung's Eranos Circle, he could not stay at what he considered to be the outward level of the psychology of religion. As he wrote in *An Introduction to Zen Buddhism* (1961: 44):

The basic idea of Zen is to come in touch with the inner workings of our being, and to do this in the most direct way possible, without resorting to anything external or superadded ... Zen professes itself to be the spirit of Buddhism, but in fact it is the spirit of all religions and philosophies. When Zen is thoroughly understood, absolute peace of mind is attained, and a man lives as he ought to live.

It remains to be seen whether Lynn White's daring prophecy will have any validity (1956: 304–5).

it may well be that the publication of D.T. Suzuki's first *Essays in Zen Buddhism* in 1927 will seem in future generations as great an intellectual event as William of Moerbeke's Latin translations of Aristotle in the thirteenth century or Marsiglio Ficino's of Plato in the fifteenth. But in Suzuki's case the shell of the Occident has been broken through.

Whether such vast claims are meaningful or not, it is clear that the work of Suzuki is in itself a partial refutation of some of Said's notions, and that Suzuki ranks with Radhakrishnan as a major eastern scholar who realised in his own person the fruits of his intellectual and spiritual quest.

Like Radhakrishnan, Suzuki had his own personal religious commitment. He had an early training in Zen; his second Zen master, Soyen Shaku, enabled him to advance spiritually and also to go to America; his study of Bankei's Zen awakening and teaching of the 'Unborn' had a deep spiritual influence upon him after the death of his wife in 1939. And so, like Radhakrishnan, he was not only the detached scholar objectively exegeting his texts. His scholarship was also an exercise in communicating a way of life he believed to be true.

Suzuki followed Radhakrishnan secondly in creatively reinterpreting his own tradition with the double aim of reforming it to serve his own culture and communicating it to the West to serve western culture. He had a lively sense of the organic continuity of the Buddhist tradition, but this meant that it was always developing, and its modern development had to take account of the global situation which demanded the presentation of Buddhism in both East and West. Suzuki's reformulation of Buddhism and Buddhist studies was therefore geared to the global situation and not only to internal Buddhist needs in the East. His main work was done in relation to Mahāyāna Buddhism, especially in his reinterpretations of Zen, but he was also influential within Buddhist ecumenical circles and in the wider interpretation of Buddhism as a whole.

Suzuki differed from Radhakrishnan in that he was responsible not
only for promoting the creative study of his own tradition but also for
presenting Zen Buddhism in such a way that it came to command the
emotional allegiance of a number of people in the West. Through
Suzuki's work, Zen Buddhism found a new vitality in Japan, and a new
arena of influence in the United States of America. It became for a
number of western students not merely a new area of study but also a
new possibility for commitment. Suzuki might state in theory that
'Buddhism and Christianity and all other religious beliefs are not more
than variations of one single Faith, deeply imbedded in the human soul'
(1921: vol. 1, 156), in practice his stress upon spiritual experience and his
interest in Zen studies led some western students to see in Zen an avenue
of religious fulfilment as well as academic endeavour. Suzuki therefore
achieved the status in some quarters of a guru in a more than academic
sense. This kind of western response to Suzuki was viewed with very
mixed feelings by western historians of religion, especially European
scholars who were trying to establish the study of religion along academically recognisable lines. However, it probably remains true to say
that more western scholars of Buddhism would be willing to view
themselves (however vaguely) as 'Buddhists' in contrast with western
scholars of other religions. Indeed the practical and theoretical implications of Suzuki's work are still working themselves out.

Martin Buber

Our next scholar, Buber, is non-Christian but not non-western. In
some ways Buber is similar to Suzuki. The latter introduced a knowledge of Zen Buddhism into the West, Buber did the same for Hasidic
Judaism; Buber had a great influence outside the confines of his own
tradition, just as Suzuki had done; like Suzuki, Buber's motivation was
religious and mystical rather than rationalistic and secular. The principle
difference between them is that Suzuki was revered within his own
community as an interpreter and exponent of Buddhism, whereas
Buber's practical influence upon his tradition was more limited. As
Epstein comments:

Buber ignores Talmudic teaching and, in fact, does not consider the observances of Jewish practices as essential to the ideal of society which he advocates. Nor does he attempt to formulate a programme indicating how these ideas are to be realized, which accounts for the limited influence of Buber on Jewish practical life (1959: 314).

Martin Buber was born in 1878 in Vienna, but brought up by his grandparents at Lemberg in Poland where he was educated, and where he had early contacts with the Ḥasidism that was to form part of his life. His main university studies were at the University of Vienna where he gained his Ph.D. in 1904. During this period he had contacts with, and worked for, the Zionist movement, although he eventually withdrew from active Zionist work in 1921. In addition to this, he began three very important activities during his student days: he commenced intensive studies of the Bible and the Hebrew language that would lead eventually to his completion of a German translation of the Tenach (Hebrew Bible) in 1961; he discovered the Ḥasidic writings which were to occupy his attention for much of his career; and he developed an interest in foreign epics and myths, including those of China, which were to give an eastern dimension to some of his thought. His first significant book on Ḥasidism came out in 1906 namely *Die Geschichten des Rabbi Nachman*; his important article on the Tao appeared in 1910; in 1913 his book *Daniel* was published which contained his first poetic formulation of man's duality; and in 1922 his epoch-making *Ich und Du* (I and Thou) appeared. From 1923–33 he was Professor at the Freies Jüdisches Lehrhaus in Frankfurt and at Frankfurt University, but he eventually left Germany in 1938 and became professor of social philosophy at the Hebrew University in Jerusalem, and it was in Jerusalem that he died in 1965. His books continued to appear throughout this period of teaching including his important work of biblical interpretation, *Königtum Gottes* (Kingdom of God) in 1932, to which he applied some of Max Weber's ideas, and his only novel *Gog and Magog* which he wrote in Hebrew in 1943.

Our first comment upon Buber must be that he was a genuinely global figure. His global outlook arose mainly out of his Jewish background, but he was also influenced by Christianity and eastern religions. We have mentioned his work for Zionism, his Ḥasidic interpretations, his lecturing for a Jewish institute in Frankfurt and a Hebrew University, his

work on Biblical translation and interpretation, and the Jewish flavour
of his work: yet these served to feed into a wider global vision. The
influence of Buber's *I and Thou* upon Christian thinking is clear. Indeed
this most famous of Buber's works may well have had a greater influence
upon Christian than upon Jewish thought, and he himself was in
continual dialogue with Christianity. It is perhaps less well known that
Buber was also influenced by eastern thought. As Friedman puts it
(1976: 411) 'his concern with mysticism in Taoism, Ḥasidism, and Zen,
and with Eastern thought, became a steady dialogue; it was an integral
part of his path, of his being.' Friedman is right to mention the word
'dialogue' in connection with Buber's development. He did not merely
accept Ḥasidism as a block of ideas, he engaged in dialogue with it
throughout his life, and the same is true to a lesser extent in relation to
Taoism and Zen. It is easier to understand two important notions of
Buber's *I and Thou*: those of the I-Thou relationship with nature and of
the free man who wills without arbitrariness, if we see the emergence of
these ideas against the background of his wrestling with Taoist conceptions of the Tao of nature and *wu-wei*. Moreover, Buber's impressive
contrast between Zen and Ḥasidism in his essay on 'The Place of
Ḥasidism in the History of Religions' shows how his grappling with Zen
enabled him to understand Ḥasidism better and vice versa.

In the second place, Buber like Suzuki was engaged in his studies
existentially as well as academically. They were not merely textual or
historical researches. Indeed Gershem Scholem attacked Buber for
interpreting Ḥasidism existentially as well as academically. In so doing,
claimed Scholem, Buber had overstepped academic boundaries and
therefore not helped the cause of a true understanding of Ḥasidism. Zwi
Werblowsky is another representative of a branch of Jewish scholarship
that would insist upon separating the History of Religions as a discipline
from existentially Jewish considerations. For Buber the separation was
not so clearly desirable or possible. His researches involved a dialogue
with as well as a study of Ḥasidism and the Bible. His stress upon
dialogue in *I and Thou* was no accident. It was both an academic category
and an existential concern.

In the third place, Buber's main concern was with man, and his basic
approach was philosophical. His methodology, if we can call it such, was

that of philosophical anthropology. His primary interest was in man's relationships with other men, with nature, and with God. These relationships could take the form of an I-It relationship with others as objects, or an I-Thou relationship with others in the immediacy of encounter. Built into this approach was an emphasis upon the primacy of personal I-Thou relationships which could not be objectified and therefore could not be studied as phenomena. For Buber, interpersonal or intrapersonal encounter could not be quantified but was nevertheless crucial. And so, as in the case of Radhakrishnan and Suzuki, Buber's philosophical and indeed mystical interests took him beyond the normal historical, sociological, psychological, and phenomenological horizons of the history of religions.

Seyyed Hossein Nasr

By contrast with the last four scholars we have examined, our fifth scholar, Nasr, is still living. He bears certain resemblances to Coomaraswamy, Radhakrishnan, Suzuki, and Buber. Like Coomaraswamy, he espouses the approach of 'perennial philosophy.' Like Suzuki and Buber, he is responsible for making a particular section of studies of his own tradition, namely Ṣūfī studies, more academically popular in the West. Like Radhakrishnan, he combines an interest in philosophy with an interest in religious experience.

Seyyed Hossein Nasr was born in Tehran in 1933, and he received his early education in Iran with its Shī'ite background. He pursued his academic studies in North America, gaining a B.Sc. in Physics from M.I.T. in 1954, an M.A. from Harvard in 1956, and a Ph.D. in the History of Science and Philosophy from Harvard in 1958. His interest in science and philosophy continued when he returned to Iran to lecture in 1958. Increasingly he became active in the field of Islamic science and philosophy as well as in the problems related to the introduction of western science and technology into the Muslim world. Not only so, he also became prolific in his writing on Islam in general and Ṣūfism in particular. His latest academic post is as Professor of Islamics at Temple University, Philadelphia.

Nasr has already written twenty books and two hundred articles. They divide into four main sections: Ṣūfī studies (*Sufi Essays* 1972, *Jalal ad-Din Rumi* 1974); more general Islamic studies (*An Introduction to Islamic Cosmological Doctrines* 1964, *Three Muslim Sages* 1964, *Ideals and Realities of Islam* 1966, *Islamic Studies* 1967, *Science and Civilisation in Islam* 1970, *Islamic Science, An Illustrated Study* 1967, *Histoire de la philosophie islamique* [with Corbin and Yahya] 1964); cultural studies (*Iran* 1966, *Persia, Bridge of Turquoise* [with Beny] 1975); and analyses of the plight of modern man containing an implicit stress upon Philosophia Perennis (*The Encounter of Man and Nature*, *The Spiritual Crisis of Modern Man* 1968, *Islam and the Plight of Modern Man* 1975, and the forthcoming Gifford Lectures entitled, *Knowledge and the Sacred*).

The keys to Nasr's thought are indicated by the basic concerns of his writings. In the first place, he is concerned for Islam and he interprets it through a perspective derived from (Shīʾite) Ṣūfism. In his *Ideals and Realities of Islam* he probes beneath the externals of Islamic practice and symbolism to the inner truths that lie beneath those externals, and he finds them reflected in Ṣūfism. As he puts it (*Islam and the Plight of Modern Man*, 1975: 58):

Sufism, being the inner dimension of Islam, shares, in its formal aspect, in the particular features of this tradition. Since Islam is based on Unity (al-tawhid), all of its manifestations reflect Unity in one way or another; this is especially true of Sufism, in which the principles of the revelation are most directly reflected.

Indeed, for Nasr, Ṣūfism is also the key to an understanding of comparative religion whereby the inner truths of other religions can be understood without their outward forms being compromised. He therefore claims (*Sufi Essays*, 1972: 38):

Sufism provides the metaphysics necessary to carry out the study of comparative religion in depth so that man can accept the validity of every detail of the authentic religions of mankind and at the same time see beyond these details to the transcendent unity of these religions.

According to Nasr, Islam and the other religious traditions of the world can be described and compared in their outward forms. These forms are unique and different, and there is no need to modify them (as he considers John Hick to do in the case of Christianity) in a misguided attempt to heal religious or cultural divisions. Religions, Nasr asserts, can also be studied in their essence 'which leads to their inner unity because the source of all reality and therefore all religion is God who is One' (1972: 130). Religions are therefore 'relatively absolute:' absolute according to the traditional doctrine of the universality of revelation, and relative according to the particularities of each revealed form. The hermeneutical key to Nasr's analysis of both Islam and other religions is therefore Ṣūfism.

He is careful to state however that Ṣūfism *as such* is intrinsic to Islam and cannot be practised outside it. Nevertheless, according to Nasr, something akin to Ṣūfism exists in other religions according to the nature of things. At the heart of intelligence there lies a divine spark which unites man with the sacred and this doctrine lies at the heart of the religious traditions of mankind. This is the perennial philosophy which amounts to knowledge of the sacred; it is 'metaphysics in its real sense, which is a sapiental knowledge based upon the direct and immediate experience of the Truth' (1975: 29). At the basis of Nasr's work there is the aspiration to extend and widen not only a knowledge of Ṣūfism but also a knowledge of the perennial philosophy previously expounded by Ananda Coomaraswamy. The point is not to extend Ṣūfism itself, as Suzuki's work had extended Zen, but to awaken an awareness of the equivalent of Ṣūfism in other religious traditions.

Like our previous four scholars, Nasr is keenly aware of deficiencies in western culture. In his *Man and Nature, The Spiritual Crisis of Modern Man* (1968), he warned about what is now termed the ecological crisis before it had become fashionable to do this. He traced it back to the secularisation of knowledge in the West whereby the study of nature had been divorced from the sacred and therefore from the Reality which is the source of all that is sacred. He points out that the same kind of divorce has occurred in relation to the study of art, history, philosophy, and even theology. As he puts it (1975: 4):

The inner history of the so-called development of modern Western man from his historic background as traditional man—who represents at once his ancestor in time and his centre in space—is a gradual alienation from the Centre and the axis through the spokes of the wheel of existence to the rim, where modern man resides.

Nasr's work therefore is motivated partly by an attempt to heal the disintegration in western culture caused by the weakening of its religious roots, and partly by an attempt to prevent the same thing happening in non-western cultures.

Although Nasr approaches his work from a Muslim angle, we see in him a similar emphasis upon philosophy, upon the inwardness of religion, upon the spiritual need of the West, and upon a particular strand within his own tradition as a key to wider understanding that we discovered in our other thinkers. Clearly by no means all scholars, western or Muslim, would agree that Ṣūfism is the key to Islam, or that the perennial philosophy is the key to understanding world religions. Many students of religion would be reluctant to agree that the study of religion must go beyond the study of religious phenomena and forms to the inner realities that lie behind them. Nor would a number of scholars feel that the study of religion has, as part of its task, the motive of diagnosing or healing the ailments of the West or of other parts of the world. These concerns would be seen to be outside the purview of the scholar of religion. It is nevertheless significant that the non-Christian and non-western scholars we have examined *do* dwell upon these themes.

John Mbiti

John Mbiti, like Nasr, is still an active and developing scholar. He is African and Christian, and he is devoting his energies to an investigation, from an African perspective, of African traditional religion and African Christianity. This development in ·African studies of African religion is distinctively post-war, and it is almost certain to grow in importance. As we shall see, although scholars of African religion such as Mbiti are aware of wider initiatives in Christian theology they are less likely to be cognisant of studies of other world religions, especially eastern ones.

John Mbiti was born in Kenya. His studies began at Makerere

University College and after a spell at Barrington College, Rhode·Island, he eventually took a doctorate of theology at Cambridge. He served for a time in an Anglican parish, and was a visiting Lecturer at Selly Oak Colleges, Birmingham and at Hamburg University. However, he returned to Africa in 1964 to become lecturer and later professor of religious studies at Makerere University in Uganda. More recently he has served as Principal of the Ecumenical Institute at Bossey in Switzerland. Like Radhakrishnan, Suzuki, and Nasr he has therefore taught both within his own culture and in the West.

In addition to his many articles Mbiti has written a number of books, including *Akamba Stories* (1966) in the Oxford Library of African Literature, *African Religions and Philosophy* (1969), *Concepts of God in Africa* (1970), *New Testament Eschatology in an African Background* (1971), and *The Prayers of African Religion* (1975). Mbiti's method can best be seen in an analysis of his *African Religions and Philosophy*. He begins this work by pointing out the all-pervasive nature of religion in Africa, and the many varieties of African traditional religion which constitute 'a reality which calls for academic scrutiny' (1969: 1). He reflects upon past methods of studying African religion. He dismisses earlier attitudes which assumed that African beliefs and culture were borrowed from elsewhere, that African religion was 'animism,' that African religion could be termed 'primitive religion' and put at the lower end of a religious evolutionary scale, and that African religions amount to ancestor worship or magic. He comments, 'it is only around the middle of the twentieth century that these subjects have begun to be studied properly and respectfully as an academic discipline in their own right' (1969: 6). Mbiti then goes on to trace four modern approaches to the study of African religion. The first of these approaches is represented by P. Tempels (1946, 1969), J. Jahn (1958, 1961), and J.V. Taylor (1963) writing respectively in French, German, and English. They are more sympathetic than earlier western scholars in their attitude towards African religion. Tempels, in his book *Bantu Philosophy*, analyses Baluba religion and philosophy and interprets it in terms of the 'vital force,' the essence of which is being. Jahn, in his book *Muntu*, points out that Africa has something of philosophical value to offer to the world, and in his reflection upon Muntu and three other categories he widens Tempels' notion of 'vital force.' Taylor, in his book *The Primal Vision*, attempts to get inside the primal world of African religion from a Christian perspective, and largely succeeds in doing this, albeit somewhat uncritically. He, Tempels and Jahn see African religion as an integral part of the whole life of African people.

The second modern approach, represented again in English, French, and German by Parrinder (1954), Deschamps (1960), and Dammann (1963), attempts to treat African religions systematically and to bring together material from various African peoples. Parrinder's book *African Traditional Religion* was especially important, as an early example of this genre, as valuable in its own right, and as a spur to African scholars such as Mbiti who followed a basically similar method.

The third current approach is that of fieldwork oriented anthropologists such as Evans-Pritchard (*Nuer Religion*, 1956) and Lienhardt (*Divinity and Experience: the Religion of the Dinka*, 1961). They represent a strand of western anthropological scholarship that concentrates upon the religions of individual peoples and treats them in depth and in relation to the integral situation of the people concerned.

The fourth approach is that of African scholars themselves who may either take a particular religious topic and treat it in depth within a single area (Danquah 1944, Nketia 1955, Kagame 1956, Idowu 1962), or, like Mbiti, take an overview of a single topic throughout African religion. Mbiti's approach is 'to treat religion as an ontological phenomenon, with the concept of time as the key to teaching some understanding of African religion and philosophy' (1969: 14). His thesis is that it is misleading to think of Africans classifying time into past, present and future in a western fashion. Using two Swahili terms, *sasa* and *zamani*, he divides time into two categories: *sasa* the 'now-period,' the micro-time, of immediate experience; *zamani* the past events, the macro-time, that *has* been experienced. He claims that the African view of time is backward-looking, with the future having no significance, and he works out this thesis in great detail as being relevant to a true understanding and a full comprehension of African religion.

Certain premises underly Mbiti's general thinking. First, he stresses the importance of religion as a key to understanding Africa and as a force for creating a new Africa. 'Singly, jointly or in comparison,' he writes, 'the religions in Africa should be able to exert a force and make a contribution in creating new standards, morals and ethics suitable. for our changing society' (1969: 274). It is only religion that is truly sensitive to the fullness of man's dignity, nature and potentialities; man cannot live by politics and science alone. Second, Mbiti treats African religions as a whole. He emphasises the unity of African religions and philosophy and gives an overall picture of their situation. He considers that there is a basic understanding, mind-set, perception and logic behind the manner in which Africans think, speak, or act that makes it meaningful to talk about African religion as a generic phenomenon. Third, he is not content to describe and deal with the beliefs, ceremonies, rituals, religious leaders, and other data of African religion. He is concerned with the philosophy that lies behind the words and actions and outward data. That philosophy is not present as a 'philosophical system,' it is arrived at by interpretation, and yet it is crucial. Fourthly, while being sympathetic to Islam and African indigenous religions, Mbiti stresses the role of Christianity in Africa. He claims that it is traditionally African and indigenous and that it therefore has a greater potentiality for 'meeting the dilemmas and challenges of modern Africa, and of reaching the full integration and manhood of individuals and communities' (1969: 277). Once again, therefore, we have in Mbiti a thinker who recognises his own religious commitment, and who is concerned that religion, his own and that of others, should be ready to tackle the problems and challenges of the modern world.

It is possible to criticise Mbiti on five different but interrelated counts. His interest in ascertaining the concepts of God, the prayers, or the view of time in African religion in general makes him vulnerable in relation to the exceptions that inevitably occur within particular areas. He stands on firmer ground when he speaks about the Bantu African religion of south and east Africa, but he has less knowledge about west Africa which in subtle ways is different from Bantu Africa. His concern to determine the general nature of African philosophy and religion tends to involve him in statements that are not only general but also abstract and therefore a stage removed from the concrete particularities of actual peoples. His efforts to understand and engage in dialogue with African religion are applauded by Christian theologians, but the liberation theologians among them tend to question what they consider to be Mbiti's over-concern with religious theory and underconcern for everyday praxis. Finally, his basic thesis that there is no future time in African thought, and his implied notion that there is a monolithic view of time of African thought, have both been brought into question (Horton 1967: 177; Parratt 1977). However, Mbiti is representative of a new movement among Africans to comment academically upon their own religion. He is typical of an increasing endeavour among African scholars to research their own religion both for its own sake and for the light it throws upon the wider religious scene.

Wing-Tsit Chan

One of the most representative scholars of Chinese religion in recent times has been Wing-Tsit Chan. He was born at Canton, and obtained his B.A. degree at Lingnan University. He later finished a Harvard doctorate, and after teaching in China he became professor of chinese culture and philosophy at Dartmouth College in 1942. He subsequently became professor of philosophy at Chatham College, Pittsburgh and during his long teaching career in the United States he has written many articles and books.

Wing-Tsit Chan's writings fall into three broad categories. He has been notable firstly for the quality and prolific nature of his translations. The most widely-known example of this translation work is *A Source Book in Chinese Philosophy* (1963), the whole of which was translated and compiled by Chan. This work covers the ancient, medieval and modern periods of Chinese philosophy and includes material from the Confucian, Taoist, and Buddhist traditions, and it represents a monumental feat of translation requiring not only linguistic but also hermeneutical expertise. As Chan comments, his new translations provide consistency of style and language, he is able to make use of recent research works and commentaries, and he is able to render more exactly a number of problematical Chinese technical philosophical terms. Other important translations by Chan include: *Instructions for Practical Living, and Other Neo-Confucian Writings of Wang Yang-Ming* (1963), *The Way of*

Lao Tzu, a Translation and Study of the Tao-te ching (1963), and *The Platform Scripture, The Basic Classic of Zen Buddhism* (1963).

In the second place, Wing-Tsit Chan has written on the whole gamut of Chinese religion and philosophy. In his *Historical Charts of Chinese Philosophy* (1955), he gives a chronological chart of the whole development of the Chinese philosophical tradition. *A Source Book in Chinese Philosophy* covers, in forty-four sections, the entire unfolding of Chinese thought from pre-Confucianism to present-day communist China. He deals in succession with the ancient period (from Confucius to c. 200 BC) which includes various Confucian strands, early Taoist thought, Mo Tzu, the Logicians, Yin Yang, and Legalism; the medieval period (covering the thousand years to about 800 AD) which includes Han Confucianism, Taoist, and Neo-Taoist strands, the various Buddhist schools, and the Confucian revival under Han Yu and Li Ao; and the modern period in which he examines Sung Neo-Confucianism, Ming Neo-Confucianism, Ch'ing Confucianism, and eventually Communism. It is worth noting that he has a real concern for the contemporary period within China. His *Religious Trends in Modern China* (1953) analyses developments within the present century up to the time of the communist revolution, and his *Chinese Philosophy in Mainland China, 1949–1963* brings the story closer to present-day. A more detailed review of Chan's works than we have time for now would show a general interest in various aspects of Chinese religion and thought throughout its history.

In addition to his broad concerns, Wing-Tsit Chan has concentrated wherever possible upon the neo-Confucian element in Chinese philosophy. He has helped to develop a wider academic interest in the neo-Confucian giants, Chu Hsi and Wang Yang-Ming, as well as in lesser-known facets of neo-Confucian thought. He sees the development of neo-Confucianism as being in continuity with earlier developments of Confucianism, with the added advantage that it incorporates within a new synthesis elements taken from the Buddhist and Taoist traditions. The titles of a number of his articles indicate the importance Chan attaches to neo-Confucianism: 'The Evolution of the Confucian Concept *Jen*' (1955), 'How Buddhistic is Wang Yang-Ming?' (1962), 'The Neo-Confucian Solution of the Problem of Evil' (1957), 'Neo-Confucianism and Chinese Scientific Thought' (1957), 'Synthesis in

Chinese Metaphysics' (1951), 'Wang Yang-Ming' (1960), 'Chu Hsi's Completion of Neo-Confucianism' (1973), 'Patterns for Neo-Confucianism: Why Chu Hsi Differed From Ch'eng I' (1978), 'The Evolution of the Neo-Confucian Concept Li as Principle' (1964), and 'Chinese and Western Interpretations of Jen (Humanity)' (1975). It is especially interesting to reflect upon the way Chan develops the neo-Confucian interpretation of the Confucian concepts of *Li* and *Jen*. He regards the concept of *Li* as principle to be the most important in Chinese thought in the last eight hundred years, and yet there is discontinuity in its interpretation because the concept of *Li* had not been 'central in Confucianism from the very beginning' (1964: 123). By contrast, 'the concept of *Jen* (humanity, love, humaneness) is a central concept of Confucian thought and has gone through a long evolution of more than 2,000 years' (1975: 107). One has the feeling, in reading Wing-Tsit Chan, that he sees neo-Confucianism as the syncretic fulfilment of earlier Chinese religion, as the basic religion of the Chinese intelligentsia, and as an ongoing phenomenon in China in that it is 'extremely naturalistic, rationalistic, and humanistic ... free from myths, supernatural deities, and irrational miracles' (1953: 260). For him, neo-Confucianism is the intellectual equivalent of Vedānta for Radhakrishnan, Ḥasidism for Buber, Ṣūfism for Nasr, and Zen for Suzuki.

In reviewing Chan's thought we see that, like our other thinkers, he has a concern for philosophy. His concern for the technicalities of philosophy converges with that of Radhakrishnan in that they both take seriously the history as well as the structure of philosophy, they both review their philosophical tradition in length as well as in depth, and they both have a critical predilection for a particular philosophical viewpoint (Vedānta for Radhakrishnan, neo-Confucianism for Chan). Chan's interest in philosophy is not as existential as that of Buber, Nasr, or Suzuki. He sees it rather as an academic area of interest and an academic tool.

Like Coomaraswamy, Chan's academic career has been exercised mainly in the West. This has been necessitated by practical considerations and for this reason he does not rank as a typical representative of contemporary Chinese scholarship in the cultural sense. Nevertheless, unlike Coomaraswamy, he is concerned about the contemporary religious situation in his own land as it is developing indigenously *now*, and he is less inclined to react unfavourably to western culture or religion. 'No one doubts the positive character of the Christian teaching,' he states (1975: 120).

There is a certain resemblance between Wing-Tsit Chan and Mbiti in that their objects of study, Chinese religion and African traditional religion, have undergone an ostensible decline in the contemporary situation. It is hardly as feasible for members of other cultures to become adherents of Confucianism or African religion as it is for them to become adherents of the major renascent religious traditions. Moreover, the element of mysticism is not as present in neo-Confucianism and African religion as it is in Ḥasidism, Ṣūfism, Vedānta, or Zen. It is therefore more likely that Chinese religion and African religion will be seen as objects of study rather than vehicles of commitment or religious experience.

The value of the work of Chan and Mbiti, although they are not uninterested in other religions, lies mainly in their ability to use their knowledge of the language, literature, and ethos of their own religious traditions to interpret them academically in a way that would be difficult for western scholars who lack their indigenous background.

Implications of the Work of non-western Scholars of Religion

We have analysed briefly the work of seven scholars: Coomaraswamy, Radhakrishnan, Suzuki, Buber, Nasr, Mbiti, and Chan; they are respectively Celanese, Indian, Japanese, Austrian, Iranian, Kenyan, and Chinese; their expertise lies respectively in Indian religion (the first two), Buddhism, Judaism, Islam, African religions, and Chinese religion. All are clearly important scholars. Opinions may differ as to whether they are truly representative of scholarship in their traditions. It is also true to say that four of them, Coomaraswamy, Radhakrishnan, Suzuki and Buber, did some work before World War II and that their work therefore covers a long time-span. The conclusions that we draw from their work must therefore be limited. Nevertheless, because they are eminent scholars who approach the study of religion from (except for Buber) a non-western standpoint, it is instructive to examine the implications of their work. Our findings must be tentative, they will not necessarily be unimportant.

(1) All these scholars study, first and foremost, their *own* religion. This may seem a trite point to make, it is nevertheless a significant one. As Ursula King points out in an earlier chapter, much western study of religion has stressed the study of religions other than Christianity. On the whole the study of the main western religion, namely Christianity, has been seen as the province of theology and the findings of theology have been *used* by students of religion rather than systematically researched by them. Insofar as this is the case, the time is now ripe for a religious studies perspective to be brought to bear more directly upon Christianity and for scholars of religion to study more closely its ideas and values as well as its social structures, rituals, denominations, and scriptures. Although our seven scholars may have had an interest in the study of other religions, their primary concern has been with their own. All of them have combined a general interest in the whole of their own tradition with a particular concern for part of it: Indian art (Coomaraswamy), Vedānta (Radhakrishnan), Zen (Suzuki), Hasidism (Buber), Ṣūfism (Nasr), Bantu Africa (Mbiti), and neo-Confucianism (Chan). Many of them have been active in the translation of important texts of their own religion or in the providing of collections of stories in translation. Suzuki, for example, did important work on the *Laṅkāvatāra Sūtra* (1930, 1932), on Aśvaghosa's *Discourse on the Awakening of Faith in the Mahāyāna* (1900), and on exegeting Zen texts, in addition to providing hermeneutical insights into the Buddhist tradition. One of the values of their work has been to enrich our knowledge of the language, texts, and interpretation of their own traditions through a personal concern in what they were studying. In smaller or greater degree, they have not only advanced but transformed the academic study of their own religion.

(2) Our seven scholars share an interest in and a concern for the major living religions of the world. All of them belong to living world religions and these world religions delimit the scope of their studies. In other words, they have little or no academic curiosity about archaic religions that are dead. With the partial exceptions of Mbiti and Chan

who concentrate more narrowly upon their regional (yet still multi-religious) concerns, the others have a wider interest in other world religions. This is in contrast to much western study of religion which tends to focus more upon archaic religion, primal religions (which although living are not major and are not usually able to respond in dialogue), and the historical, sociological, psychological, and more outward aspects of western religion.

(3) A third and related point is that our eminent authors have a creative awareness of the present situation of their own and other religions. All of them are interested in speaking to the present age. Their expertise and research are not confined to an investigation of the past history or ancient texts of their tradition. They are concerned creatively to re-interpret their own religion in the light of the modern situation. The contexts may differ. For Chan, it is communist China, for Mbiti independent Africa, for Coomaraswamy and Radhakrishnan renascent Ceylon and India, for Suzuki modern Japan, for Buber pre- and post-holocaust Judaism, for Nasr modernising Islam, and for all of them the secularising West. They diverge over the nature of their attempts to reinterpret the classical forms of their religious traditions. Coomaraswamy and Nasr aim to recover the perennial philosophy of past tradition to transform the present, Mbiti desires to create an indigenous African theology, Chan wrestles to see the continuity between neo-Confucianism and the developing China, and Radhakrishnan, Suzuki and Buber imaginatively renew important aspects of their developing traditions to speak to contemporary needs. The point is that their academic concern is with the present as well as with the past.

(4) All of them share a relationship with the West. Each of them has studied or taught in the West: Coomaraswamy in England and Boston, Radhakrishnan at Oxford, Suzuki in the United States, Nasr at Harvard and Temple, Mbiti at Cambridge and Bossey, Chan at Dartmouth and Chatham. Although to some extent influenced by the West, to a greater or lesser degree they·all react against it. This reaction is less obvious (although still there) in Chan and Mbiti. It is extremely complex in Buber who was a German Jew before and after the Nazi Holocaust in the West. Coomaraswamy, Radhakrishnan, Suzuki, and Nasr are responding noticeably to what they consider to be the weakening effects upon religion

of western secularisation. It is significant that the response towards the West adopted by these scholars is threefold. In the first place, they are commenting implicitly upon western approaches to the study of their own tradition. While generally not disapproving of the work of western scholars, their suggestion is that this work needs to be supplemented by that of scholars belonging to the traditions themselves. Their strictures upon western scholarship are less radical than those of Said. They are not implying that western scholars are influenced by quasi-political concerns but that western cultural presuppositions make it less easy for westerners to understand the language and world-view of the people concerned. In the second place, they are responding to the general educational ethos of western scholarship. Their feeling is (less obviously so in Chan) that the western tendency to stress empirical and rational categories derived from a science-based model makes it less easy for western scholars to understand what Vedānta means to a Hindu, Ṣūfism to a Muslim, Zen to a Buddhist, or ancestor worship to an African. Third, and relatedly, they are responding to the general impact upon the wider world of western civilisation with its basic emphasis upon technology, material progress, scientific specialisation, the accumulation of data, and so on. At this point, their concern is not so much with the effect of the West upon the study of religion but with the effect of the West upon religion as such.

The implications of the ambivalent attitude towards the West on the part of these seven scholars are both varied and debateable. We have time to mention only two. The first implication revolves around the thorny topic of dialogue. All of these scholars see the need for 'dialogue' although they are not united in their view of what it means. At one level, dialogue simply means academic dialogue between western and non-western scholars in order to clarify intellectually and comparatively the meaning of terms, and the place of those terms within wider worldviews. An example of this approach is Chan's comparative analysis of *jen* and humanity within the Chinese and western traditions. At another level, dialogue may involve a debate between scholars who consider themselves to be in some degree representatives of their religions. With the possible exception of Chan, our seven scholars have sometimes engaged in this type of discussion. The aim of this kind of exercise is to clarify areas of agreement and disagreement between religious traditions seen as such. This view of dialogue converges with a similar notion present within Christian theology, and 'dialogue' in this sense is sometimes viewed as a Christian theological approach. This is not necessarily the case, and it is a moot point as to whether dialogue in the Christian theological sense was initiated by Christians or was a response to the work of men such as Radhakrishnan, Suzuki, and Buber. In this type of dialogue, the scholar operates as Christian, Buddhist, Muslim, Hindu or Jewish scholar rather than as 'neutral' scholar. At a third level, dialogue may involve a dialogue between scholars as representative of cultures. When Coomaraswamy, Radhakrishnan, Buber, Nasr, Suzuki, Mbiti, and occasionally Chan operate in this fashion they are not in debate with Christianity but with western culture which is seen to have partly abandoned its roots in Christianity. They are concerned to portray the spiritual crisis of western culture and to suggest by implication how non-western religions and cultures can alleviate the western cultural crisis. Dialogue may be seen, fourthly, as the internal dialogue within the scholar. This view is especially evident in the work of Buber who placed the notion of dialogue within and between persons at the centre of his thinking. According to this view, the scholar cannot remain completely detached from the material or the tradition he is studying: he or she will be influenced by the very fact of engaging in dialogue with the data (as well as the people) of other traditions. Failure to differentiate between these different meanings of 'dialogue' is sometimes responsible for lack of mature academic discussion of this topic. It is likely that the increasing realisation that 'dialogue' has to do with the study of religion as well as with religion, and that the motivation for dialogue arises not only from within Christian theology but from within the ranks of academics of other religions, will lead to a fresh definition of, and interest in, the concept of dialogue.

The second implication of the involvement of non-western scholars of religion in the West revolves around the notion that the study of religion in our global context should have some relevance in regard to the pursuit of world harmony. The recognition that western science has unified the world materially, but that the world is not yet united humanly and spiritually, is seen to be a global problem that cannot be shirked by the study of religion.

(5) The scholars we have studied all have an interest in philosophy. They are not content to remain at the levels of sociology, psychology, history, phenomenology, comparison, science, anthropology or mythical and textual studies. They ask wider questions of their material, and they are interested in philosophy as such. Three of them, Radhakrishnan, Chan, and Nasr, are specialists in philosophy; three others, Suzuki, Buber, and Coomaraswamy have a concern for metaphysics in a more general sense; and Mbiti, although studying the non-philosophical African tradition, is exercised to discover the basic ideas, the 'African Philosophy,' lying behind that tradition. As we have implied, their concern for philosophy is a dual one. They are interested in the religious concepts of the religions they are studying; they are also interested in what those concepts mean to the people concerned, they are interested in *meaning*. They are generally unconcerned about the social sciences with their emphasis upon action and social behaviour. They are more stimulated by ideas-related areas such as spirituality, ethics, and (with Coomaraswamy) aesthetics. Although most of our scholars have done their fair share of translation or textual work, their major concern is for the philosophy, meaning and value lying behind religious texts.

(6) With the exception of Chan who does not parade his religious commitment, our scholars are not concerned to hide their own religious position. It is clear that Coomaraswamy and Radhakrishnan are Hindus, Suzuki a Buddhist, Buber a Jew, Nasr a Muslim, and Mbiti an African Christian. They approach their work from a viewpoint of religious commitment, and although their ideas have been in constant evolution that evolution has advanced within a religious framework that is 'given.' This does not mean that their commitment is narrow or unhelpful. Indeed their commitment may well be part of the reason for the fruitfulness of their theories. That commitment is twofold. It is first to the study of religion itself, for they are primarily students and scholars; it is second a personal religious quest fulfilled through the medium of their study of religion. There is a dialectical relationship between their study of religion and their religion. They see no necessary separation between

commitment and academic responsibility, personalism and objectivity, and *homo religiosus* and *homo academicus*. This is reflected partly in their academic concerns. We have mentioned already their interest in philosophy. This is accompanied, in general, by an interest in religious experience as an area of academic research.

(7) Finally, they all express an interest in what we may term the 'transcendental' as well as the historical structures of religion. The greater part of this book has concentrated upon an investigation of what we may call the historical-immanental structures of religion or religions. The historical, sociological, anthropological, psychological, and textual approaches bracket out transcendental categories; likewise the phenomenological approach, although it classically conceived of a single fundamental essence common to all religions, does not depend upon a transcendent reality revealing itself through religion. In contrast, transcendental structures are more basic to the thinking of the seven scholars we have discussed. Coomaraswamy and Nasr stress the perennial philosophy they see lying at the heart of all religions; they regard it as revealing the Truth as a living reality which provides the archetypal categories whereby men and women can live transcendently as well as immanently. For Radhakrishnan, idealism is the key whereby the structure of ultimate reality can be unfolded. In Suzuki's case, mysticism is the life of religion and the key to its understanding. Buber prefers to stress the I-Thou relationship as central to a true insight into the nature of God and man. Mbiti's framework of thought either stresses or presumes that all African people have a notion of God as Supreme Being. For Chan, Chinese life and culture are closely related to Chinese philosophy the perennial problems of which, knowledge, human destiny, human nature, heaven, and the like, provide the 'transcendental' structure for his thought.

And so we see, with the partial exception of Chan, that our seven scholars conform to a general pattern. They research their own religion, their interest is in the living religions, they have a concern for the present as well as the past, they have an ambivalent relationship with the West, their general approach is philosophical, they do not hide their own commitment, and the structures they investigate are 'transcendental' as well as historical.

Our conclusion must be that in general they do not substantiate Said's thesis. His contention is that Orientalism served the interests of western imperialism rather than pure scholarship. Our findings are that the work of these seven scholars does diverge from some of the presuppositions of western historically-oriented scholarship but on academic and cultural rather than imperialistic grounds. Moreover, their work has begun to bear fruit within the general discipline of the study of religion, especially in the United States. One example of this is the notion that the study of a particular religious tradition can gain useful and even necessary help from scholars of the tradition concerned. This principle was first incorporated effectively into an ongoing project by Kenneth Morgan of Colgate University. In his *Religion of the Hindus* (1953) Morgan used his extensive personal contacts to persuade a number of Hindu scholars to write about various aspects of their own religion. He used the same principle in his *The Path of the Buddha* (1956) and *Islam—The Straight Path* (1958) which were books on their own religious traditions written by Asian Buddhists and Muslims respectively. Wilfred Cantwell Smith has introduced the allied principle of verification whereby he suggests that members of religious traditions that are studied should be consulted in regard to works written on their own traditions. The point at stake is whether western scholars should be able to comment with impunity upon other religions without being subject to the informed opinion of members of those other religions concerning the general appropriateness and accuracy of those comments. This verification principle goes further than the general phenomenological emphasis upon *Einfühlung* which encourages empathy on the part of the scholar for the religious tradition he is studying—it requires that the scholar should keep in mind the fact that he is writing for a wider than western audience. His criteria for writing are not confined, then, to a consideration of how western scholars will respond to his thought; he will have to bear in mind also what scholars and members of the tradition he is studying will have to say about his ideas. If taken seriously, this would involve a subtle change of perspective and orientation. A further sign of the times is the practice in some universities, especially in North America, to appoint adherents of certain religions to teach those religions.

A second example of the implicit or explicit influence of foreign scholars such as those we have examined is the rise of centres for study of religion in different parts of the world. While stressing the academic nature of the study of religion these centres have drawn together experts on different religious traditions and often from different parts of the world to share together in the scholarly task of studying and interpreting religion. The assumption of these centres is often that the major living religions of the world are the main focus of the academic study of religion. They also symbolise by implication the view that academic dialogue is a desirable thing. One of the leading exponents of this viewpoint is W.C. Smith. In a celebrated article, 'Comparative Religion: Whither—and Why?' (1959), Smith outlined his position by tracing the progress of the history of religions in various stages. The first stage saw the accumulation and analysis of facts. At first this was the impersonal accumulation of facts about 'it,' a religion so-called. Then it became the accumulation of facts about 'they,' the people of a religion, by people still personally uninvolved. The next stage saw the personalisation of the work so that 'we' as scholars were studying 'they' as people. A further step came when it was seen that personal contact with others was an important part of the study of religion, and that discussion with others not as 'they' but as 'you' was relevant. This was the stage of dialogue. The final step involved going beyond dialogue to 'colloquium,' the academic co-operation of an international group of scholars writing for a world audience and if possible studying together. The implicit idea of Smith's work was that centres should be set up around the world where such groups of scholars could work together. This has not proved to be possible in any major way, but in a number of places around the world including McGill, Chicago, Ankara, Ibadan, Patiala, Tokyo, and Harvard centres of one sort or another have been formed to accomplish similar aims. Indeed it is difficult to be unaware, in reading Smith's work, of the similarity between some of his ideas and some of those of the seven scholars we examined earlier; it is hard to imagine his work unless it had been preceded and accompanied by theirs.

The influence of non-western thought upon the study of religion is a complex topic and there is not the space in this present work to discuss it more deeply. Any discussion of it is made more difficult by the fact that this thought is neither concentrated within one academic discipline nor confined to the study of one particular religion, and therefore its impact is diffuse rather than concrete. We shall remain content with three final comments.

A. It is clear that the main influence of non-western scholarship upon the study of religion has been in the Anglo-Saxon world of North America and Britain rather than in continental Europe. European scholars have generally remained satisfied with the textual, sociological, anthropological, psychological, historical, and phenomenological approaches we have described in this book. The more daring hermeneutical theories have emerged in North America, and to a lesser extent in Britain, in the work of scholars such as Smith and Eliade who lived in non-western countries and knew their thought. An alternative stream of European thought arising out of the work of Otto and van der Leeuw has maintained closer links with theological work than is commonly found elsewhere in Europe, but this theological work is western. It is outside Europe that the impact of Asian and African thought has been most obvious. The influence of cultural factors, such as the residual contacts forged by the British Empire, the force of the English language, and the Asian links established by the United States after the second world war, should not be minimised in this context, neither should the impact of the thinkers we have described who were influenced by the Anglo-Saxon world. To this extent, Said's thesis is susceptible to radical reinterpretation in the light of the apparently reverse influence of the religions of other cultures upon the scholarship of the imperial forces that worked upon them, whereas the less imperial continental European countries remained more wedded to the presuppositions of western scholarship.

B. A second comment is that western scholarship and indeed western culture has provided the agenda and the framework for reactions from thinkers outside the West. Perhaps this is the hidden thrust of Said's work in contrast to some of the more flamboyantly explicit remarks that he makes. The present global situation is witnessing the rise of other spheres of political and cultural influence in other areas of the world such as Japan, China, the Muslim world, the Soviet block, and the third world which are no longer subject to western hegemony in the old sense. The question implicitly raised by Said is whether scholarship in these developing regions will continue to respond to western problems and concerns or whether scholars from these parts will wish to provide their own agenda and framework independently from the West. To phrase the problem in a different way, to what extent is the western framework for the study of religion western rather than universal? Can scholars from other cultures fit with adjustments into a framework that is universally valid, or are the presuppositions at present governing the study of religion so hidebound by western thought-forms that they must be radically modified in order to become universal? Dr. King in her chapter distinguishes five major areas with different cultural, religious and scholarly traditions which are involved in the study of religion: western Europe, North America, the socialist countries, Africa, and a cluster of Asian countries. She rightly states that it is regrettable that we have so little information about what is going on in some of these areas. This chapter has attempted to fill part of the gap by summarising the work of seven of the well-known scholars of religion from other cultures. We have not tried to summarise *all* the work done by Hindu, Buddhist, Jewish, Muslim, African, and Chinese scholars; we have selected some of the most eminent and shown how their work has been dialectically related to western scholarship especially in the Anglo-Saxon world.

It is difficult to answer the question we have asked as to whether the western superstructure for the study of religion is too culture-bound or whether it is universally applicable. Perhaps four things can be said.

(a) Insofar as we do live in a global world, it is vital that we have more information about what is happening globally in regard to the study of religion, and that there is more scholarly dialogue between scholars from different cultures. It is not just a matter of discovering what scholars from different regions are writing in their own languages about the minutiae of their own traditions but also of examining their general approach to their studies. In other words, it is important to extend the exercise begun in this chapter of analysing seriously the implications of the work of non-western scholars. And from now on they are less likely to be working in the West than was once the case.

(b) There is a glaring lack of information about the study of religion in socialist and communist lands. Diligent gleaning of magazines can turn up articles such as: 'Religion and the Marxist Concept of Social Formation' by Marko Kersevan, '*Une lecture marxiste du prophétisme*' by Daniel Vidal, 'A Marxist Analysis of the Religion of East African Herdsmen' by Pierre Bonte, 'Marxist Analysis and Sociology of Religion' by Otto Maduro (*Social Compass*, XXII, 3–4, 1975), 'Investigate Religion and Criticize Theology' by Ren Jiyu (*Ching Feng*, 20, 1977), and so on. More needs to be done by way of research, exchange, and academic dialogue to increase our global knowledge in this area, especially through the medium of a growing knowledge of the works of scholars in communist lands (as a complement to the work of western scholars on communism, for example, see Thrower's forthcoming book on 'Marxist-Leninism').

(c) Insofar as trends are becoming apparent, there appear to be three developments. On the one hand, there is a tendency among some scholars in countries such as East Germany, in part of the Jewish world (as seen in the work of men such as Neusner), and in Chinese scholarship outside China, to emphasise the critical-historical 'scientific' approach; on the other hand, there is the further development of the tendency we have seen in Coomaraswamy, Radhakrishnan, Suzuki, Buber, Nasr, and Mbiti for scholars of other cultures to use the treasures of their own tradition in order to inform their academic work, and this holds true in a different way of Ren Jiyu's article which is informed by dialectical materialism. In addition, as we have seen, non-western scholars may eschew their own cultural tradition and follow a critical-historical method, they may utilise their own tradition and yet share in a theory of the study of religion that has wider valency, as Coomaraswamy and Nasr share the approach of Philosophia Perennis, or they may study their own tradition less critically. The global situation is therefore a shifting one containing different cultural centres for the study of religion, fluid approaches to the study of religion, and a centre of gravity derived from but no longer stationary within the West.

(d) It is vital that there should be more intercultural and interdisciplinary knowledge and discussion about the whole gamut of problems in religious studies, especially method and theory. One of the reasons why the researches of foreign scholars have not revolutionised the study of religion in the West to the extent that might have been imagined is the fact that western approaches to the study of religion have themselves been uncoordinated. Specialisation in particular religious traditions or particular approaches to the study of religion has countered the possibility of obtaining an overview of the contemporary approaches to the study of religion within the West. So non-western scholarship has not been responding to a monolithic western approach but to a plethora of western approaches depending upon whether a particular approach favoured a sociological, anthropological, historical, phenomenological, philological, psychological, textual/mythical, or even philosophical (or theological) slant—or a combination of them. Western presuppositions concerning academic study have been present in the field of religious studies; an overarching synthesis, such as Said's idea of western Orientalism, was not. The lack of such a sovereign synthesis may, in some quarters, be regretted. By the same token, this lack presents the opportunity to construct a general view of religious studies that can incorporate insights from other cultures.

C. A third and brief comment upon non-western study of religion is that there remains a difference between apologetic defence of one's own religion or proselytisation and the study of religion. In some instances, for example, in some of the work of Suzuki and Radhakrishnan we described, there was evidence of a tendency towards apologetic or proselytisation or both. At this point, they crossed an invisible boundary separating the study of religion from another enterprise that would come more properly under the general heading of 'theology.' Equally, to the extent that they dwell explicitly upon the nature of ultimate reality, they are engaging in a more 'theological' enterprise. It is legitimate to employ hermeneutics, to research from a position of commitment, to engage in academic dialogue with scholars of other religions, to engage in philosophy, and to use 'transcendent' structures, provided that in so doing one is not engaging in advocacy or defence of a particular religious tradition or a particular view of transcendence over against other religious traditions or other views of transcendence. As I have written upon this topic elsewhere in the volume there is no cause to dwell upon it now.

The Global Context of the Study of Religion

In this chapter we have glanced at the contribution of non-western or non-Christian scholars to religious studies. Our final assignment is to look more directly to the global context of that study. In attempting this task, we will concentrate not so much upon the global situation *per se*, with its escalation of nuclear weapons, growth of world population, increasing gap between richer and poorer nations, urgent problems of medical ethics, ecological crisis, and so on (although increasing attention is beginning to be devoted to the study of 'applied religion' in religious ethics), but rather upon the global educational situation within which the study of religion is purveyed. It is clear that given the fact of our global problems, there is the need for sensitive interdisciplinary investigation in depth; there is the need for acute minds from different cultures to wrestle with these questions. There is the need for intellectual agonising, for rigorous scholarship, for academic commitment, in the realisation that the 'we' involved in this discussion is not just our family, our community, our nation, our religious tradition, our academic discipline. This is a global matter, and the 'we' involved is mankind.

Considerations of space permit us to glance only briefly at this complex topic. In order to situate the study of religion in its contemporary educational framework, we shall trace it back briefly to its basic educational roots. We begin our analysis with a consideration of the rise of learning in the western world, a rise that produced, for better or for worse, the modern notion of a university. The beginnings of this development go back to Greece and it was continued and put into clearer form by Rome (*Graecia capta Romum captum ferit*). For 2,500 years Greece and her successors have thrown up a number of areas of study, of disciplines, of specialisations, but at different periods three dominant models have emerged that have suggested implicitly or explicitly the superiority of one area of knowledge over the others. The first dominant model was the Graeco-Roman one of *humanitas*, what we would call the humanities or liberal arts. The main stress in this model was upon literature and man, and the studies of religion and science were subsumed within this wider category. Philosophy was not neglected either, but, as Otto Bird has pointed out (1976: 12–15), Cicero's quarrel with

Socrates was not that the great man was lacking in wisdom, but that Socrates had elevated philosophy into a 'discipline' independent of man's general literary-humanistic, social, and political concerns. The danger was that philosophy would become a specialisation in its own right and if that were to happen truth would be seen to lie not in man nor in the public weal but in philosophy as an intellectual pursuit independent of its practical influence upon humanity and public affairs. It is hard not to interpolate at this point an anticipation of the rise of modern disciplines wherein truth is seen to lie in the discipline, wherein one writes 'for the discipline and one's peers in the discipline' rather than for man. In a classical phrase, Aristotle, describing a person with *paideia* (the Greek equivalent of *humanitas*), comments that he is one, 'who in his own person is able to judge critically in all or nearly all branches of knowledge and not merely in some special subject' (see Bird 1976: 15). The Graeco-Roman model then was that of *humanitas*, with its stress upon the aesthetic value of words both written and spoken, with its stress upon the cultural value of studying another language, with its stress upon the value of the great traditions of the past, with its stress upon the moral and political value of true learning.

This model was inherited and not completely lost during the Christian medieval period. The fall of Rome, the symbol and upholder of the ancient ideal, was responded to by St. Augustine in his *City of God*. St. Augustine and Thomas Aquinas were representative figures of the new European model of learning which was based upon theology rather than *humanitas* as such. As a preparatory means for understanding, Augustine outlined the *humanitas* model that he had inherited (grammar, languages, history, geography, astronomy, dialectic, mathematics, and rhetoric) together with the philosophy of Plato (who had influenced him through Plotinus). However, there was no disputing that the basic axis of his model had now changed: it was God rather than man. The theological nature of the model became even clearer in the thought of Aquinas, who architectonically incorporated Aristotle's system into his full-blown model of theology which became known as the queen of the sciences. As religious thought and the natural sciences had remained the handmaids of *humanitas* during the Graeco-Roman period, *humanitas* and the natural sciences remained the handmaids of theology during the medieval

European period. There was a certain integration of thought during both these periods but within the overall sovereignty of a dominant model.

The third dominant model in the development of western thought was that of the scientific ideal of the modern age. As we have seen, the notion of science is not a purely modern notion (and as we have seen throughout this book 'science' can have different meanings). Nevertheless, the fact remains that the seventeenth century breakthrough in science (Butterfield 1949) constituted, for better or worse, one of the turning-points in the development of human thought. The notion that effective knowledge is available through induction by experiment rather than deduction from given premises; the notion of scientific verification of hypotheses and theories by continual experiment; the notion of isolating particular problems for specialised solution; the notion that pure science can be applied at the technological level; the notion that scientific research is necessarily good come what may; the notion that the modern is new and the new must become newer—have constituted until recently the presuppositions, even the myths, of western thought. And these presuppositions have spilled over into research in the arts and social sciences. The basic source for the application of the scientific ideal was nature, just as the basic source for the application of the literary-humanistic ideal was man, and the basic source for the application of the theological ideal was God. Just as the *humanitas* model had been dominant in Graeco-Roman thought, and the theological model had been dominant in medieval thought, so the natural scientific model became dominant in modern western thought.

However, for a number of reasons, a humbler and more self-conscious attitude towards science as an intellectual model is arising in our own day. There is the realisation that applied science has not only solved some human problems but that it has also fed into other emerging problems of mankind such as those highlighted in a spectacular way by groups such as the Club of Rome in regard to issues such as energy, natural resources, population, food production, urbanisation, climate, pollution, and ecology. There is the sense that it is no longer good enough for scientific research to go 'whither it may' on the supposition that scientific research must be either helpful to mankind or at worst neutral. There has been the thought-provoking research of non-conformist prophets such as Schumacher (1974), Mumford (1970), Illich (1973), Heilbroner (1974), and the like. More importantly, as we have seen, scientific positivism has been eroded partly by the soul-searching work of scientists themselves: for example in Einstein's comments about 'the free creations of thought which cannot inductively be gained from sense-experience' (Schilpp 1944: 287); in Bohr's realisation that the only way for a scientific observer to be uninvolved with his apparatus is if he observes nothing at all; and in Heisenberg's statement that 'we cannot observe atoms as they are in themselves ... we can only seize them in the act of observation, and we can say meaningful things about this relationship only' (see Urban and Glenny 1971). The awareness has also arisen that the dominance of the scientific model, unlike those of the *humanitas* and theological models, was not achieved within a wider integrated intellectual framework but that the accompanying scientific stress upon isolating particular sets of problems for solution within discrete disciplines led to specialisations within knowledge that detracted from its wholeness. Knowledge is ultimately integral and overleaps the disciplinary boundaries that we erect around it. Finally, although natural science claimed, and in technological practice achieved, universal significance, it remained an ineluctably western creation. It contains little sympathetic awareness that our planet contains other cultural and spiritual universes not centred upon western notions, and the fact that this mind-set, though accepted everywhere, is changing is another example of the passage of the times. We therefore stand at a point in intellectual history when our global problems are pressing and evident, when the scientific process that helped to produce them is less self-confident in its ability to solve them, when human knowledge is multidimensional and yet requires greater integration, and when western hegemony of the mind can no longer be taken for granted.

It may be asked, what has this to do with the study of religion? The answer is that, in prospect, it has a great deal to do with the study of religion because it represents the general climate and context within which the study of religion must continue to evolve. It is not our purpose to enter into prophecies of the future. Each chapter of this book has attempted a review of future prospects in its own particular area, and it would be hazardous to predict confidently developments at the global and integral educational levels which are necessarily more complex. Our comments must therefore remain tentative.

We have talked explicitly about the rise of *western* dominant models of knowledge as though they were by definition universal, and implicitly about the influence of western universities. Much hings upon what we mean by a 'university.' A case of sorts can be made for the existence of 'universities' prior to those in the West at the Buddhist centre of Nālanda in the early centuries of the Christian era, at al-Azhar in Muslim Cairo in the tenth century, or possibly (but less convincingly) at the Greek Academies before the Christian era, or at the Confucian centres in early medieval China. It would be interesting to look at the question of the history and dominance of educational models through the eyes of those of other cultures and other religions, and it is part of the task of comparative religion to enable us to do this. The present educational problem produced by the spread of western science and by the disintegration of knowledge into discrete specialisations within western universities is not merely a western problem but a global problem. In order to solve it we need a global vision and a global integration in which western disciplines, western universities, and western science may play an important but not a lone part. It is not enough to think in terms of integrating western educational models and their parts that have become sundered; the global problem is wider than that. Insofar as the study of religion is intrinsically global in that it includes the study of *all* the world religions, it is in a better position that most other academic endeavours to assimilate insights from the educational and spiritual universes of other cultures and religions and therefore to enable us to obtain a global vision. In this book, the present chapter and the previous chapter by Whaling, and the chapters by Bolle, Smart, and King make preliminary references to this topic.

It seems reasonable to assert that the three models we have outlined, although western in provenance, refer to three basic areas of educational and human concern, namely man, transcendence and nature. It is significant that the study of religion, although primarily a human 'science' centred upon man has a stake in the other two areas as well. The social scientific approaches to the study of religion make a partial use of natural scientific methods of experiment and quantitative analysis, and the study of religion has a direct interest in man's ecological and cultural perspective on nature; the phenomenological view of *Einfühlung* intimated by Ninian Smart, the hermeneutical view of myth intimated by Kees Bolle, and the phenomenological and comparative chapters by King and Whaling, all make reference, in different ways, to the notion of transcendence. Clearly 'transcendence' can mean different things. It can refer to the notion that our own human nature has a transcendent dimension; it can refer to human intentionality in regard to transcendent reality whether this be viewed as God, Allah, Yahweh, Brahman, or whatever; it can refer to an ontology of the sacred; or it can refer to the western post-positivistic search for transcendence in thinkers such as Reich (who sees transcendence as personal liberation, 1970). Marcuse (who sees transcendence as the possibility of historical alternatives, 1968), Laing (who sees transcendence as a psychological creation *ex nihilo*, 1960), Bloch (who sees transcendence as future, 1970), and Jung (who sees transcendence as self-realisation, 1938). The study of religion can hardly eschew any concern for 'transcendence' and therefore, although its basic concern is with man, it straddles the models that deal with natural, human, and transcendent dimensions. This gives it a potentially creative educational role as a catalyst of thought. We referred earlier to the fact that the study of religion operates more as a field of studies than as a watertight academic discipline. This may give it an advantage in the contemporary global situation insofar as, if it were a circumscribed discipline, it would be less able to exercise a mediating, catalytic and integrating function.

The study of religion, however, remains primarily the study of man, rather than the study of nature, or the study of transcendence—even though it retains an interest in man's view of nature and man's view of transcendence. To conceptualise (or reconceptualise) who he is, man is called upon not merely to renew his imaginative powers and his vision of himself through the traditional western humanities of literature, history, geography, art and philosophy, and through the social sciences of sociology, psychology, anthropology, economics, and politics, he is also called upon to take seriously the worldviews existing in other cultures. Seeing the universe empathetically through the eyes of one's fellow men in other cultures is helpful in renewing one's own world view and it is also helpful in seeking a unity within the diversity of global world views. The study of religion is likely to be significant in conceptualising both the multifacetted nature of man's complex being and mankind's global unity in diversity insofar as its work straddles many of the disciplines that deal with man and all of the religions that lie at the heart of human cultures.

Finally, we have implied the need for a greater integration within and between the educational areas that focus upon nature, man, and transcendence. On the one hand there is some force in Heidegger's statement (*Existence and Being*, 1970, p. 326):

The fields of the sciences lie far apart. Their methodologies are fundamentally different. This disrupted multiplicity of disciplines is today only held together by the technical organisation of the universities and their faculties, and maintained as a practical unit of meaning by the practical aims of those faculties.

On the other hand there is equal force in Winston King's comment (1954: 19), 'Religion may be considered to be the most ambitious of all human attempts to unify the diversity of experience.'

During the course of this book, we have summarised in detail a number of diverse contemporary approaches to the study of religion. These approaches are different in the ways that we have analysed within these pages. At the same time as we have summarised these differing approaches to the study of religion we have also sought for new integrative points within this total area of human concern. There is a sense in which the search for integration within the study of religion represents in microcosm the more macrocosmic search for integration within the university of knowledge as a whole.

We have stressed within this chapter the important links that can and should exist between the study of religion and wider areas of academic concern. Ancillary to and complementary with this wider task, there is the need to gather together, at various places around the world, experts within the different areas of the study of religion: scholars in Christian studies, Buddhist studies, Hindu studies, Jewish studies, Muslim studies, Chinese religious studies, African religious studies, primal religious studies, history and phenomenology of religion, comparative religion, mythical and hermeneutical studies, anthropology of religion, sociology of religion, psychology of religion, philosophy of religion, integral science of religion. Through the teamwork of those trained in different specialisations within the study of religion but possessing some overview of and a desire to integrate the whole there will be benefit not only for the study of religion itself but for a far wider academic audience. There is a continous task of reconceptualising through interdisciplinary and interreligious teamwork what we mean by the study of religion, and how we carry it out in our global context. This book is a contribution towards that end. As we wrote in the introduction, the study of religion should play a creative role in contemporary scholarship not only for the sake of the study of religion itself but also for the sake of the world of learning in general, especially during this period when we are confronted with global issues affecting the whole planet earth.

Bibliography

Apel, K.O. (1980), *Towards a Transformation of Philosophy*. London: Routledge.
Ayer, A.J. (1936), *Language, Truth and Logic*. London: Gollancz.

Bachelard, Gaston (1934), *Le Nouvel Esprit Scientifique*. Paris: Presses Universitaires de France.
Bird, Otto (1976), *Cultures in Conflict*. Notre Dame, Indiana: University of Notre Dame Press.
Bloch, Ernst (1970), *Man On His Own*. New York: Herder and Herder.
Bloor, D. (1971), 'Two Paradigms of Scientific Knowledge?' *Science Studies* 1: 101–15.
Bohm, David (1971, 1973), 'Quantum Theory as an Indication of a New Order in Physics' in *Foundations of Physics*, Part A: 359–81; Part B: 139–68.
Bohr, Niels (1958), *Atomic Physics and Human Knowledge*. New York: Wiley.
Bonte, Pierre (1975), 'Cattle for God: An Attempt at a Marxist Analysis of the Religion of East African Herdsmen.' *Social Compass* XXII (3–4): 381–96.
Buber Martin (1906), *Die Geschichten des Rabbi Nachman*. Frankfurt: Rütten and Loening.
— (1908), *Die Legende des Baalschem*. Frankfurt: Rütten and Loening. (1955: The *Legend of the Baal-Shem*, tr. M. Friedman, New York: Harper.)
— (1913), *Daniel. Gespräche von der Verwirklichung*. Leipzig: Insel. (1964: *Daniel. Dialogues on Realisation*, tr. M. Friedman, New York: Holt, Rinehart and Winston.)
— (1922), *Ich und Du*. Leipzig: Insel. (1937: *I and Thou*, tr. R. Gregor Smith, Edinburgh: T. and T. Clark.)
— (1932), *Königtum Gottes*. Berlin: Schocken. (1967: *Kingship of God*, tr. R. Scheimann, New York: Harper and Row.)
— (1948). *Hasidism*. New York: Philosophical Library.
— (1949), *Gog und Magog. Eine Chronik*. Heidelberg: Lambert Schneider. (Hebrew edition, 1943.)
— (1962–63), *Complete Works:* I. *Schriften zur Philosophie*. II. *Schriften zur Bibel*. III. *Schriften zur Chassidismus*. Munich: Kösel; Heidelberg: Lambert Schneider.
— (1965), *Nachlese*. Heidelberg: Lambert Schneider.
Butterfield, Herbert (1949), *Origins of Modern Science*. London: Bell.

Chalmers, A. (1978), *What is This Thing Called Science?* London: Open University Press.
Chan, Wing-Tsit (1951), 'Synthesis in Chinese Metaphysics,' in Moore (ed.), 163–77.
— (1953), *Religious Trends in Modern China*. New York: Columbia University Press.
— (1957), 'The Neo-Confucian Solution of the Problem of Evil.' *Bulletin of the Institute of History and Philology Academica Sinica* 28: 773–91.
— (1957), 'Neo-Confucianism and Chinese Scientific Thought.' *Philosophy East and West* 6: 309–32.

— (1960), 'Wang Yang-Ming,' in *Encyclopaedia Britannica*, vol. 23, 320—21.
— (1962.), 'How Buddhistic is Wang Yang-Ming? *Philosophy East and West* 11: 203—16.
— (1963), *A Source Book in Chinese Philosophy*. Princeton: Princeton University Press.
— (1963), *Writings of Wang Yang-Ming* (translated with notes). New York: Columbia University Press.
— (1963), *The Way of Lao Tzu, A Translation and Study of the Tao-te Ching*. New York: Bobbs-Merrill.
— (1963), *The Platform Scripture* (translated with introduction and notes). New York: St. Johns University Press; (also 1971).
— (1964), 'The Evolution of the Neo-Confucian Concept of Li as a Principle' *Tsing Hua Journal of Chinese Studies*, 123—48.
— (1966), *Chinese Philosophy in Mainland China 1949—63*. Honolulu: East-West Center Press.
— (1967), *Reflections on Things at Hand, the Neo-Confucian Anthology, Compiled by Chu Hsi and Lu Tsu-ch'ien* (translated with notes). New York: Columbia University Press.
— (1969) *The Great Asian Religions: An Anthology*. New York: Macmillan.
— (1973). 'Chu Hsi's Completion of Neo-Confucianism,' in *Études Sung in memoriam Etienne Balazs*. Series II, Part I, ed. Francoise Aubin, 59—90.

Droscher, Vitus B. (1971), *The Magic of the Senses*. New York: Harper and Row.
Duhem, P. (1962), *The Aim and Structure of Physical Theory*. New York: Atheneum.

Eliade, Mircea (1979), 'Some Notes on Theosophia Perennis: Ananda K. Coomaraswamy and Henry Corbin.' *History of Religions*, 167—76.
Epstein, Isidore (1959), *Judaism: A Historical Presentation*. Harmondsworth: Penguin.
Evans-Pritchard, E.E. (1956), *Nuer Religion*. Oxford: Oxford University Press.

Feyerabend, Paul K. (1968), 'On the Improvement of the Sciences and the Arts, and the Possible Identity of the Two,' in *Boston Studies in the Philosophy of Science*, vol. 3, ed. R.S. Cohen and M.M. Wartofsky. Dordrecht: Reidel.
— (1975), *Against Method: Outline of an Anarchistic Theory of Knowledge*. London: New Left.
Foucault, Michel (1971), *The Order of Things*. New York: Random House.
— (1971), *The Archaeology of Knowledge*. New York: Tavistock; (also 1976 New York: Harper and Row).
Friedman, Maurice (1955), *Martin Buber: The Life of Dialogue*. London: Routledge and Kegan Paul.
— (1976), 'Martin Buber and Asia.' *Philosophy East and West* 26: 411—26.

Gadamer, Hans Georg (1975), *Truth and Method* (translation edited by Garrett Barden and John Gunning). New York: Seabury. (Original *Wahrheit und Methode*. Tübingen: Mohr. 1960.)

Habermas, Jurgen (1963), *Theorie und Praxis; sozialphilosophische Studien*. Neuwied am Rhein: Luchterhand. (*Theory and Practice*, tr. J. Viertel, Boston: Beacon. 1973.)

— (1968), *Erkenntnis und Interesse*. Frankfurt: Suhrkamp. (*Knowledge and Human Interests*, tr. J.J. Shapiro, Boston: Beacon. 1971.)

— (1973), *Legitimationsprobleme im Spät Kapitalismus*. Frankfurt: Suhrkamp (*Legitimation Crisis*, tr. T. McCarthy, Boston: Beacon. 1973.)

Hanson, N.R. (1958), *Patterns of Discovery*. Cambridge: Cambridge University Press.

Heidegger, M. (1970), *Existence and Being* (translated by Werner Brock). Chicago: Regnery (Gateway).

Heilbroner, R.L. (1974), *An Inquiry into the Human Prospect*. New York: W.W. Norton.

Heisenberg, Werner (1971), 'Rationality in Science and Society,' in Urban and Glenny (eds.), 73–88.

Hesse, Mary (1980), *Revolutions and Reconstructions in the Philosophy of Science*. Brighton: Harvester.

Hiroshi, Sakamoto (1978), 'D.T. Suzuki as a Philosopher,' *Eastern Buddhist* XI(2): 33–42.

Horton, R.F. (1967), 'African Traditional Thought and Western Science,' in *Africa* 37: 155–87.

Huxley, Aldous (1946), *The Perennial Philosophy*. London: Chatto and Windus.

Idowu, E.B. (1962), *Olodumare: God in Yoruba Belief*. London: Longmans.

Illich, Ivan (1973), *Celebration of Awareness*. Harmondsworth: Penquin.

Jahn, Jankeinz (1961), *Muntu: an Outline of the New African Culture* (translated by M. Greve). New York: Grove. (Original *Muntu: Umrisse der neoafrikanischen Kultur*. Dusseldorf: Diederichs, 1958.)

Jiyu, Ren. (Chi-Yü, Jen) (1977), 'Investigate Religion and Criticise Theology,' *Ching Feng* 20: 170–76.

Jung, C.G. (1938), *Psychology and Religion*. New Haven: Yale University Press.

Kagame, Alexis (1956), *La Philosophie Bantu-Rwandaise de l'Être*. Brussels: Académie royale des sciences coloniales.

Kerseven, Marko (1975), 'Religion and the Marxist Concept of Social Formation,' *Social Compass* XXII (3–4): 323–42.

King, Winston Lee (1954), *Introduction to Religion: A Phenomenological Approach*. New York: Harper.

Koertge, Noretta (1971), 'Inter-theoretic Criticism and the Growth of Science,' in *Boston Studies in Philosophy of Science*, vol. 8, ed. R.C. Buck and R.S. Cohen, 160–73. Dordrecht: Reidel.

Kuhn, Thomas (1962), *The Structure of Scientific Revolutions*. Chicago: Chicago University Press.

Laing, R.D. (1960), *The Divided Self*. London: Tavistock.

Lakatos, Imre, (ed.) (1968), *The Problem of Inductive Logic*. Amsterdam: North-Holland Publishing Company.

— (1974), 'Falsification and the Methodology of Scientific Research Programmes,' in I. Lakatos and A. Musgrave (eds.), *Criticism and the Growth of Knowledge*. Cambridge: Cambridge University Press.

Laszlo, Ervin (1978), *The Inner Limits of Mankind*. Oxford: Pergamon.

Lienhardt, G. (1961), *Divinity and Experience, the Religion of the Dinka*. Oxford: Clarendon.

Lipsey, Roger, (ed.) (1977), *Coomaraswamy*. Vol. 1, *Selected Papers: Traditional Art and Symbolism*; Vol. 2, *Selected Papers: Metaphysics*; Vol. 3, *His Life and Work*. (Bollingen Series LXXXIX). Princeton: Princeton University Press.

Maduro, Otto (1975), 'Marxist Analysis and Sociology of Religion.' *Social Compass* XXII (3–4): 305–22.

Magee, Bryan (1973), *Popper*. London: Collins Fontana.

— (1974), 'Karl Popper: The World's Greatest Philosopher?' *Current Affairs Bulletin* 50(8): 14–23.

Manheim, Werner (1974), *Martin Buber*. New York: Twayne.

Marcuse, H. (1968), *Negations: Essays in Critical Theory*. Boston: Beacon.

Mbiti, John (1966), *Akamba Stories*. Oxford: Clarendon.

— (1969), *African Religions and Philosophy*. London: Heinemann.

— (1970), *Concepts of God in Africa*. London: SPCK.

— (1971), *New Testament Eschatology in an African Background*. London: Oxford University Press.

— (1975), *The Prayers of African Religion*. London: SPCK.

Medawar, Peter (1969), *Induction and Intuition in Scientific Thought*. London: Methuen.

Moore, Charles A. (1944), *Philosophy East and West*. Princeton University Press.

— (1951), (ed.) *Essays in East-West Philosophy*. Honolulu: University of Hawaii.

— (1962), *Philosophy and Culture—East and West*. Honolulu: University of Hawaii.

Morgan, Kenneth (1953), (ed.) *Religion of the Hindus*. New York: Ronald.

— (1956). *The Path of the Buddha*. New York: Ronald.

— (1958), *Islam—The Straight Path*. New York: Ronald.

Mumford, L. (1970), *The Myth of the Machine: The Pentagon of Power*. New York: Harcourt Brace Jovanovich.

Murti, T.R.V. (1955), *The Central Philosophy of Buddhism: A Study of the Mādhyamika System*. London: Allen and Unwin.

Musgrave, Alan E. (1974), 'Logical Versus Historical Theories of Confirmation,' *British Journal for the Philosophy of Science* 25: 1–23.

Nagel, Ernest (1961), *The Structure of Science*. New York: Harcourt Brace.

Naravane, V.S. (1964), *Modern Indian Thought: A Philosophical Survey*. Bombay: Asia Publishing House.

Nasr, Seyyed Hossein (1964), *Three Muslim Sages.* Cambridge: Harvard University Press.
— (1964), *An Introduction to Islamic Cosmological Doctrines.* Cambridge: Harvard University Press.
— (1964), *Histoire de la philosophie islamique* (with H. Corbin and O. Yahya). Paris: Gallimard.
— (1966), *Ideals and Realities of Islam.* London: Allen and Unwin.
— (1966). *Iran.* Paris: UNESCO.
— (1967), *Islamic Studies: Essays on Law and Society, the Sciences, and Philosophy and Sufism.* Beirut: Librairie du Liban,
— (1968), *Science and Civilisation in Iran.* Cambridge: Harvard University Press.
— (1968). *The Encounter of Man and Nature; the Spiritual Crisis of Modern Man.* London: Allen and Unwin.
— (1968), *Sufi Essays.* London: Allen and Unwin.
— (1974), *Jalal ad-Din Rumi. Supreme Persian Poet and Sage.* Tehran: High Council of Culture and Arts.
— (1975), *Islam and the Plight of Modern Man.* London, New York: Longman.
— (1975), *An Annotated Bibliography of Islamic Science.* Vol. 1. Tehran: Imperial Iranian Academy of Philosophy.
— (1975), *Persia, Bridge of Turquoise* (with R. Beny). Toronto: McClelland and Stewart.
— (1976), *Islamic Science—An Illustrated Study.* London: Thorsons.
— (1981), *Knowledge and the Sacred.* Edinburgh: Edinburgh University Press.
Nketia, J.H. Kwabena (1955), *Funeral Dirges of the Akan People.* Accra.

Parratt, John (1977), 'Time in Traditional African Thought.' *Religion* 7 (2): 117–26.
Parrinder, E.G. (1954), *African Traditional Religion.* London: Hutchinson's University Library.
Polanyi, Michael (1946), *Science, Faith and Society.* Oxford: Oxford University Press; (also Chicago University Press, fifth impr. 1973).
— (1951), *The Logic of Liberty.* London: Routledge.
— (1958), *Personal Knowledge.* London: Routledge.
— (1969), *Knowing and Being.* London: Routledge.
Popper, Karl. R. (1935), *Logik der Forschung zur Erkenntnistheorie der modernen Naturwissenschaft.* Wien: J. Springer. (*The Logic of Scientific Discovery*, London: Hutchinson, 1968.)
— (1962), *Conjectures and Refutations.* New York: Basic Books.
— (1972), *Objective Knowledge.* Oxford: Oxford University Press.

Radhakrishnan, Sarvepalli (1918), *Philosophy of Rabindranath Tagore.* London: Macmillan.
— (1920), *Reign of Religion in Contemporary Philosophy.* London: Macmillan.
— (1923, 1927), *Indian Philosophy,* 2 vols. New York: Macmillan.
— (1927), *Hindu View of Life.* London: Allen and Unwin.
— (1932), *An Idealist View of Life.* New York: Macmillan.

— (1933), *East and West in Religion*. London: Allen and Unwin.

— (1938), *Gautama the Buddha*. London: H. Milford.

— (1939), *Mahatma Gandhi*. London: Allen and Unwin.

— (1939), *Eastern Religions and Western Thought*. Oxford: Oxford University Press.

— (1947), *Religion and Society*. London: Allen and Unwin.

— (1948), *Kalki*. Bombay: Hind Kitabs; (original, 1929).

— (1949), *Great Indians*. Bombay: Hind Kitabs.

— (1950), *Dhammapada*. Oxford: Oxford University Press.

— (1966), 'Fellowship of the Spirit,' In Rouner (ed.) *Philosophy, Religion and the Coming World Civilisation*.

— (1967), *Religion in a Changing World*. London: Allen and Unwin.

Reich, C. (1970), *The Greening of America*. New York: Random House.

Rescher, Nicholas (1973), 2nd. ed. (1979), *Conceptual Idealism and Cognitive Systematization*. Oxford: Blackwell.

Rouner, Leroy, ed. (1966), *Philosophy, Religion, and the Coming World Civilisation*. The Hague: Martinus Nijhoff.

Rykwert, Joseph (1979), 'A.D. Coomaraswamy.' *Religion* 9: 104–15.

Said, Edward W. (1978), *Orientalism*. London: Routledge.

Scheffler, Israel (1967), *Science and Subjectivity*. New York: Bobbs-Merrill.

Schilpp, Paul Arthur, ed. (1944), *The Philosophy of Bertrand Russell*. Evanston and Chicago: Northwestern University.

— (1952). (ed.) *The Philosophy of Sarvepalli Radhakrishnan*. New York: Tudor.

— (1974). (ed.) *The Philosophy of Karl Popper*. La Salle, Illinois: Open Court.

Schmitt, Charles B. (1966), 'Perennial Philosophy: From Agostino Stenco to Leibniz.' *Journal of the History of Ideas* 27: 505–32.

Scholem, Gershom G. (1946), *Major Trends in Jewish Mysticism*. New York: Schocken.

Schumaker, Ernst Friedrich (1973), *Small is Beautiful: A Study of Economics as if People Mattered*. London: Blond and Briggs; (also Abacus, 1974).

Smith, Wilfred Cantwell (1959), 'Comparative Religion: Whither and Why?' in M. Eliade and J.M. Kitagawa (eds.) *The History of Religions: Essays in Methodology*. Chicago and London: University of Chicago Press.

Stove, D.C. (1973), *Probability and Hume's Inductive Scepticism*. Oxford: Oxford University Press.

Suzuki, Daisetz Teitaro (1900), *Translation of Aśvaghoṣa's 'Discourse on the Awakening of Faith in the Mahāyāna'*. Chicago: Open Court.

— (1907), *Outlines of Mahayana Buddhism*. London: Luzac; (also New York: Schocken, 1963).

— (1914), 'The Development of Mahayana Buddhism,' *Monist* XXIV: 565–81.

— (1916), *Zen no tachiba kara (From the Standpoint of Zen)*. Tokyo: Kōyū-Kan.

— (1927), *Essays in Zen Buddhism*. First Series. London: Luzac.

— (1930), *Studies in the Laṅkāvatāra Sūtra*. London: Routledge.

— (1932), Translation of '*Lankāvatāra Sūtra*'. London: Routledge.

— (1949), *The Zen Doctrine of No-Mind*. London: Rider.

— (1953), 'Zen: A Reply to Hu shin,' *Philosophy East and West* 3: 25—46.

— (1955), *Studies in Zen*. New York: Philosophical Library.

— (1957), *Mysticism: Christian and Buddist*. New York: Harper.

— (1969), *Suzaki Daisetz Zenshū (Complete Works of Suzuki)*. Tokyo: Iwanami Shoten.

Takakusu, Junjirō (1947), *The Essentials of Buddhist Philosophy* (ed. Wing-Tsit Chan and C.A. Moore). Honolulu: University of Hawaii.

Taylor, John V. (1963), *The Primal Vision*. London: SCM Press.

Tempels, Placied (1946), *Bantoe-filosofie*. Antwerp: De Sikkel. (*Bantu Philosophy*, Paris: Presence africaine, 1969—translation of French version of Bantoe-filosofie.)

Toffler, Alvin (1980), *The Third Wave*. New York: Morrow.

Urban, G.R. and Glenny, M., eds. (1971), *Can We Survive Our Future?* London: Bodley Head.

Vidal, Daniel (1975), '*Une lecture marxiste du prophétisme*,' *Social Compass* XXII (3—4): 355—80.

Waardenburg, Jacques (1973), *Classical Approaches to the Study of Religion*, 2 vols. The Hague: Mouton.

White, Lynn. T. (1956), *Frontiers of Knowledge in the Study of Man*. New York: Harper.

The Authors

Kees W. Bolle, Professor of History, University of California, Los Angeles. He studied at the universities of Leiden and Chicago. Author of *The Persistence of Religion* (1965), *The Freedom of Man in Myth* (1968), the article 'Myth and Mythology' in the *Encyclopaedia Britannica* (1974); various articles in journals on the general history of religions and Indic studies. Among recent work is *The Bhagavadgītā, A New Translation* (1979). General Editor of 'Hermeneutics, Studies in the History of Religions'.

Ursula King, Ph.D. (London), M.A. (Delhi), S.T.L. (Paris), is Senior Lecturer in the Department of Theology and Religious Studies, University of Leeds. Her research interests include methods and problems in the study of religion; the comparative study of mysticism; Teilhardian studies; modern Hinduism; women and religion. Publications: contributions to American, Canadian, English, German, Indian and Italian journals and books, including *Christlicher Platonismus* (trl. from Latin into German, ed. P. Hadot), Zurich: Artemis Verlag 1967; *Towards a New Mysticism. Teilhard de Chardin and Eastern Religions*, London: Collins 1980.

Ninian Smart teaches half of each year at the University of California at Santa Barbara, and half at the University of Lancaster, where he founded England's first Department of Religious Studies. He has taught philosophy in the University of Wales and as a visiting professor at Wisconsin, the history and philosophy of religion at University of London King's College, theology as H.G. Wood Professor at Birmingham, and has been visiting professor of religion in the universities of Princeton, Otago, and Queensland. He has taught and researched in India and Sri Lanka. His books include *Reasons and Faiths* (1958), *Doctrine and Argument in Indian Philosophy* (1964), *The Science of Religion and the Sociology of Knowledge* (1973) and the Gifford Lectures, *Beyond Ideology* (1981). He helped to plan and execute the television series on world religions 'The Long Search' (1977).

Frank Whaling read History and Theology at Cambridge and later lived
for four years in India. After completing his Doctorate in Comparative
Religion at Harvard in 1973 he became the co-ordinator of the religious
studies programmes and degrees at Edinburgh University. He is
Chairman of the Scottish Working Party on Religions of the World in
Education. He has been a visiting professor or fellow at Dartmouth
College, the Peking Institute for Research into World Religions, and
Calcutta University, as well as lecturing at various other places. He has
written or edited *An Approach to Dialogue with Hinduism* (1966), *The Rise
of the Religious Significance of Rāma* (1980), *John and Charles Wesley* in the
Classics of Western Spirituality (1981), *Religions of the World* (1984),
Contemporary Approaches to the Study of Religion: The Social Sciences (1984),
The World's Religious Traditions: Current Persectives in Religious Studies)
(1984), *Comparative Religion* (1984–5). *Christian Theology and World
Religions* (1984–5). He has also written a number of articles on many
facets of religious studies.

Index of Names of Scholars
*All Indexes compiled by Frank Whaling.

Index of Other Names and Foreign Terms

Index of Topics

Belief 111, 117, 123, 140, 169, 184, 190,
229, 342, 368, 419.
Believer 122, 131, 368. (See Faith).
Benefactor/Fool 331.
Bible 191, 259, 275, 411.
Biblical Exegesis 108–9.
Biblical Interpretation 40.
Biblical Scholarship 310, 366.
Biblical Texts 310.
Bibliography 4, 6, 9, 10, 30, 32, 57–72,
153–63, 265, 299, 308–9, 349–63,
445–51.
Binary Contrasts 227–30, 330–1.
Biology 322, 329.
Biotope 255.
Birds 227.
Birth 227.
Body 192, 270, 318.
Bonzes 328.
Book, Holy 200.
Boon 222.
Bootstrap Theory 277.
B.B.C. 302.
Buildings, Sacred 210.
Burials 256.

Calendars 313, 316.
Car(s) 9.
Card-Indexes 10.
Cargo Cults 306, 344.
Caste System 229, 252.
Causality Criterion 133.
Celebration 140, 321.
Centres for the Study of Religion 431,
442–3.
Change, Religious 18–21, 87, 150, 334,
382.
Chapel 275.
Charismatic Leaders 233.
Chastity/Sexuality 227.
Church History 205, 298, 334, 365.
Church Life 315.

Church Offices 140.
Church/Sect Typology 230, 233.
Civilisation, Rise in the Middle East
244–6.
Civilisations and Religion 245–6.
Civil Religion 270.
Classical Period in Religious Studies
1–28.
Classification 39–40, 103–4, 326–7, 376.
Climates 227, 255, 438.
Cognitive Function of Religion 131.
Coherence 382–3.
Collaboration of Religion Scholars 76,
349, 443. (See Teamwork).
Collective Unconscious 345.
Colloquium 184–5, 431.
Colonialism 19, 22, 148, 347, 371, 395,
430, 432.
Commitment 15, 26, 66, 121, 182–3, 273,
366, 368, 403, 405, 409–10, 419, 423,
428–9, 435.
Commitment, Levels of 182–3.
Communications, Improved & Religious
Studies 9–10, 19.
Communication Theory 385.
Communism 26, 171, 246, 392, 434–5.
(See Marxism).
Comparative Associations 327–8.
Comparative Ecology of Religion 255–7.
Comparative Ethics 279.
Comparative Hermeneutics 114–5.
Comparative Mysticism 115–6, 254,
277–9, 407–8.
Comparative Mythology 221–3, 339–40.
Comparative Philosophy 279.
Comparative Philosophies of Religion
241–2, 276, 279.
Comparative Religion 2, 6–8, 11, 17, 24,
27, 42–3, 54, 60, 66, 71, 73, 75, 88, 90,
93, 96, 98, 125, 149, 165–282, 365,
370–1, 393, 400–1, 414, 426, 428, 431,
440–1.